Streams of Gold, Rivers of Blood

Onassis Series in Hellenic Culture

ONASSIS
FOUNDATION
USA

ANTHONY
KALDELLIS

Streams of Gold, Rivers of Blood

The Rise and Fall of

Byzantium, 955 A.D. to

the First Crusade

OXFORD
UNIVERSITY PRESS

OXFORD

UNIVERSITY PRESS

Oxford University Press is a department of the University of Oxford. It furthers the University's objective of excellence in research, scholarship, and education by publishing worldwide. Oxford is a registered trade mark of Oxford University Press in the UK and certain other countries.

Published in the United States of America by Oxford University Press
198 Madison Avenue, New York, NY 10016, United States of America.

© Oxford University Press 2017

Library of Congress Cataloging-in-Publication Data
Names: Kaldellis, Anthony, author.
Title: Streams of gold, rivers of blood : the rise and fall of Byzantium, 955 A.D. to the First Crusade / Anthony Kaldellis.
Description: New York, NY : Oxford University Press, 2017. |
Includes bibliographical references and index.
Identifiers: LCCN 2016037388 | ISBN 9780190253226 (hardback) |
ISBN 9780190253240 (ebook)
Subjects: LCSH: Byzantine Empire—History—527–1081. |
Byzantine Empire—History—1081–1453.
Classification: LCC DF591 .K36 2017 | DDC 949.5/02—dc23
LC record available at https://lccn.loc.gov/2016037388

9 8 7

Printed by Sheridan Books, Inc., United States of America

to the memory of all who have perished crossing the Aegean in hope of a life without war, and to the islanders who have so desperately tried to aid them

CONTENTS

MAPS

Map 1 Byzantine Italy

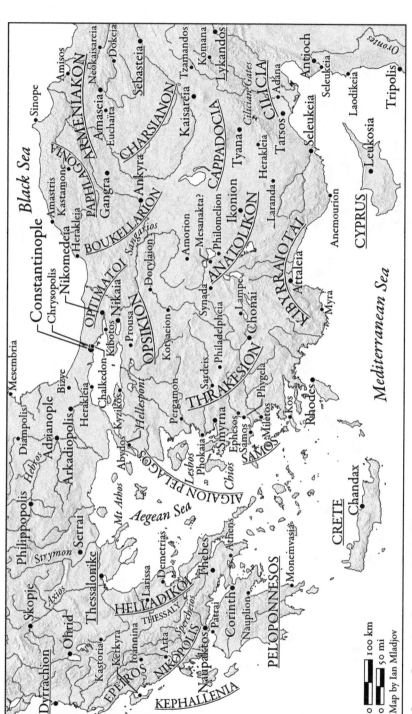

MAP 2 Byzantine Greece and Asia Minor

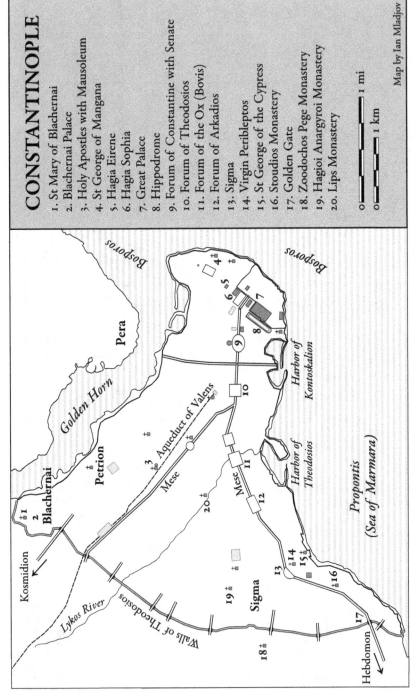

CONSTANTINOPLE

1. St Mary of Blachernai
2. Blachernai Palace
3. Holy Apostles with Mausoleum
4. St George of Mangana
5. Hagia Eirene
6. Hagia Sophia
7. Great Palace
8. Hippodrome
9. Forum of Constantine with Senate
10. Forum of Theodosios
11. Forum of the Ox (Bovis)
12. Forum of Arkadios
13. Sigma
14. Virgin Peribleptos
15. St George of the Cypress
16. Stoudios Monastery
17. Golden Gate
18. Zoodochos Pege Monastery
19. Hagioi Anargyroi Monastery
20. Lips Monastery

Map by Ian Mladjov

0 [scale] 1 mi
0 [scale] 1 km

Bosporos

Bosporos

Pera

Golden Horn

Kosmidion

Blachernai

Petrion

Aqueduct of Valens

Mese

Mese

Mese

Sigma

Lykos River

Walls of Theodosios

Hebdomon

Harbor of Kontoskalion

Harbor of Theodosios

Propontis
(Sea of Marmara)

MAP 3 Constantinople

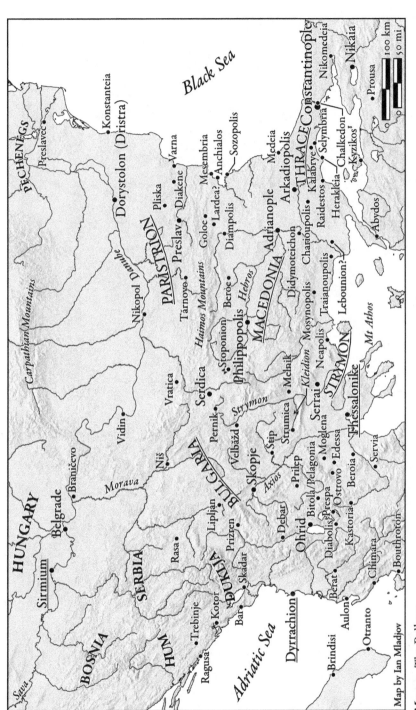

MAP 4 The Balkans

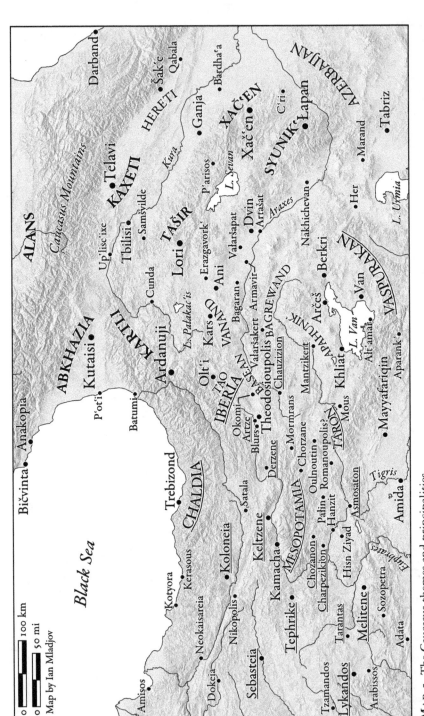

MAP 5 The Caucasus themes and principalities

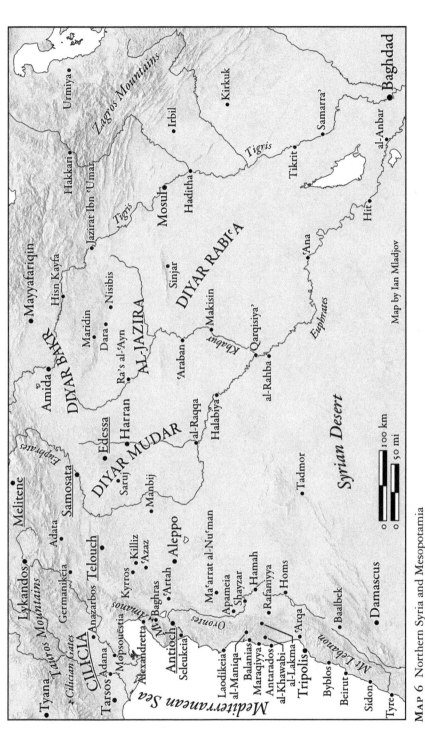

MAP 6 Northern Syria and Mesopotamia

GENEALOGIES

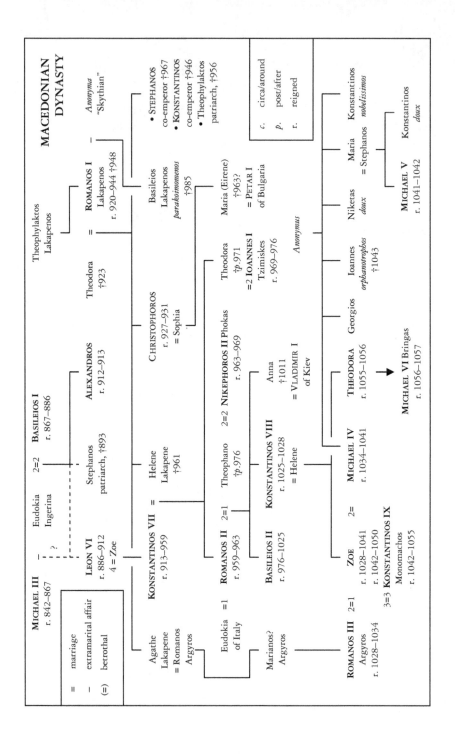

MACEDONIAN DYNASTY

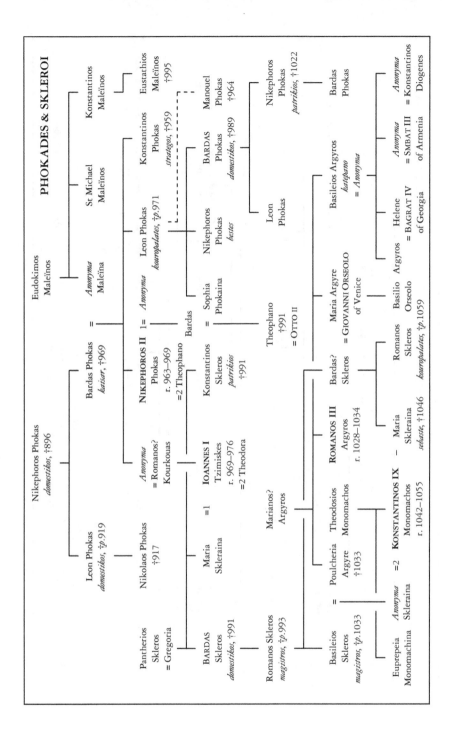

PHOKADES & SKLEROI

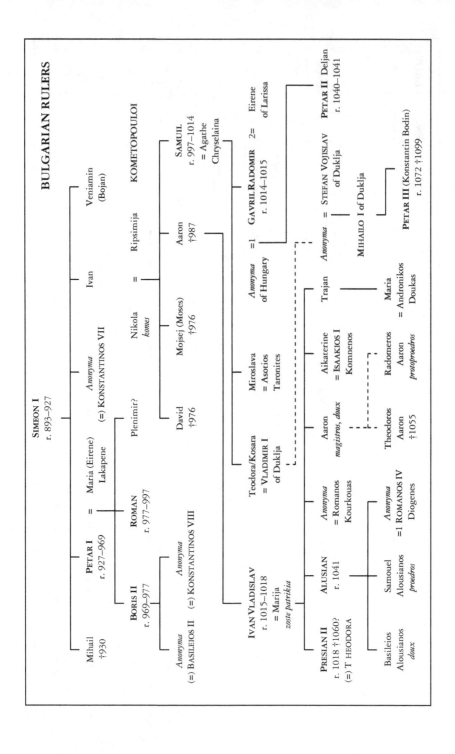

BULGARIAN RULERS

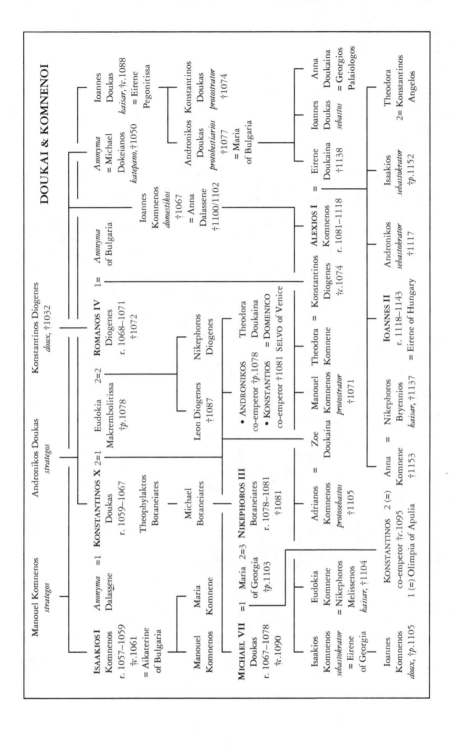

DOUKAI & KOMNENOI

HAMDANIDS

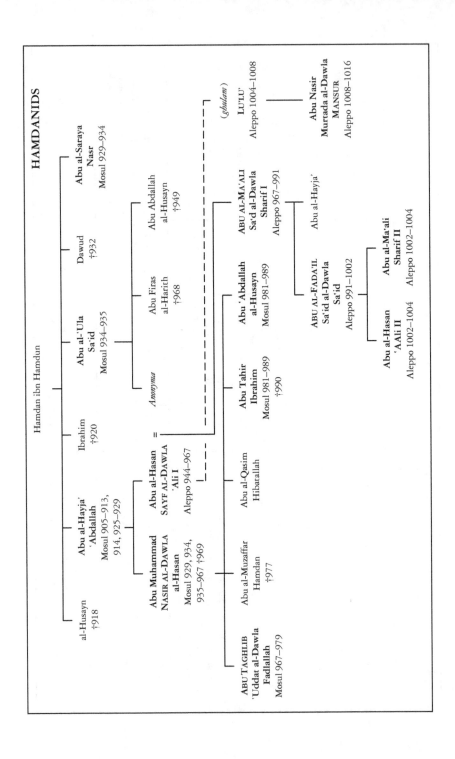

Hamdan ibn Hamdun

al-Husayn
†918

Abu al-Hayja'
'Abdallah
Mosul 905–913,
914, 925–929

Ibrahim
†920

Abu al-'Ula
Sa'id
Mosul 934–935

Dawud
†932

Abu al-Saraya
Nasr
Mosul 929–934

Abu Muhammad
NASIR AL-DAWLA
al-Hasan
Mosul 929, 934,
935–967 †969

Abu al-Hasan
SAYF AL-DAWLA
'Ali I
Aleppo 944–967

Anonyma

Abu Firas
al-Harith
†968

Abu Abdallah
al-Husayn
†949

(ghulam)

LU'LU'
Aleppo 1004–1008

ABU'TAGHLIB
'Uddat al-Dawla
Fadlallah
Mosul 967–979

Abu al-Muzaffar
Hamdan
†977

Abu al-Qasim
Hibatallah

Abu Tahir
Ibrahim
Mosul 981–989
†990

Abu 'Abdallah
al-Husayn
Mosul 981–989

ABU AL-MA'ALI
Sa'd al-Dawla
Sharif I
Aleppo 967–991

Abu al-Hayja'

Abu Nasir
Murrada al-Dawla
MANSUR
Aleppo 1008–1016

ABU AL-FADA'IL
Sa'id al-Dawla
Sa'id
Aleppo 991–1002

Abu al-Ma'ali
Sharif II
Aleppo 1002–1004

Abu al-Hasan
'Aali II
Aleppo 1002–1004

PREFACE

THE BYZANTINES WERE not a warlike people. They did not typically raise their children to fight with weapons, as happened in many societies around them. Their strategy was famously cautious and defensive. They preferred to pay their enemies either to go away or to fight among themselves. Likewise, the court at the heart of their empire sought to buy allegiance with honors, fancy titles, bales of silk, and streams of gold. Politics was the cunning art of providing just the right incentives to win over supporters and keep them loyal. Money, silk, and titles were the empire's preferred instruments of governance and foreign policy, over swords and armies. And the Byzantine state and bureaucracy could generate a larger cash flow than any other Christian realm at the time. Even in 1080, with half its territory lost to the Turks, "fountains and streams of gold gushed forth" from the court of a new emperor desperate to establish his position.[1]

That desperation stemmed from the dark side of Byzantine politics: the emperor was always vulnerable to the ambitions of domestic rivals, who resorted to murderous plots and civil war. If gold failed to make an emperor popular, or if he was perceived as weak, the "hands of sons were stained with the blood of fathers, and brother would strike down brother."[2] Sitting on the throne in Constantinople was a dangerous and precarious business—but it was business-as-usual. Our period, however, was exceptional in two other ways. It began with a burst of violence aimed at the empire's neighbors, as Byzantine armies went on the offensive and conquered more land and people than had ever been subjected to the Roman yoke since the conquests of Justinian in the sixth century. A new generation of aggressive soldiers, trained to fight from youth, slaughtered, sacked, and conquered until the empire no longer faced credible rivals. When Tzimiskes cut down the five thousand survivors of a battle, in 963, the blood ran down into the fields, and the site was renamed "the Mountain of Blood." One emperor came to be known as "the White Death of the Saracens," another as "the Bulgar Slayer."

The tide would turn during the eleventh century. Three new enemies—the Normans, Pechenegs, and Seljuk Turks—would fall upon the empire and strip it of many of its conquests. It was now the turn of the Byzantines to suffer horribly, as "rivers of blood flowed through" their provinces.[3] The present book recounts this sudden rise and fall of an empire on the cusp of the millennium, an empire torn by its own contradictions and threatened by the powers that would fashion a new world. It tells the story of how the streams of gold were drowned by the blood of politics and war.

The years between 955, when the general Nikephoros Phokas was placed in command of the army and launched a strategy of aggressive conquest, and 1081, when the general Alexios Komnenos seized the throne amidst imperial collapse and political chaos, were a pivotal period in Byzantine history. During this time, Byzantium embarked on a series of spectacular conquests, first in the southeast against the Arabs, then in Bulgaria, and finally also in Georgia and Armenia. By the early eleventh century, the empire was the most powerful state in its geostrategic environment and seemed to have no credible rivals. It was also expanding economically, demographically, and, in time, intellectually too. Yet imperial hegemony came to a crashing end in the third quarter of the eleventh century, when political disunity, fiscal mismanagement, and defeat by the Seljuks in the east and the Normans in the west forced Byzantium to fight for its very survival. It gradually had to settle for being one power among many, and just over a century later it was conquered and dismembered by the crusaders. Byzantium fell behind the curve of history and would never catch up to its peers, especially in the west. Such dramatic fluctuations had not been typical of its past history. How did this happen? What strategies, policies, and personalities shaped the rapid rise and even more rapid collapse of Byzantine power in less than 150 years?

This story, which fascinates those interested in Byzantine history because of its dramatic qualities, has to be told anew. It seems to have fallen off the radar of historians. The last to reconstruct the events of this period in detail, by using the primary sources, was Gustave Schlumberger, over a century ago (1890–1905). Yet he did not cover the eleventh-century collapse, reaching only as far as 1056, the end of the Macedonian dynasty. Schlumberger's work, moreover, which is outdated in many respects and tended toward a Romantic narrative style, has not been translated into English. After him, we have mostly general surveys, many of which are good, but they tend to look at events from a greater distance than one would sometimes like and tend to recycle the view pushed by an early twentieth-century school of thought according to which the history of Byzantium in this era was driven by a particular socioeconomic transformation. That view, however, is highly doubtful. For these reasons, we need a new narrative history of Byzantium in this era. We now have more sources than were available to Schlumberger, we know more about their limitations, and we are hopefully free of many of the preconceptions that shaped past scholarship. Yet past conjectures with little support in the evidence have also become hardened facts or common wisdom. They need to be tested against the evidence. The problem is that much specialized research is now taking place against the background of an implied master narrative of this period that is recycled with minor variations from one survey to the next. This narrative frames and limits research into more particular areas, and often predetermines the scope of their methodology.

Here, then, is what *Streams of Gold, Rivers of Blood* hopes to accomplish.

It offers a narrative reconstruction of the political and military history of the empire and points to a new understanding of the socioeconomic changes that took place in this period. The narrative focuses mostly on the decisions made by the court and their implementation on the frontier. As these decisions were not made in a vacuum, the narrative also tries to expose their structural constraints. On the domestic front, we are dealing not so much with "policies" as with attempts to reward supporters and protect each regime against potential rivals. Emperors in Byzantium were never safe; they needed to reaffirm their legitimacy constantly, and this governed imperial decisions on all levels.

This is also an "international" history in the sense that it tries to explain who the people were with whom the Romans of Byzantium were interacting, and what constraints operated along each stretch of the frontier. Though there are notable exceptions (especially Mark Whittow for this period), many of our surveys are excessively Byzantinocentric; they point the spotlight at Byzantium and do not illuminate what was going on around it. Enemies along the frontier are named, but little is said about them or the dynamics that were driving their relationship with Byzantium. After many years of heavy reading in Byzantine history, I found that I was still unable to explain to myself who the Hamdanids were or what Davitʿ of Tao was trying to accomplish. We should no longer write history that way. This book, therefore, takes a different approach: as each area becomes central to the narrative, I introduce the internal dynamics and goals of the Hamdanids, Fatimids, Normans, or Seljuks. As I am not at all committed to Byzantine imperial projects, I have tried to avoid a pro-Byzantine bias.

The narrative was also written out of a direct and critical engagement with the primary sources, including literary texts, documentary records, inscriptions, coins, and seals. Modern surveys of this period often rely on previous reconstructions, and they in turn on their predecessors. This sometimes makes it hard to find what primary source ultimately buttresses specific claims. Here, by contrast, the sources will be cited directly, so that readers know the basis for any assertion and can follow the trail. By returning to the sources and starting anew there, this history clears away a number of fictions and misunderstandings that have entered the record. Like most Byzantinists today, I make extensive use of both western and eastern sources. The "foreign" ones are sometimes better for Byzantine history than the Byzantine ones, but they must all be used critically and skeptically. There is too much gossip, political bias, and rhetorical invention in them. Some Byzantine sources reflect specific authorial projects as well as the influence of subsequent events and the pull of classical models of writing. There is less factual history in them than one might assume, and some of them are too focused on the capital and Roman politics rather than on foreign lands, or even the frontier. I will not survey the main sources here (a guide to the main ones appears at the end of the book). No mere summary can do justice to the problems and temptations that they pose to scholars, so I have written a separate study outlining the many ways in which these literary texts are both more and less than an accurate recounting of facts.[4] One device that they use, and that still tempts modern historians, is to psychologize the actions of individuals or groups. This definitely makes histories more exciting, but resisting it, as I have done here, hopefully makes them more sober, fair, and accurate. Unlike most of our sources, I try not to take sides, glorify, or condemn.

By following *all* the sources in detail and in tandem, I saw clearly for the first time patterns of imperial behavior that shaped both domestic and foreign policy. I also came to surprising conclusions, sometimes the opposite of what I expected to find. This was especially the case regarding the imperial collapse of the eleventh century. For example, I was forced, against a Psellos-induced bias, to rehabilitate the military leadership of Konstantinos IX Monomachos. I also came to a completely different understanding of the behavior of the patriarch Michael Keroularios during the fateful summer of 1054. But more importantly, beyond the actions of specific individuals, I came to question a particular model of socioeconomic transformation that some historians sought to impose on this period. According to this model, the imperial "state" ruled by the Macedonian dynasty was challenged by the landowning "magnates" of Asia Minor, who were powerful "families" that were eating up peasant lands and angling to run the empire in a way that benefited their own class. As far as I can tell, this picture is fictitious. It leads to tendentious interpretations of events and individuals that serve a modern agenda, specifically to show how and when Byzantium became "feudalized." When we view those events and individuals against the narrative patterns of Byzantine imperial history, a different picture emerges, one of emperors systemically vulnerable to potential enemies and rivals, including most prominently their own courtiers and generals. In sum, political-military history will here point to a different understanding of the socioeconomic history of this period. This is elaborated in the Introduction and the General Considerations that conclude the three parts of the book.

This book does not focus on general cultural, literary, intellectual, artistic, religious, or economic developments that took place during this period, to which a narrative approach is not ideally suited, but it does include material from those categories. Trade, painting icons, and sending embassies were always occurring in the background, but do not need to be mentioned in banal instances (which are the majority). Major changes in trade policy (especially with the Italian cities) occurred only after the period covered here. And although I am fascinated with the rise (or return) of the scientific study of the climate and of environmental history, which will contribute new insights in the coming decades, it is unclear how its conclusions can interface with the history of events, as at some point they must. Recent efforts to write narrative history from a climatological angle seem to be reductive and fail to explain Byzantine expansion in an age of supposed regional collapse.

During our period, Byzantium flipped its geographical presence. In 955, it controlled most of Asia Minor, southern Greece, and the corridor from Greece to Thessalonike and Constantinople. By 1081, it was an almost entirely Balkan state, having in effect exchanged most of Asia Minor for Bulgaria, holding both only briefly (1018–1071). The gravest domestic threat to the emperors at the beginning of our period was the armies of Asia Minor and their officers, such as Phokas, whereas toward the end the greatest threat came from the armies and officers of Macedonia, such as Bryennios. In this sense, little changed in the underlying structural dynamics of imperial power, only their geographical orientation. Thus this history will focus on the assets and vulnerabilities of imperial authority, on how emperors sought to win support and stave off enemies, first, in a phase of rapid imperial expansion; then during a phase of consolidation and equilibrium; and finally during a sudden defeat and rapid decline.

As with the title of the book, the chapter titles have also been borrowed from expressions in contemporary sources that seemed strikingly relevant.[5]

ACKNOWLEDGMENTS

I AM GRATEFUL to many friends and colleagues whom I consulted during the writing of this book. I thank Ilias Anagnostakis, Cliff Ando, Scott Kennedy, Dimitris Krallis, Eric McGeer, Gerasimos Merianos, Charis Messis, Christian Raffensperger, Paul Stephenson, and Denis Sullivan. Audiences at many universities, including Ohio State, Chicago, Cambridge, Oxford, and Birmingham, provided thoughtful comments, corrections, and suggestions. Ian Mladjov deserves special thanks for reading through the entire book carefully and correcting many mistakes and infelicitous expressions. In addition to his detailed knowledge of history, he is also the best cartographer and genealogist a Byzantinist could know. I thank also Paulos Kosmetatos for decades of prodding (even if this is not exactly the book he had in mind), and Stefan Vranka at Oxford University Press for his interest in this project, invaluable guidance at all stages, and wit.

A NOTE ON TRANSLITERATION

A S A RULE, I transliterate Byzantine names from the Greek (e.g., Ioannes and Theodoros) rather than Latinize or Anglicize them, which is a mildly offensive practice that persists almost uniquely in the case of Byzantium. Public discourse in recent decades increasingly strives to recognize cultural distinctiveness and use foreign names out of respect. Renaming everyone for convenience projects cultural dominance (or, worse, assumes it). Thus filling Byzantium with people falsely named "John," however innocuous it may have once been, is a convention whose time is up. (Note that transliteration captures spelling, not phonology.) I have tried to do the same with names from all the cultures that appear in this book, only I do not mark long vowels in Arabic (just as I do not in Greek either). One exception to this approach is for individuals who are already well known by the English forms of their names, such as Justinian and Basil II (a rough standard for "well known" is whether that name is used in two or more English book titles). The same goes for place names. Another exception is for the western leaders of the First Crusade, for whom I have also used conventional names.

Introduction

The Byzantine Empire in the Tenth Century

Romanía

In the tenth century, what we call Byzantium was still just the eastern Roman empire, with Constantinople as its capital. After the invasions by Arabs, Avars, Slavs, and Bulgars in the seventh century, its territory had been reduced to Asia Minor, Thrace, southern Greece, and southern Italy. But it was still the Roman empire. More accurately, it was "the empire of the Romans." It had a proper name, *Romanía*, which had been in use since the fourth century. Its ruler was the *basileus* of the Romans, which in Greek just meant king, but we call it an empire because it was descended from the ancient *imperium Romanum*. The Byzantines also ranked themselves and their ruler as superior in standing, prestige, culture, antiquity, and world-historical importance (even on a theological level), a claim that was often accepted by their neighbors, especially smaller Christian powers. The Byzantine *basileus* was not like any other king.

By the tenth century, however, Byzantium was not much of an empire by the most common modern definition of that word, namely rule by one ethnic or religious group (a minority of the population) over a multiethnic majority of subjects. In Byzantium, a Roman was anyone who was raised speaking Greek, was Orthodox Christian, and considered himself a member of the polity of the Romans as defined by its laws, customs, religion, and state institutions. This accounted for the majority of the population, approximately ten million people, though not everyone: there were still unassimilated Slavic groups in the Peloponnese and Greece, Armenians and Georgians in the eastern provinces, foreign contingents in the army, Paulician heretics, and Jews, all of whom could be more or less assimilated to the dominant cultural norms. Overall, Romanía looked more like a Roman kingdom that had minorities than a true multiethnic empire, though in the later tenth and eleventh centuries the balance would shift toward imperial rule over recently conquered or annexed foreign territories. Still, the boundaries between Roman and barbarian were never as stark as our sources suggest. The Byzantines were xenophobic and generally prejudiced against outsiders, but at the same time it was easy for foreign individuals and groups who entered the empire to assimilate to Roman ways and, by the second or third generation, to become Romans with no distinguishing traits. Over the centuries, Goths, Huns, Slavs, Arabs, Persians, and people from many other backgrounds were assimilated, usually through military service or land settlements. Being Roman was a cultural-political identity that could be taken on. In addition, the emperors claimed hegemony over smaller Christian states in Italy, the Adriatic coast, and the Caucasus. In practice, these were mostly autonomous, but in the eyes of Constantinople they were satellites, and some would be ceded or just annexed in the age of conquest.

By ancient or medieval standards, and for a realm of its size, Byzantium was culturally homogeneous, socially integrated, and unified by exclusive and sovereign state institutions. It is important to stress how different it was in this respect from western medieval kingdoms. Unlike the lands of the former western Roman empire, the core territories of the realm were not quasi-autonomous domains ruled by hereditary local lords, with whom the emperors had to engage in internal diplomacy to obtain support, tribute, or soldiers. They were rather administrative provinces governed by magistrates sent out from the capital for brief periods in rotation. Taxes, recruitment, law, religion, and salaries were fairly standardized and administered across imperial territory by bureaus that were headquartered in Constantinople. These grids of administrative coherence (including the Church) were parallel, hierarchical, and centralized, and they bound the provinces to the capital in overlapping ways. In the tenth century, Byzantium was second to none in the efficiency of its taxation, the resources that it could generate for use by the state, the sophistication and complexity of its bureaucratic apparatus, and the authority that the state could claim in governing the lives of all Romans.

The Roman people, moreover, were not divided by law or custom into castes or fixed classes; nor was nobility claimed as a right of blood by a handful of families. The same law—a Greek version of Roman law—applied to everyone, and families became powerful only when they succeeded in court politics and managed to retain imperial favor. Thus, even though some benefited from inherited connections, prestige, and wealth, there was also considerable political mobility and turnover. In a law, the emperor Basil II speculated that the life span of a powerful family was between seventy and one hundred years (though some lasted longer), but at the same time a poor man could become powerful by rising up and obtaining court titles.[1] In Byzantium, then, "nobility of family" was a rhetorical way by which to praise the rich and powerful for as long as they remained in power. It corresponded to no legal fact or fixed social reality but rather reflected a desire for a certain kind of social image. It is probably better to speak of a ruling elite who were powerful because they held offices at the court, in the army, and in the Church, and whose membership changed over time, often due to shifts in imperial favor. It was an aristocracy of service, not blood, despite the occasional rhetoric, and it "organized power through title and office rather than through family."[2] Likewise, imperial power itself was as much institutional as based on personal relations, a fact that historians have forgotten recently. We will see, for example with the Paphlagonians, that nobodies could step into positions of authority and command obedience—until they became unpopular, like anyone else.

This picture so far gives the impression that emperors were all-powerful. The monarchy did control all institutions of the state and could usually impose its will on the Church as well, so long as it did not try to change fundamental aspects of doctrine or ritual practice. There was no independent court of appeal, no legal limit to an emperor's power. But in practice, the emperors were highly vulnerable and insecure for reasons relating to the nature of the monarchy since its creation by Augustus and stemming in part from its elective ideology; there was no hereditary or absolute right to power. Accession to the throne was accomplished politically or militarily, but either way one had to obtain the consent of the Roman people, especially the populace of Constantinople, the army, magistrates, court, clergy, and whatever special-interest groups were powerful at any time. Emperors were created when those elements of society agreed to acclaim them publicly. If an emperor was popular, he could arrange this on behalf of an heir or successor. But if the emperor was unpopular, it was only a matter of time until someone else rose up, through a palace coup or military rebellion, to take his place. Thus, both emperors and rivals, i.e., potential emperors, looked to the legitimating power of Roman society, a broad social field. They always tried to remain popular and monitored public opinion as closely as they could, for it could promise opportunity—or spell doom. Legitimacy was not won once and for all; it had to be maintained politically in an ongoing process.

Dynasties were only provisional arrangements of power, vulnerable to challenge and liable to be suspended or overthrown. There were no guarantees in the transmission of imperial power, as no one had a right to inherit the *res publica* (*politeia* in Greek), the public affairs of the Roman people, which could not be privately owned. This was the "republican" basis of the imperial monarchy: the emperor was answerable to the polity (the *politeia*).[3] To mitigate this systemic insecurity, the monarchy promoted the narrative of divine election, and most Romans were happy to regard their *basileus* as God's favorite. But when their mood soured, God never rescued any emperor. Thus, the throne was up for grabs and the emperors were always trying to preempt or suppress rivals and protect themselves against plots and rebellions. This framework for the exercise of power shaped the empire's military and foreign policy for, in effect, there were two main political arenas in Romanía: Constantinople and the frontier armies. The emperors had to be watchful of both, which feature prominently in our sources. Given that the armies, especially ambitious officers, posed a great threat to the survival of any regime in Constantinople, military policy aimed as much to mitigate that threat as to defend the empire from foreign enemies. The history of Byzantium was to a great degree shaped by the tension between the court and the armies, which played out against a backdrop of foreign war. Let us look more closely at these two major sites of contestation.

Imperial governance

Constantinople, also known as New Rome or just the City, was the beating heart of the eastern empire, situated on the Bosporos at one of the most strategic and beautiful locations in the eastern Mediterranean. As a city and imperial capital it surpassed in size, power, and sheer magnificence any other place in the Christian world. Its monumental architecture and core layout were still those of the late antique capital built by Constantine, Theodosius, and Justinian, though damage from fires, riots, and earthquakes would everywhere have been apparent. Still, the Byzantines spared no praise for it. For them Constantinople was The Eye of the World and the Reigning City, monumental visual proof that the empire itself occupied a higher place in the cosmic order. Between the massive walls, paved boulevards, tall spiral columns, sprawling palace, and golden dome of Hagia Sophia, foreigners who came to the City were left speechless by what they saw, an impact skillfully exploited in Byzantine diplomacy. As a poet enthused in the midtenth century:

> After a long and wearisome journey, the traveler sees from a distance towers rising high into the air and, like strong giants in stride, columns that rise up to the highest point, and tall houses and temples whose vast roofs reach to the heights—who would not become instantly filled with joy? . . . And when he reaches the wall and draws near to the gates, who does not greet the City, lower his neck, kneel to the ground, grasp the famous earth, and say, "Hail, Glory created by the Cosmos"? And then he enters, full of joy.[4]

The City did not impress only foreigners and provincials. Its public spaces and monuments were effectively a series of stages on which imperial power was performed in full sight of the City's populace. The *Book of Ceremonies* compiled at the court of Konstantinos VII (d. 959) provides directions for many processions, ceremonies, acclamations, and public acts that together defined the civic and ecclesiastical calendar. The population of Constantinople, too, was enormous by medieval standards, perhaps around 250,000 or more. Given the high mortality rates of medieval cities, to maintain this population and to grow, as it did during our period, the City needed to import thousands of people every year from the provinces along with massive quantities of food. People were constantly moving to the capital to make their fortune, and the bureaucracy and ruling class there were admitting new men from the provinces. Constantinople was a magnet for the most talented and well-connected, but also the most destitute, for it was there that imperial and Church philanthropy was most bountiful. It was a place of opportunity. The founder of the reigning Macedonian dynasty, Basileios I (867–886), was a peasant who went to the City to escape poverty, and maneuvered his way to the throne.

To remain safely on the throne, emperors had to ensure that they were perceived by their subjects as just, pious, merciful, and compassionate, and by potential enemies, both domestic and foreign, as formidable; they had to defend the empire from barbarian attack, enforce the law fairly, and maintain support among the ruling elite. To a considerable degree this was accomplished through propagandistic images, but it also required the skillful use of the mechanisms of imperial governance. Roughly speaking, these were of three types: permanent institutions that operated in the background regardless of the degree of interest an emperor showed in them; the cultivation of political support through the system of court titles and offices, which shaped the upper echelons of imperial society; and personnel decisions that created a regime around the emperor. Let us consider these in turn.

The three permanent institutions that were most important in terms of their administrative apparatus and impact on the rest of society were the army, the Church, and the tax system. We will discuss the army in more detail below, but we should note here that it was by far the most dangerous concentration of power in the empire. In the midtenth century, the (nominal) rolls may have included 140,000 men, a number that grew during the age of conquest, though expeditionary forces were normally small, around 5,000. Even so, at more than 1 percent of the population, the army accounted for roughly 5 percent of adult males and consumed the largest part of the imperial budget (though figures are lacking). Simply keeping up its numbers would have required the recruitment of about 5,000 men each year, or more if additional units were being created. Its demographic impact was major and its organization required a complex bureaucratic apparatus that linked the court to the provincial headquarters.

The Church also had a large bureaucracy, for managing its extensive properties and personnel and for resolving the legal questions that arose from the application of canon law to society. The clergy numbered in the thousands, with thousands more in the monasteries that were scattered across the empire, some of which had extensive properties and trade interests. The Church was heavily involved in providing ideological support for the imperial order, and some bishops and even monks were deeply involved in politics. The emperor generally dominated the Church on the mundane level of administration. He could depose or appoint patriarchs of Constantinople, who, in our period of interest, were mostly administrators serving at the emperor's pleasure. The exceptions were Polyeuktos, who actively lobbied for episcopal prerogatives, and Keroularios, who meddled in regime change, to his undoing.

Whereas the army was the most expensive and dangerous institution in the empire, the tax system produced most of the revenue, though it could make an emperor unpopular if its power was abused. The emperors generally liked to keep tax collecting out of the hands of the local generals, to limit their options and keep them dependent on the court for funding. We need not discuss here all the bureaus involved in the collection of a complex array of taxes, fees, imposts, and such, not all of which are well understood today. Suffice it to say that they formed the basis for the imperial order, enabling the emperor to pay the army, magistrates, titulars, and other expenses, and it also tied local populations and their lands to the imperial organization of society. Taxation was efficient, if not ruthless. The system ultimately rested on a census of taxable properties that, periodically updated, created yet another bureaucratic grid linking the capital to the provinces. The tax collector was a ubiquitous figure and emblematic of an inevitable order. He appeared in the Byzantines' dreams, and the definition of a remote place was one that he did not visit in his rounds, such as mountaintops. There were no "isolated" peasants untroubled by dealings with the state. Lobbying at the court by all classes of society mostly aimed at obtaining tax exemptions.[5]

The court also shaped the upper echelons of imperial society, through its assignment and distribution of offices and titles. The two must be distinguished. Offices were salaried positions in the administration or army that required the performance of specific functions (e.g., a *strategos* or general; *protasekretis* or head of the secretariat). Titles, by contrast, were salaried honorifics that fixed one's status in the court hierarchy, but had no functions and were for life. To simplify to those that we will encounter, there were ranks associated with the emperor himself, such as *kaisar* (Caesar), *nobelissimos*, and *kouropalates* (the latter also bestowed on foreign rulers viewed as clients), followed by titles such as *proedros, magistros, patrikios*, and *protospatharios*. The holders of the higher ranks together formed the senate. Both offices and titles entailed a salary, or *roga*, personally paid to the highest ranks by the emperor at a special ceremony in the palace: he literally handed out bags of gold coins and silk garments. They also entitled bearers to additional gratuities, perks, and privileges.[6] Generals were expected to maintain their retinues and guards from these salaries. The emperor thus not only selected but financially maintained a courtly, senatorial, and military elite. Titles (and their salaries) were also given to foreign rulers, both local lords and even kings, to bind them to the empire. The court system thus extended beyond the frontier, blurring the lines between court politics and foreign policy. It was also possible to purchase titles from the court, pending approval by the emperor, by paying a sum of gold and then receiving the annual salary. Even though one would likely not recoup the original sum, titles conferred valuable social advantages.[7] We do not know all the titles for which this could be done, though the system probably resulted in a net gain for the fisc. It was crucial for the maintenance of the imperial order, and its apparent abuse in the eleventh century exacerbated the state's fiscal problems, as we will see.

The social value of court titles and the sheer presence of these overlapping layers of bureaucracy across the provinces is strikingly reflected in the Byzantine lead seals (Figure 1). These were hammered shut on a string that bound a folded document. They typically featured an inscription of the official's name, office, and ranks, thereby establishing his status, along with an

FIGURE 1 Lead seal of Basileios, imperial *protospatharios* and *chartoularios* of the *dromos* of the Armeniakoi (tenth century). The inscription on the obverse says "Lord, help your servant," while that on the reverse gives Basileios' name, rank, and office. Basileios was an administrator or secretary (*chartoularios*) in the provincial branch office of the Byzantine bureau for transportation, roads, and the post (*dromos*). © Dumbarton Oaks, Byzantine Collection, Washington, DC (accession no.: BZS.1955.1.1380).

image, usually a saint or the Virgin. The documents have been lost, but the lead seals tend to survive. More than sixty thousand have been recovered, from all provinces, and each seal represents an instance of a transmitted document. This was an empire with busy lines of communication and a robust bureaucracy. (Lead seals are also important to historians because they preserve the names, offices, and titles of officials in a more comprehensive way than do the literary sources. They provide not only "big data" but also the "metadata" of the imperial bureaucracy.)

Sitting atop these instruments of governance, emperors faced two main dilemmas. First, they needed competent men to fill the highest positions, especially the army, but the most competent men tended to be ambitious and so posed a danger. Second, they needed to govern through formal and impersonal institutions but also had to find ways to assert personal control over them so as not to be sidelined by them. In response, emperors had developed a range of strategies, which we see in our period. Generally, they marginalized collateral relatives, especially brothers and sisters, who were nuclei of potential challenge from within the dynasty. Byzantine emperors did not traditionally rule through their families. The exceptions in our period were Nikephoros Phokas, Michael IV, and Konstantinos X Doukas, whose regimes were extremely different from each other, though after Alexios I Komnenos (1081) family rule became the norm. Military commands were gradually divided into smaller regions and assigned in rotation, and generals were usually not posted to their home province, so that no one person or family could build up a power base. Multiple commands meant that powerful officer families could be used to check each other, as for instance the Argyros and Kourkouas families against the Phokas and Maleïnos families, or, later, Phokas against Skleros.[8] The smaller professional armies (*tagmata*) were used to check the larger provincial forces (*themata*) and non-Roman mercenary armies used to check regular Roman forces. Of course, it was possible for an emperor to form a relationship of trust with a general and then give him or his family extraordinary power. This is how our story begins, with Konstantinos VII and Nikephoros Phokas, but it was rare. Another solution was for the emperor to take command of the armies in person, an option taken to an almost paranoid extreme by Basil II.

In addition, emperors needed to ensure their popularity among the people of the City and the political class, because that made it difficult for usurpers to justify their cause. In the eleventh century, as emperors enjoyed dwindling dynastic continuity, this resulted in the fiscally disastrous policy of distributing expensive gifts at the beginning of every reign to buy political support, including state salaries. Emperors also preferred to give extraordinary powers to men who could not take the throne, especially eunuch administrators. Many emperors had a eunuch "prime minister," who often held the position of *parakoimomenos* (i.e., chamberlain) and was placed in charge of the civilian administration, but in the end emperors could appoint any member of their cabinet to this role, even their personal eunuch-stewards, who did not hold formal office in the administration. This "informal" flexibility at the top was a mechanism by which emperors could dominate the bureaucracy, which could use inflexibility to otherwise limit the power of emperor. Alternately, they used bishops for this role, or even eunuch-monks. During the eleventh century, emperors increasingly used such figures to command the armies, so great had imperial insecurity become. Let us turn, then, to the Roman army of this period, a constant protagonist in our story.

The army and war

The Byzantine emperors excelled at projecting soft power. They allowed foreign rulers to compete for the privilege of marrying into the Byzantine elite; they bestowed court titles and prestige items of Byzantine culture as tokens of favor; educated foreign princes in Byzantine ways; overwhelmed ambassadors with elaborate ceremonies, gifts, and monuments; and used spies, suborned foreign notables, and harbored defeated rebels from foreign states. State receptions in particular were meant to be overwhelming. To receive the envoys of Tarsos (in Cilicia) in 946, the reception hall and its surroundings were decked out with silk hangings, laurel wreaths and flowers, and silver chains, and the hall was covered with Persian carpets and sprinkled with rose water. The entire court, thousands of people, stood in a prescribed order in full ceremonial regalia, acclamations were chanted to the accompaniment of organs, and the emperor sat on a throne that was imagined to be a replica of that of the Old Testament king Solomon. It was flanked by mechanical moving animals, including roaring lions and warbling birds, and could be lifted up into the air while the envoys were prostrate on the floor.[9] This was soft power, and it also served to introduce Konstantinos VII as the new sole ruler of the empire. But the tenth-century empire was also prepared for war.

The tenth-century Roman army had two tiers: the *themata*, local defense forces based in the provinces (called "themes"), and the *tagmata*, the smaller, elite, professional units that were originally posted around Constantinople but, over time, came to be posted closer to the frontiers as well. The thematic armies were the descendants of the late Roman field armies that were pulled back into Asia Minor during the crisis of the seventh century. Hence the old big themes were named in the plural genitive after those armies, e.g., Anatolikon ("of the Orientals," i.e., the army of *Oriens*). Each of these armies was under a general (*strategos*), who gradually took on the functions of a provincial governor too. But over time the themes were divided up into smaller units, so that there were more and more of these general-governors, each with smaller jurisdiction and forces. As the empire began to regain ground in the east during the tenth century, each small new acquisition was made into a separate district around a fort or fortified town, whose general commanded only a few hundred men. Some of these new districts were settled by Armenians colonists and so were called "the Armenian themes" (as opposed to the large, older Roman themes). By 970, this process had reached its logical conclusion and a new system had to be devised, which we will examine in due course. In 955 the forces of the Anatolikon, Armeniakon, and Cappadocia remained the backbone of the army in the eastern provinces.

The thematic armies contained a core of full-time, salaried soldiers as well as a majority of soldiers on the rolls who were supported by the military lands. We are not concerned here with the (controversial) origins of this institution. By the tenth century, certain lands in the provinces had come to be designated as military in that their proceeds contributed to the upkeep of a soldier. A greater extent or quality of land was pegged for the upkeep of a cavalry soldier than for an infantryman. Local communities were expected to support and supply the armies near them in a number of ways, but this was counted toward their regular tax obligations. The "military lands" were a different arrangement: in exchange for supporting a soldier linked to this land (*strateia*), its owners paid only a basic tax and were free of additional impositions. The burden was thereby linked to the land, not the person. The soldiers themselves also received salaries (smaller in comparison to their full-time counterparts), campaign pay, a variety of one-off gifts, and social privileges. Military lands could be divided up among owners, who need not have included the soldier himself, but it may have been common for thematic soldiers to engage in farming when they were not serving. In the tenth century, it became ever more possible to fiscalize the *strateia*, that is pay full taxes in exchange for not providing a soldier. We do not know how widespread this option was. The idea was that the state would use that money to hire full-time soldiers, who were fewer but presumably better, i.e., the *tagmata*.[10]

The *tagmata* consisted of full-time soldiers and contained a higher ratio of elite cavalry. They had been formed in the eighth century as a counterweight to the large thematic armies of Asia Minor, which too many generals had used in their efforts to gain the throne. There were a number of tagmatic armies, such as the *exkoubitores, hikanatoi*, and, the most important one, the *scholai*, each of which had only a few thousand men. The most important officer of the *tagmata* was the captain of the *scholai*, called a *domestikos*, who often assumed the overall command of campaign operations. This is the position from which, as we will see, the Phokas family dominated the armed forces for almost half a century. In addition, the Roman army always employed foreign soldiers, either barbarian mercenaries or units lent by or hired from neighboring client states. We have to be careful with these. Our sources, Roman and foreign, love to enumerate the colorful ethnic names of these units, partly in order to caricature Roman armies,[11] and this has misled many historians into thinking that the Byzantine army was fundamentally multiethnic. Yet these units rarely had more than a few hundred men, and were useful because they practiced specific types of war. A long list of such units does not mean that all claimed an equal fraction of the army as did Romans. In a speech to the army in 958, the emperor Konstantinos VII reminds his officers (of both tagmatic and thematic forces) that there are "some units" of barbarians fighting alongside them, so the rest should fight bravely to impress these visitors with the courage of "our people ... the Roman people."[12] A military manual of that period imagines a large campaign force as consisting of 11,200 heavy infantry (including both tagmatic and thematic forces, both Romans and Armenians), 4,800 light infantry archers, 6,000 cavalry (500 heavy cavalry), and a few hundred Rus' auxiliaries (some of these groups overlapped).[13] Most expeditionary forces, however, would have been much smaller, usually only a few thousand. This was not an age of massive armies.

The present narrative begins in 955 when the empire's high command, meaning primarily Nikephoros and Leon Phokas, had decided to switch from a primarily defensive posture to an offense aimed at permanently conquering territory in the southeast (i.e., Cilicia and Syria). For centuries, imperial military doctrine prioritized safety and defense by generally avoiding battle with equal-sized armies of raiders, harassing them from the hills, and ambushing them in passes. Leon Phokas specialized at this type of warfare, which is codified in the treatise *On Skirmishing*. But starting in 955, a strategy of conquest was put into motion against the most dangerous enemies in the southeast, the Cilician cities (such as Tarsos) and the Hamdanid emirate of Aleppo under Sayf al-Dawla. The exponents of this brutal new phase of war were Nikephoros Phokas and Ioannes Tzimiskes. Their approach is partly reflected in a treatise attributed to the former, called the *Praecepta militaria*.[14] Historians often assume that the conquests were carried out by the *tagmata*, whereas the themes were the defense forces of the past. Yet as we will see repeatedly, the offensive armies were mixed, and the themes likely still provided the majority of the soldiers. However, if the *strateia* was increasingly commuted to cash, generals in offensive operations may have come to rely more on full-time soldiers, whether tagmatic or thematic. The distinction between the two would have gradually become moot, and we lose sight of it during the long reign of Basil II (976–1025) as *tagmata* came to be posted in the provinces.

How did palace-based emperors control this powerful war machine? First, their decisions were not bound by a rigid chain of command. Emperors managed the army with the same flexibility and ad hoc appointments that they used for the civil administration. They could, and did, appoint anyone to take overall command, including eunuchs, courtiers, or even former monks, in addition to the "bearded" officer class, and could create extraordinary positions for them to fill (e.g., *stratopedarches* for eunuchs, *stratelates* for non-eunuchs, both of which just mean generically "army commander").[15] When we begin, Konstantinos VII was using the *domestikos* of the *tagma* of the *scholai*, Nikephoros Phokas, as the commander-in-chief of both the *tagmata* and *themata* in the campaign, even though the *domestikos* technically ranked beneath the general of the Anatolikon. Alternately, these command positions could just be left vacant. They were filled (or not) depending on what the emperor thought was expeditious and safe—safe for himself as much as for the empire.

Rather than survey them here, we will discuss the empire's geostrategic challenges and neighbors individually as they become important in the narrative. Each front was different and emperors reacted according to evolving situations. A word is necessary here on the cultural aspects of war, especially the religious aspects. Much attention has been paid recently to the question of whether the Byzantines had a concept of Holy War. The question is somewhat distracting, as it requires us (again) to view Byzantium through a western prism, one that is itself derived from a particular (and problematic) view of the Crusades. This is not to say, of course, that religion did not color the practice of war. Orthodoxy was a fundamental aspect of Byzantine identity and shaped the perception of history and current events. War was certainly viewed in religious terms and provoked religious reactions. The military defense of Romanía was accordingly suffused with religious associations, images, and practices, and understood as a defense of the faith, especially when the enemy was a pagan or Muslim. The armies were sent off with prayers and litanies, accompanied by priests and religious symbols, and exhorted with strongly religious rhetoric. However, religion did not predetermine or even shape imperial strategy and military objectives. There was no difference in how Roman armies treated Muslims or Christians (though the former were often expelled from conquered territories). The Byzantines never thought of freeing the Holy Land or destroying Islam by force, and they were as likely to wage war against each other as against the infidel. They were not encouraged by either secular or religious authorities to take up the sword against the infidel, but defending the empire was a patriotic duty. Orthodoxy was the rhetoric or cultural style in which otherwise pragmatic policies were expressed. This book will focus on the latter.

"Landed aristocracy"? "Anatolian magnates"?

The military history of this period had a different trajectory from the economic. On the military side, the empire expanded dramatically after 955 and quickly lost ground between 1064 and 1078. But the period overall witnessed economic and demographic growth. More land was probably brought under cultivation and trade increased, resulting in more production and revenues for the state.[16] There were occasional downturns within this picture of otherwise steady growth, such as droughts and famine (localized in time and space), and the loss of Asia Minor caused extraordinary hardship in the 1070s. It might one day be possible to write a history of this period in which the political and the economic are more closely and horizontally integrated.

For now, however, we must push back against a specific socioeconomic meta-narrative that was imposed on the political history of Byzantium and still holds sway in some quarters.

In the first half of the twentieth century, prominent Byzantinists sought to normalize the empire's history within its broader medieval context by finding the point when it became "feudalized" and thereby joined the mainstream of western history by moving from a bureaucratic-Roman stat-ist mode of existence to a proper medieval one. They fixed that point in the tenth and eleventh century on the basis of two assumptions. The first is that there was a tension, or open war, between the central bureaucratic state and aristocrat-landowners in Asia Minor, the latter providing also the empire's "military families." This phenomenon is described as the "take-over of the state by the aristocratic families," resulting in the regime of the Komnenoi and the feudalized empire of the Palaiologoi. The second is that these rich men or the socially "powerful" (*dynatoi*) were gobbling up the lands of smaller landowners and thereby also imperiling the basis of military recruitment. By 1081, these "Anatolian magnates" or "aristoc-racy" owned much or most of the land and had imposed feudal orders on the Byzantine countryside. Two of the leading proponents of this picture, the Russian historians A. Vasiliev and G. Ostrogorsky, embedded it into the standard histories of Byzantium that they wrote, which were translated into many languages. The idea was picked up by scholars in the west (espe-cially France) who wanted to approach Byzantium as a medieval society, with an emphasis on land and socioeconomic relations rather than politics and "mere" narrative.

"Feudalization" lies at the core of this paradigm and infects the whole of it. I say infects because, in the end, feudalism turned out to be more trouble than it was worth in the Byzantine context, and has now even been rejected by many western medieval historians too. Even if scholars avoid the term and use only its surface concepts, such as the "landed magnates" who ran the army, these notions too make sense only within the narrative provided by feu-dalization, which they were designed to push historically. In the rest of this introduction, I will argue that most of this paradigm is a modern fiction, in both its hard and "lite" forms. The political history of Byzantium certainly played out against a background of socioeconomic structures and transforma-tions, as all societies always do, but there is little proof for this specific one. The feudalization paradigm becomes especially problematic the closer it is brought to bear on the events that it aims to explain. Those events are better explained within the known features of the Byzantine political scene, where potential rivals financially maintained by the court were always looking to seize power within a stable system, rather than as symptoms of far-reaching socioeconomic changes.

There were definitely wars between the emperors in Constantinople and their rivals in the provinces, but there is no warrant for calling the latter "landed magnates"; nor were the "emperors threatened on many occasions by powerful Anatolian landowners."[17] The emperors were threatened not by landowners but by army officers. Some were no doubt landowners, but there is no evidence that they were dangerous because of their property—in other words, that they were so rich that they could challenge the imperial state by means of personal resources, something that was possible in the West. Instead, they were dangerous because they could subvert the loyalty of the armies through the military prestige that they had acquired through service.[18] In the revolts that we know the most about (963, 1043, 1047, 1057), we see nothing but officers canvassing support among the army. These officers did not have private armies, as is often implied. They had retinues, but this was expected of generals, to be maintained from their salaries. Their household staff could never threaten a regular army unit.[19] Nor did they have private forts, only army installations in the territories that they controlled as generals or rebels. To seize power, they had to act subversively from *within* the imperial system, not leverage it from the outside. And we need to be completely honest about this: apart from a dubious anecdote,[20] we have no idea of the scale of the properties of the officers or "families" in question. They may have owned most of Asia Minor, or had more modest holdings, "wealthy" only in relation to poorer neighbors. Recent studies have even suggested that the wealth of the officer class may have derived from their salaries, not their lands.[21] There is only one high official (not a general) whose properties we can estimate, the judge and historian Michael Attaleiates, and he tells us that he bought them with his state salary.[22] As Mark Whittow put it already in 1996, "landownership was relatively divorced from political power."[23] He too found no evidence for provincial power bases that could challenge the government.

Social scientists would be surprised to learn that Byzantinists have been postulating fundamental socioeconomic conflicts and transformations based on such meager—in fact, nonexistent—data. It is so dire that we sometimes resort to data from literary fiction, yet we still confidently call these alleged aristocrats a "conquering socio-economic force."[24] "Aristocracy" is another problematic term. Byzantinists have produced no model in which this term adds anything to what we already know existed: a ruling elite of state and Church office holders. This elite was marked by high turnover and had no hereditary right to office or titles, and no legal authority over persons and territories except that which came from office. Ultimately, historians use the term *aristocracy* just because in the eighth century our sources begin to record second names. Perhaps not coincidentally, it is also in the late eighth century that we begin to have sources.[25] But sporting a surname does not necessarily make one an "aristocrat" according to any specific social model; nor can we prove that Byzantium in 950 was more aristocratic than it had been a century earlier. We have more family names for later periods, but the numbers are small and subject to the limitations of our sources. As suggested above, "aristocracy" better describes the rhetoric used by some of these people while they held power. But taking it at face value as a socioeconomic category, we risk turning the political ambitions of generals and courtiers into a narrative of class conflict against "the state" that led to feudalization—a fiction.

A powerful refutation of that narrative is the fact that, whenever these "surnamed" types (whether generals or "aristocratic" courtiers) seized power, they pursued the same policies as the Macedonian emperors, that is, protecting small landholders and distrusting the "powerful" (*dynatoi*). Nikephoros Phokas followed the same policies as Basil II, the enemy of the Phokades. And later, when the Komnenoi seized power in 1081, they had already lost all their lands in Asia Minor. They could not have leveraged private assets to take control of the state, as is so often implied, but the reverse: they used their positions in the army to take over the state because they had no other recourse against extinction. And Alexios ruled through his family not because he was an "aristocrat" (and that, presumably, was what aristocrats did) but the reverse: an aristocracy of family emerged in the twelfth century precisely because Alexios, for contingent reasons, had decided to rule through his extended family.

What, then, about the land legislation and the grasping of the so-called powerful?[26] In the famine of 927–928, some small landowners and members of village communes (taxed as units by the state) were compelled to sell their land cheaply to owners of larger estates (which were taxed outside the commune system), including to monasteries and the churches. The emperor Romanos I Lakapenos (920–944) sought to protect the weak by passing two laws that made it difficult for the powerful to acquire such lands and gave villagers the ability to reclaim them under certain circumstances. This legislation was maintained and progressively strengthened by subsequent emperors, who also took care to ensure that the service function of the military lands was fixed and inalienable. It is on the basis of these laws that historians have postulated a narrative of agrarian transformation in Byzantium, with the "aristocracy" gobbling up the lands of the villages and small landowners. But we have to be skeptical about this alleged transformation, as no sources prove or even indicate that it actually happened. We have no data about the size, shape, or internal articulation of the economy, or how the population was distributed into economic categories. We do not have figures for the extent or distribution of land ownership, whether in absolute or relative terms, or how it changed over time. Socioeconomic changes require *some* evidentiary basis, but here there is none. Large estates may have grown, but how much? Some scholars estimate that small holdings remained the norm, whereas others think that large ones expanded dramatically.[27] These are guesses.

Ultimately, it all rests on the testimony of Romanos I and the decision of his successors to maintain and add to his provisions. Romanos, moreover, was dealing with a unique crisis caused by a famine, so we have to ask: How many cases would induce him to issue this law? Ten? Five? We do not know what data the emperors had, or the degree to which their actions and policies responded to data rather than to anecdotal evidence or personal experiences. This is a sobering amount of ignorance. Moreover, the emperors may have had more than practical legal issues in mind, for the situation allowed Romanos to pose as a protector of the weak against the strong, a traditional theme of political paternalism; in the Christian Roman empire, the strong were always understood to be oppressing the poor. Romanos was echoing previous imperial rhetoric and legislation that sought to protect the weak against the powerful, with Justinian as a prominent precedent for using the same language.[28] This stance made emperors look good, and the emperors of the Macedonian dynasty in particular modeled themselves on the ancient lawgivers. And ṛhe emperors—our sole source for this problem—may also have had an interest in exaggerating the scope of the problem in order to check precisely those elements of society that could potentially give them the most trouble. So even though we should not deny that abuses were taking place, there are limits to how much actual history we can extract from the rhetoric of such laws. We need to approach them with greater caution.

The nature of the powerful must also be considered. They were not some private interests newly created by inscrutable and unstoppable economic forces operating "out there" in the provinces but, as defined in the laws themselves, state officials, title holders, high-ranking churchmen, and rich monasteries.[29] In other words, the emperors were facing a socioeconomic problem that the imperial order itself had created and was maintaining, an old story. Moreover, I suspect that the worst offenders among the land-grasping powerful were in fact the monasteries and Churches, not individuals, families, and the officer class. Emperors repeatedly tried to check the expansion of the wealth of religious institutions above and beyond their general attempts to limit the problem of the *dynatoi*, and sought ways to ensure that churches and monasteries contributed their fair share in taxes (e.g., Basil II's *allelengyon*). Even in the case of powerful individuals who are said to have amassed much land, for example, the eunuch chamberlain Basileios Lakapenos, those acquisitions usually took the form of endowments for a monastic foundation (and Lakapenos was not an "Anatolian magnate"). In other words, the two pillars of the feudalization narrative may not have been connected after all: the wars between the emperors and the generals had little to do with the emergence of a feudal aristocracy, while the growth of large estates was caused more by churches and monasteries. Yet Byzantinists have not developed ways of talking about tensions between the court and religious institutions. For ideological reasons, we are too accustomed to seeing them as conjoined pillars of the same imperial "Orthodox" regime. But it turns out that the emperors of this period tried to keep them at arm's length.

In sum, this narrative will not replace socioeconomic history with political and military history. Rather, it will challenge one specific reconstruction of the socioeconomic history of Byzantium—a view according to which vast private forces arose from nebulous sources in the economy and life of the provinces, and then "took over" the state—and it will replace this view with a different model of the economic and political workings of Byzantine society. The imperial state lay always at the heart of any transformation taking place, both enabling emperors to rule and funding their potential rivals. The state structured society on so many levels that it could give rise to contradictory forces. Finally, when Asia Minor was conquered by the Turks and its former "aristocracy" had lost their lands and wealth, it is to the late Roman state that they turned, once again, to ensure their own survival.

PART I | Conquest and
Consolidation

CHAPTER I

"Avengers of Rome"

The First Phase of Conquest in the East (955–963)

The cast of the conquest: The final years of Konstantinos VII (d. 959)

The "Macedonian" dynasty was the most long-lived and successful in the history of the Roman empire. It was named after the origin of its founder, Basileios I (867–886), in the Byzantine theme located around Adrianople in what we would call Thrace. He was an intimidating man of humble origins who charmed and murdered his way to the top. His son, Leon VI the Wise (886–912), was a learned emperor who wrote laws and a military manual, and delivered sermons. Leon had to marry four times before he produced an heir in 905, Konstantinos VII, but four marriages violated the rules of Church and state. The Four Marriages scandal (Tetragamy) tore the Church apart, and when Leon died in 912, Konstantinos was a child. There followed a succession of regencies headed by the patriarch, the empress, and eventually the admiral Romanos Lakapenos, another man of humble birth. Romanos had displaced his rival Leon Phokas, the head of a military family that had provided loyal service to the Macedonian emperors. Romanos now entrenched his family in power. In 919, he married his daughter Helene to the young heir Konstantinos, and the next year he took the throne alongside him, allegedly for his own protection and to deal with the Bulgarian threat.

Romanos I would steer the ship of state ably until 944. He associated his own sons in the imperial power and relegated Konstantinos to ceremonial roles and the patronage of learning. The Phokas military family was also sidelined, but the Romans continued to reclaim territories in the east under the leadership of Ioannes Kourkouas, the greatest general of the age.[1] In 934, Kourkouas conquered Melitene, turning it into a theme. Melitene (modern Malatya, in eastern Turkey) was the nexus of the Roman, Arab, Armenian, and Syriac worlds. Control of Melitine would be essential for further expansion to take place in any of those directions. Yet in December 944, Romanos was deposed by his sons, made a monk, and exiled to an island. They aimed to establish their own dynasty, but had badly misjudged their popularity.

The people of Constantinople lived for palace rumor and turned out in large numbers whenever trouble was afoot. This time it was the false report that Konstantinos VII himself had been killed. They gathered around the palace and began to protest, until the Lakapenoi relented and allowed the forty-year-old heir to the throne to show himself to the crowd.[2] It was now only a matter of time: one side would oust the other. According to later reports, the Lakapenoi planned to kill Konstantinos at a dinner, but the plot was betrayed. Konstantinos struck first on January 27, 945, ambushing their men, arresting the two brothers, and packing them off to join their father Romanos in exile. Helene sided with him, her husband, against her brothers. She had already given him a son and heir, Romanos II, who would soon be crowned co-emperor. The throne thus reverted back to the Macedonians, now intermarried with the Lakapenoi. Konstantinos' life had been determined from the start by dynastic weakness. He had not wielded power for the half-century during which he wore the crown.

In transitions of power, emperors tried to keep as many people "onside" as possible. Konstantinos now brought back old Macedonian clients but retained some of Romanos' power brokers. The new governing coalition included two children of Romanos, Helene and Basileios, the latter an illegitimate son born to a "Skythian" (probably Bulgarian) slave and castrated as a child. Between 945 and 949, Konstantinos appointed Basileios his *parakoimomenos*, a highly trusted and influential position. Basileios Lakapenos was a patron of the arts and literature. The sources agree that he was capable and dynamic, and grew rich as a middleman, selling influence. He would be briefly sidelined by a rival under Romanos II, but otherwise survived the longest among Konstantinos' new team.[3] Another Lakapenos in office was the patriarch of Constantinople Theophylaktos, a son of Romanos who had been invested by his father when only sixteen. He is presented as frivolous, more interested in horses than religion.

On the military side, Konstantinos brought back the Phokas family, who supported him in his coup against the Lakapenoi. He appointed Bardas

Phokas, who was already an old man, as *domestikos* of the *scholai* (Bardas was the brother of Leon, the old rival of Romanos I). He also appointed Bardas' three sons to key positions in the thematic armies: Nikephoros to Anatolikon, Leon to Cappadocia, and Konstantinos to Seleukeia, effectively entrusting the eastern armies to this family.[4] Another key ally was Marianos of the Argyros family, a former monk and confidant of Romanos I. He had helped the Lakapenoi princes depose their father in 944, then switched sides to join Konstantinos VII in 945, and would be entrusted with military and diplomatic commands.

Konstantinos himself is described as tall, broad-shouldered, and fair-skinned with a long face, beak nose, and friendly glance.[5] This is a flattering picture. The chronicle tradition contains both positive and negative evaluations of his performance as emperor, especially his decisions and motives in making appointments.[6] He is remembered today and studied more for the contributions of his court to scholarship and the literary image of his own dynasty. Through compilations such as the *Book of Ceremonies* (a manual on how to conduct court ceremonies and religious festivals) and the *De adminis-trando imperio* (a hodgepodge of notes on the foreign nations that surrounded Romanía), along with historical narratives such as the Continuation of Theophanes (a set of imperial biographies that covers the years 813–867) and the *Life of Basileios I* (the founder of the dynasty), his court shaped how we still view much of Byzantine culture and history. Other scholarly projects included a vast, multivolume series of passages excerpted from ancient and Byzantine histories and arranged by topic (e.g., on embassies, plots, etc.). This is still a major source of fragments from otherwise lost authors. In a way, Konstantinos was trying to put the brand of his reign and dynasty on many major branches of learning, including separate compilations on agriculture, imperial expeditions, and the antiquarian lore of the empire's themes (i.e., provinces). These projects were certainly expensive, but their ideological thrust remains elusive; nor, being kept in few copies in the palace, could they realistically function as propaganda except among a tiny circle.

In 955, the empire faced four potential fronts, though not all were active simultaneously: Bulgaria in the north; the Muslim emirate of Crete in the south; the emirates of Tarsos (in Cilicia) and Aleppo in the southeast; and the emirate of Sicily, which threatened southern Italy. We will discuss the last two in this chapter, because they were active in the 950s. Specifically, we begin with the turn of the tide in 955, when Nikephoros Phokas replaced his father Bardas in command of the empire's strategy and launched an aggressive policy of conquest.

Turning the tide in the southeast

The border with the caliphate had changed little in the two centuries after the Arab conquests. It still ran diagonally across eastern Asia Minor from the Tauros mountains to the eastern coast of the Black Sea past Trebizond.[7] Byzantium began to annex territories along the middle portion of this line when the Abbasid caliphate began to decline during the ninth century. In 879, Basileios I captured Tephrike, the stronghold of Paulician heretics (a religious community of Romans and Armenians that had broken away from the empire, whose leaders aspired to a pure state). The number of border themes gradually multiplied, and in 934 Kourkouas conquered Melitene. Our sources say little about how new territories were annexed, but it does not seem that local populations merely exchanged rulers and carried on as before. The raids that led up to conquest were not chivalric contests but systematic state violence, an effort to "inflict maximum damage to the enemy's economy and material infrastructure—enslavement or killing of populations, destruction of fortifications and urban installations, devastation of the countryside."[8] The Byzantines had long been on the receiving end of this tactic, but were now inflicting it with a vengeance. A military manual recommends that for a city to be taken by force it helps to first send multiple raids, destroy crops, block all trade, and drive out the farmers.[9] Religious difference gave the violence an additional edge.

When forts were pulled down, the surrounding population would often have to leave until an Arab emir tried to rebuild them. Melitene and Samosata were sacked a number of times before the Romans finally conquered them. When they decided to stay instead of just ravage and pull back, it seems that they either expelled most of the Muslim population, enslaved them, forced them to convert, or recruited them into the army (usually sending them to serve in other parts of the empire).[10] They then repopulated these regions with Roman and Armenian colonists. These small new frontier units were collectively labeled "the Armenian *themata*" as opposed to the "great Roman *themata*." Lands were distributed among settlers with the obligation of military service attached (or paying the cash equivalent to the state). Some of the new lands were settled with deserters from the caliphate itself, including, in 935, some ten thousand fighting men of the tribe Banu Habib, the losers in an internal Arab struggle (against the Hamdanids, on whom more below). They had defected to the empire, had converted, and were settled around newly conquered Melitene.[11] When these groups are not heard of later, it generally means that they assimilated to Roman norms and ceased to be distinguishable. At the same time, Christians from Syria began to enter imperial territories, including both Melkites (Byzantine Orthodox) and Jacobites (Monophysites), who established their own churches and monastic centers, bringing economic ties to the Muslim lands.[12] Conversely, Muslims who were expelled became refugees in Islamic lands, where beggars even pretended to have been mutilated by the Romans to gain sympathy.[13]

By the 950s, the middle stretch of the border had been extended down to the upper Euphrates, within striking distance of northern Syria and al-Jazira. This left the Cilician plain accessible to Roman forces through the Tauros passes and also from northern Mesopotamia. The Cilician cities, the largest and most powerful of which was Tarsos, had been established long ago by the Abbasids as defensive bulwarks for Syria and as forward bases from which to raid Romanía through the Cilician Gates. In addition to Mopsouestia and Adana in Cilicia, these also included Germanikeia (Maraş) and Adata (Hadath) in northern Syria. The fleet of Tarsos often raided into the Aegean. Apart from their regular garrisons, the cities attracted thousands of volunteer fighters for Islam who came from the caliphate, were given lands, and were subsidized by the rest of the Islamic world by donations. These outposts of military-religious zeal were known as *thughur*. Annual raids were likely their main occupation in prior centuries, and special barracks accommodated the volunteers, though the influx of cash and men had diminished during the tenth century, especially after the Hamdanids took northern Syria, separating Cilicia from the caliphate.[14] Many had now turned to trade, and the population included a Christian element, which would prove more amenable to Roman rule, when the time for that came. More importantly, in Cilicia and Antioch there were by now powerful factions that favored peace and trade with the empire rather than war, and were open to Roman overtures.[15] They were not prepared, however, to break over this with Sayf al-Dawla, the Hamdanid emir of Aleppo, as they would likely be unable to maintain their independence from the empire without his backing. At this time, Tarsos and the Cilician cities were loosely and not reliably under his authority.

The Hamdanids were an ethnic Arab family that maneuvered its way into key positions in the northern provinces of the disintegrating caliphate, at Mosul and Aleppo. They were quasi-independent of Abbasid control. Their history is a complex series of appointments, revolts, counterrevolts, imprisonments, and displacements within the crumbling Abbasid system. In our period, the leading representatives of the dynasty were al-Hasan and Ali, who ruled the emirates of Mosul and Aleppo respectively and are better known by their honorific titles Nasir al-Dawla and Sayf al-Dawla: *Defender* and *Sword* of the (Abbasid) Dynasty. Although the Romans saw Sayf al-Dawla as only a ferocious Muslim warrior against themselves, and he projected that image to the Muslim world to rally support, his standing was tenuous. For most of his career he was entangled in the conflicts that were taking place to his south. Raiding Romanía brought him prestige, as did his patronage of the arts and literature, but his main political objective was to secure control of Aleppo and its territory. This he first gained in 944, then lost, then regained in 947, and he struggled to hold it against tribal unrest, the instability of the Abbasid regime, its Turkish generals, the rise of the Buyids in Mesopotamia, and al-Ikhshid, the ruler of Egypt who intervened in Syria until 947. Sayf al-Dawla relied primarily on hired Bedouin and mercenary Turkish armies, and his state was oriented more toward Mesopotamia than the Mediterranean. By 950, he held Aleppo, Emesa, and the district Diyar Bakr, whose capital was Mayyafariqin (Roman Martyropolis). He had failed to take Damascus. There was no political unity behind this assemblage of cities and territories, which also harbored anti-Hamdanid factions. But Sayf al-Dawla carefully cultivated the image of the heroic warrior and employed men to celebrate his raids "against the crosses and the churches" of the Romans, including one of the greatest poets of the entire Arabic tradition, al-Mutanabbi. In rank, Sayf al-Dawla was subordinate to his brother Nasir al-Dawla, but the balance tipped in his favor over time, as Nasir al-Dawla was often driven out from Mosul by internal rivals, and there was tension between the two brothers.[16]

Yet beyond seasonal raids for plunder there was little that Sayf al-Dawla could accomplish against the empire. He tried repeatedly to close the gap of Melitene, but the pattern in the early 950s basically remained that of raid and counterraid, followed by a Roman embassy to arrange a peace, or a defined truce, and then an exchange of prisoners. Sayf al-Dawla rejected Roman appeals for peace because it would jeopardize his standing, even though peace would have enabled him to deal with domestic challenges. Moreover, after the disaster of 950, the Cilicians lobbied for peace at his court. In that year, Sayf al-Dawla had led a large force of contingents from Aleppo, Cilicia, and tribal auxiliaries deep into the theme of Charsianon, but on the return he was ambushed by Leon Phokas (son of the *domestikos* Bardas) and his army was annihilated.[17] In later engagements, however, Sayf al-Dawla tended to prevail. In particular, he consistently defeated Bardas in battle, in 952, 953, and 954, and the great poet al-Mutanabbi wrote verses mocking the Roman general as a coward.[18] Named Roman officers were killed, wounded, or captured in these defeats. In the 953 battle by Germanikeia (Maraş), Sayf al-Dawla captured Bardas' son Konstantinos, who died in an Aleppan prison. Arab sources claim that he died of natural causes and was given to the local Christian community for burial. But the Romans suspected poison. Bardas massacred Muslim prisoners in retaliation, including relatives of the emir.[19]

The Romans perceived that they held an overall strategic advantage and so they changed their strategy and leadership in 955. Sayf al-Dawla had repeatedly sent their embassies back empty-handed, so the emperor stopped dispatching them. It was to be war from now on. Bardas Phokas, who was almost eighty and had lost almost every major encounter, was replaced with his son Nikephoros Phokas, general of Anatolikon, in 954–955.[20] A forward command appointment (probably Mesopotamia) was given to Nikephoros' nephew Ioannes Tzimiskes, a capable general who favored bold and aggressive strategies. After 955, the tide would gradually turn against Sayf al-Dawla. This must have been due to the change in Roman leadership and approach, for in another respect the emir's position was strengthened in 955 when he suppressed a major revolt against his authority by tribal leaders and his own army officers.[21]

Sayf al-Dawla decided to refortify Maraş and Hadath and capture the Roman-held forts by Melitene, to the northeast. An expedition in the spring of 956 was able to make progress toward the former objective, but not the latter. Despite defeating a Roman force under Tzimiskes that tried to block his exit, Sayf al-Dawla pulled back so as not to be cut off.[22] Meanwhile, an army under Leon Phokas attacked a fortress between Maraş and the Euphrates and captured Sayf al-Dawla's cousin, who was rebuilding it.[23] In retaliation, Sayf al-Dawla set out later that year, in September, to invade Romanía. From Tzamandos, where he killed many, set fires, and took captives, including army officers, he moved east to Melitene and invested one of its forts (Hisn Ziyad [Harput]).[24] But the Romans outflanked him in his absence, attacking Cilicia for the first time in years, and by sea. The fleet of Tarsos was defeated by the general of the Kibyrraiotai, Basileios Hexamilites, who fought heroically in the engagement and went on to burn the city's suburbs. He was granted a triumph in the hippodrome of Constantinople.[25] Roman sources claim that the Tarsiots were the aggressors, but it was the Romans who were now widening the eastern front to include Sayf al-Dawla's allies. The emir returned in haste to Adana to ensure the loyalty of Tarsos, which was, without a fleet, even more vulnerable to Roman attack. As he did so, the Romans raided again from a different direction, this time striking at the territory of Mayyafariqin.[26] They had more armies and points of ingress than Sayf al-Dawla. This three-pronged response to Sayf al-Dawla in 956 (one by sea) reveals a more dynamic and coordinated strategy. But it did not yet aim at permanent conquest.

Hexamilites' was not the only triumphal celebration that year. When Leon Phokas sent Sayf's captured cousin to the capital, the emperor Konstantinos VII himself celebrated a triumph over him, "placing his foot on the man's neck" (a *calcatio*).[27] In the ancient Roman Republic, victorious generals were allowed by the senate to parade through the city with their army, singing rowdy songs and displaying their captives and loot. At the end, the enemy king was often executed, if he had been captured. The Byzantine victories of the late 950s led to a revival of the triumph, which celebrated the successes of the aggressive new approach, though these first instances were probably meant to shore up popular support for the regime in light of its recent defeats.[28] A chapter of the *Book of Ceremonies* appears to describe this very triumph. After a morning liturgy, the emperor proceeded to the forum of Constantine and stood on the top step of the column base. Then, to the accompaniment of hymns and acclamations, and in the presence of the victorious *domestikos* and the generals of the themes, the prisoners were brought to the column and the head of their "emir" was placed beneath Konstantinos' foot, while a groom placed the emperor's spear on his neck too. The prisoners fell to the ground, and were led away backward. The emperor was then acclaimed by the people.[29]

In June 957, Nikephoros attacked, seized, and destroyed Hadath, judging that he was not in a position to hold it; but he allowed its population to leave to Aleppo. He also bribed Sayf al-Dawla's Turkish mercenaries to betray him, but this was revealed to the emir, who used his Daylami and Arab soldiers to massacre the Turks. Sayf al-Dawla then executed his Roman prisoners in retaliation.[30] The next year, in May 958, Tzimiskes raided around Mayyafariqin and Amida. Sayf al-Dawla sent his leading general, Naja al-Kasaki, against him with a large army (allegedly ten thousand men), but Tzimiskes put him to flight and destroyed most of Sayf al-Dawla's army.[31] The emir's failure to respond in person is attributed either to his preoccupation with the Buyids (in Baghdad) or to illness (in this phase of his life, he suffered from a recurring neurological condition).[32] By now the defenses of the emirate of Aleppo were falling apart. In the fall of 958, sent off by a speech and prayer of the emperor that was read to the officers, Tzimiskes and Basileios Lakapenos besieged Samosata, which surrendered immediately. They defeated a relief army under Sayf al-Dawla, and chased him back to Aleppo. Basileios and Tzimiskes, bringing thousands of prisoners of war, were granted a triumph in the hippodrome for their joint victory at Samosata.[33] At this time, we have only generic references to honors given to Nikephoros Phokas "in the manner of the victorious Roman generals of old."[34]

In contrast to the multipronged response to Sayf al-Dawla in 956, in 957 and 958 Roman forces concentrated on the subjection of one major center, Hadath and Samosata respectively. In 959, the Romans made more inroads (always sending tendrils to attack flanking locations). Early in the year

Tzimiskes invaded Diyar Bakr and briefly invested Mayyafariqin before raiding out toward Nisibis and Dara. This led a popular preacher at Mayyafariqin to intensify his calls for jihad against the Romans. Later that year, or possibly at the start of 960, Leon Phokas attacked Cilicia, reaching almost to Tarsos itself, before turning to invade Diyar Bakr. Sayf al-Dawla engaged him, but was defeated, and more of his relatives were captured.[35] Cilicia and the emirate of Aleppo were more vulnerable now than ever, and it made sense for the Romans to press their advantage. Moreover, Mosul (the other Hamdanid emirate) was simultaneously engaged in hostilities with the Buyids in Iraq, and there was tension between Sayf al-Dawla and his brother Nasir al-Dawla and between Nasir al-Dawla and his children in Mosul. But the emperor, having reduced the Tarsiot fleet, now had a different objective: Crete. Given the scale of the expedition in 960, preparations for it must have begun in 959, including diplomatic moves to ensure the neutrality of other Mediterranean powers. It is to that broader context that we now turn.

Southern Italy

In the midtenth century, Byzantium's overseas territories in Italy consisted of Apulia (the theme of Longobardia, with Bari as its capital) and Calabria (also a theme). Here the empire governed a population that was not primarily Roman (i.e., Greek-speaking Orthodox) in its cultural profile. Moreover, these territories presented unique geostrategic difficulties. To the north they faced the Lombard duchies of Salerno and Capua-Benevento, the cities of Naples and Amalfi, and the popes. At times, these smaller players recognized the empire's nominal authority. But beyond them to the north lay the post-Carolingian kings who had in the past intervened in the affairs of the south and might even revive their dormant claims to a western "Roman" empire. To the south, the empire faced Muslim Sicily, which was not strong enough to permanently conquer territory on the mainland, but its armies could and did raid Calabria and Apulia. Sicily was a province of the Fatimid state in North Africa, which could also intervene in Italy, where it maintained trading links, especially with Amalfi. So Byzantine southern Italy was precariously balanced.

The inhabitants of the Italian themes were mostly Lombards and Latinate "natives." There was a strong presence of Greek speakers, especially in Calabria, where many had fled from Sicily. Constantinopolitan sources pay little attention to Italy. On the other hand, we have more primary documentation from there than from any other region of the empire, and the picture they paint is complex. The non-Roman population was allowed to live according to its own customs, religious practices (Latin-rite Catholicism), and even Lombard laws, which was not true or relevant in Romanía proper. In other words, the central government was here engaged in an "imperial" relationship with its subjects. Its personnel formed a thin layer on top that ruled through the cooperation of Lombard lords, who carried the title of *gastald*. Modes of administration differed accordingly. It is more likely that the Byzantines took over and gradually modified local means of governance than that they imported their own from Asia Minor. Religious life was also complex, as both Greek and Latin rites were in use, but there are no signs of polarization or group conflict before the eleventh century. Most of the ascetics who were active and venerated in southern Italy, including by the Lombards, were "Greeks."[36]

In the Lombard duchies outside the direct control of Byzantine officials, especially at Naples and Amalfi, imperial culture was prestigious, but the use of court titles by the local lords did not mean that they were or regarded themselves as subjects of the empire, even if emperors liked to claim that. At times they nominally recognized the emperor, but only to accept titles, which brought them prestige and money. The use of Greek in official documents and bilingualism in Naples and Amalfi did not signify political subordination or the existence of pro-Byzantine factions; it was part of the local culture, with ancient roots. In practice, the Byzantine governors defended the two themes against the Lombards, the Muslims of Sicily, and the occasional Magyar raid. Constantinople viewed Italy as a lower priority after the Balkans and the east, yet it entailed a more complex set of diplomatic relations than those fronts, in part because of the potential for outside powers to intervene from the north or from Sicily.[37]

In the 920s the Lombards of Salerno and Capua-Benevento had captured and for years held imperial lands in Calabria and Apulia respectively, but the Byzantines had somehow managed to push them back and secured the support of Hugo of Provence, king of Italy (d. 947), who brokered a peace.[38] That peace lasted for over three decades after ca. 934. For a while there was also peace with Muslim Sicily, as the empire paid a sizable protection tax to prevent raids. But the Muslim military establishment on the island, which included many Berber settlers, was fractious and rebellious, resulting in periodic civil wars. In the 930s, one such civil war led to a prolonged period of chaos that also took the form of resistance by the majority Sunnis against the Shia Fatimids of North Africa. The Sicilians had also developed close trading links with the Italian cities, and the Fatimid raids disrupted that relationship. The empire had even supported the rebels in Sicily at that time; most of the population was Christian and in times of trouble reverted to effective autonomy and reached out to imperial authorities. In 948, however, the Fatimid caliph appointed al-Hasan as governor of Sicily, who pacified the province and established his own line of governors (the Kalbid dynasty). Al-Hasan was ordered to resume annual raids on Calabria, and the empire agreed to resume payment of tribute in 952.[39]

In 955–956, the high command in Constantinople sent a large army and fleet to the region to restore the imperial position. It should be noted that this was also when Nikephoros had replaced his father Bardas in the east and had initiated a more aggressive strategy toward Cilicia and Aleppo. Unfortunately, the events that transpired in southern Italy are documented differently in the various sources and cannot be accurately discerned. Theophanes Continuatus, here based on a text that is basically a panegyric of Konstantinos VII, says that Marianos Argyros (who had supported the emperor in his struggle against the Lakapenoi in 945) was given a large army of Thracian and Macedonian soldiers and a fleet equipped with Greek fire, and was sent to subdue Naples and the Lombards who had rebelled against imperial authority; Marianos besieged Naples and subdued it. Historians have accepted this narrative, being unsure only about its date. The text then describes a naval defeat of the Arabs, after which the "emir of Africa" sued for peace along with other infidel rulers. But the tale is suspect. The empire was not at war with Naples or the Lombards, and this siege is not mentioned elsewhere. It is reported in generic rhetorical terms, with no circumstantial detail, so it is likely to be an elaboration to praise Konstantinos for subduing "rebellious" vassals in the west.[40] Attempts to make sense of the Naples incident are speculative (that the empire was raising fleets against the Arabs, or saving Naples from an Arab siege).

While Marianos was general of Longobardia and Calabria in ca. 956, most warfare was at sea, between various Roman admirals and the fleets of Sicily and Africa. It seems that by 957 the Romans had the upper hand, though the army of Marianos was defeated in Calabria. At this time, the emperor was approached by ʿAbd al-Rahman III, the great caliph of Córdoba in al-Andalus (Spain), who was opposed to the Fatimids for religious reasons and over control of the North African coast. War had erupted in the western Mediterranean between the two Muslim states in the mid-950s. The emperor Konstantinos supported the Spaniards but was simultaneously promising the new Fatimid caliph (al-Muʿizz) to stay out of the conflict in return for peace in Italy, which was finally agreed upon in 958, after multiple embassies to Tunisia (possibly led by Marianos) had been sent back by al-Muʿizz. Fatimid sources claim that the Romans agreed to pay tribute again.[41] It should be stressed that peace treaties with Muslim powers, especially the Fatimids, were understood by them only as temporary cessations of hostilities, as truces and not permanent peace, pending the Islamic conquest of Romanía. Al-Muʿizz reminded the emperor of this in the 950s.[42] He had his eye on Egypt, which the Fatimids had already tried to acquire. The caliph expected to be dealing with the Romans in northern Syria as well: the two fronts were linked in his view.[43] In Italy at any rate, the war had changed nothing, but Byzantine fleets operating in the western Mediterranean and raiding Sicily projected power to Italian observers at the same time as the empire was expanding in the east. The fleet of hostile Tarsos had, after all, also just been destroyed.

A smooth succession: Romanos II

Konstantinos VII died on November 9, 959, while preparations for a new assault on Crete were underway. A palace-based emperor, he had just completed a pilgrimage to the holy Mt. Olympos in Bithynia, seeking advice, it was said, from the ascetics there on how to depose his new patriarch. The previous patriarch Theophylaktos, a son of Romanos I and passionate about horses, had died in 956 after a riding accident. The emperor had replaced him with an austere monk named Polyeuktos, who was now criticizing the greed of the Lakapenoi (presumably the empress Helene and Basileios Lakapenos, the *parakoimomenos*).[44] Polyeuktos would play a leading role in subsequent imperial politics.

As emperor, Konstantinos VII had been a quiet survivor, weathering the political storms to ensure the survival of his dynasty. Moreover, by the mid-950s he had set in place a cast of characters who would lead Romanía into an era of renewed conquest and whose mutual struggles would dominate its politics for thirty years. These men included Phokas, Tzimiskes, Bringas, and Basileios Lakapenos. Also, by 958, his own born-in-the-purple son and heir Romanos II had produced a born-in-the-purple heir of his own, Basileios, who would become Basil II. Basil would lead the empire to the peak of its power and reign longer than any emperor in the history of the Roman empire. But he reached the apogee of his power only after he had dismantled the team that his grandfather had put in place.

The brief reign of Romanos went off almost without a hitch. It was remembered as a time of prosperity, troubled only by a crop shortage in 960. The dynasty was secure, and Romanos a fun-loving emperor who preferred hunting and racing over governing. He is described as tall and thin with broad shoulders and sandy-colored hair.[45] He had been born in the purple in 939.

In 941, his grandfather Romanos I negotiated to marry him to a daughter of the king of Italy, Hugo of Provence, a descendant of Charlemagne. Hugo had helped the empire restrain the duchies of Salerno and Capua-Benevento in the 930s. The daughter whom he offered to the court in Constantinople, Bertha, was illegitimate, born to a courtesan. She married the five-year-old Romanos in 944 and took the name Eudokia, but died in 949. A sweet funeral speech for her was ghostwritten for the prince ("we lived together, a tender couple ... like spring calves in a flowery meadow").[46] The young couple is also depicted in a fine ivory image, 24.4 × 15.4 cm, being crowned by Christ; Romanos is beardless (Figure 2). It is possible that this ivory plaque and others like it were distributed by the court on the occasion of the co-emperor's marriage to prominent supporters of the regime, such as the Phokades. As an expensive luxury object, it encoded dynastic claims directly onto the surface of prestige items that were used to bind the elite to the court. These objects

FIGURE 2 Ivory image of the young Romanos II and his first wife Bertha-Eudokia being crowned by Christ (24.4 x 15.4 cm), made between 944 and 949 AD. The image is sometimes wrongly attributed to Romanos IV Diogenes (1067–1071) and Eudokia Makrembolitissa. Bibliothèque Nationale, Paris. *Source: Erich Lessing/Art Resource NY.*

were probably meant for private ownership and enjoyment, not public display. Abrasion on the face of Christ suggests that it was possibly kissed repeatedly over time.[47] It is worth noting here generally that the tenth and eleventh centuries witnessed a remarkable revival of the Byzantine craft of ivory carving, which produced hundreds of exquisite pieces, including triptychs, box panels, caskets, icons, plaques, and combs, with both Christian images and to a lesser degree mythological and natural themes.

After the death of Eudokia, Romanos had by 956 married the beautiful Theophano (née Anastasia). A hostile tradition later made her the daughter of an innkeeper and says that she poisoned Konstantinos VII in 959 and Romanos II in 963, which is unlikely.[48] The more positive version, promulgated by the court, claims that she was of "noble descent."[49] Indeed, she maintained a discreet presence at the court of her husband, hardly appearing in the sources at all. By 958 she had given him a son, Basil II, who would succeed him.

Following his father's instructions, Romanos entrusted the governing to Ioseph Bringas, his *parakoimomenos*. Under Konstantinos VII, Bringas had served as director of the state finances and commander of the fleet.[50] He now effectively replaced Basileios Lakapenos as the top eunuch at the court, just when the Cretan campaign was about to kick off. The new regime divided the position of *domestikos* of the *scholai* into an eastern and a western post, held by Nikephoros and Leon Phokas respectively, so between them the two brothers commanded most of the empire's elite forces. Under Romanos, Bringas seems to have been on good terms with the Phokades; we should not project their later clash back onto the beginning of the reign. The aristocracy was won over with titles and grants,[51] and there was only one, feeble challenge. It was only when Romanos died young that the cards were reshuffled, through civil conflict—the usual way in Romanía.

The conquest of Crete

The recent victories in the east and the lasting peace with the Bulgarians enabled the high command to deploy a substantial part of the army and navy for a campaign to remove a thorn in the side of Romanía: the emirate of Crete. Taking advantage of an intense and protracted Byzantine civil war in the 820s, an Arab fleet from al-Andalus had conquered Crete. From there they raided throughout the Aegean and, strategically, held the door open for other Arab fleets. This disrupted the security and commerce of the islands and coasts, and some settlements had to be relocated. In 904 the Syrian Arab fleet managed to capture and sack the empire's second-largest city, Thessalonike, selling many of their captives on Crete. The emperors had repeatedly sent fleets to retake the island, in the 820s, and again in 843, 866, 911 (part of a broader attack on the Syrian fleet), and 949, all of them ending in failure, the last a costly and humiliating disaster. Every generation knew its Cretan debacle. But this was a gap in imperial defenses that the emperors had to close. The Arabs had brought other Aegean islands under their authority, and even taxed them.[52]

Unfortunately, we know little about society and politics on Arab Crete. It was an emirate with a properly trained army and fleet, not just a pirate base; it issued its own coinage and recognized the caliph in Baghdad. The Arab elite were a minority, but seem not to have oppressed the native Christian majority; the complaints that we hear are all about their victims in the rest of Romanía. It was the Arabs who founded and strongly fortified Chandax ("the City of the Moat," later Herakleion). Crete is agriculturally productive and so desirable in itself apart from its strategic location. Arabic sources refer to extensive trade and traditions of Arabic learning there cut short by the Byzantine reconquest.[53] The emir in 960 was ʿAbd al-ʿAziz b. Shuʿayb al-Qurtubi, whom the Byzantines called Kouroupas.

Two lists of military units, equipment, and expenses associated with the failed Cretan campaigns of 911 and 949 are appended to the *Book of Ceremonies*. These are valuable sources for the administration and financing of campaigns, but the documents are confusing, inconsistent, and incomplete. Many figures have to be emended, everyone who tries to count totals obtains different results, and it is unclear how much they reflect the reality of the expeditions.[54] In the case of 949, the expeditionary force included units from many of the *themata* and *tagmata* embarked on the ships of the naval themes, all together about eight thousand soldiers and between twelve and twenty thousand sailors (some of whom were marines) on about one hundred ships. Preparations would have required many months, so the expedition of 960 led by Nikephoros Phokas was probably being planned already in 959, i.e., under Konstantinos VII. This is confirmed by a manuscript containing military treatises, including works on naval warfare (*Naumachika*), prepared for Basileios Lakapenos, who was then still *parakoimomenos*. The dedicatory poem of this collection refers to Basileios' defeat of Sayf al-Dawla (i.e., the expedition to Samosata in 958) and looks forward to his capture of Crete.[55] This does not necessarily mean that he had been placed in command of the planned expedition, only that he hoped to be. But it was not to happen. He was replaced as *parakoimomenos* by Bringas, and the command was given to Nikephoros. Bringas is presented as the motive force behind the plan, and the army was accompanied by a "political officer" named Michael.[56]

We do not have reliable numbers for the 960 expedition.[57] Presumably it was a larger force than in 949, possibly double. We will see below that the effort left the eastern frontier, and possibly also the Balkans, dangerously exposed. From stray references, we know that this expedition involved contingents drawn from various thematic and tagmatic armies in addition to mercenary units. But our sources are problematic and cannot easily be synthesized. The earliest is a heroic poem on the conquest by the deacon Theodosios, written to be performed at the court of Romanos but probably not completed until the spring or summer of 963 and rededicated to Nikephoros. It presents a series of heroic tableaux that are only nebulously connected. The extension of the *Chronicle* of Symeon models its account on Prokopios' account of Belisarios' conquest of North Africa from the Vandals (533–534), often word-for-word.[58] The *History* of Leon contains too much rhetorical elaboration and textbook knowledge of Roman strategy, tactics, and weapons. Over a century later, on a visit to the island Attaleiates recorded local memories of the conquest.[59]

The fleet mustered at the naval port of Phygela, south of Ephesos.[60] The Arabs made no attempt to intercept its arrival. The landing itself, on July 13, 960, was probably contested.[61] The Romans began to slaughter the population outside the walls, including women, children, and old men, driving them to seek refuge within Chandax,[62] which they placed under siege. But Arab armies were active in the countryside and mountains during the entire war. Nikephoros assaulted the walls but realized that he would not be able to take the city by force and decided to starve it out.[63] We cannot reconstruct the subsequent operations. The Arabs in the hinterland would attack the Roman camp(s), sometimes coordinating with sorties by those inside; the Romans would strike into the hinterland, subduing it "with fire and sword" and driving back their guerrilla opponents, though one Byzantine general was ambushed and killed (either at the beginning of the siege, or at the end).[64] Nikephoros catapulted the heads of slain Arabs inside, so that those in Chandax might recognize their relatives ("here a brother, there a father").[65] The chief of artillery even launched a lame but living donkey into the city, and Nikephoros made a joke to his men as he watched it soar above "like an eagle."[66] We cannot put these fragmented episodes into narrative order.

The emir of Crete asked for help from fellow Muslim rulers, including al-Muʿizz, the Fatimid caliph in North Africa. Arabic sources and diplomatic letters indicate that some were prepared to assist, but nothing materialized.[67] Still, Nikephoros had to dig in for a long siege. The winter was harsh and the army ran out of supplies; there was an empire-wide scarcity in 960, but Bringas sent provisions from the capital.[68] In the spring, Nikephoros battered the walls with artillery and had sappers undermine them by digging tunnels. A section of the walls collapsed. On March 6 or 7, 961, the Romans burst inside after a fight in the breach and began to slaughter everyone indiscriminately.[69] Theodosios exults in the killing of the women, children, and old men, and notes a concern that the Roman soldiers not be polluted by the rape of infidel women. Leon says that Nikephoros tried to end the slaughter.[70] The emir and his son "Anemas" were taken alive.

What followed was quintessentially Roman. Nikephoros separated off the portion of the spoils owed to the public treasury (a fifth or a sixth), and selected the items and prisoners he wanted for his triumph. The rest he divided among the soldiers. Much of this wealth had been plundered from Roman lands, but it would not be returned to the victims of the Arab raids. After settling the island's affairs, Nikephoros returned to the capital to celebrate a triumph, parading the captured gold, silver, and captives, including the emir and his family. It was said that the emperor gave the emir lands on which to live and would have enrolled him in the senate if he had but converted to Christianity (but this story is suspiciously similar to that told about the Vandal king Gelimer in 534, and may be a literary elaboration).[71] Yet the emir's son Anemas did convert and joined the Roman army; his descendants included generals.[72]

As for the Arabs of Crete, those who were not massacred or enslaved were probably expelled, drafted into the Roman army, or required to convert. A late twelfth-century Arabic source says that "Christian despotism visited them [the Muslims of Crete] with one painful circumstance after another ... they were all constrained to turn Christian."[73] Nikephoros tore down the walls of Chandax (at least partially), reorganized the island's defenses, and settled it with Armenians, Romans, and others.[74] Crete became a theme under a *strategos* (first attested in ca. 1000).[75] As our sources turn away from the scene of the conquest and follow the generals to their next targets, we must make do with scraps. The emirate has left no archaeological traces, which probably reflects the aggressive re-Christianization of the island. Yahya says that Nikephoros demolished the mosques, the news of which incited riots against churches in Egypt.[76] Soon after the conquest, Crete was visited by the itinerant preacher Nikon nicknamed "Repent!" His concern was that the islanders' faith was contaminated by Islam, but his *vita* is vague on this point.[77] Nikon spent seven years on Crete, encouraging the people to build churches. He is sometimes seen as an imperial agent, but there is no proof for that. Byzantines from other parts of the empire gradually moved back to the areas that had been vacated because of the fear of Arab raids. For example, Kythera seems to have been resettled only in the eleventh century by colonists from Lakonia.[78] And an interesting letter survives in the Cairo Genizah, a huge collection of Jewish manuscripts found in the storeroom of a synagogue in Cairo. It was written by a Jew named Moshe Agura who had left Crete after it had been "overthrown." He went to Rhodes, which he hated, and was trying to join family in Egypt. This possibly relates to the conquest of 961.[79] Imperial conquest had rearranged ethnic and religious balances.

The conquest of Cilicia (phase I)

In 961–965, the Romans conquered the plain of coastal Cilicia, eliminating the raiding strongholds of Tarsos, Adana, Mopsouestia, and Anazarbos, and they permanently reduced the power of the emirate of Aleppo. The conquest of Crete was a pivot between the destruction of Sayf al-Dawla's defenses in 957–959 and the Romans' conquest of his allies in Cilicia.

In 960, Sayf al-Dawla took advantage of Nikephoros' campaign against Crete, and its diversion of many eastern units, to attack Romanía. He sent his general Naja al-Kasaki to attack a fort in Armenia, where he defeated the commander of Hanzit. Meanwhile, Sayf al-Dawla himself led a large army into Asia Minor, the last of its kind, with allegedly thirty thousand men.[80] His target was the theme of Charsianon, and he seems to have had ample time to plunder extensively "with impunity," for the emperor sent Leon Phokas, *domestikos* of the West, against him only after news of the raid had reached the capital.[81] It was possibly earlier that year (960) that Leon had defeated a large raiding party of Magyars (Hungarians) who had crossed the Danube. Lacking adequate forces to confront them directly, he crept up and fell upon them at night, annihilating them.[82] Transferred now to the east in place of his brother, he joined up with the generals of themes,[83] but still did not have enough soldiers to face Sayf al-Dawla; his army here too was "small and weak," as most of the empire's mobile soldiers had been redeployed to Crete. Imperial defenses in both the west and east consisted now of whatever Leon Phokas could improvise. Fortunately, he was an expert in ambush warfare, a traditional tactic that he had used to inflict a devastating defeat upon Sayf al-Dawla in 950; it was also one on which treatises were being written at this time with Sayf al-Dawla in mind.[84] Leon ambushed him on November 8 at the Adrassos pass, destroying most of his army, though Sayf al-Dawla escaped with a few men. The allied contingent from Tarsos had warned Sayf al-Dawla against such passes and had themselves departed by another route, avoiding

Leon's noose.[85] Leon then distributed most of the spoils to his men—as most of it came from Sayf al-Dawla's plunder,[86] this amounted to a redistribution of wealth from provincials to soldiers. He returned to the capital, where he celebrated a triumph in the hippodrome.

By mid-961, the units that had participated in the conquest of Crete seem to have returned to their stations, for Marianos Argyros, as commander of the Macedonian and western armies, faced and defeated another Magyar raid.[87] Meanwhile in the east, in 961, Naja al-Kasaki raided again into Roman Armenia from Mayyafariqin, defeated ʿAbd Allah, a Roman ally who led the forces of the theme of Melitene, and returned to Aleppo laden with plunder.[88]

When Nikephoros returned to the east in late 961, he marched directly into Cilicia and, after a number of battles, forced the surrender of Anazarbos in February 962. Eastern sources say that he massacred a part of the population, expelled the rest, and demolished the walls. Tarsos had in the meantime ceased to recognize Sayf al-Dawla, who was possibly in negotiation with the Romans. Its governor (ibn al-Zayyat) marched out against Nikephoros but his army was utterly destroyed, and he committed suicide when he returned home, jumping from a high tower. In these engagements the Romans probably enjoyed crushing numerical advantages. Nikephoros reduced many forts, uprooted plantations, and then retired to Kaisareia.[89] He had effectively "created a wasteland between Syria and Cilicia that broke the lines of supply between the two regions."[90] After spending Easter 962 at Kaisareia, he struck against cities in Hamdanid territory while Sayf al-Dawla restored his authority in Tarsos, rebuilt the walls of Anazarbos, and sent a raid into the empire, probably through the Cilician Gates.[91] But Sayf al-Dawla's absence, and perhaps his trust in the ongoing negotiations, left Aleppo itself fatally exposed to a surprise attack. In November, the Romans sacked Hierapolis (Manbij) and captured its governor, the poet-warrior Abu Firas, a cousin of Sayf al-Dawla who was eventually sent on to Constantinople. He was there treated as a prince and wrote his exilic *Roman Poems* (*Rummiyyat*), which indicate that Manbij was taken by surprise (he was released in 966 in a routine prisoner exchange).[92]

An even greater surprise was to come. In December 962, a large army split between Nikephoros and Tzimiskes marched for Aleppo, which was unprepared to resist. Tzimiskes defeated a force under Naja, who retreated and joined Sayf al-Dawla. The emir closed in on Aleppo, but was also defeated and chased to the Euphrates by Tzimiskes. After initial resistance by the garrison, public order in Aleppo collapsed and Nikephoros entered on December 24. The Romans looted the place for a week, inflicting as much damage as they could (except for the citadel, which was steep and defended by a formidable

Daylami garrison).[93] The Romans withdrew, their goal of destabilizing the emirate achieved. They took thousands of captives with them.

Aleppo was the spear-tip of jihad and Sayf al-Dawla a romantic hero. The brutal sack of the city stunned the Muslim world and broke the emir's power. He would now face internal rebellion until his death in 967, and his subordinates began to fight among each other.[94] In 964, five thousand volunteers from Khurasan came to fight against the Romans, but Sayf al-Dawla could not support them and they left.[95] The Cilician cities had lost their most powerful ally. Another triumph for Nikephoros Phokas was in order. But on his return from the front he learned that Romanos II had died suddenly on March 15, 963; he was buried in the imperial mausoleum by the church of the Holy Apostles. Foreign war was now suspended, and its place was taken by fierce domestic politics.

The rise of Phokas

Roman and Byzantine emperors did not traditionally rule through extended family networks. Wives and sons were trusted, other relatives generally not. In 963, the Macedonian dynasty found itself in a precarious position. Romanos II had forced his five sisters to be tonsured, probably so that they could not marry potential rivals.[96] His wife Theophano held the rank of Augousta, and his sons Basil and Konstantinos (a child and an infant) were invested with imperial rank. There had been only one plot against Romanos, but it had been betrayed and the conspirators were arrested, tonsured, and (temporarily) exiled.[97] Two days before Romanos died, Theophano had given birth to Anna. His death called for a regency, consisting usually of the patriarch, empress, and other high officials, in this case especially Bringas. The initiative was taken by the patriarch Polyeuktos, who had Theophano, Basil, and Konstantinos reacclaimed as emperors, to confirm their position.[98] Byzantine regimes required periodic popular ratification.

In April, Nikephoros Phokas arrived in Constantinople to celebrate his triumph over Aleppo. Our sources now begin to project later events onto this moment, engaging in mind reading: Nikephoros had already decided to rebel (but why then return to the capital?),[99] or Bringas tried to block the triumph (which would instigate a civil war).[100] Bringas' position was far less secure now that Romanos was dead, and he may have feared Nikephoros, whom the people honored with chants of "Victor."[101] This was probably when Theodosios the deacon rededicated to Nikephoros his poem on the capture of Crete, comparing him to ancient Roman generals.[102] Nikephoros had a reputation for ascetic piety, and his parade of spoils from Aleppo included a relic of John the Baptist.[103] Later, as emperor, Nikephoros would regularly bring holy relics back from his wars. This can be seen as personal piety,[104] but it was also a Christianized version of the ancient Roman triumph, accounts of which the Byzantines were studying carefully in this period. Ancient triumphs featured religious paraphernalia and sometimes introduced new forms of worship to Rome.[105]

The sources present a tense relationship between Nikephoros and Bringas, but we should not believe anecdotes about their encounters, especially the story that Bringas tried to have Nikephoros blinded (which likely derives from later pro-Phokas propaganda). In reality, the patriarch, senate, and Bringas renewed Nikephoros' appointment as *domestikos* of the East and sent him to Cappadocia; he was, however, required to sign an oath that he would not rebel against the two children, "inasmuch as they were proclaimed emperors by us and all the people." He was reassured that he would be included in deliberations, which, however, reveals a level of mutual mistrust. The civilian government was placed in the hands of Bringas the chamberlain, Michael the finance minister (*logothetes*), and Symeon the head of the secretariat (*protasekretis*), probably the historian.[106]

The armies had assembled in Cappadocia for the next round of attacks on Tarsos and Aleppo. On July 2, at Kaisareia and at the instigation of the highest-ranking officers, especially Tzimiskes, the armies acclaimed Nikephoros emperor. We should reject the story that Bringas had previously sent a letter to Tzimiskes promising him power if he would betray and arrest Nikephoros, and that Tzimiskes revealed the plot to Nikephoros (his uncle).[107] Not only would this have been too risky a move for Bringas, it is refuted by the letter sent by Nikephoros to Bringas, the patriarch, and the senate formally announcing his elevation. This makes no mention of a plot even though it would have strengthened the rebel's position by proving that the agreement had been broken. The whole story was likely invented later to blacken Bringas. We should also not trust later stories that Nikephoros lusted after Theophano or that they had exchanged secret messages; as we have seen, Theophano became something of a lightning rod for romanticized revisions of history.[108] The usurpation was really an attempt in time-honored Byzantine fashion to capitalize on a general's popularity at a moment of dynastic weakness.

Nikephoros sent men to secure the straits by the City in advance of the news of his proclamation and appointed Tzimiskes *domestikos* of the East. He was now acting as emperor in his own right.[109] This was followed by the letter to Bringas, the patriarch, and the senate, in which he asked to be accepted as co-emperor and promised to respect the rights of Romanos' sons and to benefit the republic, i.e., exactly what he had sworn to do in his oath.[110] There is no reason to think that he and Bringas had previously been on bad terms, but this usurpation caused a rupture. Bringas locked down the City and proclaimed Nikephoros a public enemy. The rebel's father Bardas sought refuge in Hagia Sophia while his brother Leon disguised himself as a workman and slipped out through a drainage pipe, crossing the straits to join Nikephoros, whose army had now arrived.[111] Bringas canvassed support among some military types, especially Marianos Argyros, the former general in Italy who defeated the Magyars in 961. With a Macedonian unit, they were to block Nikephoros from crossing.[112]

The race was now on to win over the people of the City. Nikephoros was already popular, but Bringas, for all that he was a capable administrator, was not easily approachable and "was totally incapable of flattering and swaying public opinion in adverse circumstances."[113] The people had gathered in Hagia Sophia to defend Bardas Phokas (who was over eighty) and violently threw out Bringas' men, who were trying to seize him. When Bringas himself arrived to speak to the patriarch, on the morning of Sunday, August 9, he spoke in anger to the crowd and threatened to starve them out; he actually went to the bakers and ordered them to stop making bread. This did not go over well. The next day, the people and Bringas' supporters came to blows, and the latter, including the soldiers and some hastily armed Arab captives, were routed. A woman threw a pot from the roof on Marianos' head, killing him. The crowd started to plunder the mansions of Bringas' supporters. Nikephoros was now being acclaimed as emperor in the alleys. Into this opportune moment stepped Basileios Lakapenos, the former *parakoimomenos*, who added three thousand men to the rioters and destroyed Bringas' own house. The former master of the state now fled for sanctuary. Leon Phokas came across, and Basileios and the senate sent the fleet. On August 16, Nikephoros was conveyed across to the Golden Gate, where he was acclaimed co-emperor by the people in a procession culminating in Hagia Sophia. There, at the age of fifty-one, he was crowned by the patriarch. The senate and the people of Rome were with Phokas—for now.

CHAPTER 2

"The White Death of the Saracens"
Nikephoros II Phokas (963–969)

The new regime

Nikephoros Phokas was the first emperor to come from the military families of this period. His grandfather, father, uncle, brother, and nephews had all held high positions in the military command and had campaigned in the west, north, and east. Yet his agreement with the patriarch, senate, and people was that he would not found a dynasty but rule on behalf of the two heirs, Basil II and Konstantinos VIII, who were children. We cannot know whether he intended to honor this commitment. The recent precedent for this situation was Romanos I, who had indefinitely extended his tutelage over the dynastic heir Konstantinos VII and had tried to supplant him with his own family, but failed. There were no fixed rules in this game. Nikephoros could expect that events would present him with new opportunities—or limit his options. In 963, his popularity was high. But it was also fragile; he had not been tested as a politician.

Nikephoros' popularity was based on his conquests. He had spent the past decade on campaign. Now he spent a year in Constantinople, consolidating his regime. He made his elderly father Bardas *kaisar* ("Caesar"), a title that had not been used in decades. It had once been used to designate heirs to the throne or honor an important relative of the emperor. As no one regarded Bardas as a potential successor, the title was honorific, meaning that he ranked above the *magistroi* (his previous title).[1] A hostile western visitor to the court five years later saw Bardas at an official dinner: "a man, it seemed to me, born a hundred and fifty years before."[2]

Tzimiskes, the principal backer of Nikephoros' rebellion, was appointed *domestikos* of the East; he seems to have remained in the East during the regime change in Constantinople. Leon Phokas was placed in charge of the state finances (as *logothetes*) and given the high title *kouropalates* (which is how he is identified in most sources). Bringas was exiled to Paphlagonia, and eventually to a monastery, where he died two years later.[3] He was replaced as *parakoimomenos* by Basileios Lakapenos, who had provided critical assistance to the Phokades during the coup. A new title was invented for him, *proedros* ("president") of the senate.[4]

On September 20, 963, Nikephoros married Theophano, the widow of Romanos II and mother of the heirs to the throne. This was done to bind the families together and ensure dynastic stability, but the marriage also created problems. Nikephoros had ascetic traits, including vegetarianism, either out of religious conviction or in mourning for a son from a prior marriage who had died in a hunting accident years ago. The emperor's image makers now had to square this with marriage to the attractive Theophano. The patriarch Polyeuktos also had demands. As he proved to nearly every emperor, Polyeuktos, a eunuch since childhood, could take a firm stand on moral grounds, but he never pushed it beyond the point where he could get what he wanted. Now he demanded the two-year period of penance required of all who married for the second time, which soured his relations with Nikephoros. And a scandal broke out when it was alleged that Nikephoros had stood as godfather for one or both of the two child-heirs. As spiritual relationships were the same as biological ones in the eyes of the Church for the purposes of marriage, the validity of union to Theophano was called into question. A Church committee was formed, witnesses testified that it was not so, and rules were economized so that it did not matter even if it were; the marriage was validated.[5] But we know nothing of the couple's private life together, not even whether they had one.

Nikephoros is described as dark, with thick curly hair, and stocky, with broad shoulders like Herakles.[6] The western envoy Liudprand wrote a racist satire of his appearance within those parameters.[7] The coexistence of strikingly positive *and* negative images of Nikephoros is an interesting feature of the reign. Nikephoros was a military hero who managed to alienate powerful sectors of Roman society (starting, as we saw, with the patriarch), especially through his fiscal policy, which was meant to support his constant wars. The Phokades and their dependents produced many texts that portrayed the emperor positively, while his enemies did the opposite. These images were the stuff of politics; we should not be looking for a single true one.[8]

Failure in Sicily

Nikephoros set out in person for the east in the spring of 964. First, he sent a fleet to attack Sicily and aid its Christians. Some background is necessary.[9] It was not until ca. 950 that the Fatimids in North Africa managed to subdue the island after the civil wars and rebellions of the 930s. The caliph al-Mu'izz now proposed to make its administration more direct and efficient, curtail local autonomy, expand the Muslim presence, and bring the Christian communities under tighter control. The Christians were concentrated in the east of the island (the Val di Noto and Val Demone). During the time of troubles, they had seized some strongholds, including Taormina and Rometta. The Byzantines in Calabria had helped them in the 940s. In 962, the governor's son Ahmad besieged and reduced Taormina, selling its entire population into slavery and resettling the area with Muslim colonists. In 963, his brother besieged Rometta, which now appealed to the emperor. Nikephoros, unwilling to continue paying tribute to the Fatimids, equipped a fleet, possibly including veterans of Crete, and placed it under the command of the pious eunuch Niketas. The cavalry was commanded by the emperor's nephew, Manouel (possibly an illegitimate son of his brother Leon). With hindsight, the Roman sources call him impulsive and unfit for command.[10]

In October 964, the siege of Rometta was reinforced by the governor al-Hasan himself, with another Berber army. According to the historian Leon the deacon, the Romans landed and captured Syracuse, Himera, Taormina, and Leontini without bloodshed, whereupon they marched into rougher terrain and were ambushed. This is fiction; the Arabic sources are better.[11] The Romans crossed the strait, landed at Messina, and made for Rometta. They were set upon by the Muslims, defeated, and routed. Manouel was killed. The fleet was attacked and destroyed when the surviving soldiers tried to cross at Messina, and Niketas was captured. The Arabic sources recount an incredible operation of frogmen booby-trapping the rudders of the Roman ships by attaching incendiary devices underwater.[12] The rout was complete. Rometta fell in May 965 after a long siege and suffered the fate of Taormina. The Fatimid policy of Muslim colonization proceeded as planned and the island was fortified against future attacks. In 965, the governor of Longobardia and Calabria, Nikephoros Hexakionites, ordered the towns of Calabria to provide ships, but Rossano preferred to burn them instead and kill the local captain. This is presented as a rebellion against a requisition, but it has been suggested that the coastal towns did not want their trading relations with Sicily disrupted by another imperial war. This episode was allegedly quieted by the mediation of the local saint Neilos.[13] In 965–966, Hexakionites was defeated and killed in a naval battle with the Arabs near Reggio.[14] His objective remains unclear.

The emperor was now ready for peace. A treaty with the caliphate was signed in 967. Al-Mu'izz was planning his invasion of Egypt and wanted to secure the Sicilian front, though he had long doubted that Romans kept faith with their treaties. Nikephoros also sent a ransom to redeem Niketas and other captive officers, and sent also a Muslim relic, a sword of Muhammad, that he had taken in the Syrian wars.[15] In captivity, Niketas had copied out sermons of the saints Basil the Great and Gregory of Nazianzos. We have this manuscript, which he later donated to a church, noting that he had written it in an African prison.[16]

The conquest of Cilicia (phase II) and Cyprus

Phokas' usurpation had given Tarsos and Aleppo an opportunity to raid into Roman territory in the fall of 963. In September, Naja raided around Melitene for eighteen days. Sayf al-Dawla was incapacitated by a stroke before he could enter Roman lands, and had to be carried back. Then, in October, the Tarsiots invaded as far as Ikonion but had to fight their way back through an ambush in a pass. Altogether, they seem to have pulled in little plunder, and it is not clear whether these two raids were coordinated.[17] The sack of Aleppo at the end of 962 had weakened Sayf al-Dawla's authority: he had little money, his lieutenants were quarreling, and tribal revolts began again after a ten-year hiatus. However, when the Roman high command turned its attention back to this region, it set its sights on the conquest of Cilicia, not Aleppo. Aleppo had been weakened so that the Romans could attack their principal target without distraction.[18]

In December 963, Tzimiskes attacked Adana. He defeated the joint army of the Cilician cities, then cut down five thousand survivors who made a final stand on a nearby hill. Their blood ran down into the fields, so this was afterwards called "the Mountain of Blood." Tzimiskes then besieged Mospouestia in early 964, but a scarcity of food caused by widespread famine in the area forced him to leave after seven days. Along his departure, he burned the suburbs of Mospouestia, Adana, and Tarsos, and sent a message to the inhabitants, saying that he would return to kill them all. Carried in a litter, Sayf al-Dawla came in February with an army of volunteers from Khurasan, but the Romans had left, and he could not feed his army either, which dispersed.[19] At this point, Arabic sources refer to diplomatic contacts between the Romans and Sayf al-Dawla, which may have led to a truce, as the former no longer attacked Aleppo, concentrating instead on Cilicia, and the latter moved his court permanently to Mayyafariqin and effectively lost control of Aleppo itself to tribal rivals.[20] It is possible that Sayf al-Dawla gave up on the *thughur*—the Muslim militarized zone bordering on the empire—to focus on domestic challenges. Cilicia was now alone and vulnerable.

In the spring of 964, Nikephoros returned in person to the eastern front, interestingly bringing Theophano and the children with him, but leaving them in a fort inside the border. That summer he made multiple raids and, it seems, an attack on Tarsos itself. But the city was massively fortified and well provisioned, and held out. Nikephoros did, however, capture Anazarbos (again) and Adana before withdrawing to Roman territory.[21] In November of the same year (964), he returned to besiege Mospouestia, where the inhabitants of Adana had sought refuge, but again withdrew to Kaisareia. Contingents of the Roman army are recorded as raiding all the way to Antioch.[22] The sources are confused on details and dates, because each was recording only part of a broader on-off offensive. But the stage was now set for the decisive conquests of 965.

It was probably in the first half of that year that the Romans asserted their rights over Cyprus and expelled from it the representatives of Arab powers. For more than two centuries, the island had been under a unique regime that historians have called a "condominium" in that its tax revenues were shared between the Romans and the caliphate. The reality, however, was not so balanced. The vast majority of the population was Roman, and the empire had never ceased to think of Cyprus as an integral part of its territories, in fact a regular theme; it just paid protection money to spare it from further attacks. Unfortunately, we know little about how it was governed or the Muslim presence. Also, there is a puzzling gap between its sparse archaeology and the claims in reliable sources that it was a prosperous trade center.[23] Nikephoros sent Niketas Chalkoutzes with a fleet to expel the Arabs, which he seems to have accomplished easily (it is unclear which Muslim power they represented at this time).[24] Yahya claims that this move was resisted by an Egyptian fleet, which was annihilated by the Romans.[25] It is possible that Nikephoros' intention was precisely to deprive Egypt of access to timber for its fleets, and the conquest was followed as usual by the settlement of Armenian colonists.[26]

With the destruction of the Tarsiot fleet, the conquest of Crete, and now the total subjugation of Cyprus, the Romans finally regained mastery over their sea space. Roman naval power had not been as great since late antiquity.

The final offensive against Cilicia was launched in the summer of 965, and all three big guns came out: the emperor, Tzimiskes, and Leon Phokas. The governor of Tarsos, Rashiq al-Nasimi, loosely affiliated with the Hamdanids, sent envoys offering the city's nominal submission, and Mopsouestia did the same, but Nikephoros rejected the offer, promising them his sword instead.[27] While he and Tzimiskes attacked Mopsouestia, his brother invested Tarsos. The former fell on July 13, 965, after the Romans secretly tunneled under, and then collapsed, part of its walls. The inhabitants who were not massacred during the capture were enslaved. Nikephoros then joined Leon at Tarsos. The city had strong fortifications but had exhausted its provisions and surrendered on terms, on August 16. A large Egyptian fleet with supplies arrived three days too late, and was chased away by imperial ships. The Muslims of Tarsos who would not convert were expelled and escorted to Antioch.[28] Nikephoros made its mosque into a stable (though this could just be Muslim polemic) and began to repopulate the city with Romans and Armenians. Eventually, some of its original inhabitants returned and converted to Christianity.[29] Both cities became mini-themes under generals, and Germanikeia (Maraş) fell later that year. The *thughur* was finished. Later Arab writers imagined Nikephoros boasting to the caliph that "nothing is left in your *thughur* except ashes."[30]

In October, Nikephoros triumphed again in Constantinople. The spoils on display included Roman battle standards recovered from Tarsos and the gates of the two captured cities, which were gilded and set up as permanent victory monuments. The people were treated to chariot races and spectacles.[31] These victories were commemorated in the provinces too. A church at Çavuşin in Cappadocia is decorated with a scene that includes the emperor, his brother, father, Theophano, and Tzimiskes, and was probably painted in connection with the events of 965.[32] Nikephoros also came to an arrangement with the Syrian Jacobite Church. According to Michael the Syrian, its patriarch and historian in the late twelfth century, the emperor sought out the patriarch Yuhannan VII Sarigta and made a deal with him ratified with the emperor's seal: Nikephoros would tolerate their Church if the patriarch relocated permanently to Melitene. Yuhannan did so, followed by many of his people, who now began to build churches and monasteries in that province.[33]

Coastal Cilicia was now in Roman hands, a territory roughly the size of Cyprus. In the first part of 966, Nikephoros and Sayf al-Dawla arranged for an exchange of prisoners at Samosata on June 23, 966. Abu Firas and other Hamdanid princes were among those returned, but Sayf al-Dawla did not have enough Romans to exchange, so he had to ransom the remaining Muslim captives. It was embarrassing; he had to give his jewels as collateral and his secretary as a hostage.[34] But another prize now enticed the Romans: the city of Antioch.

In late antiquity, Antioch was one of the three great cities of the eastern Roman empire. It was the seat of a patriarch, a center of Christian and Greek culture, and, at times, an imperial residence. In the early sixth century, however, it was struck by earthquakes, sacked by the Persians (who deported a large part of its population), and visited by the plague. It never fully recovered. Under Arab rule it is not mentioned much and its social and political history are obscure. Though it continued to have a large Melkite Christian population (i.e., Byzantine Orthodox), over time it became mostly Arabic-speaking. The city has even been called a "provincial backwater" of the Islamic world.[35] It had come under Sayf al-Dawla's authority in 944, but his weakness in the 960s and withdrawal to Mayyafariqin had cost him direct control over the city. A party opposed to Hamdanid rule favored unification with the empire, and had won over Rashiq al-Nasimi, the former governor of Tarsos who had migrated to Antioch. This party approached Nikephoros with an offer of nominal recognition of Roman suzerainty, an offer that was still on the table while the emperor and Sayf al-Dawla were discussing terms for a peace in 966. Rashiq was killed in an effort to take Aleppo, and Sayf al-Dawla reasserted his authority over Antioch in June, imprisoning his enemies.[36] Nikephoros was apparently still in contact with members of the anti-Hamdanid party and broke off his negotiations with Sayf al-Dawla. The war would now go deeper into Syria. Part of the Muslim population fled in anticipation.[37]

The details of the campaign are difficult to reconstruct, especially as the Byzantine sources conflate it with that of 968 (with Leon placing both in 968 and Skylitzes in 966).[38] Nikephoros besieged Manbij (Hierapolis) on October 6, but left after a few days when he received from it the *keramidion*, the holy tile on which Christ's holy features had been impressed. Sending out raiding parties, he swung past Aleppo for Antioch, still in communication with the pro-Roman faction. He reached it on October 23, but found it closed against him. The ancient fortifications of Antioch were virtually impregnable to direct assault. Nikephoros spent a week before the city but no one opened it to him, and he was running out of supplies, so he left for Tarsos.[39] Nikephoros returned to the City on or before January 24, 967, with the holy tile.[40]

Nikephoros had achieved little on this campaign, and it would be a year before he retuned to the east. But the situation would then be different, as Sayf al-Dawla died on February 8, 967, at Aleppo. The combative relationship between Rome and Aleppo was about to be transformed to one of patron and client. But that step would be taken by Nikephoros' murderer and successor.

The annexation of Taron

Since antiquity, the Roman empire could acquire territory by means other than conquest, when rulers along the periphery bequeathed or ceded their lands to Rome in exchange for personal enrichment, titles, and the opportunities of imperial service. This is what happened now, in 967 or 968, with the Armenian realm of Taron, situated between the Roman district of Melitene and lake Van. It was approximately 185 miles long, therefore somewhat longer than Crete, and reached north about 125 miles to Roman Keltzene. At this time, the Armenian lands were divided among a number of principalities, some of which were ruled by branches of the ancient Bagratid family, as was Taron. Armenians had always been pushed and pulled between Rome and the major eastern power, whether Parthian, Persian Sasanian, or Muslim Arab. After the Arab conquests, Armenian leaders alternated in alliance between Rome and the caliphate, taking part in their wars against each other and their occasional civil wars. However, in the tenth century, and with the caliphate's decline, Rome and the Armenian realms were generally at peace.[41] For the period covered here, the empire did not need to worry about hostilities along this stretch of its frontier, and could therefore concentrate its forces in the southeast (at least until the Seljuks arrived from Central Asia in the mideleventh century). In the tenth century, the Caucasian principalities recognized the empire's superior standing, even if not yet its sovereignty, and many Armenians took up service under it, joined its aristocracy, and were settled in its recently conquered territories, even as far as Crete and Italy. Despite what most medieval Armenian literature would have us believe, many Armenians did not define themselves religiously by opposition to the Council of Chalcedon of 451 (the Armenian Church rejected that Council and was considered "Monophysite" by the Byzantines).[42]

Ašot III of Taron died in 966, and his sons preferred to cede the realm to the emperor in exchange for lands, titles, and opportunities for advancement in the empire, especially the military. They and their descendants would be known as the Taronitai (though they were not the only ones with that name).[43] Their decision had precedent, for their ancestors and relatives had long received court titles, were on the imperial payroll, had visited Constantinople (as had their father Ašot), and were sometimes assigned palaces there. In exchange for these favors and recognition, the emperors came to treat the rulers of Taron as their own "military governors" within the Roman system, and sent officials to interfere in the affairs of the principality. Under Romanos I (920–944), Ašot's cousin Tʿorʿnik had left his portion of the realm to the emperor in his will, but Ašot had successfully pleaded with Romanos to accept a fortress instead (Oulnoutin, or Oğnut, in the west).[44] The exact date of the annexation of Taron is not known, but it is attested as a Roman command by the 970s.[45]

After ca. 944, the Romans generally did not seek to annex Armenian lands by force. Instead, they assimilated Georgian and Armenian elites from a distance, probably in order to keep them friendly, but this also prepared the ground for smooth political unions. Peace with Armenia enabled the Romans to point their armies at Cilicia and Syria. But there were Muslim pockets along the Armenian frontier too, especially the Qaysid emirates in Mantzikert, Khliat, and the other towns around lake Van (in the region of Apahunikʿ). In the late ninth century, the Qaysids were subject to the Armenian kings, though by the midtenth they recognized the Romans, paying tribute but otherwise enjoying autonomy. Konstantinos VII had marked them out as essential buffers between Romanía and the emirate of Azerbaijan. In 966, that emirate was taken over by Sayf al-Dawla in pursuit of his general Naja al-Kasaki, who had rebelled against him in 964.[46] This made the cities legitimate Roman targets. Bardas Phokas, Nikephoros' nephew and a future rebel against Basil II, first appears as the *doux* of the theme of Chaldia leading an attack in 968 against Apahunikʿ. He besieged, captured, and destroyed Mantzikert.[47] It was only a punitive raid, and eventually part of Apahunikʿ would be picked up by a new power, the Kurdish-Arab Marwanids, who displaced the failing Hamdanids in Diyar Bakr. This region, however, would in time become an integral part of the imperial defenses—and a factor in their collapse in the eleventh century.

Declining popularity

Nikephoros spent most of 967 and 968 in the capital. Not all was well at home, and the more he stayed in Constantinople the worse it got. By promoting the interests of soldiers, his tactless response to popular criticism, and his laws on the finances of Church and state, the emperor gradually alienated his subjects, both people in the street and political enemies who passed a negative image of him to posterity. In the history of Skylitzes, that image takes the form of a series of articles of indictment.[48]

The oath of loyalty required of Nikephoros before his rebellion and the challenges posed to his marriage with Theophano already revealed tensions between him and the patriarch Polyeuktos, which the emperor's laws and policies regarding the Church aggravated. Skylitzes reports that he canceled subsidies that previous emperors had paid to churches and monasteries; barred churches from acquiring more lands, so that more support could go to the poor and to soldiers; required his approval for the appointment of bishops; and sent imperial agents to audit the records of every diocese upon the death of the bishop and confiscate wealth in excess of expenses.[49] We have the text of the decree that Nikephoros issued in 964 forbidding endowments for new monasteries and charitable foundations and banning gifts of real estate to old ones, including churches (donors could, however, sell land and give cash or movable goods). The problem was that Church lands were inalienable, but were either underutilized or belonged to institutions that were becoming wealthy, even business-oriented. This was locking too much land away from state use. The emperor zealously argued that monks should live up to their ideals of poverty and self-denial, and he blasted their worldly preoccupations and the vanity of donors who wanted new foundations. Still, Nikephoros admired those ideals and made an exception for *laurai*, a form of quasi-solitary asceticism practiced by his uncle, the saint Michael Maleïnos, and the latter's disciple, saint Athanasios of Athos, who was also Nikephoros' spiritual advisor. The emperor thus pitted the ascetics against a "worldly" Church, even though he knew that those ascetics were busy amassing landed properties of their own, in part with his own generous help. Some have even seen the hand of Athanasios behind the decree of 964.[50]

Skylitzes also reports that Nikephoros demanded that soldiers killed in battle with the infidel should be treated as martyrs by the Church, to which the bishops responded with outrage. This notice had fueled an extensive discussion about possible Byzantine notions of Holy War, but it is too brief and polemical as reported to bear much weight. It might even be invented propaganda to slander Nikephoros for valorizing the military life at the expense of the traditions of the Church.[51] Nikephoros was a strict disciplinarian on campaign, but he tolerated abuses that his soldiers allegedly inflicted on civilians. He deflected complaints by putting it all down to a few bad apples, but they were "mistreating the very citizens who had made no small contribution to his rise to power."[52]

At Easter of (probably) 967, this exploded in the emperor's face. There was a bloody brawl between his Armenian mercenaries and some sailors in which many civilians were killed, and the prefect of the City Sisinnios almost lost his life. This was not the first time unruly Armenians had given the emperor trouble.[53] On his way back to the palace, the people began to abuse him, and a woman threw stones at him from a window; she was arrested and burned the next day. Our sources next describe a military parade and mock performance of combat that the emperor decided to stage in the hippodrome, during the games. He may have done this to display the discipline of his soldiers and reassure the people of the city, but it all went horribly wrong. The people feared that he was turning the army against them (as Justinian had done in 532), and they fled, but many were trampled or fell from the top rows. The stampede ended only when they saw the emperor sitting calmly in his box (probably shaking his head in disbelief). Days later, while Nikephoros was returning from a celebration of the feast of the Ascension (forty days after Easter), the relatives of those killed began to abuse him, calling him a bloody murderer and pelting him with stones. Nikephoros was now alarmed for his security, and his response only deepened his unpopularity: he built a new wall around part of the palace, which required destroying some nearby property. This wall symbolized everything the people were beginning to dislike about this emperor.[54]

And the wars cost money. Apparently, the conquest was not paying for itself. Byzantine sources claim that to fund his wars Nikephoros imposed greater taxes and requisitions, and reduced the perquisites of senators. Tax officials swarmed the provinces.[55] But the soldiery was perhaps spared these additional burdens, if Nikephoros followed the suggestions made in a military manual associated with his name: soldiers, this text pleads, must be paid in full and regularly; they should not be oppressed by tax collectors, despicable characters who "contribute nothing to the common good"; and they should be judged by their commanding officers, not civilian courts.[56] This was a conflicted position, to say the least. Past Roman emperors had praised the tax system for maintaining the very armies in which Nikephoros took such pride.[57] Though he came from a wealthy family, as emperor he continued the policy of his two Macedonian predecessors of limiting the ability of wealthy landowners to acquire the designated military lands whose revenues supported the empire's soldiers.[58] He was the army's emperor, and did not champion some social or economic class; there was no narrative here of the "families versus the state." Nikephoros' tax policy probably fell heavily on his own class. A contemporary Arab geographer reported that Nikephoros became unpopular because of the oppressive taxes that he imposed to pay for his wars: "they hated him for it ... this is why they killed him."[59]

Unlike modern states, Byzantium could not borrow money to fund wars. One policy available to emperors was a partial or temporary devaluation of the coinage, and Nikephoros resorted to this. He issued the so-called *tetarteron*, a gold coin lighter than the standard one (now named the *histameon*) by a twelfth but of equal nominal value (Figure 3). The hostile tradition claims

FIGURE 3 *Nomisma histamenon* of Nikephoros II Phokas (963–969) (4.39 g,
20 mm). This was the standard-weight gold coin of Byzantium, the "dollar of the
Middle Ages." On the obverse Jesus Christ is identified in Latin as *Rex Regnantium*
("King of Kings"). On other coins, Nikephoros is shown on the reverse holding
the imperial standard, together with a youthful Basil II, but here Basil has been
displaced by the Virgin, whose assistance for Nikephoros alone the inscription
above invokes. © Dumbarton Oaks, Byzantine Collection, Washington, DC
(accession no.: BZC.1957.4.82).

that he expected to pay his obligations in the new coin and collect in the old,
but that would have driven the old out of circulation; besides, both forms
continued to circulate until the end of the eleventh century. In fact, it seems
that the state made payments in both type of coin, but treated them as equivalent. Nikephoros was effectively making an 8.3 percent profit on minting
tetartera.[60] Though the parallel circulation of a lighter coin may have caused
some inflation, he could get away with this because the market trusted in the
future solvency of the state, which hinged on its success in the wars that this
money was meant to fund. And this success Nikephoros amply ensured. But
overall the year 967, when he was not at war, was a bad year for him. He had
been a better general than he was now an emperor.

Tension with Bulgaria

As emperor, Nikephoros would lead or authorize full-scale wars only against
Muslim enemies, in the east and Sicily. Among his subjects these earned
him the name "White Death of the Saracens."[61] The conquest of Cilicia had
probably been his plan all along, even under Romanos II, and by 966 he was
pushing to retake Antioch. War there was his overriding preoccupation. But

in the last few years of the reign, tensions began to mount with the two major Christian powers, Bulgaria and the German empire, with which Romanía had complex ideological relationships. In the case of Bulgaria, Nikephoros' bellicose missteps would bring a two-front war to the empire.

In the tenth century, Bulgaria was one of the most important Christian states in Europe. The pagan Bulgars had crossed the Danube in 680, taken over the Roman province of Moesia, and gradually expanded their control over the central Balkans. The Romans never forgot that the Bulgars had occupied Roman territory. Their kings—called khans by scholars, though the title is not securely attested—alternated between warring against the empire and helping the emperors against other enemies, both foreign and domestic. The Bulgar ruling class assimilated to the predominantly Slavic-speaking subject population, a process that accelerated with conversion to Christianity in the ninth century. The pagan Bulgars became Orthodox Bulgarians and negotiated for themselves, in 870, an autocephalous Church. The most powerful ruler of Bulgaria, Simeon (893–927), raised in Constantinople as a child, used force to secure recognition of his status as *basileus* or tsar, i.e., a peer of the Roman emperor, and a patriarch for his capital Preslav. Bulgaria under Simeon could be just as aggressive toward the empire as the pagan Bulgars had once been, but in 927 a peace was concluded that would last forty years. Simeon's son and heir Petar (927–969) married the granddaughter of Romanos I, Maria Lakapene, who was appropriately renamed Eirene ("Peace"), and had at least two sons, Boris and Roman. At times, the Romans could think of Bulgarians as a fellow Christian nation, but beneath the surface there lurked stereotypes about their uncivilized, Skythian (i.e., nomadic), and pagan past.[62]

Nikephoros was to take a more aggressive stance toward Bulgaria that led, in the reign of his successor, to open warfare. Almost all scholars follow the narrative of Leon the deacon here, according to whom Nikephoros became furious when Bulgarian envoys came requesting the customary "tribute." He yelled at them, called them leather-gnawing Skythians, threatened war, and had them slapped in the face. He then assembled an army and marched to Bulgaria, capturing all the forts along the border, but then realized that those mountains were steep and densely wooded, so he returned to the capital and sent a man called Kalokyros to bribe the Rus' with a massive sum to attack the Bulgarians from behind. No date is given, but it is placed in 965–967.[63] This story appears in all discussions, but is probably fictitious.

It is hard to believe that Nikephoros would threaten war when he was clearly unprepared for it; that he would march against a state that was at peace, only to realize at the last minute that there are mountains in the

Balkans; that there was no response from the Bulgarians; that he would give more money to the Rus' to disrupt a peaceful arrangement than to the Bulgarians in order to maintain it; that he suddenly grew angry at a "tribute" that the Romans (he too) had been paying for decades, or that he would do this cynically to have a *casus belli* when he did not in fact intend to go to war. And why does Leon not tell us which forts he captured? In sum, this story bears all the marks of invention and distortion. It was likely made up by the Phokas family after Nikephoros' death, probably at a time when the Romans were at war with Bulgaria and when the Phokades themselves were out of favor or in revolt, so before 989.[64] Its aim was to show that Nikephoros played tough with the Bulgarians and stood up to them (unlike the young Basil II). As propaganda it is good; as history incoherent. Most of it consists of insults directed at the Bulgarians; the actual "campaign" is barely a line long and this "tribute," which is mentioned nowhere else, might also have been part of the fiction, to reveal the weakness of the Macedonian emperors.[65]

Skylitzes gives a briefer, more sober account. In June 967, Nikephoros toured the (Roman) forts of Thrace and wrote to Petar, the tsar of Bulgaria, asking that he prevent Magyars from raiding Roman lands. Petar disregarded this request, and even "did the opposite," whatever that means. It was then that Nikephoros sent Kalokyros, a notable of Cherson, to pay Svjatoslav and the Rus' to raid the Bulgarians' Danubian lands. Svjatoslav did so in August 968, and then returned home. Skylitzes adds that Svjatoslav repeated this in 969.[66] We will turn to those events below; what we must do is understand the origins of the tensions between Bulgaria and Byzantium. The Magyars were ranging south after their defeat on the Lech by Otto I in 955. We have seen two of their raids into Byzantium (in 960 and 961), and there may have been others that were unrecorded. It is because of this situation that Nikephoros probably went on his Thracian tour,[67] and the story in Leon is likely just a highly dramatized version of that tour. At this point, Zonaras, a chronicler of the twelfth century, provides crucial information. He says that Nikephoros protested to Petar when some Magyars invaded Thrace, and Petar answered as follows: "When they came against us, you would not help us, but now we have been forced to make a treaty with them." It is possible that Bulgaria had come to an accommodation with the Magyars, allowing them to pass through its territory in order to raid Byzantium.[68]

In sum, in 967 Nikephoros instigated a Rus' raid (to come in 968) in order to punish the Bulgarians for not blocking Magyar raids.[69] This would have dramatic and unforeseen consequences. In 967, however, this strategy may have been designed to kill two birds with one stone. It seems that Svjatoslav was threatening Cherson at that time, an overseas imperial possession in the Crimea, so the payment also relieved pressure there.[70] Punishing Bulgaria might have been a secondary objective. The western envoy Liudprand saw Bulgarian envoys at Nikephoros' court in June or July 968, and they appear to have been treated with proper respect. Liudprand wanted to make them seem more honored than he, to highlight the alleged insult to his master, Otto I, who was trying to extend his authority into southern Italy.[71] The rise of the western empire is a development to which we must now turn. It forms the background to the most entertaining, if distorted, account of Nikephoros' reign that we have, Liudprand's *Embassy to Constantinople*.

Tension in Italy with the German empire

After the end of the Roman empire in the West, it was the Franks who created a new imperial framework there, unifying the north and pushing farther into central Europe than the Romans ever had. Internally, the Franks were politically weak and disunited, but they were still more powerful than their neighbors. They set most of the trends that enabled the Latin West to emerge and recognize itself as a kind of coherent civilization, loosely coordinated to be sure but developing in tandem with the expansion of "Frankish" institutions.[72] This expansion was accomplished in part by conquest and imposition and in part by emulation of Frankish prestige in the periphery. This new Europe was diverse in all ways, but one of the instruments that allowed its component parts to speak to each other and come to a common understanding of their place in the world was the idea of Rome—its empire, history, language, and Church—which functioned as a template coordinating languages, polities, histories, and ethnicities.[73] It was inevitable that a Frank would one day be proclaimed "emperor" in Rome, even if no one in the West knew what that meant, not even Charlemagne himself. It sounded right because it gave a prestigious label to the fact of his overwhelming power. However, in the western empire that he created "Roman" corresponded to no identity—other than the people of the city of Rome—and there were no conventions governing its use. Claims to "empire" petered out in the late ninth century along with the Carolingian dynasty itself.

By the midtenth century, momentum had passed to the Saxons, in the eastern territories of the old Frankish empire, and specifically to the Liudolfing house of dukes. They claimed the kingdom of Germany (of "the Saxons and Franks"), which had evolved out of the Carolingian realm of East Francia. Otto became king of Germany in 936 and, with the prestige that he won by defeating the Hungarians on the Lech in 955, he aimed to expand the sphere of his authority. In 961 he invaded Italy and had himself crowned its king at Pavia, though not without opposition. Henceforth, the crowns of Italy and Germany were united. The following year, Otto was crowned *imperator* and *Augustus* by the pope in Rome. In later centuries, the union of crowns and titles that Otto had effected was regarded as the foundation of the Holy Roman Empire. It is unclear if his title explicitly mentioned the "Romans" (medieval titulature was never uniform). But he and his subjects understood that this imperial project had something to do with Rome, that Otto and his heirs were "emperors of the Romans." After the eleventh century their realm was called *imperium Romanum*, as in ancient Rome.[74] Its theorists eventually made the German empire the successor to the ancient Roman one, a fiction, but politically potent. In practice, the imperial title gave historical and religious prestige to the monarch, the German king, who ruled over a medley of peoples, kings, margraves, counts, bishops, cities, and such. But no consensus developed as to what was Roman about this "empire," despite its antiquarian titles, or who these "Romans" were who now had a German emperor.[75] These titles, moreover, had grave consequences for relations with Byzantium, the real empire of the Romans.

In Romanía, the equivalent titles and concepts had a different valence, making the two imperial ideologies incommensurate. There actually was a Roman people in the east, which had a strong sense of its Roman identity and continuity from ancient Rome. Their ruler was called "king" or "emperor" (*basileus*) of the Romans because they were the Romans and he was their ruler. These eastern Romans did not care much if a foreign ruler wanted to be called a *basileus*—whether that was taken as king or emperor—but they considered it an aggressive move if his title claimed sovereignty over "the Romans," because that referred to them. Otto could be a *basileus* so long as it was of the Franks.[76] When westerners wanted to annoy the Byzantines they would call them "Greeks" and assert that they had lost their claim to the Roman name by forgetting Latin or fostering heresies. In 871, Louis II was in conflict with Basileios I precisely over southern Italy, and in his letter he styled himself *imperator Romanorum Augustus* and called Basileios *imperator Novae Romae*, explaining to him that he was a Greek with no understanding of Roman tradition.[77] This hostile view would eventually prevail in the west and provide the framework for modern Byzantine studies. But it was possible at the time for western emperors to be more conciliatory. It seems that Charlemagne himself and Otto I did not use the full title *imperator Romanorum* in their correspondence with Romanía.

The Reich and Romanía were fundamentally different entities. Romanía was a single state governed by more or less uniform law and a single exclusive administrative system whose hierarchies (ecclesiastical, fiscal, military, judicial) were integrated and culminated in the capital. The majority of the population was Roman (by language, culture, religion, and political identity) and had no qualifying ethnic affiliations; the empire had as yet few peripheral or dependent territories populated by non-Romans. The Reich, by contrast, was a patchwork of locally autonomous smaller entities and aristocratic interests. The kaiser had no fixed capital and moved around with his court, reminding his subjects of his nominal authority and creating ties of dependency, which were the only unity the realm had.

In the 960s, Otto was active in Italy, attempting to incorporate the entire peninsula into his sphere of authority. The key to his strategy in the south was one Pandulf I Ironhead, the Lombard duke of Capua and, with his brother, of Benevento.[78] Otto won his allegiance by giving him Spoleto and Camarino in central Italy and by making Capua an archbishopric. The German emperor then invaded Byzantine Apulia in 968 and besieged Bari. His stated position was that Apulia had been stolen by the Greeks and had to be integrated into the kingdom of Italy. Otto withdrew when he found Bari to be impregnable. Without leaving the south, he sent Liudprand of Cremona to Constantinople. Meanwhile, the Byzantines raised Otranto to an archbishopric, which was answered, in 969, by the similar elevation of Benevento. These were games of jurisdictional one-upmanship between the two empires.[79]

Liudprand stayed in Constantinople from June to October 968. He failed in his mission and would write, on his return, the most hostile and insidious account by any visitor to the court. Its immediate purpose was to persuade the Lombard dukes to stay faithful to Otto and distrust Nikephoros' intentions toward them. Ostensibly his mission was to arrange the marriage of Otto II and Anna, the born-in-the-purple daughter of Romanos II (she would eventually marry Vladimir of Kiev). In addition, he was there to spy on the possible Byzantine responses to Otto's aggression and to secure recognition of his master's imperial title in exchange for Apulia, which Otto would "give" freely to the easterners.[80] Liudprand failed here too, and sought in this work to pin the blame on Nikephoros, whom he presented as uncouth and arrogant, and on the Byzantines generally, whom his diatribe castigates as faithless and gross. The insidious aspect of his tale is that he presents weighty issues on which east and west were beginning to disagree (for example, ownership of the Roman heritage and doctrinal differences) as mere affects of the Byzantines' deranged culture. In his debates with members of the court, they come across as haughty and he as reasonable. Liudprand's voice has been internalized by some modern writers on Byzantium. It should be contrasted to the more positive impression of the same court given in the captivity poems of Abu Firas, Sayf al-Dawla's cousin, but these are, unsurprisingly, not read in the West. The Arab poet recounts his debates with the emperor, and was struck by his knowledge of Islam.[81]

For all his bias, Liudprand provides us with fascinating glimpses of the chief personalities of the court, including the Phokades, the two child-heirs to the throne, Basileios *parakoimomenos*, and Symeon the *protasekretis* (and historian), as well as of ceremonial processions and banquets. The banquets are interesting because Skylitzes, in documenting the emperor's declining popularity, describes the food scarcities that struck Constantinople in 968, which Liudprand mentions too.[82] It is alleged that Nikephoros sold imperial stores of grain at inflated prices and his brother Leon joined in the profiteering. The people began to grumble and deride the emperor, even as the wall around his palace was going up.

As for Italy, Liudprand claims that Nikephoros threatened to bring his "slaves," the dukes of Capua-Benevento, back to imperial obedience by force, and hints were dropped about a march on Rome.[83] Liudprand witnessed the departure of a fleet from Constantinople on July 19. This was also taking gold to strengthen Adalbert, the deposed king of Italy and enemy of the Saxons.[84] We should not be fooled by Liudprand's partisan rhetoric; the responsibility for this entire conflict lay with Otto, who initiated hostilities to extract concessions and recognition. Liudprand complains that "the Greeks" would not recognize his master as *basileus*, but only as a minor *rex*. In early 969, Otto moved against Calabria, but failed to make any progress in besieging Cassano. He then returned to Apulia and attacked Bovino, but here too encountered stiff resistance. Otto returned north in May, leaving Pandulf Ironhead to press the siege. But Pandulf was defeated and captured by the imperial general Eugenios, who sent him on to Constantinople. Eugenios then invaded the duchies, besieged Capua, and was received triumphantly in Salerno. In a strange turn of events, he was recalled to the capital on account of his excessive severity as governor.[85] German armies, followed by Otto himself, returned to the south in later 969. The two empires were for now committed to war, though no decisive encounters were fought. A modern historian of southern Italy has put it well: "Each side was capable of deep penetrations into the other's territory, but neither was strong enough to make any permanent impression."[86]

It is worth remembering that the Byzantine ability to keep the Germans at bay was premised on the peace with the Fatimids signed just the year before the conflict began, in 967. Otherwise, the empire would have been facing a two-front war in southern Italy. Fortunately, the Fatimids were preparing for another major assault on Egypt. The emperors now tended to place both Italian themes under one general, e.g., Marianos Argyros in 956, and now, in 969, Eugenios was likely the first to hold the new post of *katepano* of Italy, which had overall command.[87] In the 970s, similar posts were created for the Balkan and eastern themes as well; we will examine them in the next reign.

Military victory, political failure: The final years

While he was spending those miserable four months in Constantinople in 968, Liudprand also witnessed Nikephoros' departure for the east—his final one—in late July (just as Svjatoslav was marching against Bulgaria for the first time). This was a year and half after the death of Sayf al-Dawla. Events had unfolded in the Arab states in the meantime. The Roman conquests had sparked outrage among Muslim communities, and Christians were targeted regardless of their political loyalties. In 966, the patriarch of Jerusalem, Ioannes, was burned alive and the Holy Sepulcher was damaged by a mob. In 967, the patriarch of Antioch Christophoros, a supporter of Sayf al-Dawla, was murdered on the suspicion—or pretext—of inciting the Romans. These killings were noted in Byzantium.[88] In the Arab world it may have been believed that Nikephoros' goal was the Holy Land, and then Baghdad itself.[89] But the strategy of Nikephoros was consistent and more limited: to destroy weak neighbors close to his borders, and weaken those next to them. At no point did Byzantine strategy aim to recover the Holy Land.

Sayf al-Dawla's death had unleashed civil strife within the emirate of Aleppo, which fragmented. Five thousand Khurasanis had now arrived at Antioch, under the command of one Muhammad ibn Isa, to wage war against the infidel Romans. In the winter of 967–968, they made a successful raid into Roman territory, which now presumably meant their prior *thughur*. The Muslims were now raiding their former strongholds. They followed that up with another raid in 968, but were met in battle by Petros, a eunuch of Nikephoros' household who had been given the ad hoc position of *stratopedarches* ("army commander"). Petros defeated them between Mopsouestia and Antioch and captured their leader, who was ransomed by the people of Antioch.[90] Nikephoros arrived in October 968 and raided northern Syria, killing and enslaving from Mayyafariqin to Antioch, which he reached on October 19. He left three days later, striking south to Emesa, from which he extorted the head of John the Baptist, then across Mt. Lebanon to Tripolis, which he reached on November 5, burning its suburbs. There he turned north to 'Arqa, which he besieged for nine days, captured, and sacked, as the movable wealth of the region had been stored here for safekeeping. Nikephoros captured many forts on his return, taking captives and acquiring Laodikeia through negotiated surrender; the local notable who surrendered it was placed in charge of it as general. The emperor built a fortress to face Antioch at the pass of Baghras in the Amanos mountain, thereby effectively blockading the city. He left Michael Bourtzes there with a force of five hundred cavalry and a thousand infantry as well as his retainer Petros to ravage the city's lands from a base in Cilicia. The emperor returned to Constantinople in early 969.[91] No one had come out to fight him during this invasion of Syria and the coast.[92]

When he returned, Nikephoros brought with him the patriarch Yuhannan VII of the Syrian Church and a number of his bishops. In Constantinople, they were forced to debate doctrinal matters in a synod, and when they refused to accept Roman Orthodoxy, they were exiled (though we do not know where to). Nikephoros had broken his word to preserve peace with the Jacobite Church.[93]

A new crisis awaited Nikephoros on his return. The Rus' had sailed into the Danube in the summer of 968, defeated a Bulgarian army by Dorystolon (Dristra), and set about capturing Danubian towns. Petar suffered a stroke and died on January 30, 969. The emperor now put the City on military alert, in case the Rus' should attack it with their fleet, as they had done before. It is possible that Nikephoros had heard rumors of the treachery of his own envoy, Kalokyros, who promised to pay Svjatoslav and recognize his conquests if he could place him on the Byzantine throne.[94] This situation was now alarming, spiraling out of control. Breathing space was provided by an attack on Kiev by the Pechenegs (a Central Asian, mostly nomadic people), either in 968 or 969. Svjatoslav rushed off overland to relieve the city and save his children and mother Olga. With that accomplished, in 969, he declared his intention to relocate to the Danube, "since that is the centre of my realm, where all riches are concentrated; gold, silks, wine, and various fruits from Greece, silver and horses from Hungary and Bohemia, and from Rus' furs, wax, honey, and slaves."[95]

Some suspect that the Pecheneg attack was instigated by Byzantine gold, but there is no proof for that, and Nikephoros was absent in the east during most of those events. On his return, he wanted to come to an agreement with the Bulgarians, fearing that they might join the Rus'. Boris II took his father's throne. Nikephoros sent envoys asking for princesses to marry the two Roman heirs, Basil and Konstantinos, but by the time the maidens arrived toward the end of 969, it was too late for Bulgaria.[96] Svjatoslav may have left part of his army in Bulgaria when he rushed to Kiev,[97] but now he was back, in the late summer of 969, with greater forces, including Pechenegs and Magyars. Bulgaria was in chaos, but this was a mess that Nikephoros' successor would have to clean up. We do not know how the White Death of the Saracens planned to deal with the pale nations of the north.

Before he died, Nikephoros received a momentous piece of news: the city of Antioch had fallen and was again in Roman hands. The emperor had ordered his generals to blockade the city, but make no attempt on it. Bourtzes, however, felt that it was within reach, and craved the glory. He suborned one of the Arab leaders inside and, with his help, scaled the walls on a moonless rainy night and captured a tower. He was there besieged by the Antiochenes for three days, and during these battles fires were set that damaged the city. Bourtzes sent repeated summons to Petros, who was initially reluctant to disobey orders. But when Petros finally approached with his army, on October 28, the Antiochenes pulled back and Bourtzes opened the gates. The city fell immediately, and Petros worked to extinguish the fires, even as Bourtzes raced to the capital to deliver the news. Nikephoros rejoiced but was angry with Bourtzes, dismissing him from his position. The reason cannot have been that he feared prophesies about his own death that were linked to the fall of the city; such silly tales were regularly invented after the fact. Nikephoros seems rather to have been upset about the fires: he had wanted to take the city without damaging it. The good news also coincided with the death of his father Bardas, who was, it was said, over ninety.[98]

Everyone now expected that all of Syria would fall to Nikephoros. His strategy was well understood: he would weaken a region through repeated raids in which he killed multitudes, plundered the land, set fires, and destroyed whole communities, and he would then scoop up the pieces.[99] But now he reached the end of his extraordinary career. The murder of Nikephoros Phokas, on the night of December 10–11, 969, as he slept in his own palace, surrounded by his newly finished walls, is one of the most infamous events in Byzantine history. The site of the deed was remembered as "Phokas' chamber" for centuries thereafter, and a lookout was placed on the palace walls to prevent the same from happening again; this lookout is attested still in the late twelfth century.[100] Yet even at the time, the viciousness of the deed was oddly tempered by its romanticized perpetrators and adventurous execution.

There can be no doubt about the chief plotter. Ioannes Tzimiskes, the emperor's nephew, was prominent in Nikephoros' rise to power and the conquest of Cilicia. But we lose track of him at the end of 965, after the fall of Tarsos, when he was summoned back to the capital.[101] For reasons that we are not told, Nikephoros suspected his loyalty, stripped him of his command, and placed him under house arrest in eastern Asia Minor for four years. Our sources now claim that he was allowed to come to the capital through the intervention of Theophano. We cannot discern her motive in this matter, nor the exact course of the ensuing events, for gossip and imagination colored everything afterward, and Tzimiskes, once on the throne, had every reason to blame it all on her. It is not even certain that Theophano did in fact facilitate his entry into the palace on that snowy winter night. It was he who formed a conspiracy against Nikephoros with Michael Bourtzes, the conqueror of Antioch, Leon Pediasimos, and others. Somehow they placed men in the palace, who then hauled them up the seaward side of the new wall in a rope-drawn basket. They eventually found the emperor sleeping on the floor on a bearskin that he had received from his uncle, the saint Michael Maleïnos, and cut off his head. By showing the head through a window, they paralyzed the palace staff and the bodyguards. Tzimiskes went straight to the throne room to take command, counting on the slain emperor's unpopularity to neutralize the Phokas faction. Later that day he ordered that Nikephoros' body be buried, quietly and unceremoniously, in the imperial mausoleum of the Holy Apostles.[102]

One of Nikephoros' soldiers, Ioannes Geometres, who was also a scholar, wrote poems that praised the deceased emperor: "you, the general of invincible Rome, a king by nature, a bringer-of-victories [*nikephore*] in fact." Another lists the emperor's conquests, only to conclude that he fell in the midst of the palace, despite his armies and a double wall for protection.[103] A preacher at the court of the Hamdanids, by contrast, was glad: "God was kind and arranged it so that the murder of the tyrant of *Rum* occurred in his own land."[104]

CHAPTER 3

"A Mind Full of Cares, Brave in Danger"
Ioannes I Tzimiskes (969–976)

The new regime

As a general, Ioannes Tzimiskes was known for aggressive offense. He took daring risks that we might call reckless but for the fact that he almost always won. He was one of the instigators of Nikephoros' revolt in 963, and his own usurpation was equally audacious and ruthless. But we still have to wonder how a man who had been living in virtual exile for four years could just sneak into the palace, murder his uncle, and expect to be recognized as emperor. The short answer is that Tzimiskes *always* knew what he was doing.[1] The longer answer involves the dynamics of regime change in Byzantium.

From the scene of the crime, Tzimiskes went to the throne room of the Chrysotriklinos and donned imperial regalia. Nikephoros' head in a window neutralized the bodyguard corps. The first person Tzimiskes summoned—in the middle of the night—was Basileios *parakoimomenos*, the head of the senate and director of the palace, who had a plan for securing the succession. The two men, who had campaigned together against Samosata ten years earlier, seem to have planned this in advance, as Leon the deacon claims (and Basileios may have felt that the Cretan campaign had been "stolen" from him and given to Nikephoros in 960). That night Tzimiskes was acclaimed emperor by all who were present and eventually by the entire palace, certainly including the guards. Basileios sent heralds throughout the City to announce that Tzimiskes was now emperor along with Basil and Konstantinos. This was followed immediately by a decree outlawing all looting, which commonly took place during coups. There were no disturbances; the handling was meticulous.[2] Leon Phokas missed the chance to instigate a countercoup: he fled to Hagia Sophia. He and his son Nikephoros were arrested and exiled to Lesbos, while his other son Bardas, *doux* of Chaldia, was arrested and held in Amaseia, in the Armeniakon, Tzimiskes' territory.[3] We may doubt that all this was improvised during the night of December 10–11.

From the start Tzimiskes was issuing orders and making and unmaking appointments, as emperor. Yet he had been acclaimed only in the palace, not (yet) by the people as a whole. Why did the people of Constantinople not turn out in numbers, as they usually did during such events? First, dynastic stability had been prudently ensured by the joint proclamation of the two Macedonian heirs. Second, the contest was already over; there was no ongoing struggle in which the people could intervene. In past and future coups (e.g., 695, 802, 1185), when heralds had been sent throughout the City calling for regime change, the active support of the people was being solicited in a yet-unresolved struggle. But Nikephoros was already dead. Third, the Phokades were unpopular, which was the chief premise of Tzimiskes' bid: the people would probably not have rallied to them even if they were still in play. Fourth, because of his four-year absence Tzimiskes was not associated with the most unpopular of Nikephoros' measures. But he had enormous military prestige of his own, second only to the murdered emperor, and was an acceptable candidate for the army. The patriarch had his own reasons for disliking Nikephoros. Tzimiskes is described as short but fair and handsome, with strong arms and broad shoulders.[4]

A week later it was time to cut a deal with the patriarch, for Tzimiskes still needed a formal coronation and acclamation. Our sources do not report whether during this time he appeared before the people in the hippodrome, which would have entailed popular acclamation. This cannot be ruled out, for the sources do not report every step in every emperor's accession. They focus on Polyeuktos' demands, which were that Tzimiskes should cancel Nikephoros' decree on episcopal appointments (or on all Church matters) and punish Nikephoros' murderers. Tzimiskes promptly blamed two of his minor accomplices and said that they had acted at the empress' instigation. They were exiled and Theophano was banished, first to one of the Princes' Islands and then, when she escaped and sought refuge in Hagia Sophia, she was removed by Basileios *parakoimomenos* and sent to a monastery in the Armeniakon theme. The emperor gave half of his own private property to neighboring farmers and used the other half to endow a house for lepers (St. Zotikos) by the capital. After this expiation, he was crowned in Hagia Sophia and acclaimed by the army and the people on Christmas Day, 969, two weeks after the murder.[5] Later, in November 970, the emperor married

Theodora, one of the sisters of Romanos II; she is described as unattractive but smart. This gave Tzimiskes dynastic legitimacy, through a move that we are told pleased the people; apparently, the emperor agreed that if there were children, they would rank after the two heirs.[6] This marriage also tied him to Basileios *parakoimomenos*, Theodora's uncle. The eunuch seems to have had more influence under Tzimiskes than under Nikephoros.[7]

It is not clear why Tzimiskes banished Theophano. If we believe the worst that our sources say about her, she was a lower-class seductress and poisoner of emperors. I am inclined to believe none of this, not even her alleged affair with Tzimiskes before the murder, which was probably just a palace coup facilitated by the *parakoimomenos*. But Tzimiskes needed a high-value scape-goat to serve up to the patriarch, who may have disliked Theophano for his own reasons. Removing her also effectively isolated the two heirs, one of whom, Basil, would soon be reaching maturity (he was eleven in 969). Theophano's bad press likely stemmed from the propaganda of Tzimiskes' regime, and the story of her affair with him likely came from the Phokades, when they took up arms against her son Basil II. A later vernacular poem satirized the ambitions of Theophano—"she wanted the cake" but the other woman (Theodora) ate it—while "the men with shriveled cocks and gap-ing assholes" (i.e., the eunuchs Polyeuktos and Basileios) paraded the former empress on a mule. The date of this poem is unclear.[8]

Tzimiskes granted the Armeniakon theme a major tax break and increased the stipends of the senate, which Nikephoros had lowered.[9] This was pork-barrel politics. Polyeuktos died on February 5, 970, at the age of about sev-enty, and Tzimiskes replaced him with the monk Basileios Skamandrenos, an ascetic from Mt. Olympos in Bithynia. Tzimiskes was a nephew of Phokas through his mother and also related to the Kourkouas family; his first wife, Maria, now deceased, was the sister of Bardas Skleros, the head of a military family. As a counterweight to the Phokades, Tzimiskes promoted Skleros to the all-purpose military office of *stratelates* ("army leader"),[10] setting off a rivalry between the Skleros and Phokas families that dominated Roman politics for the next twenty years. But he needed the support of these military types, such as Bourtzes, the conqueror of Antioch.

Tzimiskes also ended the persecution of the Jacobite patriarchs, who were allowed to return to Melitene. They would not be molested again by the Roman authorities until 1029.[11] The *katholikos* (chief prelate) of the Armenian church also established sees for Armenians in Roman Syria during this reign.[12] Finally, in 970 Tzimiskes diplomatically ended the pointless war with Otto I in southern Italy. The emperor released Pandulf Ironhead, the duke of Capua-Benevento who had been captured the previous year, and sent him as an envoy to Otto, who was at Bovino in August. Whatever agreement they came to then ended the war, as Otto departed for the north one month later.[13] Tzimiskes must have agreed to give the sought-after imperial bride. This role fell to one Theophano, whose exact identity is unclear; she was probably the niece of the emperor's first wife. She was escorted to the west in 971, possibly by Liudprand of Cremona, and married Otto II, who had been his father's co-emperor since 967, in St. Peter's on April 14, 972. Theophano has been discussed extensively as a figure transmitting Byzantine culture to the developing west.[14] She is never mentioned in Byzantine sources.

Meanwhile, the emperor's agents were also active in the provinces settling disputes. It was at this time that Mt. Athos emerged into the light of history as a monastic center. Today it is an autonomous polity of twenty monasteries within the Greek state from which, because of its nature, origins, and traditions, women are still excluded. We know little about its communities before the arrival of saint Athanasios (ca. 925–1003), who hailed from Trebizond. Sponsored by Nikephoros Phokas, he founded the Great Lavra monastery in 963 and wrote its Rule. This was a coenobitic community, a group of monks living together under a common set of rules. Athanasios had ambitions for his foundation, secured impressive endowments for it, expanded its properties, and began to exploit its agricultural assets. But other ascetics on Athos tended toward solitary forms of devotion and were threatened by this new development. They protested to Tzimiskes—who had, after all, eliminated Athanasios' patron Phokas—and Tzimiskes sent a monk from the capital to investigate. This inquiry resulted in a compromise solution known as the *Typikon of Tzimiskes*, a charter for the future of Mt. Athos that recognized the validity of the various types of asceticism practiced there (it finds that none of the parties to the dispute were to blame, only Satan for stirring up trouble). Tzimiskes even added to the Lavra's cash stipend. This set the stage for the spectacular expansion of Athonite foundations, recruitment, landholding, and business interests in the following centuries. Future emperors would be torn between the pious desire (and good publicity) of supporting the holy mountain with exemptions from fiscal and legal burdens, and the practical need to rein in its acquisitiveness and expansion against poorer neighbors and villages.

The defeat of the Rus' and Bulgaria

Tzimiskes is remembered as a bold general who was successful on the field of battle, yet his moves in 969–970 reveal a consummate politician. It was a perfectly executed coup, a skilful and daring leveraging of assets and connections to put a man on the throne whose career seemed finished. He then made all the right moves to stamp out potential resistance and placate possible foes by making precisely those concessions that cost him the least. As emperor, Tzimiskes would replicate this success on the field of battle too. In 970, he had to deal with threats on two fronts, a situation that the empire had not faced for many years. In the east there was a volatile situation, as the Roman conquests had caused outrage in the Muslim world, and a rising power, the Fatimids, were asserting themselves in Syria after the collapse of the Hamdanids. Meanwhile, in the north there was a potentially more dangerous threat, as the Rus' were subjugating Bulgaria; and the scarcity of food had not abated. Tzimiskes decided to handle the Balkan issue personally in 971, while his officers held the empire's position in the east until he could arrive in person.

As an emerging culture, Kievan Rus' was unlike anything on the Byzantine horizon. Rather than seek a single determinative element, it is best to see it as defined by the confluence of multiple agents and factors, resulting in a dynamic mixture. These were basically trading settlements founded along the major rivers north of the Black Sea by Scandinavians who raided for plunder as Vikings while also expanding trade routes. Over time they assimilated into the culture of their predominantly Slavic-speaking subjects. These mixed settlements grew into permanent towns by the tenth century, and the Rus' traded and raided in all directions, subjecting weaker rivals along their routes until they came up against more formidable states, which then became their trading partners, e.g., Byzantium and the Khazar khaganate, both of which contributed elements to the growing agglomeration of Rus' culture. The Rus' were pagans, though little is known about their religion. The mixed culture of their lands was not hostile to Christianity. Past emperors had boasted of converting them, but with no lasting impact. Svjatoslav's mother Olga, who had visited the court of Konstantinos VII and invited bishops from Germany, was a convert, though what that meant for the spread of Christianity is unknown. In the 960s, the Rus' were emerging as the dominant power across a huge region, under the unifying authority of the ruler of Kiev. In 965 Svjatoslav had just dealt a death blow to the Khazar khaganate to the east and was looking to expand to the southwest and along the Danube. In the past, Rus' ships had raided as far as Constantinople, making sudden attacks in large numbers, so the Romans had legitimate concerns about his invasion of Bulgaria. They could not afford to see it absorbed by an aggressive pagan power.

We have two sources for the Byzantine-Rus' war of 970–971. The first is a panegyrical narrative of Tzimiskes' victory that was used independently by both Leon and Skylitzes. This casts (or invents) episodes in the war to make its hero resemble Greek and Roman conquerors.[15] The second is the chronicle of the early Rus', the *Tale of Bygone Years* (called today the *Russian Primary Chronicle*), whose section on Svjatoslav was put together in the twelfth century. Its broad contours are historical, but many of its details are fictional. It tries to maintain that Svjatoslav won, when in fact he was crushed by Tzimiskes and killed by Pechenegs on the way home.

By late 969, Svjatoslav was in control of northeastern Bulgaria, including its capital Preslav and its tsar Boris II, and had then moved south, taking Philippopolis (Plovdiv) and intending to conquer more (western Bulgaria, we will see later, was heading in a different direction). He had with him Magyars and Pechenegs, and seems to have persuaded the Bulgarians, including their tsar Boris, to join his anti-Roman campaign; they were now fighting alongside the Rus', if not for them.[16] In early 970, Tzimiskes was busy consolidating his hold on the throne. He failed to persuade Svjatoslav to depart, so he transferred over some eastern armies and placed ten to twelve thousand men under the command of his brother-in-law, Bardas Skleros, and Petros, the *stratopedarches* and conqueror of Antioch. When part of Svjatoslav's army marched down the military road to Arkadiopolis, Skleros, using feigned retreats and ambushes, destroyed some of its units. It was a modest victory, albeit written up as an epic success.[17]

But now events in Asia Minor caused Tzimiskes to suspend the Rus' war and transfer the armies and Skleros over to Asia. Specifically, a group of officers hatched a plot to proclaim Bardas Phokas emperor.[18] Accompanied by relatives and allies, he escaped from Amaseia and traveled to Kaisareia, where he was proclaimed emperor and began to issue orders. At the same time, his father Leon and brother Konstantinos, in exile on Lesbos, planned to escape to Macedonia and rally army units there in support of Bardas. So in addition to an active military front in two theaters (the Balkans and the east), Tzimiskes faced a new challenge, which was to become increasingly distracting for the empire, namely a military revolt during a foreign war. The rebellion of Bardas was a first for the political history of the middle Byzantine period in that it involved a former emperor's relation claiming the throne through a sense of family entitlement and with the support of a network of family connections who were officers.

But the rebellion fizzled. The plot of Leon and Nikephoros Phokas was uncovered and they were arrested, turned over to the courts, and sentenced to death. The emperor commuted this sentence to blinding, and then suspended it. Skleros meanwhile proceeded to the military post of Dorylaion. After failing to negotiate Phokas' surrender—his brother was married to

Phokas' sister—Skleros secretly bribed most of Phokas' associates to abandon him and join the emperor. Phokas fled to the fortress of Tyropoion, then surrendered on terms. He was forced to become a priest and sent to the island of Chios. It seems that only one Roman died in this revolt, in the pursuit of Phokas to Tyropoion. The rebellion began and ended quickly in 970. Skleros was ordered to winter quarters back in Europe. The Rus' had hardly been checked and were plundering Macedonia. The emperor stored up supplies in Adrianople in advance of campaigning in person the following spring.[19]

In the early spring of 971, Tzimiskes sent a fleet armed with Greek fire to block the mouth of the Danube. He then marched ahead with select infantry and cavalry forces, including an elite cavalry *tagma* that he had created called "the Immortals."[20] Tzimiskes crossed the Haimos mountains and reached Preslav, apparently surprising everyone (why the passes remained unguarded remains a mystery).[21] Basileios *parakoimomenos* followed at a slower pace with the rest of the army and the siege engines. Appearing over the hill with trumpets blaring, the emperor apparently surprised a Rus' force in the fields around Preslav and defeated it, killing eighty-five hundred; the rest sought safety inside, where tsar Boris held court. Kalokyros, the former Byzantine agent, now slipped out to summon Svjatoslav from Dorystolon (Dristra). Basileios arrived the next day, and the emperor assaulted Preslav. The city fell quickly. Further action was required against a force of eight thousand that held the palace. Tzimiskes set fire to it and smoked them out. He now took Boris and the entire royal family captive, though he treated them courteously. At this point he may have still been planning to restore Bulgaria, albeit as a Roman client. While celebrating Easter on April 16, he renamed Preslav "Ioannoupolis" after himself, and it would become a theme in the imperial reorganization of the newly conquered lands. Svjatoslav meanwhile massacred three hundred Bulgarian nobles who were with him at Dorystolon (Dristra). It is unclear why he allowed the Romans to take on his army piecemeal, at Preslav and then Dorystolon. Svjatoslav appears to have been a terrible strategist.

Tzimiskes now marched north, taking Pliska and other cities along the way. The two armies met on April 23 a few miles from Dorystolon. It was a long and hard-fought battle, but the Romans prevailed. The Rus' sought refuge inside, imprisoning and binding the local Bulgarians, whom they could no longer trust, while the Roman fleet blockaded the town from the river. Petros and Skleros were assigned to guard the land gates, and repulsed a furious Rus' sortie. The next day a large Rus' force came out for a pitched battle, but pulled back after the death of its commander. It now seemed likely that the siege would be prolonged. Svjatoslav began to dig a ditch around the walls to prevent the Romans from approaching, and he sent a large force out on a moonless and stormy night in ships to gather supplies. On the way back they killed many Roman orderlies by the river. Tzimiskes was furious at the fleet commanders, invested the city tightly, cut off the roads, and settled in to starve the enemy.

Meanwhile, the plotting of the Phokades again distracted the emperor. Leon and Nikephoros had escaped from Lesbos and sailed to the capital, where they bribed some of the guards and were planning to take the palace. But the plot was revealed to Leon, the admiral of the fleet whom Tzimiskes had left in control of the City. He had them arrested and sent to a small island. They were to be blinded for good this time.[22] Thus ended the active career of Leon Phokas, the conqueror of Sayf al-Dawla.

The situation of the Rus' was dire. They had exhausted their food supplies and were being bombarded by the siege engines under Tzimiskes' cousin, one Ioannes Kourkouas. Their sorties were defeated (though they did manage to kill Kourkouas in one of them). They decided on a final stand. The battle between the two armies was fought in July, and the Romans again prevailed.[23] Among their 350 casualties was Anemas (the son of the emir of Crete), who was now serving in the emperor's bodyguard; the Rus' allegedly lost 15,500 men. Svjatoslav now sued for terms and asked for an audience with the emperor. Leon offers a striking description of the muscular Rus' leader, intended to highlight Tzimiskes' victory over barbarism.[24] He had completely shaved his beard and head, except for a long lock that hung down on one side, and he let his mustache grow long and bushy. He wore a gold earring on one ear, and was dressed only in white, like his companions. Svjatoslav pledged never to attack the Romans or their allies, invoking his pagan gods Perun and Veles[25]; in return, the Rus' would be given food and allowed to depart, and Roman envoys would be sent to the Pechengs to arrange a trilateral trade agreement. But on his return, in 972, Svjatoslav was ambushed and killed at the Dnieper rapids by Pechengs, who supposedly turned his skull into a chalice.[26] Tzimiskes celebrated a triumph on entering Constantinople, modeled on that of the ancient Roman hero Camillus described by Plutarch, except he yielded his place in the chariot drawn by white horses to an icon of the Mother of God that he had taken at Preslav, and walked behind it. The parade featured the Bulgarian royal family. At the end, in sight of everyone, Tzimiskes divested Boris II of his imperial regalia and then dedicated the Bulgarian crown in Hagia Sophia as an offering. Bulgaria was to be annexed, just as its icon was brought to protect the City and Boris was given a court title. As the monarchy had formally ceased to exist in Roman eyes, later claimants to it (such as Samuil) were regarded as nothing more than rebels and usurpers.

The administration of occupied (i.e., eastern) Bulgaria is not described in the literary sources and so is poorly understood. Our main source is a *Taktikon* known as Escorial (after the library that holds it). *Taktika* were precedence lists of all office and title holders, used by the palace staff to organize court events. Thus, they preserve snapshots of the military, civilian, and court hierarchy at a specific moment in time, in this case between 971–975. This *Taktikon* reveals the creation of new themes in the conquered territories. However, Tzimiskes made a major addition to the overall command structure. As new frontier themes in recently conquered regions were being made smaller and smaller, he began to cluster them together under the broader regional authority of a *doux* (sometimes called a *katepano*). The Balkan *doukes* attested in the Escorial *Taktikon* were those of Adrianople, Thessalonike, and a place called "Mesopotamia of the West" (possibly around the Danube delta).[27] Equivalent posts were created for the eastern front, as we will see. These overarching commands may have been pioneered in southern Italy.

However, we cannot assume that these posts, once created, were always filled. Those who produced the *Taktika* needed to know the relative rank of all *possible* office holders in order to organize their receptions, and so the lists may give a misleadingly full picture of the hierarchy at any moment. In practice, emperors made many ad hoc arrangements and appointments for the governance of the frontier regions, and the *doukes* may have been only one among various options, to be filled when needed.[28] For actual appointees, we rely on historical sources, though these are negligible for the first, brief Byzantine occupation of eastern Bulgaria (from 971 to 986). We also rely on lead seals that were used to mark correspondence (unfortunately the correspondence itself does not survive). The seals reveal the names of office holders and the offices themselves.[29] We do not know where the soldiers of the new themes came from. Some were no doubt from the *tagmata* used in the conquest, but we do not know how easily thematic soldiers could be transferred or how thematic lands were created in the new provinces to support them or newly raised forces.

It is not clear how far west Roman control now extended. Even so, in the course of three months Tzimiskes had added more territory to the empire in a single swoop than any emperor since Justinian. For the first time since the seventh century the empire extended to the Danube. Forts were renovated or built at strategic locations to control crossings and seemed to be aimed primarily at blocking future Rus' invasions. The patriarchate of Bulgaria was abolished (at least in Byzantine eyes) and replaced by a metropolitan bishopric subordinate to Constantinople.[30] Bulgaria otherwise remains dark. The region did not produce secular literature, and the tsars had not yet minted coins. The local economy and administration were not yet as bureaucratized as in the rest of the empire. But the Rus' were definitively pushed back.

Eastern incursions: Toward a new balance of power

When Nikephoros was murdered, the eastern frontier was volatile. Skylitzes says that some recently acquired cities were contemplating a rebellion, but nothing more is heard of this.[31] Antioch was strategically vulnerable to attacks from Aleppo, but after the death of Sayf al-Dawla in 967 the Hamdanids were in the midst of a succession struggle. For the Romans, this was the moment to strike and to establish a new status quo. Petros was invited to intervene by Sayf al-Dawla's former minister Qarghuya, who had repudiated Hamdanid authority and was being besieged by a rival. When Petros approached, the rival withdrew but Petros then besieged Aleppo in turn in December 969; it fell after twenty-seven days, in January 970. He was likely acting on his own bold initiative in this, unless Nikephoros had time to send immediate instructions in November 969, before he was killed (though this is unlikely). The Romans were not prepared to occupy Aleppo (Figure 4), so they made a pact with Qarghuya known as the treaty of Safar. It recognized the independence of Aleppo under his rule but now as a Roman tributary. In addition to tribute and the usual terms of a defensive-offensive alliance (though Muslims would not be required to fight against other Muslims), Aleppo ceded many lands to its northwest; an imperial agent would tax trade to the empire;

FIGURE 4 The citadel of Aleppo, one of the oldest fortified settlements in the world. Most of its extant fortifications date from the later twelfth century and after. *Source: Shutterstock, ID 42411829.*

the emperor could nominate the future emirs; the emirate would not allow Muslim armies to pass through; and religious converts would not be punished by either side.[32] Aleppo was no longer a separate power but a Roman client. Qarghuya was to rule it by Roman sufferance, and he could transmit his power to his deputy, Bakjur. The Romans now benefited directly from the high volume of trade that passed through the city, situated on the route from Iraq to the Mediterranean.[33]

Petros returned to Antioch, where he executed one of the instigators of the murder of Christophoros, the bishop of the city who had been lynched in 967.[34] The remaining Muslim population of the city seems to have been small, while the Christian population included many Monophysites and, soon, Armenians. This means that the city had many parallel ecclesiastical hierarchies, the main ones being the Melkites (Chalcedonians) and Jacobites (anti-Chalcedonians). On January 23, 970, the Synod in Constantinople appointed Theodoros II (970–976) as its own patriarch for Antioch. He was abbot of a monastery in the Armeniakon theme and was designated by Tzimiskes.[35] The city was to become the base for Roman forward control of Syria for the next century. In recent times, it had a history of self-rule and was not used to being strategically important. Thus the choice of (Byzantine orthodox) patriarchs was crucial, for rallying at least part of the local Christian population behind imperial policies. Petros was recalled to Constantinople to take part in the war against the Rus' (see above), and Bourtzes was sent back to govern Antioch, which he had captured.[36] At this point, the Fatimids, whom the Romans had so far faced only in Sicily, intervened in Syria, resulting in a new balance of power in the eastern Mediterranean.

The roots of the Fatimid movement and state lay in the sectarian divisions of Islam. Their leadership represented a branch of the Ismaili branch of the Shia. The Shia believe that Muhammad's son-in-law Ali was the heir of the Prophet and also the first Imam, that is, a religious leader possessing special insight into God's message. In effect, they did not accept the legitimacy of the Umayyad and Abbasid caliphs. Among the Shia, in turn, various groups disagreed about the genealogical succession of the imamate among the Prophet's descendants. Some believed that the Last Imam was occluded and would reappear at a future time, but others proclaimed themselves to hold that position, the Fatimids among them. They were established initially in Tunisia with mostly Berber support (and with a reach eventually to Morocco), although in theory they always aimed for universal domination over the entire Muslim world, rejecting the Abbasids and calling for jihad against the Romans. Their ruler was both caliph and Imam, an infallible representative of God, and obedience to him was a religious duty.[37]

The Fatimids made numerous attempts on Egypt during the tenth century and finally succeeded in 969, wresting it from nominal Abbasid rule, though by that point there was little resistance. The general in charge of the expedition was Jawhar, who was of Sicilian Greek or Slavic ethnic origin. It was he who founded Cairo as a base for his government and Berber army, and was in charge in Egypt for four years before his caliph, al-Muʿizz, arrived from Tunisia. The majority of the country's population were likely Coptic Christian, and most of its Muslims, although they recognized the Fatimids as legitimate rulers, did not accept their specific version of Islam. Jawhar decided immediately on the conquest of Syria. In fact, even as he was taking over Egypt in 969, his propaganda stressed the need to push back the Romans, who were just then blockading Antioch.[38] It was perhaps in part for this reason, to check the threat from North Africa, that Nikephoros Phokas had sent the sword of Muhammad to the caliph al-Muʿizz, an item he had acquired from one of the Hamdanid forts he had captured.[39]

But the Fatimids would not be deterred from holy war. In 970, Jawhar sent a Berber army north under Jaʿfar that secured Palestine and subdued Damascus. In October 970, Jaʿfar sent his slave-soldier Futuh north to prepare an attack against the Romans. He besieged Antioch for five months, until the middle of 971. Skylitzes reports that news was sent to Tzimiskes (who must have been in Bulgaria), and he sent the general of Mesopotamia and one of his own retainers, the eunuch Nikolaos, who defeated the Muslims in battle. Later Arabic sources confirm that this took place by Alexandretta, but involved only a contingent of the Fatimid army.[40] The latter had to withdraw to face a far more serious challenge to its presence in Syria. A rival Ismaili group, the Qarmatians, who were especially strong in the Arabian peninsula, attacked the Fatimids in force, defeated and killed Jaʿfar, and then invaded Egypt, where Jawhar himself barely managed to push them back.[41] This relieved the pressure on the empire. The Fatimids would return to Syria, but they never again seriously challenged the Roman presence there. In fact, until the coming of the Seljuks in the mideleventh century, the Romans and the Fatimids between them provided a framework of basic stability for the eastern Mediterranean and generally respected each other's spheres of authority.

The reign of Tzimiskes after 971 is poorly documented, especially in Byzantine sources. We know from Venetian sources that in 971 the emperor imposed a ban on the trade of weapons and lumber with Muslim states, a ban that he requested Venice, a client state of his, also respect.[42] A year later, in 972, he attacked northern Mesopotamia. We know about this incursion largely from diplomatic documents of the Baghdad court.[43] Tzimiskes crossed the border from Melitene in late September, more than a year after his triumph in Bulgaria. He captured Nisibis on October 12, where he massacred, burned, and plundered. He did not leave until he had extorted an annual tribute from Abu Taghlib, the Hamdanid emir of Mosul. An effort to muster an army in Baghdad to confront the Romans turned to rioting and infighting.[44] Tzimiskes then moved north to besiege Mayyafariqin, without success. He returned to Roman territory, leaving on the Euphrates his *domestikos* of the eastern *scholai*, Melias. With this brief campaign, the emperor turned his attention east, and was following the same aggressive policy of the recent past: ravage, destroy, and extort until the enemy is so weak that some pieces might eventually shake loose. But northern Mesopotamia, unlike Cilicia, was too exposed to the Muslim heartlands for lasting conquests to be maintained.

Probably in early 973, Melias besieged Amida. Abu Taghlib, the emir of Mosul, sent his brother against him, who defeated the Romans on July 4, 973, in a narrow pass before Amida, which neutralized the superior Roman numbers. Melias and others were captured and one thousand heads were dispatched to Baghdad for display. Melias died in captivity in Mosul in the spring of 974, before an exchange could be arranged.[45] It is unclear whether the "annual" tribute from Nisibis was continued after this. There is no proof that Tzimiskes campaigned in the east in 974.[46] We know little about what the emperor was doing between late 972 and the summer of 975, when he invaded Syria in force. It is likely that he was preoccupied with the administrative, military, and fiscal challenges posed by the conquest of eastern Bulgaria. The empire had not conquered such a large territory in more than four centuries.

We can reconstruct the emperor's romp through Syria in 975 from many sources, but one has long excited historians' imagination. The twelfth-century Armenian historian Matthew of Edessa quotes what purports to be a letter from Tzimiskes to Ašot III of Armenia (953–977) narrating the campaign in detail.[47] Although some of these details are confirmed by other sources, "Tzimiskes" here alleges that he reached as far as the Sea of Galilee, Nazareth, and Kaisareia, conquering all of those regions "intent on delivering the holy sepulcher of Christ from Muslim bondage." This is an obvious anachronism influenced by the Crusades. The itinerary described in the letter makes little sense, and the stories that Matthew recounts for that period are fanciful and garbled. Tzimiskes did not go to Palestine.[48]

The goal of the 975 incursion was to plunder; impose tribute where possible, or even client status, on cities that had been detached from broader allegiances; and soften up targets for future attack. The international scene was inviting, as Syria was extremely fragmented. Aleppo was a client state, and its emirate was split between Bakjur at Aleppo and his nominal master Abu al-Maʿali, the son of Sayf al-Dawla, at Homs (Emesa). Abu Taghlib of Mosul, the son of Nasir al-Dawla, was preoccupied in conflict with Buyid Baghdad. The Fatimids had weathered another Qarmatian invasion (974), and their control over southern Syria was unstable: Damascus was under the control of a Turkish general-for-hire, Alp Takin, who had just come from Buyid employment.[49] Nevertheless, the legitimacy of the Fatimid presence was based on a promise to push back the Roman infidels, a threat that could not be ignored.[50] Tzimiskes made a Grand Tour, replicating that of Nikephoros in 968, only in a wider circuit.

Passing by Apameia, through territory that Rome controlled according to the 970 treaty with Aleppo,[51] Tzimiskes headed for Baalbek (Heliopolis). The Turkish mercenary captain Alp Takin, who had left Baghdad to seek his fortune in Syria, had recently gained control of Damascus and expelled the Fatimids. He tried to stop the emperor at this point, but failed and retreated to Damascus. Tzimiskes besieged Baalbek, captured it on May 29, and sacked it.[52] He then moved on Damascus. The townspeople knew that they were in no position to resist, and submitted in exchange for a large payment. The Roman army was delayed there, however, as the money could not be raised easily from the war-torn city. Damascus does not seem to have been subordinated to the empire in any lasting way.[53] When it was finally delivered, Tzimiskes moved diagonally up to the coast to besiege Beirut (held by a Fatimid governor) and capture some minor forts. During the siege of Beirut, the leaders of Sidon came to offer their submission and tribute. Beirut then surrendered its governor, who was sent on to Roman lands. Tzimiskes moved up the coast, taking Byblos by force but failing, like Nikephoros before him, to take Tripolis (also in Fatimid hands). In fact, it is possible that before he set out toward Baalbek Tzimiskes had sent a contingent to blockade Tripolis, and that he rejoined it now. He ravaged the area, destroying plantations and capturing minor forts along his return route. Laodikeia seems now to have been incorporated into the empire.[54] Tzimiskes returned home in August.

Tzimiskes' Grand Tour, which involved almost no actual battles, revealed how weak the empire's neighbors were to the southeast, but also how unlikely it was that the Romans could conquer and annex additional lands in this direction. Tzimiskes was installing client rulers and establishing tributary relationships to act as buffers between Romanía and whatever came next in Syria. The threat of a Fatimid onslaught had been checked, and the terms of the treaty of Safar with Aleppo had passed a stress test. But the new relationships cannot have lasted long after his departure, especially given the civil wars that would distract the Romans for years to come. Aleppo remained secure, but for how long did tribute from Nisibis, Damascus, Beirut, and the rest flow? Possibly not at all after the initial take. Alp Takin also expanded his realm to include some coastal cities, but he was defeated (and then rehired) by the Fatimids in 978.[55] It is doubtful that he had been paying the empire until then. The main gains from the incursion of 975 probably consisted of what the Roman army brought back with it.

Just as in Bulgaria, in the east too Tzimiskes grouped the smaller frontier themes together, including the new ones that he created, under the command of regional *doukes*. So there was now a *doux* of Chaldia in the north, a *doux* of Mesopotamia in the central sector, and in the southern sector a *doux* of Antioch, controlling northern Syria and Cilicia.[56] It is possible that these positions were sometimes left vacant, and that their jurisdiction and duties changed according to need.[57] The high command was flexible, serving imperial needs.

An otherwise obscure reign

Tzimiskes fell gravely ill on the return journey to Constantinople, and arrived barely able to breathe. He died on January 10–11, 976, at the age of fifty-one. He was buried in the church of the Savior at the Chalke Gate of the palace. The story told by the Byzantine sources is that, while traversing the lands of the frontier themes, the emperor discovered that many of them now belonged to Basileios *parakoimomenos*, which annoyed him: "Are we all fighting so that a eunuch can get rich?" This was reported to Basileios, who had the emperor poisoned by a eunuch in his service.[58] But it is more likely that this story is an invention driven by a bias against Basileios (and against eunuchs in general) than that someone was in a position to know about such secret plots.

Tzimiskes enjoyed a mixed reputation in the generation after his death. The soldier-poet Ioannes Geometres, who served under him too, presented him as a tragic hero forever stained by the murder of his uncle and torn by remorse, whereas another contemporary poet castigated him as an ape who had murdered a lion.[59] In a Byzantine vision of the afterlife, Tzimiskes is seen recognizing the horror of his crime before Nikephoros.[60] In the contemporary *History* of Leon the deacon, by contrast, both emperors are heroes, though Nikephoros is portrayed as a pious ascetic while Tzimiskes liked drinking parties and sex.[61]

Even so it is striking how little later Byzantines (and therefore we too) knew about his reign. The vast majority of the preserved information is about the Rus' campaign. We do not know what Tzimiskes was doing between campaigns. The patriarch Basileios was involved in a plot against him, about which we have little information; he was deposed, and replaced in 973.[62] That no scandals or major commotions are recorded, especially by Leon, who lived through the reign and was not completely dependent on written sources, suggests that it was a quiet period at home. Tzimiskes took measures to distribute grain efficiently in the ongoing scarcity,[63] and even excused the hearth tax.[64] He was generous to churches, monasteries, and philanthropic institutions.[65] For all that he was then (and is still now) remembered chiefly for his wars, the first year of his reign revealed a remarkable ability to settle disputes, make political compromises, and deescalate tense situations. Tzimiskes was the first emperor in centuries who did not have to cope with Arab raids. The conquest of Cilicia and subjugation of Aleppo, in which he had played a leading part even before his accession, had already begun to pay off. Under this fearsome general, the empire began to enjoy a long-awaited peace.

How did Tzimiskes manage the balancing act of paying for war while still maintaining his popularity with the people? This was where Nikephoros had failed. The answer is that Tzimiskes seems to have campaigned less than his predecessor: not at all in 970, 973, and 974, and not much in 972. It is also likely that he brought in more booty. Bulgaria had been at peace for decades when war came to it, and the Rus' might have already done most of the grunt work of plundering it when the Romans swept up all their gains. Some Romans may have also plundered Bulgarian churches during the war.[66] A rich haul was also brought in from the 975 raid. Perhaps Tzimiskes spent less on war and made more from it. We know that he was a good general. It is likely that he was a good emperor as well.

CHAPTER 4

"From Spectator to Contestant"
Basil II (976–1025), Part I

The new regime

With the death of Tzimiskes, Basil II was left as the senior emperor, though he was only eighteen. His brother Konstantinos VIII was fifteen and would live in his shadow as co-emperor for the next fifty years, until the moment came for him to rule by himself. Like their grandfather Konstantinos VII, they had survived through multiple regencies and ambitious "guardian-generals," but Basil was old enough now to do without either. Though the empire was at the peak of its power, the regime faced potential threats at home, specifically the Phokades, who had held the throne under Nikephoros and had allies in the army, and the military supporters of Tzimiskes, notably Skleros and Bourtzes. Fortunately, Skleros and Phokas were at odds, and the government was in the hands of Basileios *parakoimomenos*, who was not loyal to either side (we will call him Lakapenos to avoid confusion with the emperor). Lakapenos does seem to have been in charge of the state for the first decade of his great-nephew's reign. He had led armies, conducted diplomacy, helped in at least two coups, advised three emperors, and made himself rich. He was now in a position to tutor an inexperienced young emperor, a position he may have wished for back in 959, with Romanos II. The regime's first act was to recall the emperors' mother Theophano from exile[1]; she had likely been innocent of *all* charges against her (poisoning, adultery, regicide).

Bad news for the new regime poured in from many fronts in its first year. In Sicily, Byzantine forces had apparently occupied Messina again. We do not hear about this from Byzantine sources, and so cannot gauge the strategy behind it. Was it another effort to retake Sicily after ten years of peace with the Fatimids? The Fatimid governor, Abu al-Qasim, expelled them from Messina in the spring of 976. He crossed to Calabria and extorted money from Cosenza while sending his brother to raid Apulia. In the summer of that year, Abu al-Qasim crossed over again, seized and burned Taranto, and raided the Roman province before returning to Palermo with hundreds of slaves.[2]

The second piece of bad news concerned developments in Bulgaria, specifically in the western part of its former empire. We know nothing about these regions after the conquest of eastern Bulgaria in 971. Eventually, the areas around Ohrid and Prespa formed the core of a new Bulgarian state under Samuil, though its origins are obscure. Samuil and his three older, also biblically named brothers, David, Moses, and Aaron, were the sons of a *komes* ("count") Nikola; thus they were called the Kometopouloi. Arguments that they were of Armenian origin are irrelevant, and are produced by nationalist readings of the biased history of Step'anos of Taron, who cast most important figures of his time as Armenians. As a modern historian has observed, "what is important is that Samuil called his state Bulgarian; furthermore, Byzantine sources called it Bulgarian also and treat Samuil as a ruler continuing the former Bulgarian state."[3] Roman sources claim that the Kometopouloi "rebelled" after the death of Tzimiskes in 976, which was what Romans called any action that harmed imperial interests. In reality, their rise must have entailed a complex power struggle in Bulgaria that is invisible to us. It was associated with the escape or release from Constantinople of the sons of tsar Petar, Boris II and Roman. Boris was killed along the way by a Bulgarian frontier guard because he was dressed like a Byzantine. Roman was now proclaimed tsar, despite having been castrated during his stay in Constantinople. Real power lay with the Kometopouloi, especially Samuil, who commanded the armies.

How this situation came about is unclear. Yahya and Skylitzes say that the princes escaped from Constantinople, though Skylitzes says elsewhere that they were released to check the Kometopouloi, while Step'anos of Taron claims that the Kometopouloi belonged to an Armenian army sent by Basil II against Macedonia (i.e., western Bulgaria) who defected and joined the eunuch-tsar.[4] Be that as it may, Samuil was the leading general under Roman, the eunuch-tsar, who was only a figurehead. One by one Samuil's brothers died, eventually leaving him in sole command, and he did not take the title tsar himself until 997. According to Skylitzes, Samuil took advantage of the rebellion of Skleros to raid the empire in 976, but this compresses the events of many years.[5] In the late 970s, Bulgaria did not yet require imperial intervention. Neither did southern Italy, as the Fatimids had relocated to Egypt, relieving the pressure on the Byzantine provinces. The Muslims of Sicily raided for slaves and plunder, not to conquer. The burden passed directly to the provincials, and local generals did what they could. The real threat in 976 lay closer to home.

The first rebellion of Bardas Skleros

In the spring or summer of 976, Bardas Skleros proclaimed himself emperor. He had led armies during the conquest of Bulgaria in 970–971 and had been sent by Tzimiskes to put down the rebellion of Bardas Phokas in 970. His career after that is obscure. Skylitzes reports that he had been arrested by Tzimiskes on suspicion of treason but later appointed as *domestikos* of the east (such suspicions, however, were often written back into the prior history of later rebels). After the death of Tzimiskes, Lakapenos reshuffled the military command in the east. Skleros was made *doux* of Mesopotamia, still a powerful position but one that he viewed as a demotion. Michael Bourtzes, the conqueror of Antioch, was reconfirmed as *doux* of that city, while the *stratopedarches* Petros, the other conqueror of Antioch, took over from Skleros as *domestikos* of the east. As a former retainer of Nikephoros II Phokas, Petros might be expected to check Skleros, as indeed happened.[6] From Antioch Bourtzes made a brief raid against Tripoli.[7]

Skleros' revolt exemplified the tendency of the Roman imperial system to test the regime for weakness. Skleros did not necessarily aim to overthrow the emperors, only to sideline them while he wielded power. He sent a man to fetch his son Romanos from the capital, and then seized Melitene, which gave him access to tax revenues. There he was acclaimed emperor by the Roman and Armenian soldiers. Skleros also made a marriage alliance (possibly through his son) with Abu Taghlib, the son of Nasir al-Dawla and emir of Mosul (who was based at Mayyafariqin), receiving from him auxiliary cavalry.[8] The palace responded quickly, ordering Petros to Kaisareia and instructing Bourtzes and Eustathios Maleïnos, the governor of Tarsos, to intercept Skleros. Beyond this point it is not easy to reconcile the movements reported by Yahya and Skylitzes, though the outline is clear. The palace sent the bishop of Nikomedeia to negotiate for peace, but Skleros advanced toward Kaisareia and, in the district of Lykandos, defeated the army of Petros, Bourtzes, and Maleïnos that sought to block his way. Bourtzes joined the rebel, probably under duress, and with him went Antioch. Skleros sent a converted Arab from Melitene, 'Ubayd Allah, to represent him there.[9] He advanced to Tzamandos, where he was able to collect much wealth and acquire more support, and then to Kaisareia. Another follower seized the naval station of Attaleia when its people put the imperial admiral in chains.[10] Thus, between late 976 and early 977, Skleros had opened a path to the capital.

The palace then set a second plan into motion. The court eunuch Leon was sent out with full imperial authority. He joined Petros at Kotyaeion (modern Kütahya) in Phrygia, and they tried to bribe Skleros' followers away from him. When that did not work, they circumvented him and marched into the lands of those followers, whereupon the latter began to switch sides. Skleros sent Bourtzes to harry the imperial army, but not engage it. At that point both sides received an unexpected piece of news: the emissaries of Aleppo were traveling through there (Phrygia) with the annual tribute. Such a prize could not be resisted, and the two armies came to battle. Leon defeated Bourtzes, who fled again, and the Romans in the imperial army massacred his Armenian soldiers. This situation was critical for any rebel, whereas the palace could, and did, recover from similar setbacks. To regain the initiative, Skleros sought out the imperial army, which imprudently attacked him at a place called Rageai. Leon the palace eunuch was defeated and captured, whereas Petros, the conqueror of Antioch and Aleppo, was killed in the rout. Skleros resumed his march on the capital and took Nikaia after a siege, when its commander negotiated the withdrawal of the population.[11] Meanwhile, Skleros' fleet had blocked grain shipments to the capital, which led to naval engagements in the Aegean (by Phokaia) and at Abydos in the Hellespont, which was captured by the rebel's son Romanos, though at sea the imperial forces were winning.[12] To take the capital, Skleros had to control the sea, and this the palace had denied him.

Imperial diplomacy was active in Antioch too. On the death of the city's bishop Theodoros, the inhabitants wanted as his replacement one Agapios, the bishop of Aleppo. Agapios traveled to Constantinople, where he promised that, if he were confirmed, he would bring ʿUbayd Allah over to the imperial side. The palace armed him with a letter promising ʿUbayd Allah the governorship of Antioch for life if he switched sides. The offer was duly accepted, and so Antioch proclaimed for Basil and Konstantinos in early 978. Skleros sent some of his men to reclaim it, but they were denied entry. They attempted to use force, aided by local Armenians friendly to Skleros, but ʿUbayd Allah put them to flight with the backing of the Antiochenes.[13]

In early 978, the palace set its third plan into motion, revealing the extent of its desperation. Bardas Phokas was recalled from his seven-year exile on Chios and set loose against his old enemy Skleros. He was now made *domestikos* of the *scholai*, and given an army composed of western units. But why was he appointed? It is unlikely that Romanía lacked other generals, and Phokas' own rebellion in 970 had been a farce. The thinking was probably that his name and network would disrupt the loyalty of Skleros' officers; of course, precisely that was the *risk* of appointing a Phokas. Initially, at any rate, the plan worked. By night marches, Phokas bypassed Skleros and reached Kaisareia, joining up with Maleïnos. Among those who switched sides now was Bourtzes (one of the killers of Nikephoros in 969!).[14] Skleros again had to move east. This was the imperial strategy: every time Skleros defeated a loyalist army, another would push or lure him back to central Asia Minor—one step back for every two forward.

The war between Skleros and Phokas is difficult to reconstruct because our two sources, Skylitzes and Yahya, record the battles differently. But the basic outline is clear.[15] Skleros prevailed in their first engagement, which was fought on June 19, 978, at Pankaleia near Amorion. Phokas seems to have fought in person.[16] Possibly suffering more defeats at the hands of Skleros, he withdrew ever eastward, drawing his enemy away from his objective. Phokas eventually sought refuge outside Roman territory with Davitʿ, the ruler of Upper Tao (Taykʿ in Armenian). Davitʿ (966–1000) belonged to the Kartvelian (Georgian or Iberian in Greek) branch of the Bagratid royal family and was at that moment engaged in an ambitious project to reunite Kartli. We will discuss his situation below; at this time, Davitʿ intervened decisively in the Roman civil war. He and Phokas were apparently on good terms since the latter had been *doux* of Chaldia, which bordered on Tao, in the late 960s.[17] Davitʿ sheltered the defeated imperial army during the winter of 978–979, and was persuaded to give Phokas a Kartvelian army of (allegedly) twelve thousand elite cavalry. Imperial diplomacy was at work, not just personal ties, and it produced one of the most interesting stories of the century.

The story is told in the Georgian *Life* of two saints who were monks on Mt. Athos at the monastery of Iviron (i.e., of the Georgians; Figure 5). It begins before the foundation of that particular monastery, when a high-ranking noble named Ioane left the court of Davitʿ and joined the Lavra of Athanasios on Mt. Athos during the reign of Nikephoros Phokas, Athanasios' patron. Ioane soon became the focal point for other Georgians who wished to become monks, including in ca. 970 a wealthy general of Tao named Tʿorʿnik, who was a cousin of Ioane and took the same monastic name. Tʿorʿnik had served under the Roman emperors and received the high court title of *patrikios*. In 978, at the peak of the Skleros rebellion, the palace, which presumably kept tabs on its titulars, called on Tʿorʿnik to secure help from his former lord, Davitʿ. When he received the imperial summons, he was reluctant to break his vows. His fellow monks, however, including

FIGURE 5 The Iviron monastery on the coast of Mt. Athos, founded in the later tenth century by and for Georgians (Iviron means "of the Georgians" in Greek). *Source: Shutterstock, ID 334387394.*

Athanasios, advised him to obey. The *Life* is explicit that the affairs of the palace in Constantinople were being run by Basileios Lakapenos, and an emotional appeal to Tʿorʿnik was made by the empress Theophano herself (who was, after all, the widow of Nikephoros Phokas; this is possibly her only appearance during the reign of her sons). The *Life* lists the concessions made to Davitʿ and the Georgians by the emperors, and recounts how Tʿorʿnik returned to Tao, was given the twelve thousand cavalry by Davitʿ, and attacked Skleros. The emperors later helped Tʿorʿnik and the Georgians establish the Iviron monastery on Mt. Athos and endowed it with rich properties, but we must also not underestimate the links that bound Athanasios (of the Lavra) to the Phokades. After saving the empire, Tʿorʿnik returned to the religious life.[18]

In Byzantine civil wars, the palace regime could withstand multiple defeats so long as it had additional armies to hurl against the rebel, and, even if it did not, it could barricade itself behind the walls of the City, contest his crossing of the straits, and wait him out. A rebel, on the other hand, was usually finished after a single decisive defeat. This was administered to Skleros by the joint forces of Phokas and Tʿorʿnik on March 24, 979. The location, Charsianon, is confirmed by a Georgian inscription honoring one of the participants, who later founded a chapel.[19] Skleros and his loyal adherents fled to the territory of Mayyafariqin, eventually seeking asylum in Baghdad. His story was far from over. Phokas was confirmed as *domestikos* of the east. Some followers of Skleros continued to resist in the Thrakesion theme until they were granted an amnesty in 980.[20]

Most civil wars in Byzantium ended quickly, in about a year or less, and decisively, one way or the other. They were focused around individuals, never ideologies, and most Romans quickly decided which side they would support. The first rebellion of Skleros, which lasted for more than three years, was among the longest. Skleros did not have many assets going into it, or much of a faction. He built those up through his victories, an amazing feat of tenacity, only to watch his supporters defect when the palace waved them a promise, and one decisive defeat was enough to ruin his cause. His rebellion cost the empire many soldiers, including the general Petros, and brought the troublesome Phokas back into the game. At the same time, the war revealed the dominant position that the empire had attained on the eastern stage. Neighboring powers did not seek to attack it in order to claim or reclaim territories; rather, they sought to join it in the hopes of eventual preferment by the winner. The Kartvelians sided with the palace, while the Armenians and the emir of Mosul sided with the rebel.

It is often said that Skleros cost the empire four years that might have been devoted to further conquest. Conquest, however, had been the policy mainly of Nikephoros II, between 955 and 969. In the early 970s, Tzimiskes had intervened in Bulgaria because he had to, and twice raided Syria, but he did not aggressively pursue conquest. It is not certain that the regime of Basileios Lakapenos would have sought conquest either. Now, in 979, the configuration of power in Romanía reverted to what it had been twenty years earlier under Romanos II: a largely uninvolved young emperor, a eunuch handler, and a Phokas general in the east. Precedent suggested that this was a prelude for another Phokas on the throne.

The foreign policy of Lakapenos and Phokas, 979–985

Roman, Kartvelian, and Arabic sources attest that Basileios Lakapenos was the dominant power in the palace during the first ten years of the young emperors' reign (976–985). He had more than twenty years of experience in imperial politics, and now forged a new alliance with the Phokades. With Bardas and his appointees in charge of the army, Lakapenos steered the empire's foreign policy. This section will examine developments on a number of fronts during and immediately after the civil war, including a brief resurgence of German interest in southern Italy, the ambitions of Davitʻ of Tao, the maintenance of the new status quo in the east, and the negotiations with Baghdad over Skleros.

The early 980s began with another determined attempt by the Ottonians to take southern Italy. Otto I had died in 973 and his young heir Otto II, married to Tzimiskes' niece Theophano, struggled for years to assert his authority in Germany. In late 980 he left for Italy and in early 982 attacked Calabria, accompanied by Theophano, their newborn son (Otto III), and an army of German knights. We know nothing about Theophano's views in this matter. She was likely descended from both the Skleroi and the Phokades,[21] but was given to the west by the anti-Phokas party of Tzimiskes-Skleros, so possibly she sided more with them than with the Phokades now in power in Constantinople. Otto's ostensible purpose was to drive the Saracens of Sicily from the south, but historians suspect that his main goal was to incorporate the southern provinces into his realm, because he targeted them first and spent months besieging cities there. Ottonian writers assumed that these lands belonged naturally to his empire, the only "Roman" empire they were willing to recognize.[22] Otto II took Taranto and began to refer to himself as *imperator Romanorum*. He then set out to confront a large army that was brought into Calabria by Abu al-Qasim, the governor of Sicily. In mid-July 982, at Stilo near Squillace, the Arabs, regrouping after an initial reverse, decisively defeated the Germans, killing many of their nobles, though Abu al-Qasim also fell in the fighting. His son and successor Jabir quickly withdrew to Sicily. Otto, it was said, escaped by seeking passage on one of two Byzantine tax vessels that were there, watching their two enemies so conveniently destroy each other. Otto had to disguise his identity and then escape from their protective custody, lest he be escorted as an "honored guest" to Constantinople.[23]

Otto hastened north to Verona for an emergency council of his noblemen to fill positions left vacant by the deaths at Crotone; also, parts of his empire in the Slavic lands had risen up in rebellion. The following year, 983, Otto died in Rome. His disastrous expedition suppressed German ambitions in southern Italy for a long time. There is no evidence of Byzantine-Arab collusion in his defeat, though both sides benefited from it. This was a time of general unrest among the Lombard subjects of the empire in Apulia, caused in part by imperial tax policy, which Otto may have been trying to exploit.[24] Moreover, the distant palace in Constantinople did not consider the defense of Calabria from the Arabs as its top priority, and this may have further alienated its Italian subjects. After Otto's defeat, the empire struck back.

Kalokyros Delphinas, the new *katepano* of Italy and probably already an ally of Phokas, arrived at Bari in June 982, advanced as far as Ascoli, and took it by December and then Trani by August 983.[25] Phokas was placing his people in positions of power.[26] Constantinople's reach may have extended as far as Rome itself. The throne of the papacy was regularly contested, and one of its failed claimants, or antipopes, was Boniface VII. He had spent years in exile at Constantinople, but returned to Rome in 984, imprisoned Otto's pope John XIV, and took the papal throne. Lakapenos had, after all, promised Liudprand that he would see Rome ruled according to his wishes![27] Boniface, however, lasted only for eleven months as pope. Overall, however, Italy was a success story for the new Phokas-Lakapenos regime.

In the east, concessions had to be made to Davit' of Tao, who had bailed Phokas out during the civil war. By the midtenth century, most of central Kartli (Georgia, or Iberia in Greek) was ruled by the kings of Abkhazia (or Abasgia). Davit' belonged to a Kartvelian branch of the Bagratid family, who were limited to two principalities in southwest Caucasia, Upper Tao, which was next to the Roman border, and Lower Tao, which retained the titular right to the throne of a unified Kartli.[28] Davit' II ruled Upper Tao (since 966), held the Roman court title *magistros*,[29] presided over a bicultural (Georgian and Armenian) court, and would play a leading role in the kingdom's reunification. He was engaged in that project when the emperors and Bardas Phokas appealed to him for help in 978, during the civil war. He had contrived a clever scheme to unify Kartli. Childless himself, he adopted his cousin Bagrat III, grandson of Bagrat II, the king of Lower Tao (with claim to Kartli). By 975, Abkhazian rule over central Kartli had become so destabilized that Davit' was able to occupy it and install the young Bagrat as its governor. As it happened, this Bagrat was also descended, through his mother, from the royal house of Abkhazia, which meant that he now stood to inherit Upper *and* Lower Tao (and Kartli) *and* Abkhazia. In 978–979, in other words precisely when Phokas was wintering in Upper Tao, the king of Abkhazia (T'eodos III) was deposed and Bagrat assumed his throne. This was the first step in the reunification of Kartli.[30]

These dynastic successions are important for understanding Basil II's later interventions in the Caucasus, and his relations with Davit' specifically. In 979, the palace was hugely in debt to Davit' for his loan of an army. Unfortunately it is difficult to reconstruct the terms of the land grant that the empire now made to him. To the south of Tao it included the Basean valley and Theodosioupolis (Armenian Karin, Turkish Erzurum), which had been taken by the empire only in 949 and settled, typically, with Romans and Armenians. Theodosioupolis was of crucial strategic importance and no small concession. As for the other territories listed by Stepʿanos of Taron, some cannot be identified, while regarding others, in the direction of lake Van, we do not know what their status was when they were given to Davitʿ; were they governed directly by the emperors, or had they only acknowledged imperial suzerainty (e.g., the small Arab emirates in the region)? It is also unclear whether Davitʿ was given their ownership or only the right to govern them.[31]

In 979, the star of Phokas' ally Davitʿ was rising. The opposite was true of Skleros' foreign backer, Abu Taghlib, the emir of Mosul, whose side lost in the Roman civil war while he himself was losing his realm to his own enemies. The geopolitical scene in Syria had changed dramatically during the civil war, but not because of it. To explain this development, we have to discuss briefly the arrival in northern Mesopotamia of the Buyid dynasty.

The Buyids were descended from a Daylami (i.e., Iranian) adventurer named ʿAli who established himself in Fars in the 930s with a following of his warlike countrymen.[32] He consolidated his hold there and his brothers quickly took over Iraq (including Baghdad) and Rayy. By the late tenth century, the Buyid realm was not a single state but a confederation of affiliated principalities that recognized the loose authority of family elders. Their leaders had Persian personal names but are usually referred to by their (Abbasid) court honorifics. In 967–978, Iraq was governed by ʿIzz al-Dawla Bakhtiyar, but he was unable to solve the systemic problems of the region that had caused the Abbasid decline in the first place. These included food shortages; inefficient, unsystematic, and often corrupt administration; and unruly and overpaid mercenary soldiers, mostly Turks. Baghdad was regularly in a state of chaos: "Buyid Iraq, on its own, was virtually ungovernable."[33] ʿIzz al-Dawla had also picked a fight with Abu Taghlib in 973, but was defeated and had to be rescued by his cousin from Fars, Fana Khusraw, or ʿAdud al-Dawla. The latter deposed ʿIzz al-Dawla for his incompetence, but was ordered by his father Rukn al-Dawla (in Fars) to restore him. In 977, when Rukn al-Dawla died, ʿAdud al-Dawla marched back to reclaim Baghdad. ʿIzz al-Dawla was now allied with Abu Taghlib, but was defeated and executed in 978. ʿAdud al-Dawla would be recognized as the greatest of all Buyid rulers, especially of Fars, which was always his base. He tried to set things right in Baghdad, but mostly failed. Still, ʿAdud al-Dawla was a methodical and efficient administrator. This was the power with which the Romans would have to deal in Mesopotamia now, at least until his death in 983. The Buyids now joined Romanía and the Fatimids as a regional power at the intersection of northern Syria.

In 978, after the execution of ʿIzz al-Dawla, ʿAdud al-Dawla's top priority was to pursue Abu Taghlib to the north and terminate the Hamdanid emirate. In that and the next year he took Mosul, Diyar Bakr, and Mayyafariqin. Abu Taghlib fled to Roman territory and, at Hisn Ziyad (Harput), sought the help of his ally and in-law Bardas Skleros, who had just defeated Phokas and was preparing for the next round of the civil war. Skleros had no help to give him, and Abu Taghlib would not join him against Phokas. He fled to Fatimid Palestine, where he was killed in 979; his head was sent to Cairo.[34]

Change had also come to the emirate of Aleppo since Petros had imposed the treaty of Safar on it in early 970. Sayf al-Dawla's heirs and generals had contended over it after the emir's death in 967. In 977, so again during the Roman civil war, Aleppo was taken by Sayf al-Dawla's son Abu al-Maʿali, who sought recognition from the Buyids and received the court title Saʿd al-Dawla from Baghdad.[35] Aleppo thereby became the meeting point of Roman, Fatimid, and Buyid interests. The Romans were concerned to extract Skleros from Buyid custody and enforce the treaty of Safar, including its tribute payments, on Aleppo. As we saw, Aleppo was paying tribute to the empire in 977 during the civil war, but Abu al-Maʿali seems to have discontinued it when he took over the emirate. After his defeat, Skleros sent his brother from Mayyafariqin to Baghdad to gain the support of ʿAdud al-Dawla; eventually, Skleros himself was brought to Baghdad by ʿAdud al-Dawla, who, of course, saw him exactly for what he was, a bargaining chip. Skleros had three hundred followers and relatives, who were lodged in a vacated palace, under guard.[36]

The situation called for diplomacy, as it does not appear that any of the three major powers (Romans, Buyids, Fatimids) were interested in all-out war. Many embassies traveled back and forth between Constantinople and Baghdad during the next four years, discussing terms for the return of Skleros, who was to be fully pardoned: the return of all Muslim prisoners in Romanía; the restoration of forts captured by the Romans after the defeat of Skleros as well as forts taken during the wars of conquest of the past twenty years; and the status of Aleppo, whose tribute the Romans were prepared to cede.[37] More interesting than the terms themselves is the (self-serving and probably redacted) report of one of the Buyid envoys, ibn Shahram, who visited Constantinople in 981–982, because it reflects the uneasy balance of power within Romanía.[38] Ibn Shahram was received politely in Charsianon by Bardas Phokas himself, who said that he personally had no interest in peace, though the emperor might favor it. The Romans may have been deliberately giving mixed signals, but there is likely to have been a genuine split, and ibn

Shahram claims that Phokas was thinking of rebelling. In Constantinople, ibn Shahram negotiated terms in many meetings with Basileios Lakapenos, the emperor, and the blinded *kouropalates* Leon Phokas. At just that point, the tribute from Aleppo arrived again. In November 981, Phokas had marched to the city and forced it to resume payment, though at a reduced rate compared to the treaty of Safar.[39] The gold, possibly including missed back payments, was sent to the court and shown to ibn Shahram as proof of Aleppo's obedience.

Ibn Shahram perceived that the military types wanted war, and decided to appeal for peace to the emperor, slyly arguing that only if he could override the wishes of his generals would the emperor show that he was in charge. He was assisted in this pitch by his escort Nikephoros Ouranos, one of the emperor's confidants and diplomats who according to ibn Shahram was hostile to Basileios Lakapenos, the *parakoimomenos*. It happened that Lakapenos was ill, and thus progress was made between the envoy and the emperor toward a ten-year peace. When Lakapenos recovered he was incensed at what had happened, and the emperor had to mollify him and turn him against the Phokades. This is the first sign of tension between the emperor and the chamberlain.

In 982, Ouranos was sent to Baghdad with a proposal to exchange Aleppo for Skleros. The plan was ambitious: Skleros' brother and son would be restored to their former positions and, if all went well for two years, he himself would follow, whereupon the tribute of Aleppo would revert to Baghdad. ʿAdud al-Dawla died on March 26, 983, though the treaty was apparently concluded with his son and successor Samsam al-Dawla (983–987, in Iraq). For unknown reasons, however, these terms were not implemented. Possibly they were sabotaged by the Phokades. Samsam al-Dawla was involved in a civil war with a brother until 986 and Ouranos was detained in Baghdad until 987.[40] Our sources are silent about this diplomatic front in 983–987.

The Buyids' systemic weakness in Iraq left Aleppo without support from Baghdad, so the emirate would be contested henceforth between the Romans and the Fatimids, who, under their caliph al-ʿAziz, were reasserting their authority in Palestine and Syria with raids and skirmishes along the coast. A Fatimid army took Damascus in June 983 and sent units to besiege Aleppo. This was done at the instigation of Bakjur, a Circassian general hired by the Hamdanids who was Qarghuya's deputy when Aleppo signed the treaty of Safar with the Romans. He had ruled Aleppo in 975–977 before being expelled to Homs (Emesa) by Abu al-Maʿali (Saʿd al-Dawla). Bakjur and his Fatimid army invested the city on September 12, 983, but retreated immediately when news reached them of Phokas' imminent arrival (the second in two years). Phokas encamped before the city and extracted a payment of two years' worth of tribute, presumably for 982 and 983.[41] The relationship was tense, but the Romans were in fact fulfilling their part of the treaty by protecting Abu al-Maʿali. He then directed the Roman army to attack Bakjur's base, Homs. Phokas put it to the torch on October 30, 983. Bakjur was appointed governor of Damascus by the Fatimids (until 988).[42]

A tense balance of power had been established in Syria, with intermittent mutual raiding. Let us assess the change in the overall strategic situation and, by extension, in military priorities. The empire had managed to defeat and liquidate enemies of long standing in Cilicia, annex their lands, and reduce Aleppo to the status of a protectorate; it had then managed to enforce its claims against the rival Islamic empires of Baghdad and Cairo. It was only twenty years previously that Bardas' uncle Nikephoros had sacked Aleppo, ending the regional power of Abu al-Maʿali's father Sayf al-Dawla. Yet outright conquest in the east had been the policy only of Nikephoros Phokas in the 960s. The treaty of Safar had stabilized the situation in 970, whereupon it became an issue merely of enforcement. Tzimiskes' eastern incursions had not produced extensive conquests; nor had they aimed to do so. Since 970, the Romans were maintaining the status quo, which, in this corner of the northeast Mediterranean, inland from the strategic capital of Antioch, would remain more or less fixed for a century.[43]

The empire and Aleppo came to blows again in 985–986, though the events and their causes are obscure. Yahya says that Abu al-Maʿali again ceased payment of the tribute, at which point Phokas attacked the fort of Killiz, north of Aleppo, and took its residents captive in July 985; he then attacked the city of Apameia with siege engines. In response, Abu al-Maʿali sent out Qarghuya, who attacked a Melkite (Byzantine Orthodox) monastery of St. Simeon on the border between Antioch and Aleppo, killing many monks and enslaving people who had sought refuge there in September. Phokas widened his attack against other targets, but then written orders reached him from the emperor to lift the siege of Apameia. Meanwhile, a Fatimid force had taken the coastal fort of Balanias. The emperor appointed Leon Melissenos *doux* of Antioch and ordered him to retake the fort. Here Basil first displayed the imperious severity that marked relations with his officers later in the reign. When Melissenos withdrew after an initial assault, the emperor told him to succeed or else pay for the cost of the campaign himself. Melissenos promptly took the fort on the second try. The next year (probably mid-986), Phokas and Abu al-Maʿali signed a new treaty, stipulating the same tribute. We are clearly missing crucial parts of the background story.[44] It is possible that Abu al-Maʿali had reached an understanding with the Fatimids, as he recognized their nominal authority in 986 (in place of that of the Buyids).[45]

Basil was making his own decisions because a domestic "coup" had meanwhile shaken up the imperial court. Basil had ended the unofficial "reign" of his great-uncle Lakapenos, and the position of Phokas was also compromised: removed from the position of *domestikos*, which he had held for almost ten years, he was made *doux* of the East with authority over Antioch, after Melissenos had completed his mission.[46] This reshuffling of power led to another round of civil war.

The fall of Lakapenos and the rebellion of Phokas and Skleros

In 985, Basil II was about twenty-seven years old and Lakapenos was about sixty. Lakapenos was the last surviving member of the governing team put in place by the emperor's grandfather, Konstantinos VII. It is only now, with his removal from power and the defeat of the Phokades, that governance can be said to have passed into the hands of the next generation. We can glimpse the tension between the emperor and his handler in the report of the Buyid ambassador ibn Shahram, in 981–982. Otherwise, our sources tell us only that Basil grew tired of Lakapenos' tutelage, dismissed him from his post, and confined him to house arrest. Then, seeing that he was still plotting, the emperor exiled him and confiscated his wealth. The eunuch died soon afterward. Only Yahya gives the date, 985, which is crucial for the sequence of events.[47] Basil was effecting a regime change from the throne. In a law issued much later, in 996, Basil claimed that until Lakapenos' fall from power "our opinions had no effect but his will and command prevailed in all matters." All decrees promulgated at that time would be invalid unless they were now brought to him for reconfirmation.[48]

In the aftermath of this coup, Basil tried to dislodge the Lakapenos-Phokas faction too. Phokas, as we saw, was posted to Antioch after ten years as *domestikos* of the east. He remained effectively in charge of the eastern armies, but it was a step in a gradual demotion. A similar move by Lakapenos had caused Skleros to rebel in 976. Basil also recalled the *katepano* of Italy Delphinas (he would side with Phokas in the civil war to come).[49] Leon Melissenos, the *doux* of Antioch who seems to have reacted badly to Lakapenos' fall, was summoned to the capital (he too would side with Phokas).[50] Even the soldier-poet Ioannes Geometres, who had written favorably about Nikephoros Phokas and

Basileios Lakapenos (implying that the latter was the *de facto* emperor), was dismissed from service in 985.[51]

The ensuing configuration of power had little precedent and was unstable by nature. It was one thing for a general to control the armies with a civilian ally such as a eunuch handling a cipher emperor, or for the general to be proclaimed co-emperor and rule as a guardian of a young heir. In 985, by contrast, there was an increasingly strong-willed emperor staring across Asia Minor at an ambitious general whose family and personal history was anything but reassuring, and the stand-off lacked experienced brokers like Lakapenos. This could not last for long. Basil correctly understood that the odds would tilt in his favor if he acquired military credentials of his own, thereby reassuring his subjects that Phokas' military leadership was not necessary. He wisely stayed away from the eastern front, which was Phokas' playing field. So he made the decision to strike against the Bulgarians, in the west. It made good sense, but the result would be disaster that plunged the empire into civil war and emboldened the new Bulgarian state that would trouble the empire for another thirty years.

We know little about the Bulgarian state led by the Kometopouloi, its internal politics, and its relations with Romanía. It was based more in the west, around Ohrid, than in the lower Danube, but we do not know whether Samuil recruited officials or nobles from the Bulgarian east, which was conquered by the Rus' and Tzimiskes in 971. Skylitzes gives a condensed list of Roman locations hit by Samuil before 986, including Thessaly and Greece, but, given his methods of composition, we cannot be certain of the chronology; it is almost certain that the Bulgarian capture of Larissa (in Thessaly) took place after Basil's defeat in 986.[52] There is no reason to think that any of the (eastern) Bulgarian territory conquered by Tzimiskes had been retaken by Samuil before then. The empire was not tied down elsewhere in 980–986 and could have responded with force to serious encroachments on its conquered territories. Thus, Basil's incursion of 986 may have been disproportionate to previous Bulgarian raids and probably precipitated the longer war to come.

In the summer of 986, Basil led his army to Serdica (modern Sofia) and besieged it for twenty days while Samuil prowled the surrounding mountains. Having accomplished nothing, the emperor set out for home, motivated, it was said, by a suspicion that Melissenos was planning treason in his rear. Rushing off, he was ambushed by Samuil in the pass of Trajan's Gate on August 16 (this was by the fortress of Stoponion, now Ihtiman). The army was scattered, its supply train and the imperial tent were plundered, and the emperor barely escaped to Philippopolis. We have an eyewitness account of the rout by Leon, serving the emperor as a deacon.[53] Melissenos, it turned out, was innocent, but the emperor's defeat had terrible consequences for him and the empire. The campaign was perceived as incompetent.[54] It was likely in the immediate aftermath of Trajan's Gate that Samuil recovered the original heart of the Bulgarian empire, including Preslav. He also raided into Thessaly, likely still in 986, and took Larissa by starvation. He transported its population into his realm and transferred the relics of the local saint Achilleios to a newly built church by lake Prespa (whose ruins can still be visited).[55] Within a few years, Samuil ruled a realm reaching from the Black Sea to the Adriatic and from the Danubian lands to northern Greece. Probably in 987, he executed his last surviving brother, Aaron, on suspicion of being pro-Roman.[56] Bulgarian raids intensified and are referred to in Roman sources, albeit in vague terms. The poet Geometres, bitter against Basil, wrote gloomy verses about this state of affairs, calling on Nikephoros Phokas to rise up from the grave and punish the Bulgarians.[57] One defeat had rolled the Balkan situation to where it had been under Simeon, the aggressive tsar of the early tenth century.

Worse, the defeat weakened the emperor in the cold war against his two military rivals. News of it soon reached Baghdad. As we saw, no agreement had been reached over the return of Skleros. The thinking at the court of Samsam al-Dawla was that if Skleros could not be usefully bargained away, he could be unleashed to claim the throne with Buyid support. Roman sources, by contrast, recount a heroic tale in which Skleros and his stalwart Romans, released from prison, were used in internal wars between Arabs and Persians, earning the emir's gratitude; then, after defeating the emir's enemies, they escaped from Muslim lands. These stories, however, which are not mentioned in the Arab sources, are likely fictions of pro-Skleros propaganda.[58] Two Arabic texts give a more realistic explanation of what happened. An eyewitness account of a cinematic reception for Skleros, his son Romanos, and brother Konstantinos on the occasion of their release and sponsorship by Samsam al-Dawla in December 986 is embedded in an Arabic history.[59] It summarizes the terms of a formal treaty to which Skleros agreed, the text of which is embedded in a later Arabic handbook of diplomacy: Skleros had to agree to many of the terms that the Buyids had tried to extract from Basil in the negotiations of 980–983, namely that he would release all Muslim prisoners, cease hostilities, and hand over seven forts in the northern Diyar Bakr. The text of the treaty refers to Skleros as *melik al-Rum*, "king of the Romans."[60]

The Buyids apparently did not provide Skleros with an army, so he tried to recruit tribal warriors along his return to the north; Armenians also joined his cause, as they had in 976. In February 987, he reached Melitene, whose governor opened its gates to him. There Skleros proclaimed himself emperor again, just as he had in 976, and gained the support of Badh, the Kurdish emir of the Marwanid dynasty that was to replace the Hamdanids in Diyar Bakr.[61] But in early 987, his Buyid backer Samsam al-Dawla was overthrown by his brother (Sharaf al-Dawla), and the former's advisor Ziyad, who had masterminded Skleros' release, was executed (it was now that Ouranos escaped from Baghdad to Constantinople). The Buyids nevertheless continued to support the rebellion despite their own turnover.[62] But Skleros soon learned of a greater obstacle to his ambitions: Phokas had also revolted and proclaimed himself emperor.

The court's reaction to the news about Skleros was to reappoint Phokas as *domestikos* in April, but in August or September he too rebelled, at the estate of his relative Eustathios Maleïnos in Charsianon.[63] The two rebels now entered into negotiation and concluded an agreement whereby they would both rule the empire through a partition of powers or territories, though Phokas would be the senior partner. But when Skleros arrived in Cappadocia, Phokas imprisoned him in his fort of Tyropoion. Skleros' son Romanos, however, had already defected to the imperial side (later it was alleged that this was a clever insurance policy for his father, but likely it was a genuine split); and Skleros' Arabs returned home.[64] Phokas was now the master of Asia Minor. The emperors in Constantinople had virtually no foothold there. We should recall that Phokades had commanded the army for the last forty years, from the 940s to 987, excepting the six years of Tzimiskes' reign. Bardas had likely been planning for this eventuality ever since his release from prison in 978. Moreover, the western armies had just been defeated by the Bulgarians, and Basil had little command experience and no one now to guide him. The year 987 was the low point of his entire reign. The emperor did, however, have an advantage beyond Constantinople and his legitimacy: Phokas was an incompetent commander. His rebellion in 970 had been a farce; he had been defeated by Skleros in 978 and had won in 979 only because of Davitʿ of Tao; and he had accomplished little in the east in 980–987. Skleros was by far the abler man, but he lacked Phokas' inherited prestige and networks.

Phokas' armies soon reached the straits. His ally Delphinas (the former *katepano* of Italy) and the rebel's blinded brother Nikephoros encamped across the Bosporos at Chrysopolis. Phokas attacked Abydos on the Hellespont, albeit without success, at which point he left Leon Melissenos to continue the siege. Delphinas was charged with blocking grain from reaching the capital from Asia. The emperor, however, made arrangements for shipments to be brought in by sea from cities along the Black Sea coast, as far as Trebizond.[65]

Basil also made an important foreign-policy decision: he offered Vladimir (or Volodymyr, 978–1015), the king of the Rus' in Kiev and son of Svjatoslav, his much-requested twenty-seven-year-old sister Anna in marriage, in exchange for military aid, on the condition that Vladimir convert to Christianity. Vladimir had an ambitious agenda of his own. He had imposed his rule in the dynastic chaos that followed the death of his father in 972, after recruiting a Scandinavian (Varangian) army and killing many of his relatives. He was looking for ways to normalize his rule and establish himself among the legitimate rulers of Christendom. Netting a born-in-the-purple imperial princess, an unprecedented feat—one, moreover, that had been beyond the reach of Otto I and Hugh Capet—was a tremendous coup. "An unheard-of thing," it was called to Liudprand. Earlier in the century, Petar I of Bulgaria had married the granddaughter of Romanos I Lakapenos—to the chagrin of Konstantinos VII, who decried this violation of Roman imperial dignity—but the girl (Maria) had likely not been a born-in-the-purple princess.

Moreover, Vladimir's aggressive Christianization of Rus' unified his realm and increased his power over it; he had, in fact, previously sought to consolidate his subject's paganism under his control. Also, his choice of Byzantine Orthodoxy increased his access to the west while shielding him from ecclesiastical meddling by the Catholic Franks, who tended to send their own missionaries and bishops, trying, in this way, to dominate their neighbors. Our information about his conversion is so scanty that it may have been Vladimir's intention before Basil's offer in 987: the two rulers were likely in discussion for some time.[66] Moreover, it seems that after taking Kiev Vladimir had found his Varangian mercenaries to be troublesome and demanding, so he wanted to unload them on the Romans.[67]

Basil received his six thousand Varangians in the spring or summer of 988. Probably in that year, he crossed the straits at night, took Delphinas' camp by surprise, and defeated the rebels at Chrysopolis. He hanged the former *katepano* on the spot—the second instance of Basil's severe justice—and arrested and imprisoned Phokas' blind brother Nikephoros.[68] A column was eventually set up to preserve the memory of "the condemned dolphin."[69] The emperors had simultaneously initiated an action behind enemy lines: they sent one Taronites to Trebizond by sea, where he recruited a force and set out for the Euphrates, presumably to disrupt Phokas' bases and undermine the resolve of his followers from those regions. This Taronites was likely Gregorios, the son of Ašot III of Taron who had turned his lands over to Nikephoros II Phokas in 968,[70] and he used his local contacts to good effect. Phokas countered by sending his son Nikephoros to his old ally, Davit', who gave him one thousand cavalry, and the "sons of Bagrat" brought another thousand. This was much less than the army of twelve thousand that Davit' had given to Phokas in 989—we will return to the situation in the Caucasus below—but it did the job: Taronites was defeated. Soon, however, news arrived of the defeat of Delphinas at Chrysopolis, and the Caucasian soldiers went home, claiming that they had fulfilled their duty. Nikephoros' Roman units also dissolved.[71]

Phokas intensified the siege of Abydos, hoping to cross over to Europe, but in early 989 the two emperors crossed the Hellespont with Roman and Varangian units. Phokas prepared to meet them in pitched battle on April 13, but he suddenly died before battle was joined. No one afterward knew exactly how. Basil II celebrated a triumph, displaying Phokas' head in Constantinople, and then dispatched it to the eastern cities. The rebel's son Leon surrendered Antioch on November 3, 989.[72] Thus, the alliance of Macedonian emperors and Phokas generals, begun a century before by Basileios I, and renewed by the two opponents' grandfathers in the 940s, came to an end.

That still left Bardas Skleros. He was released from captivity and resumed his rebellion, picking up many of Phokas' former followers, but he was pushing seventy and the fight had gone out of him. By October 989, he had negotiated a surrender, stipulating amnesty and promotions for himself and his supporters. Skleros would retire with the high court title of *kouropalates*. When he was finally brought before the emperor, an old and almost blind man propped up by his escorts, Basil said, "Look at this man I have so feared!" Skleros was sent to an estate near Didymoteichon in Thrace, where he died on March 6, 991.[73]

Historians have deemed this second round of concurrent revolts as both damaging to the empire and distracting from its career of conquest. It receives great prominence in histories of Byzantium. In reality, it does not seem to have been destructive. There were fewer battles than during Skleros' 976–979 revolt, and each was over with less actual fighting and few Roman casualties. Phokas did not have to fight to gain Asia Minor. The empire's eastern neighbors did not take advantage of the rebellion to attack. Baghdad, after all, had a stake in the fight, while the Fatimids were having trouble in Syria, and Basil concluded a seven-year treaty with them in 987–988 (the Fatimid caliph would henceforth be the one mentioned in the prayers of the mosques of Constantinople).[74] Nor was the empire distracted from making additional conquests, as it had not made any since the early 970s. Imperial policy in the east had since then mostly maintained existing relationships. But the war did leave some loose ends.

In the spring of 989, Vladimir attacked and captured Cherson, the Roman outpost in the Crimea. We know only that he did so, not why. One possibility is that he was trying to force Basil to fulfill the terms of the agreement and hand over Anna. Another is that Cherson had sided with Phokas and Vladimir was restoring it to imperial obedience.[75] Either way, Anna was duly dispatched to marry a still-heathen king known in the west as *fornicator immensis*. The *Russian Primary Chronicle* records that "Anna departed with reluctance. 'It is as if I were setting out into captivity,' she lamented; 'better were it for me to die at home.' But her brothers protested, 'Through your agency God turns the land of Rus' to repentance'." According to the later Rus' legends recorded there, the wedding took place in the church of St. Basil in the center of Cherson, whereupon the city was returned to the emperors. Anna's retinue included priests, who began converting the new country.[76] Meanwhile, Basil formed his six thousand Varangians into a new imperial *tagma*, which, for the next two centuries, would draw its recruits primarily among Scandinavians, who often returned home after gaining riches in imperial service (Figure 6).[77] In the Icelandic sagas, various figures boast about their service in Miklagard ("Great City" in Old Norse, i.e., Constantinople) and show off their imperial swords, gold, and garments. Conversely, they left

FIGURE 6 VARANGIAN RUNES ON THE LION OF PEIRAIEUS. The lion standing outside the Arsenal in Venice was looted from the Peiraieus in 1687 by the admiral Francesco Morosini (soon after he bombarded and exploded the Parthenon). It bears on its shoulder an elaborate inscription in Scandinavian runes, which unfortunately cannot be deciphered. It was probably carved by a Varangian guardsman or a passing pilgrim. Image from K. Gjerset, *History of the Norwegian People*, NY 1915.

the marks of their passage through "Greece," such as a long runic inscription carved on the side of an ancient statue of a lion in the Peiraieus of Athens (it was moved to Venice in the seventeenth century). They were a recognizably foreign element in Byzantine society, and paid to be fierce and intimidating. Lacking roots in the land as well as ties to its generals, they were fiercely loyal to their one employer, the emperor.

The most troubling development of the latest round of civil war was Davitʿ of Tao's support of the Phokades. He had supported Phokas also in 978–979, but that was on behalf of the court against the rebel Skleros. Still, Davitʿ had provided less assistance to Phokas in 988 compared to 979, and it was withdrawn when news arrived of the defeat of Phokas' forces at Chrysopolis. Davitʿ was possibly hedging his bets. He was, moreover, facing challenges in his ambitious plan to unify the Georgian principalities of the Caucasus. As we saw, he had managed to install his cousin Bagrat, the heir to the throne of Lower Tao and Kartli proper, on the throne of Abkhazia, and also adopted him so that he would inherit Upper Tao as well. The first round of Roman civil war (976–979) had caught him in the midst of these maneuverings. The second round came at an equally critical time. In 988–989, Bagrat and Davitʿ were at war with each other, but, perceiving that he was weak, Bagrat yielded and begged forgiveness, pretending that it was all a misunderstanding.[78] Yet this time Davitʿ had backed the loser in the civil war, even if without enthusiasm. He was exposed to retribution.

According to Yahya, Basil was angry with Davitʿ and sent an army. However, Davitʿ was swift to tender his submission and offered to bequeath all his lands to the emperor. Romans had accepted bequests of principalities and entire kingdoms since the days of the Republic, and had acquired the Armenian state of Taron by cession as recently as ca. 968. Basil accepted this proposal and granted Davitʿ the higher title of *kouropalates*, which usually went to the emperor's man in the Caucasus. In a sense, Davitʿ was being treated in a similar way to Skleros: a court title accompanied by historical obsolescence. The emperor also bestowed titles on leading Georgians, apparently planning for the transfer of sovereignty. When Davitʿ died in 1000, the empire annexed his lands without opposition. Whatever plans Davitʿ may have made previously for Bagrat III to succeed him in Upper Tao were superseded by this testamentary arrangement with the empire.[79]

Another former ally was also accused of conspiring with the Phokades: Agapios, the patriarch of Antioch, who had delivered that city to the emperor at a crucial moment in 978. He was summoned to Constantinople, confined to a monastery, and eventually replaced by a Constantinopolitan appointee (Ioannes) in 996.[80]

All in all, Phokas' rebellion had worked out well for Basil, though for two years it seemed extremely perilous. Phokas had suppressed Skleros, who was a more dangerous foe in battle, while conducting an ineffective strategy himself. His defeat recuperated Basil's military credentials and gave the emperor the opportunity to hire six thousand Varangians, dismantle the Phokas network, and secure the submission of Tao. The revolt also exposed the inability of Buyid Baghdad to interfere effectively in Roman affairs. In 989, the only cloud on the horizon was the Bulgarians, who had taken advantage of the war to raid deeply into Roman territory, though we are poorly informed about Balkan events. They pillaged the hinterland of Thessalonike and captured the city of Beroia.[81] Basil would now have to fight in the west while simultaneously defending imperial interests in the east. In the past, the second task, or even both, could be assigned to trusted subordinates, but Basil had little trust left. He would take on both challenges himself.

CHAPTER 5

"Guarding the Children of New Rome"

Basil II (976–1025), Part II

From status quo to peace in the east, 990–1001

Sources for the reign of Basil II thin out after the great revolts—with thirty-five more years to go! Eastern writers, especially Yahya, cover military conflicts in the east, but mostly in discrete, disconnected episodes. Skylitzes gives information about war with Bulgaria, but does not organize his material chronologically and leaves many gaps. And although there is coverage of the imperial periphery, there is almost nothing about the center. We have almost no information about Constantinople for the entirety of Basil's fifty-year reign. On the night of October 25, 989, an earthquake struck the capital and its vicinity, killing many and cracking the walls of the City and the domes and arches of Hagia Sophia. A rhetorical lament was composed about the damage to the cathedral, and its restoration was a major project lasting four or six years.[1] Step'anos of Taron claims that the chief architect was the Armenian Trdat, which has been taken at face value. But we must be skeptical, given Step'anos' nationalist tendency to see Armenians in the lead everywhere.[2]

The sources for Basil's reign are thin, but this does not necessarily mean that significant developments were taking place that are lost to us. Historical narratives tend to record unusual or dramatic events such as wars and political conflict. In the case of this reign, and with the possible exception of the Bulgarian war(s), we have no reason to believe that there was much happening. In other words, Basil's reign after 989 may have been a time of relative peace, quiet, and prosperity for the majority of his subjects, at least those who were not living next to his wars. The "darkness" that envelops Constantinople probably means that for some fifty years there were few famines, unpopular appointments, vexatious taxation, or abuses by soldiers. This would make Basil one of the most successful Byzantine emperors on the domestic front, and the years 989–1025 (and beyond) the most peaceful in the history of the empire. On the political front, Basil successfully protected himself from the empire's officer class, an effort we will discuss separately below. But this remained a domestic "cold war," and the sources again fail to report much by way of concrete events. Thus Basil remains one of the most enigmatic emperors. He did not marry or produce heirs, and commissioned few works of art, architecture, and literature despite amassing vast wealth by the end of his reign. He did not appoint patriarchs who gave him trouble; he even left the office vacant for 991–996.

We have little access to Basil's thoughts, goals, and personality, but it is clear that he was not one to tolerate treachery, sometimes devising cruel forms of punishment for those who betrayed him, and we will repeatedly see him inflict exemplary punishment on large numbers of foreign enemies (including blinding, amputation, and the like). In the twelfth century, Byzantines began to remember him as the Bulgar Slayer. Even if it was as a later invention, the moniker was certainly appropriate. Basil no doubt killed many Bulgarians, and it is likely that he spent most of his reign fighting against them in a war whose extraordinary length had no precedent in Roman tradition.

Later generations reinvented him in ways that catered to their immediate needs. The most compelling literary portrait was crafted by Michael Psellos in the mideleventh century. In his *Chronographia*, Psellos presented him as an inhumanly tireless commander, ascetic in a military (not religious) way. He did not care for adornment, ceremony, or literature, only the facts of power. He was aloof, even arrogant, rough, inaccessible, and inscrutable. But we must take note of the purpose of this constructed image: Psellos was offering a model of martial virtue for the palace-based, cultured, and mild-mannered emperors of his own time.[3] He devotes most of his attention to Basil's generalship, presenting him as a "scientific" commander. He had studied the manuals, knew every detail about his armies, micromanaged the battlefield and his communications, never took great risks, punished soldiers who broke formation even if they defeated the enemy, and kept his plans secret.[4] In an oration presented to Konstantinos IX in 1043, Psellos portrayed Basil as an emperor focused on strategy, a term that he mentions five times in ten lines.[5] He was no glamorous hero, but a strategist who brought home the victories. He was slightly below average in height, and his features were even and harmonious, but otherwise undistinguished.[6] You would not think he was an important person.

Along the eastern front, Basil had inherited a viable situation that needed only maintenance and enforcement. With peace secure at home after early 989, he focused on the conflict with Bulgaria, where the situation was not viable. We will recount the events in each theater separately to maintain their coherence. The emperor moved to the east only when the balance of power was sliding away from the empire. Still, by 1000, he had managed to create a more favorable status quo in the east as well, leaving him free to pursue the Balkan war.

Roman policy in Syria aimed primarily to hold Aleppo as a tributary protectorate and buffer between the empire and the Fatimids. In late 990, the renegade general Bakjur, now employed by the Fatimids, made his last attempt to regain Aleppo (the previous one had been in 983). He was defeated, captured, and executed in April 991 by Abu al-Ma'ali, the emir of Aleppo, who also had the assistance of six thousand Roman, Armenian, and Georgian soldiers brought by the newly reappointed *doux* of Antioch, Michael Bourtzes (one of the few survivors from the era of Nikephoros II). The emir had specifically requested aid from the emperor, who authorized it.[7] When Abu al-Ma'ali died in late 991, he was succeeded by his son Abu al-Fada'il, though many of the emirate's top men went over to Cairo. This transition highlighted the ill-defined position of Aleppo between Rome and the Fatimids. The latter, who had a tenuous hold on southern Syria, had not sought an all-out confrontation with the Romans in the north. This policy is attributed in Arabic sources to the vizier Ya'qub ibn Killis, whose dying advice to the caliph al-'Aziz was to avoid such a conflict.[8] But ibn Killis died in February 991. The caliph now made a determined effort to take Aleppo, which lasted for years, and failed.

Fatimid operations in 992 were commanded by the Turkish general Manju Takin from Damascus. Manju Takin moved north, took Homs, destroyed a Hamdanid force at Apameia, and besieged Aleppo for a month. Abu al-Fada'il's minister Lu'lu' wrote to Basil, who was then fighting the Bulgarians. At the same time, Manju Takin reassured Bourtzes that his target was Aleppo and that he would harm no Roman. But Basil had ordered Bourtzes to assist Aleppo, so he imprisoned the Fatimid envoy. Manju Takin therefore moved against Antioch in the summer, plundering Bourtzes' own lands along the way. Bourtzes tried to block his passage on the bridge that crossed the Orontes, with an army of five thousand, but failed and fell back to the walls of Antioch. The *doux* refrained from engaging again, as the enemy had a much larger army, said to be thirty thousand strong. Manju Takin remained at Antioch for half a day, plundering its suburbs, then returned to Aleppo and besieged it again before returning to Damascus, still in 992. Meanwhile, from Bulgaria Basil reproached Bourtzes for his treatment of the ambassador and ordered that he be set free. When the Muslim population of Laodikeia rebelled that year, Bourtzes suppressed the revolt and transported the rebels back to Roman territory, where they were resettled.[9]

It is unclear whether land operations took place in 993, though by then the Fatimids had taken Apameia and naval operations are attested.[10] Manju Takin set out again in the spring of 994, attacked the villages around Antioch, and, in the summer, besieged Aleppo. The same events as before played out: Aleppo appealed to Basil, who ordered Bourtzes to intervene and sent Leon Melissenos with reinforcements. These two harassed the Fatimids' foragers, so Manju Takin decided to confront the Romans in a valley north of Apameia, on September 15, 994. The Fatimid army outnumbered the Romans. When the units from Aleppo fled, the Romans also broke ranks, losing five thousand men in the carnage. Manju Takin returned to invest Aleppo again, a siege that lasted into 995. This time the Fatimid army did not return home.[11]

Aleppo sent another appeal to Basil, who was now "in the heart of Bulgarian territory." They told him that they had no supplies left and warned that Antioch would be next. The emperor decided to intervene in person, so he force-marched his army across the entire empire in under a month, mounting his infantry on mules and supplying his cavalry with spare horses. He reached Antioch by March 995, and headed straight for Aleppo. As soon as he learned this, Manju Takin lifted the siege (now in its seventh month), burned his camp, and fled in panic back to Damascus. Abu al-Fada'il and Lu'lu' came out and prostrated themselves before the emperor. He forgave them the tribute owed for the years of war, and then decided to stay in Syria to show the region what a real Roman army could do. He took Apameia in a day, then Rafaniyya, other forts, and Homs, burning, pillaging, and taking captives. When tribesmen attacked, Basil captured forty, cut off their hands, and let them go. No more attacked him after that. The emperor then lay siege to Tripolis, which was a key port for supplying Fatimid armies in northern Syria.[12] But the city held out for more than a month, despite having a pro-Roman faction, so Basil departed for Antarados, some 60 kilometers to the north, which he rebuilt and garrisoned with Armenians. He then returned to Antioch and departed for Constantinople.[13]

The emperor's Syrian incursion of 995 was much like that of Tzimiskes twenty years earlier: it did not change many realities, but reinforced (or restored) perceptions about relative strength. Tripolis was, it seems, the only target worth conquering. Despite his failure there, Basil appeared as a cat among mice, bringing overwhelming and terrifying force that instantly changed the balance of power. He upheld his treaty obligations to Aleppo and treated it generously. An Arab historian even comments that Basil was also famous for his justice and affection for Muslims, a rare compliment from a Muslim writer.[14] He also had little patience with incompetence: he placed Bourtzes under house arrest and appointed Damianos Dalassenos in his place as *doux* of Antioch, with responsibility for eastern defense. Bourtzes' failures had cost the emperor a season's worth of campaigning in Bulgaria. Dalassenos revealed what orders he was under when, probably in late 995, he raided Tripolis; then, three months later, in early 996, 'Arqa; then Tripolis again; and he captured the fort of al-Lakma, taking many prisoners.[15]

There was outrage in Cairo over these events, and massive preparations for war in Syria were made in late 995 and early 996. It seems that the caliph al-'Aziz was going to take the field himself, and many volunteered. But the fleet being readied to accompany the expedition burned in the harbor on the Nile in May 996. This was blamed on Amalfitan traders, many of whom were murdered before the (Christian) vizier intervened. A second fleet began to be built, using wood taken from public buildings, when al-'Aziz fell sick in August 996, and died on October 14. He was succeeded by his eleven-year-old son al-Hakim, and Fatimid energies were diverted to the succession. The expedition was canceled.[16] But Manju Takin had not remained idle. In 996, he besieged Aleppo for a few days, and then moved on to besiege Antarados, where the new fleet from Egypt joined him. But a storm wrecked the fleet just when Dalassenos approached from Antioch. Manju Takin fled and the Romans captured the surviving ships.[17]

Manju Takin's domestic position had now became untenable, as a Berber faction in the Fatimid armed forces became dominant in the transition of power. In 997, he rebelled against the new regime and marched on Cairo, albeit without success in the end. Interestingly, in this venture he sought aid from the emperor, who, however, turned him down, saying that he could not help him to wage war against his lawful sovereign. Basil surely recognized that the venture was a long shot, and what he wanted were good relations with the Fatimids so that he could devote all his attention to Bulgaria. Moreover, he might have empathized with al-Hakim, a child-heir handled by eunuchs and now threatened by generals—a position Basil knew all too well. But when Tyre rebelled against Cairo in 997 and sought the emperor's support, he granted it, because it disrupted the Fatimids' naval supply routes. The rebellion lasted into 998.[18]

The years 996–998 had, after the emperor's intervention, seen only limited operations in Syria. The Romans were successful at maintaining the status quo of 970. But a pattern emerged: the situation would gradually deteriorate, forcing the emperor to intervene, ravage enemy territory, and reestablish Roman interests. This happened again in 998–999. A fire in the citadel of Apameia gave the emir of Aleppo and his minister Lu'lu' the opportunity to retake the city, to which they were entitled according to the treaty of Safar. It had been taken by Basil in 995, and it is unclear who controlled it in the aftermath; possibly it was quasi-autonomous. They besieged the citadel for a few days but fled at the approach of Dalassenos from Antioch, who, with a large army, besieged it in turn. The lord of the city now wrote to the Fatimid governor of Damascus, Jaysh ibn al-Samsama, to come to his aid. It seems that many cities in Syria were generally discontented with outside rule at this time (as we have seen in Tyre, Apameia, and Damascus), and sought to play the major powers against each other. These cities also had corporate institutions of local self-governance with local headmen who could, at times, implement autonomous policies.[19]

Jaysh's counteroffensive aimed at a general restoration of Fatimid authority in Syria and began with the subjugation of Tyre. A Fatimid fleet repelled the Roman ships that came to its aid, and the city was taken in June 998. Jaysh then turned to Apameia. He and Dalassenos fought the battle of Apameia on July 19, 998. The *doux* broke through the center of the Fatimid army, where the Daylami where stationed, but he received a fatal wound to his side during the pursuit. The Muslims raised the cry of victory, which turned the tide. The Romans fled and more than six thousand of them (possibly even ten thousand) were killed. Dalassenos' sons and many officers were taken to Cairo, where they would remain captive for ten years. Jaysh then advanced to Antioch and sat before it for four days before returning to the fort of Shayzar (or Larissa; Basil had taken it in 995, but it had apparently reverted to Fatimid control).[20] This effectively replayed the events of 992 and 994, when, after defeating Roman armies, Manju Takin had reached Antioch. The situation again called for imperial intervention.

This did not come for a year and a half. Basil was too busy in Bulgaria, but at the same time the Fatimids had no further objective beyond imposing their authority in southern Syria. In late 998 and 999, Jaysh was busy suppressing local anti-Fatimid elements in Damascus, with much bloodshed.[21] Roman embassies were sent to Cairo to make peace, but failed.[22] So Basil appeared in Syria in person, on September 20, 999. His first stop was at Apameia, where he gathered and buried the bones of the fallen Romans, and built a church on top. There is no evidence that he attacked the fort there. He besieged Shayzar until the garrison negotiated its surrender and their departure. Basil installed Armenians in the citadel and also took a number of nearby forts. He then burned and plundered his way to Homs, which he sacked. The Varangians set fire to a church of St. Constantine, where the population had sought refuge. Meanwhile, Jaysh appealed for help from Damascus and gathered a large army, but did not seek to intercept the emperor. Basil now headed for the coast, burning ʿArqa and again attacking Tripolis, in early December. This operation was supported by the navy. But a week later the garrison attacked the imperial army, inflicting heavy casualties, so Basil returned to Antioch and named his proven general Nikephoros Ouranos as *doux*.[23] The incursion had followed the usual script, only this time the emperor wintered in Cilicia, intending to invade again in the spring.

The Fatimids were now ready to make peace, and probably realized that the emperor's objective was the same, and that despite his periodic incursions, war in the east was distracting to him. The initiative was led by Barjawan, the eunuch tutor and now chief minister of the young caliph al-Hakim. He sent one of the Roman ambassadors, who had been detained from before the war, along with Orestes, the patriarch of Jerusalem, to establish a ten-year peace, to which the emperor agreed, probably in 1000. We have a detailed account of the reception of the Roman ambassador at Cairo in 1001, when the truce was ratified, and then again for 1013, when it was probably renewed.[24] Having secured the status quo, the emperor returned to his Bulgarian war.[25] Barjawan was murdered almost immediately after this by al-Hakim, who now embarked on his reign of terror over his top officials and capricious rule over his subjects. But peace was kept with Rome.

Like all past agreements with the Fatimids, this one was defined as a temporary truce rather than a lasting peace, to accommodate their ideology of holy war. Most such agreements rarely expired before the outbreak of new hostilities. This one, however, was not only followed as agreed, it effectively lasted for as long as northern Syria was the meeting point of Roman and Fatimid interests, about another fifty years, probably by being periodically renewed. The two empires created a stable framework for the region, despite occasional provocations. The Romans did not want further conquests in this area after 970. They had directed persistent attacks only against Tripolis, showing an intention to take it too, probably because it was a strategic point in any conflict with Egypt. With that conflict over, its importance faded. Basil had turned the status quo of 970, which required enforcement and policing, into a lasting peace, a major achievement on his part. The Buyids, meanwhile, had lost power and influence in Diyar Bakr. The former emirate of Mosul had fragmented into tribal regions, smaller emirates, and autonomous cities. This "represented a thorough consolidation of the Byzantine position on the southeastern frontier."[26]

While Basil was wintering in Cilicia, he received the news that Davitʿ of Tao had died on March 31, 1000 (later sources claimed that he was poisoned by domestic enemies, but this, as always, is unlikely). Ten years earlier, after the failure of Phokas' revolt, Davitʿ had made Basil his heir in Upper Tao. Then, in the early 990s, Davitʿ had conquered Mantzikert from the emir al-Hasan of the Marwanid dynasty, which had replaced the Hamdanids in Diyar Bakr (Mayyafariqin) and also ruled the cities to the west and north of lake Van. Davitʿ resettled Mantzikert with Georgians and Armenians, but he later failed to take Khliat from al-Hasan's successor Mumahhid al-Dawla (997–1010).[27] Now that Davitʿ had died, Basil set out in the summer of 1000 to claim his rights in Tao and, through a tour, to establish his status as regional overlord along his eastern border. He was followed at a distance by Ouranos and the army of Antioch.

The emperor traveled via Melitene to Erez (Keltzene, modern Erzincan). Here, in July 1000, he was met by Mumahhid al-Dawla, who became an imperial client. Basil granted him the title of *magistros*, made him *doux* of the region, and authorized him to call the armies of Taron and western Armenia to his aid. This made Mumahhid al-Dawla the only Muslim with such authority and command status in the imperial hierarchy. Then, entering the territory of Tao, at Havčʿičʿ (i.e., the former theme Chauzizion), Basil received Bagrat III of Abkhazia, whom he made *kouropalates* in place of Davitʿ, and his father Gurgen of Kartli, whom he made *magistros*. At this place, a skirmish broke out between some nobles loyal to Davitʿ and the Varangian guard over rights to some forage; the latter won, and many of the nobles were killed. Basil then received the rulers of the Armenian principalities of Kars (Vanand, just to the east of Tao) and Vaspurakan (to the east of Van), to whom he gave gifts (but not titles); then, passing through Mantzikert, Basil came to Vałarškert (in Bagrewand), where he expected a similar visit of submission by the ruler of Ani, Gagik, the Bagratid King of Kings, but he did not come (though his nephew came to slander him). Basil then moved into the heart of Tao. At Oltʿi, its capital, he appointed his own men to the offices and commands of the realm. Presumably, these included Georgians who received imperial ranks and titles, but many were Romans; the rest of the local nobility he took back with him. It was likely now that the theme of Iberia was first formed from these lands, namely Upper Tao, Bagrewand, Theodosioupolis and the Basean valley, and Apahunikʿ (including Mantzikert). Some of these territories had been ceded to Davitʿ by the empire after the first revolt of Skleros, in 979.[28] Either now or later, Iberia would be commanded by a *doux* based in Theodosioupolis. It was possibly at this point that the emperor's coins began to feature a suspended crown over his head, a sign of victory that had not been used since the fifth century.[29]

In Byzantine eyes, Georgia was Orthodox but the Armenian Church was Monophysite. Yet many Armenians in the new provinces were Chalcedonians (Orthodox), and the imperial Church had been penetrating Armenian lands by creating new episcopal sees there (as it was simultaneously bolstering its position in southern Italy in similar ways).[30] There is evidence that Roman and Armenian rulers did not let the doctrinal position of their respective Churches hamper their rapprochement. The court of Basil had early on sent a fragment of the True Cross to enrich the holdings of the monastery of Aparank' in Vaspurakan. An account of its dedication in 983, in the presence of the three princes of Vaspurakan (two of whom would survive to meet Basil in 1000), was written by the great poet and monk Grigor of Narek sometime in the 990s. This work, while expressing standard Armenian theological views, begins with a powerful panegyric of the emperors Basil and Konstantinos and the Roman empire in general, which, "spread out like the sky across the vast surface of the whole world, will gather in its ample bosom innumerable multitudes, as a single flock in a single place."[31]

After the emperor's departure, so likely in 1001, Gurgen of Kartli attacked Tao. Step'anos claims that he was angry that Basil had bestowed a lesser title on him than on his son Bagrat. The emperor ordered Ouranos to intervene, and he reached Basean later in 1001. The two armies stared at each other during the winter, until the crisis was resolved diplomatically (though we do not know the terms).[32]

In sum, Skylitzes was wrong to say that, in contrast to his conquering predecessors, Basil "was distracted by civil wars at first, then by his efforts against Samuil, hence he did not have the opportunity of securing the eastern part of the empire properly.... All he could do was make an appearance in the east and deal with the most pressing situations before returning to his constant concern and worry: the subjection of the Bulgarians."[33] Bulgaria may have been his priority, but securing the east is exactly what he did, more effectively and lastingly than his predecessors. Skylitzes was simply unaware of most of the events on that front, which we know from eastern sources. Moreover, through his acquisition of Tao, accomplished without a war, Basil probably added more territory to the empire than Nikephoros Phokas had taken in Cilicia and Syria. And the conquest of Bulgaria added even more.

The war against Bulgaria, 991–1003

The eastern sources do not provide sustained coverage of the Bulgarian war, but they do make it clear that it was Basil's priority during the 990s and after. The Aleppan embassies always found him in Bulgaria, and he had to be pulled away from there to intervene in the east. The Arab historian al-Rudhrawari claims that Basil kept up the war against the Bulgarians for thirty-five years until he conquered them, and the Roman historian Attaleiates says that Basil fought against them for forty years. Yahya says that Basil did not appoint a patriarch for the first half of the 990s because he was too busy fighting the Bulgarians, which suggests that he did not even visit the capital during the winter. Our main source for the Balkan theater, Skylitzes, says that Basil fought against Bulgaria every year without interruption until he conquered it.[34] But Skylitzes was badly informed about the east (as we saw) and his narrative of the Bulgarian war is, frankly, not viable. It consists of fragmented episodes that give no sense of the overall strategic context of the war, and they can often be shown to be out of sequence and badly aligned with datable events in the east. Skylitzes occasionally gives dates, but we cannot assume that events he recounts after those passages necessarily happened afterward; in some cases, they demonstrably did not. A major study of Skylitzes' narrative method for this reign has proven that he sometimes clusters events by thematic affinity, not contemporaneity.[35]

Even though a full narrative of the Bulgarian war cannot be written, it is possible to attain greater clarity and resolve some long-standing problems by relying on the fixed dates in the eastern sources and Skylitzes. Before 1014, when Skylitzes returns to a linear narrative, we have only scattered and fragmentary notices that are in jumbled order. Immediately after reporting Skleros' surrender in 989, Skylitzes says that Basil marched into Thrace and Macedonia against the Bulgarians, leaving behind Gregorios Taronites (the son of Ašot III of Taron) as commander in Thessalonike. Skylitzes says nothing more about the campaign. Eastern sources say that Basil set out against the Bulgarians in early 991 and waged war for four years (i.e., until his 995 incursion in the east), capturing many forts, including Beroia, in Macedonia. Gregorios Taronites' son Asotios (i.e., Ašot) was captured in an ambush by Samuil, and Gregorios himself was killed in another ambush when he came to the rescue, near Thessalonike.[36] Scholars date these events to 995,[37] but in fact we know only that they occurred *before* September 995, when Ioannes Chaldos had taken over as *doux* of Thessalonike. In that month, he confirmed some fiscal exemptions of a local monastery. From that document, it appears that Chaldos was concurrently general of the Armeniakon and Boukellarion themes, which may signal the transfer of eastern soldiers to the Bulgarian theater; this would explain why the monks were eager to have their exemption from military impositions confirmed.[38]

We know little, then, about the first four years of the war, except that it was fought in Macedonia (understood in a broad geographical sense). We know from eastern sources that in mid-992 and again in late 993 and early 994 Basil was fighting in Bulgaria (in the later case "deep in the heart of Bulgaria").[39] It was probably also during this first phase of the war that Basil captured Skopje after defeating Samuil by the Axios (Vardar) river, and the greatest prize that came with Skopje was the surrender of the eunuch tsar Roman, the son of Petar. Skylitzes dates this later in the war, but his chronology is hopelessly confused and there are good reasons to place the capture of the Bulgarian tsar in the early phase of this conflict.[40] The emperor gave the tsar court titles and later put him in command of Abydos, on the Asian side of the Hellespont. After Skopje, the emperor besieged Pernik (near Sofia) for a long time, but eventually gave up and returned to the capital via Philippopolis (Plovdiv). This first phase of the war, then, went well for Basil. He had taken Beroia, defeated Samuil at the Axios, sacked Ohrid, captured the Bulgarian tsar Roman, and besieged Pernik.

In 995, Basil was forced to rush off to the eastern front, and in 996 his lieutenant in Thessalonike Ioannes Chaldos was captured in another ambush by Samuil. Chaldos would be not be released from captivity for another twenty-two years.[41] At this time, Samuil began raiding throughout (Roman) Macedonia and Greece, possibly emboldened by Basil's departure for the east. The emperor sent his trusted supporter Nikephoros Ouranos to replace Chaldos and take charge of the west. Ouranos seems to have held both the position of *doux* and *domestikos* (a position that Basil had ceased filling after the great revolts, and it was apparently no longer split between east and west).[42] When Ouranos took office, likely in the summer of 996, Samuil had raided south through Thessaly, Boiotia, and Attica, plundering even as far as the Peloponnese. Ouranos shadowed him, and camped across from Samuil along the river Spercheios in central Greece. The river was in flood because it was a stormy day, so the Bulgarians believed themselves to be safe during the night. But Ouranos found a ford and fell upon them, killing many in their sleep and capturing their camp. Samuil and his son hid among the bodies, and then escaped through western Greece (the Pindos) until they reached Ohrid. Ouranos sent one thousand severed heads and twelve thousand prisoners to Constantinople, and the bones of the slain could still be seen decades later.[43] According to Yahya, Samuil now sued for peace and Basil was open to negotiation. But suddenly "the king of the Bulgarians, who was held captive by the emperor in Constantinople [i.e., Roman], died," whereupon Samuil proclaimed himself tsar in his place. This is dated to 997. Samuil was trying to bolster his standing after the terrible defeat at the Spercheios. In response, the emperor ordered Ouranos to attack the Bulgarians, which he did for three months, with no opposition.[44]

We now run into an acute shortage of information. Skylitzes offers only thematically organized dossiers of material, one on defectors to Samuil and suspected traitors, and another (after three out-of-sequence items) on Samuil's generals who surrendered their towns to Basil. Scholars have wanted to assume that this material is presented in chronological sequence, but there is none; these episodes could have occurred at any time between 986 and 1014, a thirty-year span. There was not *one* year in which *all* the defections happened, and in both directions simultaneously no less![45] What we learn from this material is that the emperor's policy was to reward high-status defectors with ranks, offices, and presumably salaries in the Roman system. Among these episodes, it is likely that Dobromir, who surrendered Beroia, did so in the early 990s, when Basil took that town. Dobromir (known as Damianos to the Romans) was given important command positions.[46] It is also possible that the emperor's expedition to rebuild the forts in Thessaly that had been destroyed by the Bulgarians happened either in 991–994 or after the battle of the Spercheios (996), i.e., after the known Bulgarian raids in this area.

The two dossiers are, as mentioned, separated by three items that are out-of-sequence: they are, in order, a marriage of the sister of Romanos Argyros (the future emperor Romanos III) to the son of the doge of Venice, which we know happened in 1005/6; a second attack on Serdica by the emperor, which cannot be dated; and a Roman attack led by Theodorokanos and Nikephoros Xiphias, dated precisely to 1000/1, which took Preslav, Pliska, and the Danube delta. Skylitzes does not explicitly say that they occupied those places, so it is not clear that easternmost Bulgaria came under Roman rule again at this time (though it may have).[47] After the dossier with the defectors, Skylitzes says that when Ouranos was posted to Antioch he was replaced in Thessalonike by David Arianites; though he does not say it, we know from eastern events that this took place in 999. The next item, dated to 1002/3, is Basil's capture of Vidin after an eight-month siege (he left a garrison behind) and Samuil's concurrent attack on the fair at Adrianople, on August 15, 1003. If we antedate the Skopje material to the early 990s, as I believe we must, our information about the Bulgarian war ends there.[48]

In sum, for the years 997–1003 we have only a jumble of incoherent bits of information. The impression that emerges is of gradual Roman gains, made both by the emperor and by his generals, though we cannot always distinguish between successful raids and permanent conquests. If the Romans kept all the places they captured in the years 991–1003, which is to say, Beroia, Preslav, Pliska, Vidin, Dyrrachion, and Skopje, then Samuil would by 1003 have been confined to a small realm around Ohrid, not a major threat to the Romans. He had raided from the Peloponnese to Adrianople, but does not seem to have gained or permanently recovered ground after 990. However, *we have no information about the decade 1003–1014.* When the curtain rises in 1014, we see that the Bulgarian state controlled a fair amount of territory around Ohrid, including Skopje and Beroia (both of which must, then, have been recaptured), and toward the east as far as Serdica but not Philippopolis (Plovdiv). The Romans held eastern Bulgaria and a stretch of the Danube (as far as Vidin?).[49]

Samuil's was largely a southwestern Balkan state. Unfortunately, we know little about it, its history, and its governance. Samuil and many of his subjects probably considered themselves Bulgarians, but how exactly they understood that identity is beyond our reach, as is the multiethnic composition of his state. Samuil also entered into diplomatic relations and marriage alliances with other states in the Balkans, but they are impossible to reconstruct in detail. The same is true of Basil's alliances. We hear of a 992 agreement with Venice involving naval assistance and some Serb envoys trying to reach the emperor in 993, but these parties are not mentioned again in connection with the war.[50] It is not until 1014 that the veil of silence rises on the Bulgarian war.

The emperor and the "aristocracy"

A major theme in discussions of Basil's reign, indeed of the later Macedonian dynasty, is the tension between the emperor and the emerging aristocracy. This theme is situated at the nexus of social, political, economic, and military history, and has therefore attracted attention by historians who want to move past mere narrative and study broader social structures. In the Introduction, I argued that it is difficult if not impossible to draw reliable conclusions about socioeconomic trends from the meager information at our disposal. This section will assess the role of Basil II in the long-standing efforts by emperors to curb the abuses of the "powerful" in Byzantine society. Katherine Holmes has persuasively argued that Basil's main concern in all this was to protect himself, both reactively and preemptively, against threats to his authority and position, especially after the great revolts.[51] Thus, she reads the emperor's laws and interventions politically and not in terms of a socioeconomic ideology. The idea that Basil was at war with the "aristocracy" is overblown, and I would add that it was not defined by socioeconomic criteria to begin with; Basil, like many other emperors, was concerned specifically and primarily about army officers with clout, prestige, and connections. No one in Romanía had enough land to challenge an emperor, but an army could do so.

Traditional images of Basil's hostility to the aristocracy stem largely from Psellos' compelling character portrait. Psellos implies that Basil ruled according to the advice given to him by the defeated rebel Skleros: "Depose all who accumulate too much power; don't let generals grow too rich; run them down with unfair taxes so that they are always busy with their private affairs; don't let a woman into the palace; don't be accessible; and don't let many know what you are thinking."[52] There is actually considerable truth to this picture. Basil did not marry and remained an aloof figure. Yahya even comments that when he set out on one expedition, no one knew where he intended to go.[53] We will see that he passed measures that allowed him to beat down the powerful if he so chose. But this does not amount to a war against them, even in Psellos' portrait. Perhaps it was a cold war, a latent distrust that included the stockpiling of deterrents, even if they were not used.

To flesh out his picture, Psellos also claims that Basil gathered around him a team of subordinates who were neither learned nor of illustrious origin.[54] We have to treat this cautiously. Many emperors, before and after, relied on such "rough" men of humble origin. Psellos is highlighting this because of the specific portrait that he wants to paint of this emperor. As the preceding narrative has shown, Basil continued to employ "distinguished" men after 989, though he relied on those whom he deemed loyal and competent. He was playing politics with the leading families, not trying to abolish them or even weaken them as a group.[55] The aristocracy was alive and well (and still rich) at the end of his reign. Despite his occasional severity, Basil was open to reconciliation even with those who had acted against him. Witness the survival and even the careers (in some cases) of Melissenos, Bourtzes, Tornikes, Maleïnos, Skleros, Davit' of Tao, and even the sons of the rebel Phokas.[56] Emperors pragmatically tried to keep as many important people onside as they could, even after rebellions.[57]

In the thirty-five years between 989 and 1025, Basil passed an extremely small number of measures that might have negatively affected the aristocracy, so small that they cannot constitute a sustained policy of class warfare. These measures aimed to rhetorically strengthen the emperor's otherwise vulnerable position vis-à-vis the powerful and influential men that he needed to run the empire, especially the army. We will discuss those measures shortly.

Let us first consider other aspects of his rule that likely had the same goal. Basil did not appoint a *domestikos* of the *scholai* in the east, an office that had functioned too often in the recent past as a stepping stone to the throne, and he appointed only Ouranos to it in the west (suppressing in the process the distinction between the eastern and western offices). Basil was also the first emperor of his dynasty to campaign in person since its founder (and even he had not campaigned much). He also always took command in the most active theater of war with, probably, the largest army. His subordinates at Antioch and Thessalonike tended to be defeated in his absence, which means that they may not have been given large armies. It is likely that Basil kept most active forces with him. The Varangian Guard, made up of foreigners loyal to the emperor with no prior ties to Roman society, gave Basil another advantage in facing down potential rivals. That had been their *original* function, after all. And the emperor's own unprecedented refusal to marry may also have stemmed from a fear of creating independent sources of influence in the palace, possibly also of giving one of the families a foothold in it. Psellos' portrait was correct at least insofar as this emperor was a micromanager.

The surest way to achieve social distinction in the empire was to obtain a court title or office. In the legislation of the Macedonian emperors, most of the "powerful" whose grasping must be curtailed are those who possess titles and offices. Therefore an emperor, especially a long-lived emperor such as Basil, had control over the composition of that group. He could not abolish the titles, which were the glue of the imperial system, but he could direct them to men who won his favor. Unfortunately, apart from the highest military offices, we have no information about how he used this leverage. There is slightly more evidence about his confiscation of property. All the cases mentioned in the sources—and they are few—concern men who opposed or betrayed him or the empire before the mid-990s, e.g., Lakapenos, Phokas, Davitʻ of Tao, Bobos,[58] and Eustathios Maleïnos. Skylitzes tells a striking story about Maleïnos. When the emperor was returning from his eastern incursion of 995, Maleïnos hosted and fed the entire army at his estates in Cappadocia. This display of resources, from one who had orchestrated the acclamation of Bardas Phokas at that very estate, so alarmed the emperor that he took Maleïnos with him to the capital, treating him generously but confiscating his property when he died. Basil, says Skylitzes, then passed a more draconian version of the land legislation, his law of January 996.[59]

We may be skeptical about the story. If the confiscation was historical, it sounds like the arrangement made with Davitʻ of Tao, another of Phokas' allies in 987–989. The arrangement with Maleïnos may have been made already in 989 when the revolt that Maleïnos backed had been defeated, in which case Basil was quartering his army on land that would eventually be imperial. Let us look at the 996 law, which was actually a bundle of measures that limited the ability of the powerful to appropriate the land of the poor by extending the latter's reclamation rights, reformed procedures for registering land boundaries that were cited in legal disputes, curtailed and reversed the takeover of villages by powerful bishops through local monasteries, extended the claim by the fisc to its own lands back to the time of Caesar Augustus, reformed the penalties for murder committed by men of rank, invalidated (again) grants made by Basileios Lakapenos that had not been subsequently confirmed by the emperor, and restricted the ability of the powerful to buy up local fairs.[60]

We have little evidence for the enforcement of this law or its effectiveness over time (it remained valid after the reign).[61] Conjectures about whether or not it stemmed the tide of the "powerful" are just that. Since socioeconomic history is beyond our reach, let us look instead at the emperor's rhetoric. He claims to be motivated by compassion for the poor and a care for the common interest, and he wants to embrace justice and curtail greed. There is a broad moral and political agenda here. Basil also claims to have investigated all matters in question and acquired extensive information about patterns of abuse. His sources are his own travels through the provinces (mentioned twice), court cases that have come before him, and subjects' petitions. The emperor is trying hard to make it seem as if his reforms are based on "data," though of course his information is ultimately anecdotal. He had traveled through Asia Minor only once as an adult, i.e., in the previous year (995). He narrates at length the case of a poor man who became rich and powerful and oppressed his fellow villagers; the emperor demolished his villa and demoted him to his former status. This story is told to illustrate the consequences of violation.[62]

The emperor possibly intended to intervene in socioeconomic trends but, if so, we hear of no effort of enforcement, such as we have when emperors tried out some new heresy for example. At the very least, the law of 996 reaffirmed the supreme power of the emperor as ultimate judge and gave him a weapon that he could use if it became necessary. It was a sword that he hung over the heads of potential trouble makers. This is symbolized dramatically in the extension of the rights of the imperial fisc back to the time of Caesar Augustus. Surely there was no paperwork going back a thousand years, but the choice was deliberate, as the period coincided with the entire duration of imperial authority, precisely what Basil was bolstering. A study of early Byzantine governance has argued that conflicting instructions coming from agents of the imperial government gave the emperors more power, as it established them as the ultimate arbiters of disputes over authority.[63] Basil observes in his law that few officers of the fisc execute their job in the interests of the fisc, as most take bribes or serve the interests of the powerful. The emperor claims the authority to overturn such corrupt decisions, creating uncertainty among his potential enemies. This is precisely the advice given to him by Skleros in Psellos: keep them busy worrying about their private affairs. Likewise, grants made by Lakapenos also had to be reconfirmed by the emperor.[64] The emperor was ostentatiously arming himself, both rhetorically and legally, against the powerful. As a modern historian has written, "it was a declaration of intent and of terror."[65]

Another law issued during the patriarchate of Sergios (999–1019), who twice protested against it in vain, is lost but summarized by Skylitzes. This was the *allelengyon*, or a provision "for mutual solidarity," which made the powerful liable for the taxes of the poor who died in war, thus requiring them to contribute to the villages' collective dues. Again, we have no information as to how this was enforced, or even its exact provisions. It seems to have been designed to generate revenue for the Bulgarian war, seeing as the emperor promised to repeal it after the conquest of Bulgaria, though he did not. A big deal is sometimes made of it by historians, as if it were a radical move in a class war. In fact, since late Roman times the tax liabilities on abandoned land that belonged to a village collectivity (fiscally defined) passed to the rest of the collectivity for a fixed period, unless an exemption was granted; neighboring private estates stood outside this system of collective responsibility. Basil was now partially puncturing that separation. This too has been seen as anti-aristocratic, but it may genuinely have been driven by wartime fiscal needs, and its biggest target was likely the Church, the largest provincial landowner.[66] Then, in 997, Basil induced the patriarch Sisinnios to pass an ecclesiastical decree that introduced more restrictions on marriages to in-laws; its purpose may well have been to "inhibit . . . the accumulation of inherited wealth among small groups of aristocratic families."[67]

Emperors since late antiquity had tried to curtail the power of their own functionaries and officers and the landowning appetite and tax exemptions of the Church and large monasteries. There was nothing new here. Basil was only reaffirming traditional imperial roles, in moral terms. He also sought to protect himself not against an alleged "landowning aristocracy" but rather a powerful class of army officers. The narrative was predominantly military-political, not socioeconomic. As we have seen, emperors from the "military families" who took the throne faced the same challenges and supported the same policies, only with Basil they took on a harsher edge.

CHAPTER 6

"No One Ever Saw My Spear at Rest"
Basil II (976–1025), Part III

The missing decade and conquest of Bulgaria, 1004–1018

With peace secured in the east in 1000–1001 and the annexation of Tao, our eastern sources for the reign of Basil dry up. But this was a front where we know that little happened to report. Not so Bulgaria. Here, after the mid-990s, our information comes exclusively from the later synopsis of Skylitzes, who badly garbles the chronology of 991–1003. Then, he omits the years 1003–1014, and picks up in the middle of the action in 1014, whereupon he provides a full (and linear) account of the fall of the Bulgarian state. As for the missing decade, Skylitzes says only that Basil continued to invade Bulgaria every year.[1] The intriguing suggestion has been made that in reality Basil and Samuil agreed to a peace during that decade, and so there was nothing to report, and that this peace treaty was later covered up.[2] This is certainly possible, but Skylitzes does sound as if he is summarizing a more detailed account of the war, which he bypassed to get to the death of Samuil. Meanwhile, it seems that the Bulgarians reversed the gains made by Basil in the first phases of the war, so Skylitzes possibly wanted to hide these embarrassments. Moreover, when the curtain rises in 1014, we are in the midst of war, not a new outbreak of hostilities, and positions had apparently shifted since 1003. Beroia, taken by the Romans in the early 990s, was now in Bulgarian hands; Skopje too, though Basil may have only sacked it when he captured tsar Roman, not occupied it. The armies in the final phase of the war seem to be engaged in familiar patterns of behavior, and were led by generals who had apparently made a name for themselves in the recent past, but whom we hear of only now.[3] Something had been happening.

In 1014, the border between the two states encircled Thessalonike. Samuil controlled Beroia, Moglena, Strumica, and Melnik. The action opens at the pass of Kleidion between the Strymon and Axios valleys. Samuil, with a large army, was holding it ably against Basil, when the Roman governor of Philippopolis, Nikephoros Xiphias, found a way around it to the south and fell on the Bulgarian army from behind, on July 29. Samuil and his son escaped the rout to Prilep, but Basil captured much of his army. We now read the most macabre report in Byzantine history. The emperor blinded them all, in total between fourteen thousand and fifteen thousand men, except for one out of every hundred, who was blinded in only one eye in order to lead the others home. Samuil, about seventy, fainted when he saw this horror and died of a heart attack two days later, on October 6.[4] He was buried in the church of St. Achilleios on the island in lake Prespa (Figure 7). Samuil's tomb was apparently excavated in 1965, and his seventy-year-old bones were found wrapped in gilded chain mail and garments woven of gold and silk.[5]

FIGURE 7 The church of St. Achilleios on an island in the small lake Prespa, burial place of the Bulgarian tsar Samuil (d. 1014). His bones were discovered there in 1969 along with gilded chain mail and a garment woven of gold and silk threads. Source: Shutterstock, ID 70750807.

The historicity of Basil's atrocity has been questioned.[6] We have seen repeatedly that he could resort to harsh punishments, but the figure seems vastly inflated: fifteen thousand casualties would have decimated Bulgarian military manpower, and yet the war continued without interruption. At the same time as the events at Kleidion, the *doux* of Thessalonike, Theophylaktos Botaneiates (grandfather of the future emperor), defeated an assault on the city by another Bulgarian army, and then joined Basil's advance on Strumica. Basil ordered the *doux* to clear the fortifications in the passes to Strumica, but he was caught in an ambush and killed. The emperor pulled back, going northeast to the fortress of Melnik, which his eunuch Sergios persuaded to surrender. Basil now retired to Mosynopolis, well within Roman territory, indicating that he did not believe he had gained a decisive advantage at Kleidion. It was here that he heard the news of Samuil's death. He immediately launched back into action, invading the region of Pelagonia, capturing Prilep and Štip and burning the palace at Bitola, before he returned to Thessalonike via Edessa, on January 9, 1015.[7]

Basil was now within striking distance of the enemy heartland; in the spring of 1015 he retook Edessa, which seems to have rebelled against him, and returned to Thessalonike. Unfortunately, we know nothing of the recent history of Edessa to interpret the significance of this event; it had been taken in the first phase of the war,[8] but possibly changed hands again. The emperor then moved north and captured Moglena by collapsing the walls with fire. He sent its able-bodied men to serve in the armies of Armenia, killed the rest of the population, and set fire to the fortress—more exemplary punishment. Meanwhile, Bulgarian leadership was crumbling into factions. Samuil was succeeded by his son Gavril Radomir (also called Romanos in Byzantine sources), who seems to have made some kind of peace overture to the emperor. But in the summer of 1015, he was murdered by his cousin Ivan Vladislav, the son of Samuil's brother (and victim) Aaron. Skylitzes reports that Ivan Vladislav also offered to surrender, but the plan was somehow a trick, and the interpolator of Skylitzes adds details about a Roman plan to assassinate Ivan Vladislav that backfired. It all makes little sense, and the war was soon on again anyway. Basil invaded Pelagonia, blinding all the prisoners he took. He captured Ohrid and was set to pursue Ivan Vladislav, who was threatening Dyrrachion, when an imperial army was destroyed in an ambush by one Ibatzes. Basil turned back but failed to catch Ibatzes, so he returned to Constantinople, in January 1016, via Thessalonike and Mosynopolis; meanwhile, he sent contingents to take smaller forts near Strumica and Serdica.[9]

We still have no information about the internal history of Bulgaria or its systems of military and provincial command. Skylitzes reports only one action by the emperor after the other. By this point in the war, Basil had driven a wedge through Bulgarian territory, between Albania, northern Epeiros, and western Macedonia on the one hand and western Bulgaria (around Sofia) on the other. In late 1016, Basil unsuccessfully besieged Pernik for three months. In the spring of 1017, he moved against Macedonia again, taking and burning the fort of Longos (location unknown), dividing the loot among the Varangians, the Romans, and himself. He also sent David Arianites and Konstantinos Diogenes (the *doux* of Thessalonike and father of the future emperor) to ravage Pelagonia. Basil then advanced on Kastoria, but decided it was impregnable and turned back. He received a report that the Bulgarian commander Krakras was planning 'an alliance with the Pechenegs to attack the lower Danube. However, this was foiled, possibly through diplomatic intervention. Basil was meanwhile reducing forts in western Macedonia, including Beroia. Ivan Vladislav attempted to ambush a Roman army, but was defeated when the emperor rushed to the rescue; he lost two hundred soldiers (a plausible figure) and retreated. Basil returned to the capital via Edessa on January 9, 1018.[10]

A month later, Ivan Vladislav was killed assaulting Dyrrachion. There was now a mad scramble on the part of the Bulgarian leadership to surrender to Basil, who was more than happy to receive them, give them titles, and accept their fortresses. Krakras sent his brother and son to the emperor at Adrianople to surrender Pernik. Basil advanced to Strumica via Mosynopolis, receiving delegations of surrender from Pelagonia, Strumica, the Bulgarian Church, and many fortresses. He granted high titles to the Bulgarian generals, even that of *patrikios*, and, at Skopje, appointed David Arianites as the first *katepano* of the new regional command of Bulgaria, with plenipotentiary powers. At Ohrid the population came out to acclaim the emperor, who received the treasury of the tsars and distributed it to his army. All the surviving members and children of Samuil's extended family were brought to Basil at Diabolis, where he received them on a podium, reassured them, and gave them Roman titles, sending them on to the capital. The general Ibatzes was hauled in too, after he had been captured and blinded in a commando operation by the governor of Ohrid, Eustathios Daphnomeles (who was now promoted to Dyrrachion). The Romans who had been taken prisoner by the Bulgarians were given the chance of staying or leaving, and the former *doux* of Thessalonike, Ioannes Chaldos, was freed after twenty-two years in captivity.[11]

Basil spent the remainder of that year establishing the new themes, commands, and fortifications of the Bulgarian provinces, laying down a solid foundation for the incorporation of new territory. Accompanied as always by his Varangians, his tour through Bulgaria reminds us of his tour of Tao and the east in 1000, eighteen years previously. Former royalty had to be accommodated, and a new governing class created through Roman titles and offices. He then traveled south from Kastoria to the battlefield on the Spercheios where Ouranos had defeated Samuil, and then on to Athens, where he gave thanks for his victory at the Parthenon, now a church of the Virgin. Only one emperor had come this far south in Greece in eight centuries (Konstas II, on his way to Italy). Then, in early 1019, Basil returned to the capital, entered through the Golden Gate, and celebrated a triumph like that of Tzimiskes, which featured the captive Bulgarian royal family.[12] This celebration marked the end of the Bulgarian war. Bulgaria would remain under Roman rule for 160 years, though pro-independence factions within it would soon instigate revolts.

The extent of Basil's conquests was not limited to the areas of conflict. His armies seem not to have gone farther north than Vidin (once) or northwest than Skopje. Yet after the fall of Bulgaria, Skylitzes says that Roman authority was recognized as far as Croatia, and when the ruler of Sirmium did not submit, he was murdered by Konstantinos Diogenes, who took over his city. It is unclear how the leap was made from Skopje to Sirmium, near Belgrade. Likely Samuil's state reached that far north. Diogenes was appointed governor of this distant province, as general of Serbia or commander of Sirmium.[13] Annexing territory that reached from the lower Danube to the Adriatic Sea and as far north as Hungary posed significant logistical and organizational challenges. It was the largest conquest the Romans had made in centuries, and, even though that territory had once been ruled by them, it had long been under foreign rule and probably only a small minority of its population would have been culturally Roman. Yet eastern Bulgaria had been already annexed and reorganized by Tzimiskes in 971, and seems to have been held by Samuil only between 986 and 1001; after that, eastern Bulgaria had been in Roman hands. What about the newly conquered regions?

Unfortunately, we do not have another *Taktikon*, as we did for the reign of Tzimiskes, listing all the new offices and regional commands. We have to rely on references in the historians and on seals, but many of them are from later in the eleventh century and so we cannot be sure that the new offices were established already by Basil. The overall command structure of the postwar Balkans followed the regular system of regional *doukes* with subordinate *strategoi* (generals). The latter were based in the main forts over whose possession the war was mostly fought. In addition, then, to the *doukes* of Adrianople and Thessalonike, Basil made a *doux* for Bulgaria based in Skopje (with *strategoi* at Ohrid, Diabolis, Kastoria, and others), and another command at Sirmium, whose rank, under Diogenes and his successors, is unknown. For what it is worth (not much), the *Chronicle of the Priest of Dioclea (Duklja)*, says that the conquest included Bulgaria, Serbia, Bosnia, and Dalmatia.[14] But the effective scope of the Sirmium command is unknown. It is unlikely to have encompassed direct control over the whole of southern Serbia, and likely to have been linked to other Roman command centers via the Danube and Velika Morava rivers. Maps that give to the empire almost the whole of the former Yugoslavia are exaggerated. In addition, later in the century we hear of a *doux* for the forts along the Danube (Paradounabon, or Paristrion), which some historians believe was instituted to deal with the later Pecheneg threat, but the command, if not the name, may go back to Basil II.[15] Some of its *strategoi* were posted at Preslav, Pliska, and Varna.

This command structure was managed flexibly, as in the east: important posts could be combined (e.g., Bulgaria and Thessalonike), or not filled if not necessary. *Doukes* seem to have been posted there more regularly in the middle of the century, when troubles began again.[16] Moreover, the posting of a general to a certain fort did not necessarily entail the creation of full-blown themes, as existed in the empire's core provinces, even if seemingly thematic terminology is used in the later sources. This was, at least at first, an army of occupation, not a local defense force.[17]

Governing a conquered land entailed more than just creating commands. What about the population? Unfortunately, we have little information about the identity of most of the subjects of the former Bulgarian empire, or whether even a majority identified as Bulgarian. Whoever they thought they were, Romans would not accept them as their own. Being Roman was not—contrary to what many historians assert—an imperial identity, such that merely being subject to the empire, or serving the emperor, automatically made one a Roman, even if one were Orthodox, as the Bulgarians and most of their subjects were. There was in addition a set of cultural attributes that marked Roman identity, including the Greek language. Romans and Bulgarians remained distinct categories under Byzantine rule in the Balkans, even if there was ambiguity in many settings. So Byzantium was now a proper imperial state, with Romans ruling non-Romans to a degree that had not been seen since antiquity. Still, it was always possible, and it did happen, for Bulgarians to become Romans by taking up service and, over the course of two generations, acquiring the cultural attributes of being Roman too. As we have seen, it was the policy of Basil to encourage the Bulgarian ruling class to do just that. Just as he had done in Tao, starting ten years before its annexation, he had, even while the Bulgarian war was raging, drawn in Bulgarian magnates with Roman titles and Roman prospects.[18]

Yahya says that Basil took over their forts, treated them generously, and gave them court titles corresponding to their former ranks. Still, he placed

Romans in charge of the key forts and dismantled the rest, so that they could not become centers of resistance. He sent out officers of the imperial fisc to manage the administration, and arranged for many marriages between leading Romans and Bulgarians (including of Roman women to Bulgarian men) "in order to put an end to their former mutual hatred."[19] The Continuator of Skylitzes says that Basil wanted the Bulgarians to continue living under their own customs and native leadership.[20] Specifically, he allowed them to continue paying their taxes in kind instead of coin, though presumably their economy would gradually catch up with Roman levels of monetization.[21] He reduced the Church of Bulgaria (at Ohrid) from a patriarchate to an archbishopric, postulating it as a continuation of Justiniana Prima and retaining it as autocephalous (albeit under the authority of the emperor, of course). The first appointee was a Bulgarian, Ivan of Debar (1019–1036), though he would be succeeded by a Roman.[22] Basil also issued three charters (*sigillia*) at Ivan's request that gave or confirmed the jurisdiction of the Bulgarian Church over a large territory including Ioannina, Kastoria, and other sees along the coast of modern southern Albania; Pelagonia, Beroia, Skopje, Strumica, Serdica, Vidin, and Niš in the central Balkans; Belgrade and Sirmium in the northwest; and Dorystolon (Dristra) in the northeast. The emperor states that he intended to preserve the Bulgarian Church as it was under Petar and Samuil, indicating that this ecclesiastical jurisdiction might mirror the extent of their former state.[23] But if the Bulgarian empire had reached as far north as Sirmium, most of the lands in between seem to have contributed little or nothing to its own war effort, and did not constitute a fallback position after the Roman victories in the south. It is likely that Bulgaria exercised as loose and distant a dominion over southern Serbia as Byzantium would now.

In the aftermath of the conquest and settlement, the presence of Roman authority would have been much thicker on the ground in eastern Bulgaria and the region defined by Thessalonike, Ohrid, and Skopje. Beyond that, in what is modern Albania and Serbia, it would likely have been limited to the uppermost levels of the provincial administration, plus a garrison, while everything below that was in local hands.[24] Presumably, the emperor retained most of the prior military and administrative structures, and even some of their personnel. The border between areas of more direct Roman control and de facto local control was possibly marked by a string of forts and watchtowers that runs from Kosovo to southern Serbia.[25] Farther away, among the "Croats" who allegedly "submitted" to Basil, we are probably dealing with local lords who were given court titles as a gesture (albeit not a guarantee) of friendship, and not to magistrates sent out from Constantinople.[26] Thus, imperial control became more attenuated and even symbolic the farther one went from Constantinople. Moreover, the apparatus of the new administration would have been introduced only gradually.

In the absence of information about the crucial decade 1003–1014, the war between Romanía and Bulgaria cannot properly be evaluated. Certainly, Bulgaria was the most formidable opponent of Roman arms at this time. On the eastern front, all that Basil had to do was show up in person and his enemies would withdraw. Yet in the Balkans, we know that protracted fighting between 991 and 1003 had resulted in the recovery of eastern Bulgaria and perhaps the security of southern Greece, but no decisive advantage against the core of Samuil's state, which was able to recover remarkably from setbacks. The war here consisted of sieges and ambushes, not pitched battles, and the two sides held their forts and mountain passes tightly against each other. Unlike the eastern emirates, Bulgaria was not a crumbling foe that fell quickly after being pummeled hard for three or four years. It is possible, despite the gap in Skylitzes' coverage, that this war did last for twenty-seven years if we count from 991, or thirty-two if from 986, longer than any other war in Roman history. It was certainly atypical for the Byzantine wars of conquest of the tenth century.

The war also served to enhance the emperor's relative power within the Roman polity, and not merely through the prestige and material spoils that came with victory. First, the autocephalous archbishopric of Ohrid was now effectively under the emperor's authority, not the patriarch's. Second, a sizable portion of the Bulgarian military nobility now entered imperial service and was dependent on the emperor's favor with no ties to the officer class of Asia Minor. And, third, the ongoing Balkan struggle and its opportunities for advancement enabled the emperor to build up a *Roman* military aristocracy dependent on him in this new zone of conquest and enrichment. It was in these campaigns that we first hear the names of families that would rise to the throne in the eleventh century (Diogenes and Botaneiates; the Komnenoi also were Basil's protégés). The emperor was effectively building up his own officer class, or military aristocracy. The imperial state was still shaping the social and political landscape.

Monitoring Aleppo, 1000–1025

During the 990s, Basil was committed to the Bulgarian war. His governors in the southeast (Bourtzes, then Dalassenos) both failed to maintain the status quo and secure northern Syria against Fatimid encroachment. The situation twice built up to a critical point that required Basil's whirlwind intervention. After 1000, Antioch was in the hands of Nikephoros Ouranos. The new framework for stability included the Fatimids as partners and lasted to the end of Basil's reign and beyond, but not without some tensions. These stemmed from the decline of the Hamdanid regime at Aleppo and the fact that it simultaneously recognized both the empire and Cairo. The emirate was becoming unstable, and each side tried to impose its own solution, though always from a distance. Basil did not have to intervene in person. By 1025, the status quo had returned more or less to what it had been in 1000, with minimal expense of Roman resources.[27]

The first decade of the eleventh century was relatively uneventful. At Antioch, Ouranos spent some of his time composing a long manual of military warfare that is only partially published.[28] Skylitzes, in the midst of his garbled reporting on the Bulgarian war, includes a notice that Ouranos fought two or three battles against Arab tribal raiders. These must date to the first half of the decade, as Ouranos is not attested after 1007.[29] The Hamdanid emir Abu al-Fada'il died in January 1002 and was succeeded by his two sons, but his minister Lu'lu' expelled them in 1004 and ruled Aleppo in his own name; the former emir's brother Abu al-Hayja' fled to Constantinople. This change of power excited little interest there or in Cairo, as Lu'lu' continued to serve both powers. In 1005, one al-Asfar began to preach holy war against the Romans and attracted armed followers, with whom he made incursions into the territory of Antioch. He was met by a *patrikios* named Bigas, who defeated him and pursued him to Saruj (in the Diyar Mudar, western Jazira). Here he gained support among the Numayr and Kilab tribes. Al-Asfar managed to flee after every defeat that Bigas inflicted on him, whereupon Lu'lu' intervened in early 1007 and mediated a solution: al-Asfar would be detained indefinitely in the citadel of Aleppo.[30] This is was what loyal clients were good for.

Lu'lu' died in 1008 and was succeeded by his son Mansur, under whose rule the emirate's decline accelerated. Specifically, the Kilab tribe under one Salih ibn Mirdas nibbled on Aleppan territory. This was Aleppan history, not Roman, so we need not discuss it in detail. The Romans and Fatimids struggled to ensure that they had clients among the competing factions. Basil did not object to the deposition of the Hamdanids in 1004. Then, in 1010, he was approached by leaders in Aleppo and among the Kilab who wanted to restore Abu al-Hayja', the grandson of Sayf al-Dawla, but the emperor initially did not wish to interfere. He was eventually persuaded to release Abu al-Hayja' by Mumahhid al-Dawla, the Marwanid emir of Diyar Bakr (whom Basil had made a *magistros* in 1000). In response to the invasion by Abu al-Hayja', Mansur brought in the Fatimids and bought off the Kilab, so Abu al-Hayja' had to flee. Basil refused him reentry after this debacle, but Mansur, wanting him out of Muslim lands, petitioned the emperor to take him back. Abu al-Hayja' returned to Constantinople, where he seems to have converted to Christianity.[31] As for Mansur, he now had to face the Fatimids and the Kilab. By 1014, having broken his agreements with the latter, he was besieged by them in Aleppo. He wrote to Basil for help, and received one thousand Armenians, who drove them out. But Salih, the leader of the Kilab, also wrote to the emperor, offered his submission, sent his son as a hostage, and recounted the treacheries his people had endured at Mansur's hands. Basil now reversed his stance again, recalled the Armenians, and ordered Mansur to honor his deal with the Kilab, who would receive half the lands of the emirate.[32] The emperor, busy with the war in Bulgaria, was backing anyone who asked for his help, ensuring that the victor would be his man in any case.

In January 1016, Mansur was expelled from Aleppo by his lieutenant Fath, who called in the Fatimids from Apameia but kept the citadel for himself. The emperor's response reveals the extraordinary discipline of the Roman state at this time and its impressive infrastructural capacity: from the Balkans, Basil prohibited travel and trade between the empire and Syria and Egypt, excepting only Salih and the Kilab from this embargo; he arranged for Mansur and his relatives to be maintained with a retinue at Antioch; and strengthened that city's walls, adding an impregnable citadel that impressed the crusaders later.[33] In Aleppo, Fath was bought off by the caliph al-Hakim and gave up the citadel to the hired general 'Aziz al-Dawla Fatik, in February 1017. It looked as if the Fatimids had finally won Aleppo. But it was not to last. In an amazing reversal, between 1017 and 1021 Fatik also rebelled against the impossibly unstable al-Hakim and offered his submission to the emperor, who now reopened the trade routes.[34] The status quo of 970 had been restored with little effort—beyond the discomfort of the trade embargo.

The reasons for Fatik's defection included the damage being done to the trade economy of Aleppo by the Roman embargo and the increasingly erratic nature of al-Hakim's caliphate. Al-Hakim (996–1021) was one of the most bizarre rulers in history.[35] He issued a stream of often inexplicable laws and regulations, and regularly executed his top officials, even for minor or perceived failings. No one felt safe. He also placed restrictions on Jews and Christians (who otherwise held high positions in society and the court), and caused many of their places of worship to be demolished, including, ca. 1009, the Holy Sepulcher in Jerusalem. The Byzantine ascetic Lazaros witnessed its destruction but then left Palestine because of the persecution of Christians. There is no evidence that Basil reacted to these events or posed in any way as a protector of Christians in the caliphate; the exchange of embassies and gifts continued as before. In 1013–1015, al-Hakim allowed Christians to emigrate from Egypt and Syria to Romanía and other Christian lands. After bribing in some cases the border guards to let them pass, they settled at Laodikeia, Antioch, and other Roman cities, especially in the years 1013–1015; among them was the future historian Yahya of Antioch.[36] Along with these Christians, then, al-Hakim drove Aleppo into the hands of Rome.

By 1020, it seemed that the empire and caliphate were heading for war. Al-Hakim was preparing for it, and Basil had just concluded the annexation of Bulgaria in 1019. According to Yahya, it was around this time that Giorgi I of Abkhazia and Kartli (Georgia) approached al-Hakim with an offer of alliance; Giorgi was contesting the Roman annexation of Tao.[37] Conversely, in early 1021, the Fatimid governor of the fort of al-Khawabi surrendered it to Basil along with the ruined coastal city of Maraqiyya.[38] By that point, the emperor was already marching through Asia Minor, albeit without revealing his destination to anyone. Many expected that he would return to Aleppo, twenty years after his last Syrian incursion. Along the way, he received the news of al-Hakim's death, or more accurately of his disappearance. For years the caliph had been in the habit of wandering alone at night outside Cairo. On February 13, 1021, he did not return.

The caliph's disappearance enabled former Fatimid rebels to return to the fold, including Fatik, the governor of Aleppo. However, he was assassinated in 1022, and a series of Fatimid governors were appointed in succession.[39] The emperor evinced no concern over this development; in fact, his policy was one of non-involvement. By 1024, the tribes had united against the Fatimids in Aleppo, but when Silah of the Kilab asked Basil, his former patron, for assistance, he refused on the grounds that they were rebelling against their lords (an excuse that he had used in 997 with Manju Takin).[40] In January 1025, Silah and his allies took the city, but not the citadel, and in the summer they asked for help from the *katepano* of Antioch, Konstantinos Dalassenos. He sent three hundred men, but when Basil found out he ordered him to recall them. Salih took the citadel anyway in June, establishing the Mirdasid dynasty of Aleppo. The emirate was again lost to the Fatimids, and posed no threat to the Romans. It had gone back to being a buffer state. It would be interesting to know when it had stopped paying the tribute stipulated in the treaty of Safar (of 970). If in 1000 Basil had decided that adverse developments in Syria would sooner or later correct themselves, he was right. Moreover, he kept the trade embargo against Egypt in place. A Fatimid embassy in the early 1020s, citing the caliph's restoration of Christian properties, failed to persuade him to lift it.[41]

The war with Abkhazia-Kartli and the last rebellion, 1021–1022

Marching through Asia Minor in 1021 when he learned of the caliph's death, the emperor detoured to the Caucasus—or had planned to go there from the start to bring Giorgi I to heel. Giorgi was the beneficiary of the plan hatched more than forty years earlier by Davitʿ of Tao to unite the thrones of Abkhazia, Kartli, and Tao in the person of Bagrat III (d. 1014), Giorgi's father. In 1000, as we saw, Upper Tao was claimed by Basil, and Bagrat was made *kouropalates*, the highest rank awarded by the court in the region. It seems that Basil also ceded to Bagrat some of the lands of Davitʿ of Tao, for when Bagrat died in 1014 Basil asked Giorgi, then a teenager, to return them. Giorgi (or his regime) refused, invaded Upper Tao sometime in the late 1010s, defeated a Roman army near Oltʿi, and occupied some of the lands of Tao.[42] Therefore, in Basil's eyes Giorgi was a trespasser and, worse, had tried in 1020 to make an alliance with al-Hakim. Moreover, there was now no Bulgarian war to hold the emperor back. The ensuing war against Abkhazia-Kartli activated a military theater that, during the past century, had seen action only briefly during the civil wars at the start of Basil's reign. Emperors had not personally led armies there in centuries. The Georgian and Armenian frontier had been mostly peaceful during the empire's expansion in the southeast and Balkans. What is amazing is that anyone would find it advisable to offend Basil at this point in his reign.

According to Aristakes, the emperor reached Basean and repeatedly sent envoys to Giorgi to settle the dispute, but was rebuffed every time. When his patience was exhausted, he ravaged Okomi, just to the east of Theodosioupolis (Erzurum), sending captives to Chaldia, and then he began to march northward, into Vanand (Kars); meanwhile, Giorgi burned some estates at Oltʿi and retreated north. While Giorgi's action reflects an understanding that he was about to lose Tao, it is unclear why Basil would ravage an area that would soon be his; possibly the locals had abetted the king's occupation of Tao. The Caucasian sources claim that Basil defeated Giorgi in a battle either by lake Pałakacʿis (modern Çıldır göl) or Širimni (south of Kars), and the Georgian king fled, whereas Yahya claims that Giorgi fled without fighting across a river that the Romans could not cross (the Kura or the Kʿcʿia). Either way, the emperor ravaged the region, took captives, and killed or blinded thousands of men. This was Basil in a wrathful mode. He went into winter quarters at Trebizond and reopened negotiations. The two armies were now separated by a considerable distance.[43] Yahya says that during the winter Giorgi consented to return the lands of Tao, surrender his son Bagrat as a hostage, and recognize the emperor as his suzerain. Basil, preparing a fleet against Abkhazia, accepted and sent officials to ratify the deal in the presence of the Georgian bishops.[44] No other source confirms this, though Yahya is a reliable and, in this matter, unbiased source, unlike the Caucasian chronicles.

The eastern campaign of 1021–1022 marked deep changes in Roman-Armenian relations as well. In a replay of the voluntary cession of Taron in 966, Senek‘erim (1003–1021), the king of Vaspurakan (an Armenian kingdom southeast of lake Van), decided to exchange the troubles of governing his weak and imperiled kingdom for the security, vast wealth, and titles for himself and his family that he could have within the empire. Senek‘erim had apparently been rattled by the first Turkish raid into the eastern Caucasus, so he gave his lands and those of his vassals to the emperor. The exact date of his offer is not clear, but lies between 1019 and 1021 (the offer may have been made earlier with the actual transfer taking place when the emperor was there). Already in 1015, the emperor had transferred the Bulgarian soldiers that he captured in the fortress of Moglena to Vaspurakan, where Aristakes complains that they behaved badly.[45] Thus a conduit already existed. Senek‘erim was given extensive estates around Sebasteia in Cappadocia, likely from crown lands, and possibly even made the governor of the theme. Basil turned Vaspurakan into a *katepanaton* and sent Roman officers to take over its fortresses. The first *katepano* was Basileios Argyros, but he somehow made a mess of it and was replaced with Nikephoros Komnenos.[46] Chalcedonian ecclesiastical sees were established in the main centers of the new territory. Moreover, the territory nominally ceded to the empire by Senek‘erim included towns (such as Arčeš and Berkri along the north coast of lake Van) that were under the control of small Arab emirates. The empire would pick those up piecemeal during the following decade.[47]

Another Armenian kingdom that was pledged to Rome in the winter of 1021–1022 was that of Ani. The Bagratid kingdom of Armenia had split between two brothers, Smbat III and Ašot IV, who spent most of their time fighting each other. During that winter, Smbat III, lord of Ani, sent the *katholikos* of the Armenian Church, Petros, to the emperor with a binding pledge to cede his realm to Rome on his death (in 1041, as it turned out). Skylitzes claims that he had sided with Giorgi in the first phase of the war and was now terrified of the emperor. The latter gave him the title of *magistros* and appointed him ruler of Ani for life.[48] All this replayed Davit‘ of Tao in 990.

Another surprising development of that eventful winter was a blast from a distant and, to the emperor, wholly unwelcome past: a rebellion of army officers led by Nikephoros Phokas and Nikephoros Xiphias. The first represented the old families that Basil had suppressed, being the younger son of Bardas Phokas. He had participated in his father's rebellion of 987–989, but is not mentioned again until the spring of 1022. The second represented the new officer class that Basil had built up. He was a hero of the Bulgarian war, instrumental in the defeat of Samuil at Kleidion in 1014. In 1022 he was the general of the Anatolikon theme.[49] The two rebelled in Cappadocia in 1022, precisely when Basil was reengaging with Giorgi, and it was rumored that they sought an alliance with the Abkhazian.[50] Byzantine rebels, the Phokades in particular, had a nasty habit of rebelling when the empire was at war (which would prove disastrous in the later eleventh century). Their aim, to seize power, was straightforward. The political culture of the empire was based on periodic stress tests: emperors perceived to be weak faced challengers willing to take a risk. Given Basil's record, and in hindsight, this risk seems akin to madness. But they must have thought he was vulnerable, and not only because he was at war. Their reasoning likely had to do with the succession. Basil was now in his midsixties, had never married, and had not designated an heir. The future was unclear. Xiphias, who held office, invited Phokas to join him and lend him the prestige of his name, which would ensure continuity with the past in the eyes of the army. Phokas, a mere titular, was initially Xiphias' mascot, but soon eclipsed Xiphias, making him jealous.[51]

Basil was now caught between two hostile forces. He tried to turn the rebels against each other by dispatching Theophylaktos Dalassenos, the son of the former *doux* of Antioch, with money and letters to subvert their followers. Skylitzes says that Xiphias had Phokas killed. Aristakes says that Phokas was killed by Davitʻ, the son of the former king of Vaspurakan, Senekʻerim, who had relocated to Cappadocia and taken up with the rebels, but now changed sides. Either way, Phokas died on August, 15, 1022, suggesting that he was taken at a religious event (that is the date of the major festival of the Assumption of Mary). His head was sent to Basil, who displayed it to the army, confirming the loyalty of his soldiers, many of whom were wavering. Dalassenos arrested Nikephoros Xiphias and sent him in chains to Constantinople, where he was tonsured by one Ioannes (the eunuch brother of the later emperor Michael IV). At this time, and possibly also when he returned to Constantinople in 1023, the emperor executed some conspirators and confiscated their property. Allegedly he fed a chamberlain accused of trying to poison him to a lion. In the end, as Aristakes said, the revolt had been built on sand.[52]

Phokas' head was sent on to Giorgi of Abkhazia. This signaled the emperor's belief that the king had also been involved in the rebellion, thereby canceling the agreement made between them the previous winter.[53] The war with Abkhazia-Kartli was on again. Basil marched into Basean, capturing forts that had been granted to Davitᶜ of Tao for the duration of his lifetime but that had been seized by various Georgians since 1000. He sent envoys to Giorgi demanding that the other forts be surrendered as well. The king agreed, but this was only a ruse as he planned to ambush the emperor. The ambush was badly executed, with the Romans routing and slaughtering the Abkhazians and Georgians. Basil seized the royal treasure and allegedly ordered his men to cut off the heads of the slain and pile them up in heaps. This was in the fall of 1022. Giorgi now sued for peace, gave up his son Bagrat among the hostages as had been agreed during the previous winter, and surrendered the requested forts. The emperor made no additional demands, and promised to release the hostages after three years (which he did). All things considered, Giorgi got off lightly. Before his death in 1025, Basil even released the young Bagrat.[54]

It was certainly at this time, if not already in 1000, that Basil created the *katepanaton* of Iberia (Georgia in Greek). From the site of his victory, Basil marched to Vaspurakan, probably to put its administration into order and deal with whatever problem had been troubling Senekᶜerim before his abdication. This problem lay in the plain of Her (Khoy, north of lake Urmia, Iran), but the identity of the enemy ("Persians") remains unclear. The local emir agreed to pay tribute, whereupon Basil returned to Constantinople, probably in early 1023.[55] In 1024 (probably), the *katepano* of Vaspurakan, Komnenos, annexed Arčeš, on the north coast of lake Van, from its (unspecified) Muslim ruler.[56]

The apogee of Byzantine Italy

The long reign of Basil witnessed the ultimate extension and consolidation of Byzantine power in southern Italy.[57] The defeat of Otto II's effort to conquer the south in 982 had ruined the Saxon cause, temporarily halted Arab raiding from Sicily, and cowed the Lombard duchies. The *katepano* had advanced to Ascoli and Trani, and a pro-Byzantine pope, Boniface VII, had briefly imposed himself in 984. In the ensuing peace, the Byzantines consolidated their position, though Arab raids were always a fact of life in southern Italy.[58]

In 992, the emperor made a treaty with Venice, which was beginning to expand its trading interests eastward under doge Pietro Orseolo II (991–1008). The Venetians received favorable toll rights at Constantinople and Abydos in exchange for helping to transport imperial armies to Italy.[59]

Venice was already one of the most important centers for trade between east and west, benefiting from the disruptions caused by the Magyars to the overland route, and it was positioned to dominate the Adriatic, which, in 970, ibn Hawqal called the Bay of the Venetians.[60] It is unclear to what degree the Venetians yet believed that they were a fully autonomous political community, though they did make separate deals with the western and eastern emperors. From the Byzantine point of view, they were a minor if useful peripheral power well within the orbit and the rights of the empire. Their ruler (a *doux*) was occasionally rewarded with court titles just as were his Armenian and Georgian counterparts in the east.[61] The "treaty" of 992 took the form of a concession of benefits from the emperor to foreigners (*extranei*) who were loyal to the empire, not a deal between equals. The Venetians did help lift a siege of Bari by the Arabs of Sicily in 1002, an intervention that is still celebrated in Bari in the Vidua Vidue festival: "Look, Look! The Venetians are coming!" This was in the latter's interests, of course, but it was rewarded. In 1004–1006, the doge's son Giovanni was made a *patrikios* at Constantinople and married to Maria, sister of Romanos Argyros (the future emperor); it should be noted that the Argyroi siblings were descended, like the emperor himself, from Romanos I and could therefore be considered part of the extended dynasty. Maria was pregnant when the couple came to Venice and gave birth to a son who was named Basileios after his uncle or even the emperor, but the entire family died in an epidemic in 1006.[62]

The emperor made overtures to his western counterpart, Otto III, the son of Theophano, Otto II's Skleraina bride (who had died in 991). These took place against the backdrop of events at Rome involving Ioannes Philagathos, one of the colorful figures of this period. Philagathos was a Byzantine from Rossano who rose at the court of Otto II through Theophano's patronage and was appointed bishop of Piacenza. In 995, he was dispatched by the fifteen-year-old Otto III to Constantinople to secure a marriage alliance, and he stayed there until 997. He returned to Rome and joined the Crescentii faction that drove out pope Gregory V, Otto's own cousin. With the support of the Romans and, it was rumored in the west, of the Byzantine emperor, Philagathos was proclaimed pope as John XVI. This was the second pope in the past two decades to come directly from the court in Constantinople. We happen to have the letters of Leon of Synada, Byzantine envoy to Rome, who participated in the intrigues that placed Philagathos on the papal throne, though he knew that the man was a scoundrel: "I know that you're laughing at me but I suspect that you'll roar when you hear that I appointed Philagathos pope—when I ought to have strangled him and said 'serves him right!'" Leon claimed that he wanted to see Basil II rule in Rome, but admits that publicizing his own missives would embarrass the emperor. At any rate, ten months later, in 998, Otto III came to Rome in person and deposed this "antipope," mutilating him badly.[63] He made no move against Byzantine territory and continued the negotiations for a bride. These paid off by January 1002, when a bride was brought to Bari. She was a daughter of the co-emperor Konstantinos VIII, either Zoe or Theodora. At Bari, however, the delegation received the news of Otto's premature death, and so the princess went home.[64] Whichever she was, she was destined to play a crucial role in the politics of the empire.

Overall, momentum in Italy was on the Byzantine side, even during the Bulgarian war. "It was now that Byzantium began truly to leave marks on the landscape and culture of southern Italy."[65] However, the symbiosis of Lombards and "Greeks" in Apulia was always tense. Local chronicles record the murder of imperial officials by Lombards in Bari in the 980s and 990s and the retribution by other officials. There was even an abortive attempt by one Lombard to turn Bari over to the Arabs.[66] Unfortunately, it is impossible to identify factions, parties, or political-ideological goals behind these events. The most significant challenge to the Byzantine order was the two-part rebellion of one Melo of Bari (Meles in Greek), who was later claimed as a Lombard liberator and an Armenian (as are all Byzantines sooner or later).[67] Melo rallied enough supporters to occupy Bari in 1009 and defeat imperial armies. The *katepano* Ioannes Kourkouas died during the rebellion and was replaced by Basileios Argyros-Mesardonites, the brother of Romanos Argyros and Maria (who had recently married the Venetian doge's son). Mesardonites retook the city in June 1011 and Melo fled to Benevento, but his wife and infant son Argyros were captured and sent to Constantinople (that son would play a prominent role later on). Mesardonites fortified the governor's headquarters (*praitorion*) by the harbor at Bari. We have an iambic inscription by Mesardonites likely dedicating this construction.[68]

But Melo was not finished. After seeking help in the German empire, he made a second attempt in 1017, this time with the endorsement of pope Benedict VIII. While infiltrating the Byzantine provinces, he also made some new friends, Normans who were said to be returning from a pilgrimage. Though the meeting was embellished by later legend, his use of Norman mercenaries was a baneful sign of things to come. In battles at Arenula, Civitate, and Vaccarizza, reported differently in the Latin sources, the armies sent and then personally commanded by the *katepano* Leon "Kontoleon" Tornikios failed to defeat Melo. Tornikios was recalled—the emperor Basil was now wrapping up the Bulgarian war across the Adriatic—and replaced by Basileios Boioannes, one of the most able officers of the age. He brought money and Varangians, and crushed Melo in battle near Cannae in October

1018, the site of the famous defeat of Rome by Hannibal. The rebel fled to Bamberg, where the German emperor Heinrich II optimistically made him *dux Apuliae*, but Melo died in 1020.[69] We see that with the end of the Bulgarian war, money and armies were being sent to the other trouble spots along the periphery, including Italy and then Georgia.

Boioannes would govern the south until 1028, an unprecedented tenure. He fortified many sites and established settlements along the border with the north and the main roads to prevent further invasions; these included Troia, Dragonara, Melfi, and Civitate, and the region would become known as Capitanata. He encouraged Lombards from outside the empire to settle there and live under their own laws, though according to the contemporary French monk Adémar of Chabannes he closed the border to Norman pilgrims, even arresting any who reached it and sending them to Constantinople (it is interesting to note that the emperor had at that very time closed the eastern border with Egypt and Syria too).[70] Boioannes made an alliance with Pandulf IV, the duke of Capua, who recognized the emperor's suzerainty and in 1021, on the *katepano's* orders, captured Melo's brother Datto, who was holed up at Garigliano. Even Salerno seems to have been won over. All this worried the German emperor Heinrich II, who rushed to the south in 1021–1022. However, his expedition achieved little. For three months the German army made no progress against the walls of Troia. At Capua, Heinrich replaced the pro-Byzantine Pandulf IV with the pro-German Pandulf V (the count of Teano), taking the former with him back to Germany. But Heinrich died in 1024, whereupon Pandulf IV was released and regained his duchy in 1026, with the *katepano's* blessing and the help of Norman mercenaries. Capua returned to the Byzantine fold, and Byzantine sources boasted that all of Italy up to Rome was now subject to the emperor.[71]

In 1023, Boioannes built new fortifications at Mottola after an Arab attack on Bari that year. In 1024, the *katepano* took an extraordinary step: he crossed the Adriatic and invaded Croatia. He captured the wife and son of king Krešimir III (1000–1030) and sent them to Constantinople (whose hostage housing was filling up with the families of enemies and rebels from Bulgaria, Croatia, Aleppo, and Bari, among others). Why Croatia? The background was likely the emperor's plan to invade Sicily next. Having prevailed in every other corner of his empire, Basil wanted to bring the war to Sicily, as Nikephoros Phokas had twice tried to do. The far west was always the last priority. Boioannes' aim was probably to subject Croatia and resolve the dispute that had flared up between it and Venice over the coastal Dalmatian towns. For the emperor to convey a large fleet across the Adriatic, that sea would have to be pacified. Boioannes then fortified Reggio and crossed to

Messina. An advance imperial force, including Varangians and Bulgarians, arrived under the *protospatharios* Orestes.[72] But news then arrived that the emperor had died, in December 1025, and the expedition was canceled. Boioannes stayed in Italy until 1028. He was one of the most competent officials of Basil's reign and laid down the foundation for a twenty-year peace in the south past his own tenure of office.

The end of an era

Basil died on December 12, 13, or 15, 1025, at the age of sixty-seven, while preparing for the Sicilian campaign. In his last days, he summoned his brother Konstantinos VIII, who was living outside of Constantinople, and asked not to be buried in imperial regalia or, as had been planned, in the imperial mausoleum of the Holy Apostles. Instead, he was to be buried by the church of St. John the Theologian at the site known as the Hebdomon, the military mustering grounds seven miles from the city, from where the army began its triumphal processions to the Golden Gate of the City.[73] This marked the military, rather than Constantinopolitan, tenor of his reign. His verse epitaph survives, and highlights his tireless execution of the duty to protect his people:

> The emperors of old allotted to themselves different burial-sites: some here, others there; but I, Basil the purple-born, erect my tomb in the region of Hebdomon. Here I rest, on the seventh day, from the numerous toils I bore and endured on the battlefield, for from the day when the King of Heaven called upon me to become emperor, the great overlord of the world, no one saw my spear lie idle. I stayed alert throughout my life and protected the children of New Rome, valiantly campaigning both in the West and at the outposts of the East, erecting myriads of trophies in all parts of the world. And witnesses of this are the Persians and the Skythians, together with the Abkhazian, the Ismaelite, the Arab, and the Iberian. O man, seeing now my tomb here, reward me for my campaigns with your prayers.[74]

Soon after his death, and certainly during the chaos and defeat of the later eleventh century, Basil came to be regarded as one of the greatest emperors of all time. By the twelfth century he was being called "the Bulgar Slayer," a name that stuck.[75] Ultimately, however, Basil's mind, and even his personality, remain inscrutable. He often resorted to exemplary and cruel punishment, but his first instinct was usually to woo adversaries into submission and to reward them with titles and offices. Basil did his job well, preferring obedience over praise from his subjects and actual power over its trappings and theater. He was known for his loud belly laughs and witty sayings.[76]

It had been an extraordinary half-century. Basil reigned longer than any emperor before or after him and had wielded power in person longer than any since Justinian in the sixth century. Like Justinian, he "looked closely into every matter, whether great or small."[77] Roman politics, as we have seen, were driven by a dynamic competition of interests and powers, but his reign witnessed an unprecedented concentration of power into the hands of one man. All the other voices, which expressed alternative articulations of power, fell silent. The people of Constantinople were quiet; the patriarchs were docile non-entities; there were no palace coups or eunuch handlers after 985; there were no empresses, mistresses, or heirs to cause trouble; and the army was brought to heel, excepting the surprising revolt of 1022. This was a reign stripped down to the essentials: just the emperor and the army, both away from the capital much of the time. By 1025, few would be alive who remembered the politically turbulent reigns of Phokas and Tzimiskes. Basil outlived that generation and buried its last representatives. He created his own ruling group, which was loyal to him and would provide the empire's leadership for the future. He conquered Bulgaria and parts of Armenia and Georgia, and absorbed their elites into the imperial system. In true Byzantine fashion, he posted Iberians to the Balkans, Bulgarians to Vaspurakan, and kept Varangians, some of them still heathens, always by his side.

What about high culture? Almost half a century after Basil's death, the historian Michael Psellos looked back to him as a model emperor when it came to the army and the treasury, but noted that he generally scorned literature and intellectual life. There were men of letters during the reign, Psellos says, only the emperor did not sponsor them. But this is not entirely true. We have a brief speech praising him by Leon the deacon (who was hostile to him in his *History*), and Ioannes Sikeliotes refers to an address that he gave at the emperor's express command.[78] The poet Ioannes Geometres continued to write after the end of the rebellions but was not favorably disposed toward him. Byzantine scholarship produced some major works at this time, including the classical dictionary *Souda*, featuring more than thirty thousand entries on words, people, authors, and phrases. This was the belated fruit of the project set in motion by Konstantinos VII, and it is still a standard reference work among classical scholars. However, its editors appear to have received no help from Basil II. Probably the most important writer of the reign was Symeon (949–1022), later canonized as the New Theologian (meaning "most recent," to distinguish him from the Apostle John and also Gregory of Nazianzos). Symeon was a monastic leader who wrote hymns and treatises and was among the first Byzantines to make the case for a direct, personal, and spiritual apprehension of God under the aspect of divine light, what today is typically called "mysticism." There is no evidence that the emperor took an interest in his career or thought. Instead, Symeon had powerful enemies in the Church, and in 1009 they brought about his downfall and exile from the capital.

By contrast, a work possibly commissioned by Basil II toward the end of the tenth century was a new edition of 148 saints' lives by Symeon Metaphrastes (possibly the historian and high official who flexibly served both the Macedonian dynasty and Nikephoros II). The goal of this ten-volume *Menologion* was not only to collect but to upgrade the stylistic register of many texts, arranged around the liturgical calendar. There are two other famous liturgical manuscripts associated with Basil II, and in this one area of Byzantine life we may approaching the emperor's cultural interests. One manuscript (Vat. gr. 1613), often called the "Menologion of Basil II," is actually a *synaxarion*, i.e., it consists of brief entries on the saints in the order of the liturgical calendar. Some 430 of them are illustrated in lavish color and can now be viewed online through the Vatican library website. One is struck by the repeated emphasis on gruesome violence inflicted by Roman authorities on Christian martyrs, similar to the violence that Basil himself had inflicted on obstinate enemies throughout his reign. The other manuscript (Marc. gr. 17, Venice) is a Psalter (a liturgical book with hymns). On the frontispiece, it contains the famous image of Basil II in military attire (Figure 8). Basil is holding a spear, crowned by an angel, surrounded by military saints, and towering over prostrate subjects. This used to be seen as the moment of his triumph over the Bulgarians, but it is probably a generic image of the emperor's power. The people on the ground before him can be defeated (Roman) rebels or his subjects generally.[79] It is a fitting image indeed for the way the regime evolved after 989.

The history of Roman society in the core provinces of the empire during this half-century is an almost complete blank, with the exception of stray details provided by saints' lives.[80] In part, this was because historians were generally drawn to dramatic conflict, and there was little of that within the empire after 989. This was an era of peace and prosperity, especially for Asia Minor, despite the military nature of the regime, which was waging the longest war in Roman history. Yahya says that Basil left behind 6,000 *qintar* (*kentenaria*) of gold in the treasury (i.e., 43.2 million coins) whereas he had found only 4 *qintar* when he took power.[81] Psellos similarly claims that just by cutting expenses Basil amassed 200,000 talents (i.e., 14.4 million coins) to which he added the plunder of his foreign wars and the confiscated

FIGURE 8 Image of Basil II from the frontispiece of his Psalter (Marc. gr. 17, Venice). Source: Werner Forman/Art Resource NY.

properties of defeated rebels. The emperor constructed spiral underground vaults in which to store his treasure, and hardly spent any of it.[82]

Yet Basil only subdued the rival centers of power that emperors normally confronted; he did not eliminate them. They would return in force in the eleventh century as soon as they sniffed weakness around the throne—and all subsequent emperors were weaker than Basil II.

General Considerations
The Age of Conquest

B Y 1025, THE empire had almost three centuries of gradual expansion and consolidation of territory behind it. The Isaurian emperors of the eighth century held ground against the Bulgars and Arabs, and their successors in the ninth and tenth reabsorbed Greece and Romanized most of its Slavic settlers. Basileios I conquered Tephrike in 879, and Kourkouas conquered Melitene in 934. But the conquests of 955–1025 were on a different scale. The empire reaped the benefits of its superior military organization and administrative infrastructure in a time of economic expansion, and faced enemies in decline, especially in the east. But if we look closely, we do not find a coherent policy of imperial expansion; there was no dream of empire or enduring love of conquest. What we find are variable and contingent responses to geostrategic opportunities. The three main zones of expansion—the Muslim southeast, the Armenian and Georgian east, and Bulgaria—had little in common in terms of strategy, history, and outcome. And different emperors had different priorities and approaches.

Specifically, the regime of Nikephoros Phokas (both before and while he was emperor) identified the emirates of Crete, Cilicia, and Aleppo as threats to imperial security. Their fleets and armies raided Roman provinces, disrupted economic life, and took captives. They also threatened major cities. In contrast to his father Bardas, as *domestikos* Nikephoros decided on their systematic and total destruction, which he achieved, except in the case of Aleppo, which was reduced to a tributary state. In a remarkable concentration of sustained violence over the course of fifteen years, Phokas defeated Sayf al-Dawla, took Crete and Cyprus, ravaged

Cilicia, seized and plundered Aleppo, and finally conquered Cilicia and Antioch. Truces were only temporary in this struggle; it was to the death. The Muslims of Cilicia were mostly expelled or converted, and the new military themes settled with Romans, Syrian Christians, and Armenians. Few Arabs were brought onside with offices and titles, unlike what would happen later in Bulgaria and Georgia-Armenia.

Phokas was murdered by Tzimiskes, so we do not know what he would have done next. I suspect that he would have stopped the Roman momentum along this front, just as his associate Tzimiskes did. To hold Cilicia he needed Antioch, which was, moreover, a tempting target in itself with a large Christian population. But that was likely as far as Phokas would go. The Romans took Aleppo twice, but the emirate could not realistically be conquered. It was too large, exposed to Mesopotamia, and overwhelmingly Muslim. At best, Aleppo could be neutralized as a tributary buffer state, which is what it became. The Romans made no move to change this arrangement after 970. Basil II could have easily conquered Diyar Bakr and Aleppo, but he showed no interest in this: the costs and complications would have outweighed the benefits. But Tzimiskes also was not interested in permanent conquest here. Like Basil, he too raided Syria (twice) only to intimidate and plunder. In sum, despite the occasional fanfare, the burst of conquest along this front had limited objectives. The Romans resumed their defensive strategy as soon as they established a more practical and advantageous status quo. As part of the new arrangement, they remained on good terms with the Marwanid emirs of Diyar Bakr. Mumahhid al-Dawla was given a high title and Roman office, and brought onside. The emperors wanted to secure Romanía against attack, not conquer Muslim lands, which would have excited more holy war against the Christians.

Bulgaria was a wholly different situation. There was no need for Rome to be at war with it, and in fact the two states had enjoyed peaceful relations for more than forty years before Tzimiskes' invasion of 971. Moreover, that invasion was aimed primarily at the Rus' and we can hardly blame the Romans exclusively (as is often done) for the Rus' presence south of the Danube. Tzimiskes' war left the Romans in control of eastern Bulgaria, which was now exposed to attack from the reconstituted Bulgarian state in the west. It is unlikely that this tense situation could have been resolved peacefully without the Romans' surrendering eastern Bulgaria, and this was unlikely to happen. Unfortunately, we know nothing about any substantive communications between the two states after 971. We do not know what Basil and Samuil had to say to each other. Put differently, we do not know why each of them thought that he was at war, which is why this war has been so often psychologized as a personal obsession of Basil brought on by his defeat in 986.

In reality, initial hostile moves on both sides would have led to a cycle of counterraids. We also know little about the actual course of the war until 1003 and nothing about it in 1004–1013 (even whether it was still being waged). Still, the differences with the conquest in the east are striking. Bulgaria was a peer state and a far more formidable opponent than anything in the east. Also, one of the emperor's main tactics was to woo Samuil's nobles away from him with titles and offices. This also did not happen much in the east. And the postconflict settlement required no changes in the demographic and religious makeup of the new territories. In summary, Tzimiskes was sucked into a partial conquest of Bulgaria in 971, and this unresolved situation pulled the Romans into a broader conflict. Although we cannot begin to fathom Basil's strategy and objectives during those thirty years, it has been suggested that annual campaigns in the Balkans helped him to consolidate his own hold on the Roman army, which was the main threat to his throne, and keep it preoccupied far from the bases of its traditional officer class.[1]

The Georgian-Armenian frontier, by contrast, had been peaceful since the wars of Ioannes Kourkouas in the area. The Romans had no reason to expect a hostile move from this direction. They played a completely different game with the Georgian and Armenian realms, which had always oscillated between Rome and its eastern neighbor, but with the dramatic decline of the Abbasid caliphate during the tenth century they had inevitably drifted further into the orbit of Rome. We see in Konstantinos VII's *De administrando imperio* that the court was developing a language of imperial suzerainty over some of them—a fiction, certainly, but one that could prove advantageous in the right circumstances and facilitate cooptation. Even before our period, the emperors were happy to receive the service of Georgian and Armenian elites and to settle their peoples in the new smaller themes along the frontier. Religious differences were ignored in these processes, though biases persisted; the average Roman held negative stereotypes about Armenians. He and they were not by any means interconvertible, as many historians assume.

There is no evidence that the Romans had a master plan to annex the Caucasian principalities, as is sometimes alleged.[2] There were many moments during this period when they could have done so by force, but did not. In fact, they never expressed a desire to place them under direct Roman rule. Taron and Vaspurakan were, as far as we can tell, voluntarily surrendered by native rulers who thought that they were getting a better deal by exchanging them for wealth and status within the empire. We know almost nothing about their prior circumstances, so we cannot cross-check their cost-benefit analysis. Kekaumenos, the author of a book of maxims written in the 1070s, advised local lords to keep their lands rather than trade them for money and titles; better to be free and small than a lordly subject, he argued. So do not visit the court often, he added, because they will induce you to come back with more gifts and then one day you will find that you cannot leave.[3] But this moralizing works better in theory, and the author may not have understood the challenges these local lords faced at home. At any rate, there was no imperial violence in the case of Taron and Vaspurakan, while the empire presented irresistible attractions to their rulers.

Tao and Ani were given up in a different manner: their rulers picked the wrong side to back in a Roman war (though for Ani in 1022 only Skylitzes claims that), and they bequeathed their lands to the empire, the transfer to take effect when they died. Here too we do not see a Roman imperative to conquer, only an administrative arrangement, as if this were a real-estate transaction made in a buyer's market. These were mergers, not conquest, and took place because local elites hoped to benefit. Integration was already advanced. The Bagratid kingdom did not mint its own coins; after the reign of Nikephoros Phokas, it had relied almost exclusively on Roman ones. In the meantime, before transference, the emperors had already built up a body of native title holders by which to govern the new provinces but also to govern other regions of the Roman empire itself. These were lucrative opportunities for local lords. It is not clear, on the other hand, what emperors gained through these annexations. Strategically, there was no enemy in this direction—at least not yet—and the Romans were taking on the task of administering and governing fractious lands. If there was profit to be made here, we cannot calculate its worth. We know of no Roman who got rich through these new acquisitions. One benefit for the emperors would have been a new pool of potential army officers to counterbalance and disrupt the entrenched domestic officer class.

In sum, the strategic dimension and driving dynamics of conquest were entirely different in the Muslim southeast, in Bulgaria, and in Georgia-Armenia.

Let us consider now the effect on the empire itself. In 955, Romanía was relatively homogeneous. There were some Slavic ethnic minorities in Greece and the Peloponnese, Lombards in Apulia, and some Armenian and other foreign populations along the eastern frontier, but otherwise the population of the so-called empire consisted overwhelmingly of Greek-speaking Orthodox Romans (in Greek, one can take the *basileia* of the Romans to be the national kingdom of the Romans). Unlike actual empires, there was no ethnic, religious, linguistic, or cultural distinction between rulers and the vast majority of subjects. By 1025, however, the balance had moved in the direction of multiethnic empire. The territory ruled from New Rome had expanded by a third. Crete and Cyprus were mostly Roman in population already. But most inhabitants of the Bulgarian state were not Roman, and neither were those of Armenia and Georgia. Antioch was mostly Chalcedonian Christian, albeit Arabic-speaking, mixed with Roman settlers and immigrants from Syria and Egypt.[4] There were also Syrian Monophysites and Muslims. Many small frontier themes were settled by Romans and Armenians. Byzantium was more of a multiethnic empire now than it had ever been, even though in relative terms it still did not match the diversity of most multiethnic empires in history.

The Roman polity had a long record of absorbing and assimilating foreign people, and making Romans out of them. After all, this had happened already in antiquity to the ancestors of the Byzantine Romans, the inhabitants of Greece and Asia Minor. Over the centuries since, the empire had taken in numerous foreign groups, settling them on its lands and registering them in its army and tax rolls. After converting to Orthodoxy and learning Greek, these groups often disappear from the record after a few generations, i.e., they were absorbed into the general Roman background.[5] It is a legacy of nineteenth-century racial nationalism that historians still ethnicize the Byzantines, saying for instance that some general or emperor "was really" an Armenian on the basis of a conjecture about the etymology of his name, even when his family had been in the empire for centuries; when his cultural profile was Roman; and when there is no evidence of Armenian identity or cultural traits. (Race is essentialized in this way only for the putative ancestors of modern nations, not, say, for assimilated Goths or Pechenegs.) But if there was one thing that Romanía was good at compared to all other empires, it was successfully fostering "a more or less homogeneous set of political values and ideological identities out of a range of different sociocultural formations."[6]

We observe the initial stages of this process during the conquest itself. Basil won over many leading Bulgarian nobles, and some descendants of their royal family would become thoroughly Romanized. The same processes had long been at work on Georgian and Armenian elites, and were intensified by the annexations of this era. Yet Byzantine Romanía had now bitten off far more than it had ever tried to chew and digest in the past. These were established and constituted realms, not refugees from the caliphate or decentralized bands. It is unclear whether Romanization could advance deeper than the elite stratum, or how widely it could spread even there. Such transformations required time, and the empire's eastern presence was cut short in the eleventh century. As for the Balkans, after a century and a half of Roman rule there is little evidence that the Bulgarians—however exactly their identity was constituted at this time—came to identify fully with the Roman order. Antioch was Christian and its population supported the Roman order; indeed, its leading families had taken over when the Romans displaced the previous Muslim ruling class. But the city was also mostly Arabic-speaking, which put a distance between its population and other Romans.

Imperial governance, that is Roman rule over non-Romans, was flexible and adaptive. In annexed territories Roman officers were often posted to take over forts from local commanders, but sometimes locals were left in place, and Roman taxation and administration were introduced gradually. This happened in most of the lands of the Bulgarian state and partially also in Taron, Tao, and Vaspurakan. Large imperial estates—"crown lands"—were formed in the territories conquered from the Muslims in the east and in Upper Tao. Their administration was entrusted to imperial officials, but they possibly sat atop structures manned by locals.[7] Local nobility continued to be employed in high command positions and also to carry out middle and lower functions of governance. The emirates of Cilicia were probably dismembered and reconstituted as imperial territories, but Antioch had developed civic institutions that the Romans retained. Powerful men from Syria, including Aleppo, had previously played leading roles in Antiochene politics, and they continued to do so under Roman rule. A Christian Arab (Kulayb) was put in charge as *basilikos* of the governance of first Antioch and then Melitene. Another ('Ubayd Allah) was given lifelong rule over Antioch in exchange for his timely assistance during the civil war in 978. But after him, as early as 985, the *doukes* were Romans.[8] His appointment was a concession to a moment of weakness, not a policy. But political control in Antioch was generally maintained through the powerful local Christian, Arabic-speaking families.[9]

Annexation was a state project that elicited flexible approaches. In fact, the empire's command structures had been adjusting all along to new circumstances. A new hierarchy had emerged during the conquest. The tenth century witnessed the creation of many smaller new frontier themes, some of which were heavily militarized, consisting only of a fortress and its hinterland. A group was called the "Armenian themes" in contrast to the older "Roman themes." Until 963, the highest commander for campaigns was the *domestikos* of the *scholai*, assisted by the generals of the older themes of Asia Minor, such as Anatolikon and Armeniakon, and the generals of the new border themes. The Phokades used the position of *domestikos* as a stepping stone to the throne, which compromised the position. After 970, ad hoc posts become more common. If they did not lead the armies in person, the emperors appointed a loyal follower to a command position such as *stratelates, strategos autokrator*, or *stratopedarches* (the latter for eunuchs, e.g., Petros). Around 970, the *katepanata* (or *doukata*) grouped a number of themes under the command of a senior officer, the *katepano* (or *doux*), who also commanded units of the *tagmata* posted in his area. It was a notable development that *tagmata* were now posted near the frontier zone, instead of mostly around Constantinople, and detachments of them were commanded by the *doux* or other ad hoc commander-in-chief. The empire was investing more resources and status along the frontier.

It does not seem that a *doux* was always appointed to every *doukaton* that existed "in the books." Gaps in tenure might have been real and not only due to the poor state of our sources. In southern Italy, for example, in the gaps between the appointment of *katepano*, supreme command seems to have been held by the senior officer of the *tagmata* there.[10] Conversely, commands over various *doukata* and themes could be created in an ad hoc way. In sum, the top military positions were only options that emperors could activate, cancel, break up, and combine as necessary, according to the balance of power in *domestic* politics. Also, the scope of the authority invested in these positions seems to vary every time we glimpse them in action. The system was flexible, always adapting to circumstances.[11] However, two key positions that were almost always filled were the *doukata* of Thessalonike and Antioch, the command headquarters for the Balkans and the southeast. Antioch, a backwater under Muslim rule, now regained the strategic importance that it had held in late antiquity.

The themes, especially the larger older ones, presumably had a *strategos* (general-governor) at all times. It is traditional to assert that during the age of conquest the army came to rely so heavily on tagmatic forces that the thematic forces withered away, to such a degree that the empire's inability to defend itself in the later eleventh century can be partially attributed to this development. But there does not seem to be any proof for this assertion, certainly not before 1025. Granted, the *tagmata* became more important in this period, in part because the empire shifted to a mostly offensive stance. The sources document that thematic armies fought in the wars of the 960s and 970s, especially the themes of Thrace, Macedonia, Thrakesion, Anatolikon, and Armeniakon. After that, they provide less detailed information about the composition of the armies, especially for the generation after 989, in part because there is less evidence overall. Still, there is no proof for any dramatic change. The military manual that Nikephoros Ouranos wrote, probably in Antioch in the early 1000s, assumes that expeditionary forces will consist of both tagmatic and thematic units. Granted, he was copying older manuals, but he updated or adapted them when they were out of date.[12] Toward the end of Basil's reign, a Rus' raiding fleet was destroyed by the thematic navies of the Kibyrraiotai and Samos and the *doux* of Thessalonike.[13] The author of another manual implies that soldiers in border themes were more prepared than the rest, and that if muster calls were not based on accurate lists, then some soldiers might not show up, but we do not know how anecdotal this information is.[14] It is unlikely that the themes "atrophied" under Basil. By contrast, the *tagma* of the "Immortals" created by Tzimiskes in 970 is mentioned again only toward the end of the eleventh century; its existence is unlikely to have been continuous in the meantime.[15]

The purpose of flexible command structures was to enable emperors to control the Roman army itself as much as the conquered territories. By far the biggest threat to the emperors at this time were Roman rivals with prestige and authority in the army. This brings us to one of the most overblown issues in Byzantine history, the alleged struggle between the "state" and the "powerful." Twentieth-century historians preferred to see events—the stuff of "narrative"—as merely surface reflections of deeper socioeconomic upheavals with dramatic overtones of class struggle over land and social power, and with the state competing against the magnates or some putative "landed aristocracy" over control of the peasantry. In reality, all we have is a conflict of personalities at the higher ranks of the army over command of that army and, by extension, over the throne. Top officers tried to maneuver themselves into the position of co-emperor when the dynastic heir was a minor, or sought to overthrow him in a rebellion. There was nothing new about this. There was no "magnate class" beyond the army officers who appear in or are implied by the narrative sources. Some of them were rich, of course, but we do not know just how rich. None of them had private resources that could challenge the power of the state, either individually or even as a group. Their power came from office. Emperors could suppress them and their families (e.g., the Phokades and Maleïnoi) merely by denying them offices and commands, and they could elevate others to take their place. This was still an aristocracy of service, and under Basil it brought in Bulgarians, Armenians, and Georgians.

On the one hand, the emperors were trying to protect themselves against their own army. On the other hand, they were trying to protect small landowners and villagers from the encroachments of the "powerful." The latter were a fairly diverse group of provincial economic interests, mostly court titulars, magistrates, local patrons, bishops, monasteries, and certainly some of the military families too. The state had reasons for taking this stance, among them to safeguard its tax and recruitment base. Unfortunately, we again have no data about the extent of the problem, its fluctuations, or the effect of the emperors' response. Historians of socioeconomic trends assume that the pre-modern state was almost always powerless to stop these allegedly "deeper" transformations from taking place on the ground, but there is no evidence for or against this assumption either. For all we know, the problem was over-stated by the emperors to begin with (their laws are our main evidence for its existence), or effectively suppressed by them. What we should not do is conflate this issue with the officer-class problem. Historians who conflate the two have never been able to explain why emperors who came from the alleged magnate class (Phokas and Tzimiskes) failed to repeal the antipow-erful land legislation. No matter their background, *all* emperors sought to protect themselves against rivals while safeguarding the tax and recruitment basis of the imperial army, especially against the Church and the monasteries.

In part, these were two separate issues: first, a political problem of con-trol over the army, which was resolved politically or militarily; and second, a socioeconomic problem of unknown extent that the state addressed legally. It is not clear how much they overlapped. Many historians see everything in light of the alleged struggle between the state and the magnates. But when you hold a hammer, everything starts to look like a nail. For example, the establishment of imperial estates in the conquered territories in the east has been repeatedly seen as a deliberate move by the emperors to keep out the magnates and limit their power.[16] But this dynamic is imported from the model that we are by now used to employing, and has no basis in the sources. There is no evidence that officers were pushing to acquire the new lands or that such acquisitions—to whatever degree they took place—were viewed as imbalancing their power relative to the throne. We know about these estates only from the seals of officials in charge of them. The only person noted for acquiring lands in the new territories was the *parakoimomenos* Basileios Lakapenos (and in a questionable anecdote at that). If we strip away the story about "magnates," its is entirely obvious and predictable that crown lands should be formed in the newly conquered territories. What else would we expect, given that the imperial armies were doing the conquering?

There was one frontier region where Roman garrisons were likely noth-ing more than remote outposts, namely around Sirmium (at first under Konstantinos Diogenes). Here, outside areas of direct occupation (e.g., in Serbia), imperial authority was present in the form of titles bestowed on local rulers, and there is no reason to think that it was more than nominal. Modern maps that show the empire encompassing the whole of the former Yugoslavia are wildly overblown. Emperors did sometimes pretend as if bestowing titles made peripheral rulers into their subjects, but I doubt anyone took this literally, including the court. Such nominal "subjects"

ringed the periphery of the empire and could include the Lombard duchies in Italy, Venice, the Serbian and Dalmatian lordships, the Georgian
and Armenian rulers, the emirs of the various Muslim states along the
southeast (e.g., the Marwanids of Diyar Bakr), and the client city-state of
Aleppo. Some were more and some were less likely to obey imperial orders.
At either extreme, they could turn against the empire or be absorbed by
it. So the frontier consisted of a series of concentric zones, moving from
predominantly Roman areas to areas where Roman or native officers governed mostly non-Roman subjects, and finally to foreign client states.
This did not, however, mean that imperial borders were necessarily fuzzy
and fluid. People and goods could not just casually enter territory under
Roman control without passing through the proper customs and check-
points. Strategic flexibility and outsourcing to local agents did not make
Romanía an open house.[17] The emperors could effectively close the border
when they wanted to, and immigrants and travelers are often reported as
having to get past border guards. It is fashionable to call borders "zones of
interaction," and they certainly were that (because every place is), but they
were also zones of exclusion, depending on imperial policy. Byzantium was
not a liberal fantasy of open borders.

The sway of the court extended beyond the zone of foreign dependencies,
but in progressively more attenuated ways. The eastern Roman empire was
now the oldest, most powerful, most prestigious, and wealthiest Christian
monarchy in the world. It was obviously going to be widely emulated and
imitated when it came to the titles, narratives, insignia, images, rituals,
and aspirations of imperial power. This adoption of Byzantine forms by the
emerging kingdoms of Europe—usually unacknowledged, but an important
form of "soft power" nonetheless—has been extensively studied. It should
not, however, be equated with control or even cultural dominance. Foreign
kings may have emulated Byzantine ways but were not aware that they
belonged to a "Byzantine Commonwealth," a modern idea founded on Slavic
and Orthodox biases. The Rus', who accepted Byzantine Christianity, were
not closer to Byzantium than the Ottonian Germans, who aped Roman imperial forms. Both sought imperial brides and occasionally fought against the
empire. The conversion of the Rus' is often hailed as one of the great achieve-
ments of Byzantium, but those words give a misleading impression and are
deeply colored by hindsight, namely the later division of the Christian world
between Catholic and Orthodox realms. At the time, the conversion was a
choice and a feat of Vladimir and his court. The Byzantines themselves paid
little attention to it, hardly mentioned it in their literature, and never ceased
to regard the Rus' as barbarians, just as with the Bulgarians. The Church of

Constantinople did have a say in appointing the bishop of Kiev, but it is not clear what, if any, advantages or sway this gave to the emperor over the Rus'.

Byzantium did not stop acquiring territory in 1025. It continued to expand right up to the moment in the 1060s when it was surprised to realize that it was about to contract dramatically. At that point, they looked back and longed for the "virtue," i.e., overwhelming violence, of Phokas, Tzimiskes, and Basil II.[18] But what had changed in the meantime? It is not clear that any kind of "decline" set in soon after the death of Basil II. What we can say is that without him to suppress the political scene of Romanía, power was gradually reclaimed by the other elements of the polity, including the extended palace, the political and military elites, the populace of Constantinople, and even one patriarch. The return of politics, which required the renegotiation of domestic priorities, coincided with the unforeseen appearance of new enemies on the international scene. To these developments we now turn.

PART II | New Enemies and the
Return of Politics

CHAPTER 7

"Intrigues of the Women's Quarters"

From Macedonians to Paphlagonians

Konstantinos VIII (1025–1028)

The sole reign of Konstantinos VIII, now in his midsixties, was an unremarkable coda to that of his brother. Konstantinos ruled through a combination of "new men," or, rather, "new eunuchs," and the officer families that Basil had created. One difference was that he governed from Constantinople, and his choice for the succession, put off repeatedly until it had to be forced through in his final days, began the dispersal of Basil's consolidated authority to the other elements of the republic. The reign thereby bridges two periods of political history.

We do not know what Konstantinos did during his brother's long reign. He claimed credit for slaying Phokas at Abydos in 989, and one report says that he accompanied the eastern campaign of 995, urging a hawkish policy against Aleppo.[1] There is no sign that Basil entrusted him with any authority. When he lay dying in 1025, he had to summon Konstantinos from a palace outside Constantinople; Aristakes says it was in Nikaia, and the guards were reluctant because they did not want him to rule.[2] The Greek sources, Psellos and Skylitzes, are negative about Konstantinos. They say that he was devoted to horse races, gambling, comedy shows, and hunting, and ruled through vile eunuchs rather than men of birth and merit. Afflicted by gout, he preferred to ride everywhere rather than walk, though he was extremely tall and strong of body. He suspected plots and was quick to blind potential enemies. This hostile picture may have been promulgated later by the Komnenoi because he blinded one of their own.[3] The eastern sources are positive. They say that on his proclamation as sole emperor, Konstantinos freed prisoners, as was customary, including those who had been implicated in the revolt of Xiphias and Phokas.[4] Skylitzes accuses him of collecting two years of back taxes that Basil had forgiven, in addition to the taxes owed during his own three years and despite a widespread drought, but Yahya praises him for remitting back taxes and not collecting them on abandoned land (i.e., a partial abolition of the *allelengyon*, the solidarity tax). Skylitzes places the abolition of the enhanced *allelengyon* under the next emperor, Romanos III, saying that Konstantinos intended to do it but never got around to it. We should probably trust Yahya here.[5]

As we will see, Konstantinos appointed eunuchs to the *doukata* of Antioch and Iberia and other key military posts.[6] He also employed men from his brother's officer families, to good effect. Georgios Theodorokanos, general of the naval theme of Samos, defeated an Arab fleet (from where?), probably in 1026. In 1027 Konstantinos Diogenes, commander of the Roman outpost at Sirmium (and father of the future emperor Romanos IV), was made *doux* of Bulgaria and drove back a Pecheneg raid. The fate of Sirmium after that is unknown, but it was in Roman hands in ca. 1070. As for Illyria, it is not clear exactly what kind of presence the empire maintained west of the line Dyrrachion-Skopje-Niš.[7] Romanos Argyros (the future emperor Romanos III) was prefect of the City. Nikephoros Komnenos was *doux* of Vaspurakan, but in 1026 he fell under suspicion of plotting against the emperor with king Giorgi of Abkhazia-Kartli. He and his associates were arrested and blinded. Konstantinos would have remembered that the Phokades had sought Georgian allies in their own rebellions.

The emperor took no chances with the descendants of the leading officers of the 970s and 980s, whom he accused of treason and blinded. These included Konstantinos Bourtzes, son of the conqueror of Antioch; Bardas Phokas, grandson of the rebel of the 980s; Basileios Skleros, grandson of the other rebel; Romanos Kourkouas, scion of that distinguished family; and leading Bulgarian officers who had been brought onside by Basil. None of these men appear to have held office, and their families effectively drop out of the leadership. In a brutal way, Konstantinos was wrapping up his dynasty's unfinished business. He issued a law jointly with the patriarch Alexios Stoudites and the Holy Synod excommunicating anyone who plotted against the throne, joined in a rebellion, or gave counsel to a rebel. This was yet another (failed) attempt to protect the throne against the political sphere by using religion. But ambition could not be suppressed in this way, and even churchmen objected to separating people from Christ for political reasons.[8] Konstantinos also had a punitive streak. When the people of Naupaktos (in western Greece) rose up and killed their oppressive governor, he punished many and even blinded the city's bishop.[9] There were more conciliatory ways of handling local grievances. These were signs of a growing weakness.

Konstantinos appointed eunuchs from his personal retinue to important military posts for the same reason other emperors had: he could trust them more than the bearded types with families. Chief among them was Nikolaos, the *parakoimomenos* now appointed *domestikos* of the *scholai*, the first eunuch to hold that office. These were not bad appointments, as events proved. In 1027, Giorgi of Abkhazia-Kartli died and his realm was governed by his wife Mariam of Vaspurakan, mother of the child Bagrat IV, who had just spent three years as a hostage in Constantinople. We have two versions of a brief Roman-Georgian war that broke out then. According to Yahya, Mariam seized some of the forts that Giorgi had ceded to the empire after the previous war, whereupon Nikolaos *parakoimomenos* invaded and devastated her lands in 1028 until she sued for peace, returning the forts. According to the nationalist Georgian version, Konstantinos attacked by dispatching Nikolaos in 1028 after a number of Georgian lords defected from Bagrat and went over to the emperor. According to this version, the Romans captured some forts while others were surrendered by their lords, but Nikolaos was recalled by news of the emperor's terminal illness.[10]

The most pressing problem, of course, was the succession; both Basil and Konstantinos had put this off until the last moment. Apparently, it was all arranged in haste when Konstantinos fell ill in November 1028. His first choice was Konstantinos Dalassenos, the former *doux* of Antioch (who had spent ten years in Fatimid captivity after the defeat of his father Damianos in 998). He was in retirement on his estates in the Armeniakon theme, but either there was no time to recall him or other interests intervened. The next choice was the prefect of the City Romanos Argyros (also known as Argyropoulos and descended, like the emperor, from Romanos I). He was summoned to the palace and given a stark choice: either separate from his wife, marry Zoe (one of Konstantinos' three daughters), and ascend the throne—or be blinded. He chose Zoe and the throne. But divorce was not easy in Byzantium. To make it legal, his first wife had to be coerced by the patriarch Alexios to voluntarily join a convent, and an ecclesiastical synod then had to declare that Romanos and Zoe were not too closely related to marry. This was the first of many irregular marriages that prolonged the Macedonian dynasty in its twilight.[11] But it did not solve the underlying issue, as Romanos had no heirs and Zoe was almost fifty. So the problem was only postponed, and would contribute to the return of political contestation. Konstantinos died on November 11 or 12 and was the last emperor to be buried in the imperial mausoleum of the Holy Apostles.

Konstantinos VIII was not a bad emperor. He was cruel to some members of the aristocracy, whether justly or not, but we need not write history from their perspective. The empire was secure. Konstantinos engaged diplomatically with the Fatimids, asking for the restoration of the Holy Sepulcher and the right of Christians, who had been forced to convert under al-Hakim, to return to their faith.[12] Yet Konstantinos' reign also inaugurated a structure of imperial governance that proved detrimental in the long run, as Psellos clearly realized, especially when the empire later came under fiscal and military strain.[13] It can be delineated as follows: a mostly civilian emperor residing in the capital and rewarding his mostly civilian courtiers, including eunuchs, from the proceeds of a growing and increasingly monetized economy, while army officers posted to the frontier backwaters began to feel starved of favor, access, money, men, and opportunities. This alienated them from the regime and contributed to the return of political strife.

Romanos III Argyros (1028–1034): The same insecurity

Romanos was socially distinguished but his career was unremarkable. Before the prefecture of Constantinople, he had overseen the finances of Hagia Sophia and served as a judge in a province and the capital.[14] He was now about sixty, with no heirs or military credentials, and his dynastic legitimacy was newly minted and tenuous. Potential rivals included men with experience in Basil's armies, and social peers who were also but a wedding away from the throne. Romanos is often depicted by scholars as a representative of an alleged aristocracy, ruling in its class interests, but this was not the case. In reality, he was an insecure ruler who sought to fill Basil's boots by acquiring military prestige, resulting in a fiasco. He also tried to buy the favor and support of his subjects, but ended up ruling more or less as had Konstantinos VIII, by relying on eunuch-generals and suspecting plots against him from the officer class. Romanos was a more affable but weaker version of Konstantinos, except that he tried (and failed) to imitate Basil, and for these and other delusions he was mocked by Psellos.[15]

Romanos' first strategy was to buy the favor of his subjects by handing out offices, titles, gifts, exemptions, and benefactions. He increased the income of Hagia Sophia, abolished the *allelengyon* (assuming Konstantinos had not done so already), released prisoners held for debt, forgave unpaid taxes, paid off private debts himself, and ransomed captives taken by the Pechenegs. He even honored some of the victims of Konstantinos VIII with titles. There is no proof that some aristocratic "faction" or "class" was behind all this, only the emperor's desperate need to be popular. His opening moves of appeasement were thus reminiscent of the reign of Tzimiskes. But Romanos' advisors quickly restrained his profligacy, and the flow of money dried up. The inflation of titles was causing problems: bishops came to blows on the day of Pentecost over their seating arrangements, because the emperor had given the same high title (*synkellos*) to too many among them.[16]

Romanos took another page from the playbook of Tzimiskes and quickly patched up a foreign conflict in a way that established his family internationally. He offered his niece Helene to Bagrat IV of Abkhazia-Kartli and so pacified this corner of the frontier. The regent Mariam, the *katholikos* Melchisedech, and some Georgian nobles traveled in state to Constantinople to receive the bride and the title *kouropalates* for Bagrat. Their reception allowed Romanos to showcase his international prestige.[17] Between 1030 and 1032, he married another niece to the nominal king of Armenia Smbat III (1020–1040, in reality confined to Ani by his brother).[18]

But the sharks were circling, probing for weakness—or at least Romanos thought so. Presian (Prousianos in Greek) was the son of the Bulgarian tsar Ivan Vladislav, had briefly been recognized as tsar himself before the kingdom's fall, and had then entered the Roman command. He was now accused of conspiring to seize the throne with Theodora, the younger sister of the empress Zoe. Presian was confined to a monastery and blinded; a year later he voluntarily became a monk. His mother Marija, who had been given one of the highest court titles for women, was expelled to the Boukellarion theme and the princess Theodora herself was confined to a convent. In a separate incident, the experienced general Konstantinos Diogenes, *doux* of Thessalonike, was imprisoned on suspicion of treason (for all that he was married to the emperor's niece), and his accomplices arrested and exiled. These included some of Basil's other officers: Eustathios Daphnomeles, two more grandsons of Bourtzes, and others, including Georgians co-opted by Basil.[19] Romanos' reign was playing out just like Konstantinos'. It was not looking good. What he needed was military prestige and closer ties to the army.

The debacle at Aleppo and the capture of Edessa

Antioch and the southeast were restless for both religious and military reasons. The Roman conquests and the Armenian settlements had brought large groups of non-Chalcedonian Christians (Monophysites, including Syrian Jacobites) into the empire. Imperial policy had been tolerant since Tzimiskes, but in the eleventh century the imperial Church pressured these minorities to conform to Roman Orthodoxy. After a petition by Ioannes, the Chalcedonian bishop of Melitene, complained of heretics in his region, the patriarch Alexios opened a formal investigation. In 1029, he and the emperor summoned the Jacobite patriarch Yuhannan VIII bar Abdun, who was residing at Germanikeia (Maraş), to the capital, along with some of his bishops. Yuhannan was accused of posing as the patriarch of Antioch and pressured to recant his views and join the Orthodox fold. He did not, and was exiled to Mt. Ganos in Thrace, but some of his bishops complied. When he died in 1034, the Jacobites in the east elected a successor who fled to Diyar Bakr rather than be arrested. The period of Orthodox tolerance for the Jacobites that had lasted since Tzimiskes' prudent accommodation seems to have ended, but the persecution affected only Syrians, not Armenians—yet.[20]

In 1030, Romanos decided to attack Aleppo. His generals advised against it,[21] a sure sign that his motives were political and domestic. The founder of the Mirdasid dynasty of Aleppo, Salih (emir, 1024–1029), led the fractious but strong Kilab tribe of northern Syria, which had made Hamdanid rule in the region so difficult. Salih opposed the Fatimids, from whom he took Aleppo, and was killed fighting against them. This rivalry suited the Romans, though we know of no agreement between them and Salih. After his death, his sons Nasr and Thimal were in a weaker position facing the Fatimids, and were not a threat to Rome. Yet the *doux* of Antioch, Michael Spondyles, invaded Syria in 1029 on his own initiative to capitalize on Salih's death. He was checked by Nasr and Thimal, and had to make peace with them. The emperor repudiated this agreement and took the field in person. This was his chance to gain military prestige. A series of delegations from Aleppo sued for peace, but Romanos claimed that the brothers were too weak to protect Aleppo from the Fatimids; it seems that he intended to replace them with their old enemy, Mansur b. Lu'lu', who accompanied him.[22]

Romanos arrived in Antioch on July 20, 1030, and departed for Aleppo on the 27th. He had apparently mustered a huge army, but our sources agree that it was poorly trained and suffering from the heat—the sorts of things that they say with hindsight. Romanos did not head directly east for Aleppo but went north, setting up a camp with palisade near the fort of 'Azaz, in an enclosed and dry location. Strategically, it is unclear why he came here. Once encamped, Romanos sent out the tagma of the *exkoubitores* to reconnoiter on August 8, but they were ambushed by Nasr's cavalry—only one thousand men—and dispersed. The Arabs now surrounded the Roman camp, cutting it off from its water source. Konstantinos Dalassenos was sent out to break the siege, but he was defeated and retreated in disorder to the camp. The high command now decided to retreat, but the Armenians began to plunder the baggage camp and soldiers abandoned their posts. A sudden Arab charge broke up the Roman column, which dispersed and fled in confusion. The Romans regrouped only once they had crossed the border at Kyrros. Though only a few were killed or captured, Nasr seized the imperial tent and its riches. Romanos returned in haste to Constantinople, leaving two eunuchs in charge, Symeon as *domestikos* of the *scholai* and Niketas of Mistheia as *doux* of Antioch—both of them Konstantinos VIII's men.

The Romans got their act together quickly. Georgios Maniakes, general of Telouch (a theme just north of the border from 'Azaz) was approached by Arabs pursuing the Roman army and ordered to surrender his city, which he could not now hope to hold. He agreed and sent them wine, then attacked them at night and killed all eight hundred of them, sending their noses and ears to the emperor in Cappadocia.[23] The emperor duly promoted him to *katepano* of lower Media (possibly around Samosata). We will hear more of him. Then, in December 1030, Niketas and Symeon invaded Aleppan territory and captured and ravaged 'Azaz, the site of the defeat.

Moreover, the Mirdasids failed to exploit their victory. Nasr and Thimal quarreled and had to divide their territory, with Nasr holding Aleppo. The tribal coalition began to disintegrate, and the Fatimids were a looming danger. Nasr thereupon wrote to the emperor: in exchange for Roman protection, he pledged his submission, military service, and annual tribute according to the treaty of 970. The new treaty was signed in 1031.[24] Through sheer geostrategic circumstance, a major defeat had no negative impact. Paradoxically, events played out as if the Romans had won. Aleppo became a vassal state of the empire—which of course displeased the Fatimids.

There was another area of concurrent conflict in the southeast to which the sources devote considerable attention.[25] In 1028, a war captive named Nasr b. Musharraf had persuaded Spondyles, the *doux* of Antioch, to allow him to build a fort at al-Maniqa, in the mountains between Laodikeia and the emirate of Tripoli; from there he would keep the local Muslims under control. Spondyles arranged for him to receive the title *patrikios* and one thousand soldiers to carry it out. When it was finished, however, Nasr declared his independence and invited in forces from Tripoli and the Fatimid governor of Damascus, al-Dizbiri. In 1030, they killed the Romans and planned raids into the empire. By this point local Muslims were building fortresses all over this region, which was slipping out of Roman control. This was another embarrassment, and Romanos, as he was leaving Syria after his defeat, ordered Symeon and Niketas to fix it. Niketas captured a number of these forts in 1031, but failed to take al-Maniqa. The emperor sent Theoktistos, general of the tagma of the *hetaireia*, to take command; an alliance was also struck with al-Hassan ibn al-Mufarrij, emir of the tribe of Tayy and enemy of the Fatimid governor al-Dizbiri. Our sources differ on the course of the fighting, but by December 1031 Niketas had pacified Phoenicia, taken al-Maniqa with many captives, and Nasr b. Musharraf had fled and was soon to die. Niketas captured Apameia too, whose men were raiding across the border, and gave it to Aleppo. In 1032, al-Hassan was honored grandly in Constantinople. This reception also enabled the emperor to showcase his international standing before his subjects.[26] Major embarrassments had strangely morphed into a series of triumphs.

Another windfall had also just occurred. Maniakes and Sulayman, the Turkish governor of Edessa, had begun secret negotiations over the surrender of the city to the empire, in exchange for which Sulayman would receive lands and money, the usual deal.[27] Edessa was being torn apart by factions and ethnic tensions between Arabs and Kurds. Sulayman had previously gone over to the Marwanid emir of Mayyafariqin, Nasr al-Dawla, but he had failed to impose order. He turned now to Maniakes, who took over the citadel one night, in October or November 1031. Sulayman conveyed a sacred relic to the emperor, the original Syriac correspondence between Jesus and Abgar of Edessa. This relic was received in another public ceremony and added to the palace collection. But the Roman takeover did not go unchallenged. The Muslims, aided by Marwanid forces, attacked the Romans, destroying part of the walls and setting fires, and many of the inhabitants likewise took up arms in what appears to have been a complicated urban standoff that lasted for months. In the end, with the help of reinforcements Maniakes prevailed and pacified the city in 1032. This was the only breach—and a temporary one—in the otherwise stable alliance between the empire and the Marwanids, who still continued to serve Roman interests along the frontier.[28]

Roman control now extended even deeper into northern Mesopotamia. Maniakes began to send annual tribute from Edessa in 1033, which means that a tax system was already up and running. Maniakes was destined for greatness. He is described by contemporaries in the most intimidating terms as a giant of a man, with huge shoulders and arms, and a voice like thunder; he was not only an able general, but fought in the front rank and instilled terror in the enemy.

Diplomacy and dynastic instability

Romanos had been astonishingly lucky. The debacle at Aleppo improved the empire's security. The Roman armies were still the most formidable, and had suffered few casualties. But Romanos' prestige domestically must have suffered, especially in the eyes of army officers. Konstantinos Diogenes was preemptively tonsured and placed in the Stoudios monastery, where the patriarch Alexios had been abbot. In September 1031, at the Petrion convent, a place for disposing of unwanted empresses and princesses, the empress Zoe forcibly tonsured her sister Theodora on suspicion that she was plotting. The next year, a plot was alleged between her and Diogenes, who was planning to rally his supporters in the Balkan armies. Diogenes was tortured by the eunuch-monk Ioannes (who would soon play a prominent part in imperial politics), and hanged himself in his cell.[29] This was beginning to look ugly. To present a better picture of himself, Romanos started building a church of the Virgin known as the Peribleptos ("Admired by All"). It was on the Marmara coast not far from Stoudios (its foundations are known) and it featured a hospital, but the taxes and corvées that it required caused complaints. In stark contrast to the generosity that marked the beginning of his reign, Romanos had now become an oppressive tax collector.[30] He also renovated the aqueduct, cisterns, and other hospitals of Constantinople, some of which had suffered damage in recent earthquakes.[31]

In the summer of 1032, Romanos undertook a second eastern expedition, though he did not go past Mesanakta in central Asia Minor. He does not appear to have had any strategic objective, and possibly his purpose was only to keep the armies busy and in his presence. Romanos returned in August; along the way he gave aid to large groups displaced by famine and pestilence from the central and northern provinces of Asia Minor.[32] In 1032 or 1033 Romanos' own brother-in-law, Skleros (who had been blinded by Konstantinos VIII), was convicted of plotting against the emperor, so he was expelled from the City along with his wife.[33]

The situation in the east had stabilized enough toward the end of the reign for diplomacy to kick in.[34] The Romans (especially Niketas), the Mirdasids at Aleppo, and the Fatimids (especially al-Dizbiri) exchanged envoys in 1032–1033 while they mobilized armies, but nothing was agreed. Romanos wanted to restore the Holy Sepulcher, appoint a patriarch to Jerusalem, and protect the Christians of the caliphate (demands initiated by Konstantinos VIII); he also wanted no more Fatimid attacks on Aleppo or support for the raiding of the Arabs of Sicily (the general of Nauplion, Nikephoros Karantenos, had just defeated a major attack on the Adriatic coast and sent five hundred Arabs in chains to the emperor).[35] But it was Aleppo that proved to be the sticking point. Meanwhile, its ruler Nasr sent the emperor a lock of the hair of John the Baptist—this was good for another public event before the people in Constantinople. Romanos granted him the title *patrikios* in a public ceremony before the envoys of the caliph al-Zahir.[36] The emperor even sent a fleet under one Tekneas to raid Egypt, of all places; he captured and plundered some ships by Alexandria and returned unharmed.[37] This was an audacious projection of Roman power, or a trivial act of piracy, but no Arab source mentions it.

The empire made two more Caucasian acquisitions in 1033–1034, between the end of Romanos' reign and the start of Michael IV's. The first was the town of Berkri (Perkrion, modern Muradiye) in the northeastern corner of lake Van. It was a quasi-independent emirate that had not been absorbed at the time of the annexation of Vaspurakan. Our sources disagree about the course of the fighting and the general responsible for its capture. As always, there was a local faction that invited the Romans, and others who brought in the emir of Azerbaijan. There was a massacre of thousands of captured Romans at one point, but in the end the imperial armies prevailed; most of the Muslims were expelled (as usual) and the region partially resettled by Christians.[38] The Romans had now almost closed the gap north of lake Van, from which Persian (Azerbaijani) forces might enter.[39] All that remained was Khliat, but that was in the friendly hands of the Marwanids of Diyar Bakr. The second acquisition was the voluntary surrender of the fortified Black Sea town of Anakopia, on the coast of Abkhazia where the mountains meet the sea.[40] This now became a remote Roman theme, including Bičvinta (ancient Pityous), giving the empire direct access to Abkhazia.

Early in his reign, Romanos picked up a mistress—we do not know who—and ceased to care about Zoe. Psellos presents Zoe as a lustful woman who acquired a young lover too, one Michael, the brother of the eunuch Ioannes.[41] These were money changers of undistinguished origin from

Paphlagonia, and Michael was handsome, albeit an epileptic. Psellos claims that Ioannes cynically introduced his brother to the empress' affections. The affair might have lasted for most of the reign, though Psellos' black comedy focuses on psychology rather than dates and facts. Romanos did not care that this was going on; he even took pity on Michael because of his illness. But in early 1034, Romanos fell sick, lost his hair, beard, and weight, and acquired a deathly pallor. It was inevitably suspected that he was poisoned by the empress and Ioannes. On April 10 or 11, during Holy Week and after personally distributing the senate salaries, he took a bath in the palace and died; there were more rumors that he was murdered. Romanos was buried in the monastery of the Peribleptos that he had built. "But then the best men rushed to the new emperor and forgot all about Romanos," a contemporary poet noted.[42]

There is no evidence for the standard claim that Romanos III had acted in the interests of an "aristocracy," much less a landed aristocracy. He ruled as had Konstantinos VIII, through eunuch-generals and in fear of the officer class, even within his own family. He tried to acquire military prestige, to make the basis of his authority more like that of Basil II, but failed. Nevertheless, his reign witnessed notable successes due to the weakness of the Mirdasids in Aleppo and the ability of his generals Maniakes, Karantenos, and Niketas of Mistheia. The empire was at peace and still expanding, with no menacing enemies on the horizon. Romanos began his reign by making lavish gifts and concessions, but ended it as an unpopular tax collector. The surplus painstakingly acquired by Basil had likely been drained already, but the empire was experiencing general economic and demographic growth. The money could be raised. The question was rather, on what would it be spent? And the issue of the succession remained unresolved, fueling the ambitions of courtiers and generals.

Michael IV (1034–1041): Family rule

The regime of the Paphlagonians illuminates some fundamental truths about the workings of power in Byzantium. These were understood by the eunuch Ioannes, who orchestrated the transition of 1034.

On Thursday night of Holy Week, during the liturgy for the Crucifixion, the patriarch Alexios was pulled out of church and summoned to the palace. When he arrived at the Chrysotriklinos, he learned that Romanos had died and Zoe now asked him to marry her to Michael. Alexios was speechless, given their scandalous affair; also, women were required by law to grieve a full year before they could remarry.[43] But affairs of state pressed: imperial legitimacy, at this juncture, was best secured through a marriage to Zoe, and Michael was her choice. His brother Ioannes paid Alexios fifty pounds of gold and the clergy another fifty, and so, with typical Byzantine pragmatism, it was done. Before any resistance could be organized, the court was brought in to acclaim the couple as partners in empire. Who could resist? The news was publicized and the senate summoned early the next morning; they too acclaimed Michael. The people were happy to be rid of Romanos, and Michael was good-looking. Romanos was buried on Friday, and the festivities of that week offered opportunities for popular acclamations of the new emperor. The context was perfect for subduing feelings of sedition and instilling respect.[44] The mechanisms of power could, therefore, legitimate a bunch of nobodies. And the impersonal institutions of governance could enable them to rule.

Ioannes duly promoted key senators and made concessions to the people. Again a regime began with a burst of generosity, only to scale it back later. The family was from Paphlagonia, a region with a bad reputation since antiquity, especially for its eunuchs. Three of the brothers had been eunuchs since infancy (Ioannes, Konstantinos, and Georgios) and two were young men: Michael IV, aged about twenty, and Niketas, a teenager. They had a sister, Maria, married to one Stephanos with two sons, Michael (V) and Konstantinos. These people were not major landowners and had no social prestige, or even a surname. But they were in the right place at the right time.[45] The brothers and in-laws were quickly given the highest court titles. The young Niketas became *doux* of Antioch, and Konstantinos (the nephew) *doux* of Thessalonike. Ioannes is known as the *orphanotrophos*, which used to refer to the director of an orphanage, but over time came to refer to a person with a broad fiscal remit. Zoe was placed under close surveillance, and the emperor, who was subject to epileptic fits that had to be concealed behind a screen at a moment's notice, left much of the administration to Ioannes.[46] Psellos wrote a striking portrait of this eunuch-monk, an exacting and hard-working micromanager. He was intimidating and observant but not malicious.[47]

The "secret of empire" in Byzantium—to paraphrase Tacitus—was that almost any Roman could become emperor. No right to the throne came from family, social class, virtue, achievement, law, or religious fantasy. Such claims helped, but only as rhetorical arguments to justify a takeover. In reality, emperors were made when they had secured sufficient backing from other elements within the republic, given the specific circumstances that had brought them to the throne. Legitimacy was a function of popularity, of gaining support and countering opposition. But it could just as easily be lost if the balance tilted the other way. Ioannes had temporarily secured complacency, which was good enough for the moment, and Zoe provided a dynastic connection. But there were better arguments than "I happened to be there, the empress likes me, and my brother is a good administrator." A counterargument was made by Konstantinos Dalassenos, again on his estates in Armeniakon. It is recorded that "he wondered aloud why, when there were so many excellent men of distinguished families, a vulgar and threepence-a-day man should be preferred." These words apparently echoed the sentiments of others, so Ioannes proceeded carefully: he had to contain Dalassenos but not create more opposition. Thus, in an elaborate show, the emperor sent a pledge to him accompanied by wood of the True Cross, Jesus' letter to Abgar of Edessa (recently recovered), and an icon of the Virgin. Dalassenos came to Constantinople and was honored but required to stay there. He had to be kept away from the armies.[48]

When the young *doux* Niketas reached Antioch, he found the city closed against him. The people had killed an oppressive tax collector and demanded that Niketas swear amnesty oaths before entering. He did so but then executed many of the townspeople and arrested the leading citizens, sending them to Constantinople and accusing them of conspiring in favor of Dalassenos (who had once governed the city). Ioannes promptly imprisoned Dalassenos. Konstantinos Doukas, his son-in-law (and future emperor), protested this violation of the sacred guarantee, so he was imprisoned too. Other rich men were arrested and their goods confiscated. It had quickly turned ugly. The *doux* Niketas died soon after (of unknown causes) and was replaced by his brother Konstantinos.[49] Michael IV and Ioannes understood that they had to stabilize the situation and so—probably in 1034 or early 1035—they released the captive Antiochenes and did something that had not been done since the 960s: they designated a successor, specifically their nephew Michael (V), the captain of the imperial bodyguard, who was now elevated to the rank of *kaisar*. As this was a dynastic matter, Zoe was first persuaded to adopt him at a ceremony in the church at Blachernai. Zoe was popular and her support was crucial at this juncture, though Psellos alleges that Michael had stopped sharing her bed, because of his guilt (he was now spending his time with monk-confessors). The emperor also gave alms to the poor, built monasteries, and engaged in other public works involving lepers, prostitutes, and monks. This was seen as contrition for his sins under Romanos, but it was also a way to buy popularity. The new *kaisar*, moreover, was kept on a tight leash and not allowed to enjoy imperial honors.[50] In 1038, the entire Dalassenos clan was sent into exile.[51]

Michael IV was popular, but his brother Ioannes drew criticism. Psellos and Skylitzes present different images of the regime. Psellos has the emperor take active part in the administration, especially foreign policy, while Skylitzes presents him as a nonentity. Skylitzes was hostile to the regime, and punctuates his narrative with earthquakes, famine, hailstorms, and oppressive taxes. But one interesting aspect emerges: the imperial family traveled to the provinces, which was novel. Michael seems to have spent a good part of his reign at Thessalonike, allegedly seeking a cure from St. Demetrios, but possibly for political reasons too. We do not know how he held court there, though an episode is told in which he intervened with the archbishop Theophanes, who was not giving his priests their allowance during a famine. Ioannes traveled to Myra in Lykia after it was sacked by Arab pirates in 1034 or 1035; he sought a cure from St. Nikolaos and rebuilt the city walls while he was there. The *kaisar*'s mother Maria also traveled to Ephesos on pilgrimage in 1040. And one brother was always *doux* of Antioch.[52] A contemporary poet compared the four brothers to the three points and center of a cross: each sat at one point of the compass.[53] The family wrapped its many arms around the empire as tightly as it could.

Frontier integrity

The Paphlagonians maintained the integrity of the empire, but we notice a turn toward an increasingly defensive posture. The major exception was the conquest (and then loss) of Sicily, discussed below. Here we will survey the frontier and the state of the provinces.

Bagrat IV's Roman wife Helene had died around 1033. We have scattered notices of Georgian aggression against the empire in 1035 (probably in Tao) and 1038 (in Vaspurakan).[54] A key figure in the conflict to come was the formidable Georgian general Liparit, lord of Trialeti and Bagrat's main supporter (the king was only about twenty). Liparit fell out with the king when he was prevented from conquering Tbilisi and, in 1039, invited a Roman army into Georgia, which brought Bagrat's half-brother, a pretender to the throne. After some sieges deep in Georgia and further defections, the king made peace.[55] We will be hearing more of Liparit.

In the southwest, two attacks were made on Edessa. In 1034, Maniakes had been transferred from there to Vaspurakan, and the new governor was Leon Lependrenos. The city was attacked in 1036 by the combined forces of the emirs of Mayyafariqin and Harran and it would have fallen had Konstantinos, the *doux* of Antioch, not sent an army to relieve the garrison, which was blockaded in the citadel. For this intervention, he was promoted (concurrently) to the position of *domestikos* of the *scholai*. Another, more amusing, attempt to infiltrate Edessa was made in 1038 by (otherwise unknown) armed men hiding in merchant bales, but it was discovered.[56] Moreover, the standoff with the Fatimids in Syria was resolved. Negotiations were in progress while Aleppo vacillated between the empire and the caliphate. Finally, the long-desired treaty between the two was signed in late 1035 (a ten-year "truce" in the Muslim fashion), though we know few of its actual terms. Michael was given the right to intervene in Jerusalem, but otherwise Aleppo ceased to be a major concern.[57]

Turning to the Balkans, Pecheneg raids across the Danube became more frequent. One group reached Thessalonike and another captured some lesser commanders. There is, apparently, widespread evidence of the destruction that they caused, especially along the Danube, but these raids seem to have stopped in 1036, so perhaps a deal was struck.[58] Among the south Slavs, to the west and north of the areas of direct Roman control, the emperors cultivated a clientele of local lords (*župans*) through titles, salaries, spiritual ties, and visits to the capital, which led to more gifts and impressive ceremonies. But relations could sour. One Serb lord refused to return the gold that he took from the wreck of an imperial ship, while a lord of Zadar and Split was detained on his third visit to the capital and his cities seized by imperial soldiers.[59] Meanwhile, a success was scored against raiders from Arab Sicily. In 1035 they were defeated by the admiral of the Kibyrraiotai theme, who sent another five hundred captives to the capital and impaled thousands more along the Aegean coast as a trophy and a warning.[60] It is likely that the Aegean navy was boosted in this period by a unit of Varangians recently brought by Harald Sigurdsson, or Hardraada, the future king of Norway (1046–1066). At this time he was only twenty years old. His first attempt to reclaim the Norwegian throne had failed and he had escaped to Rus', after which he sought his fortune in imperial service. Later Norse sagas recount how, at the start of his service, he fought for Michael IV "in the Grecian sea," which fits these naval raids well. In fighting Arabs, then, the Roman navy was now being helped by history's last Vikings.[61]

For the empire's core provinces, the eleventh century was a period of demographic and economic expansion. It took a long time for historians to recognize this fact, but it is now documented, well studied, and accepted.[62] The end of the long war against Bulgaria, and the security brought to Greece by its conquest, also facilitated this expansion by freeing up resources and energies for investment in civilian life. As always, it is the churches that survived the later vicissitudes of history, but they provide a good indicator

FIGURE 9 HOSIOS LOUKAS. Church of the Virgin (right) and Katholikon (left) of the monastery of Hosios Loukas (Greece), seen from the east. Source: Shutterstock, ID 244945084.

of what must have been a general trend. Athens, for example, witnessed a boom in church construction during the eleventh century, both in the city itself (e.g., the Kapnikarea church) and in the surrounding hills (e.g., the monastery at Kaisariani). Moreover, some of these new buildings were quite large, for example the Daphni church (on the way from Athens to Eleusis), the *katholikon* of the monastery of Hosios Loukas (in western Boiotia; Figure 9), and the Nea Moni (on the island of Chios). Many were also adorned with impressive mosaics and frescoes that took Byzantine art in new directions.

From the historical point of view, it is worth pointing out two trends. The first is the gradual reclamation of the Aegean islands. Before the conquest of Crete, they were the targets of Arab raids and were conceived in the Byzantine literary imagination as desolate places, good for exiling enemies. Now they were places of investment and growth. The second is the belated arrival and expansion of monasticism in Greece. A late convert to Christianity, southern Greece had not developed notable monastic traditions before this time. But this changed during the eleventh century especially, when towns and the countryside were dotted by new foundations, many of which survive to this day. Moreover, some of these imperially sponsored monastic foundations, such as the Nea Moni endowed in the 1040s by Konstantinos IX Monomachos, were used as regional organizational nodes that tamed these newly pacified lands and extended the network of direct imperial patronage to them. Similar trends can be observed concurrently in Asia Minor, though its future development along these lines would be cut short later in the century by the Turkish invasions.

The conquest, and loss, of Sicily

The regime of the Paphlagonians was not content to merely defend the frontiers. Ioannes decided to solve the Sicilian problem first through diplomacy and then by direct assault, which resulted in the Paphlagonians' greatest success—brief though it was. In southern Italy, the *katepano* Boioannes (1018–1028) had firmly established Byzantine hegemony, especially over the Lombard principalities, but his successors fared badly against the Arab raiders of Sicily.[63] As we saw, the Arabs had expanded their raids along the Balkan and Aegean coasts, where they were regularly defeated by the imperial fleets. But meanwhile a civil war had broken out in Sicily, between the emir Ahmad al-Akhal and his brother Abu Hafs, which reflected deep divisions over tax issues and between "African" and "Sicilian" Muslims, though we do not know how those groups were defined. Ahmad and Ioannes opened negotiations and made a treaty in 1035: Ahmad was made a *magistros* and his son was received in Constantinople. This implied some kind of Roman sovereignty over the island and was apparently the final straw for the Zirid rulers of North Africa, who sent an army into Sicily in 1036 under ʿAbd Allah to attack Ahmad. Ahmad accordingly called on his Roman allies for assistance. At this point, Constantinople must have decided to reactivate Basil II's plan of ten years before to conquer Sicily, and Ioannes appointed none other than Maniakes to take command, with Stephanos, the father of the *kaisar* Michael, as admiral. In the meantime, in 1037, the *katepano* of Italy Opos crossed over to Sicily with a makeshift army, defeated the Africans, and reached Palermo. We do not know what happened next, but Opos returned to Italy after freeing many captives, though this action did not in the end save Ahmad; he was killed by his African enemies, who took over the island.[64] The moment was ripe for a more ambitious intervention.

Maniakes and Stephanos arrived in Italy in 1038 with a large army. From scattered references in the sources, we know that it included units from the Anatolikon, Armeniakon, Thrakesion, and Opsikion themes (though whether thematic or tagmatic soldiers stationed in those themes is unclear); Varangians, including Harald's men; three hundred or five hundred Norman mercenaries under one Arduin, a Lombard from Milan; other mercenaries; and recruits from southern Italy.[65] Given the apparent demilitarization of the Balkan provinces that we will observe during the Bulgarian revolt of 1040, it is likely that the army included units from there too, not just the Roman east. And again, a major western campaign was put into motion only after a major treaty was signed in the east, here with Egypt.

This was to be Byzantium's last Sicilian venture, so it is fitting that it left its mark on European memory. Maniakes was by himself a terrifying figure, maybe the only Byzantine who could stare down a Norman knight or Viking prince, and he provided a foil for their later self-glorification. Maniakes was remembered in the west because of his role in the rise of the Normans in Italy, recounted by their later court writers, and in the adventurous story of Harald, celebrated by the Icelandic writer Snorri Sturluson in his *Heimskringla: The Lives of the Norse Kings*. These sources exaggerate the minor feats of their countrymen in what was in fact a Byzantine military operation. The expedition thus marks a symbolic moment, when the European west emancipated itself from Byzantine dominion.

Maniakes crushed the African army at a battle by Rometta, which opened the island to conquest. During the next two years he took many towns in eastern Sicily, where the Christian population was concentrated, and finally Syracuse. A second battle was fought in early 1040 at Troina, west of Mt. Etna, and Maniakes again defeated ʿAbd Allah, who fled by ship. Maniakes had ordered the admiral Stephanos to guard the coasts, blamed him for the emir's escape, insulted him, and even struck him with a whip on the head. Stephanos promptly wrote to his brother-in-law the *orphanotrophos*, accusing Maniakes of rebellion. Maniakes also fell out with his Norman mercenaries regarding the division of the spoils, allegedly stripping and whipping their leader Arduin. The Normans, who later depicted themselves as the heroes in all the action (as did the Norwegians, perhaps in imitation of the Normans), departed in anger for Italy. But imperial politics was the bigger problem: orders came from the capital that Maniakes was to be arrested, brought back in chains, and replaced with the eunuch Basileios Pediadites. Stephanos and Pediadites now managed to lose all the gains made by Maniakes—we do not have a narrative—and withdrew to Italy, in part because of the local rebellion brewing there with Norman help. Only Messina held out under Katakalon Kekaumenos, general of the Armeniakon, possibly until 1042.[66]

It is easy to conclude that Sicily was lost because of petty infighting, and that Maniakes would have finished the job. But the problem was endemic to the imperial system: all emperors, especially the Paphlagonians, were vulnerable to the ambitions of other powerful Romans. And there was no bigger menace than a victorious, intimidating general, even one who seemed to have no political skills whatsoever. Moreover, at exactly that time, in 1040, the empire was facing its most dangerous threat since the early days of Basil II: a Bulgarian uprising. We know that Harald fought in it under Michael IV in 1041,[67] so it is likely that the emperor recalled much of the army from Sicily to face the Bulgarians and had to suspend operations in Sicily. Stephanos and Pediadites may not have been as incompetent as later sources made them appear, if their army was recalled from under them. Still, this was the chance for the Romans, at the peak of their power, to regain Sicily. That prize, lost in the ninth century, would now remain forever beyond reach.

The Bulgarian revolt

While expeditionary forces were occupied in Sicily and Italy, in 1040, the Balkans erupted in rebellion and war. The main action is depicted in the Greek sources—the only ones we have—as a Bulgarian national uprising that subsumed other acts of resistance. The leadership was provided by descendants of the Bulgarian imperial family and the officer class of the former empire. As we saw, Basil II coopted Bulgarian officers and royalty into the Roman hierarchy, often marrying them to the sons and daughters of his leading officers. But we have also seen that many of these top-tier Bulgarians suffered in the purges of Konstantinos VIII and Romanos III, for example Presian, son of Ivan Vladislav. The central figure in the rebellion was one Deljan. Escaping from Constantinople, he went to Belgrade, where, possibly with Hungarian support, he announced that he was a grandson of Samuil and proclaimed himself tsar Petar II. He advanced through the lands of the south Slavs, rallying support and killing all the Romans he encountered. The forces of Dyrrachion under Basileios Synadenos moved to intercept him, but Synadenos was denounced to the emperor by one of his officers, imprisoned in Thessalonike, and replaced by his accuser, who quickly lost control of his army. That army—likely made up of soldiers of Bulgarian origin—decided to rebel too and proclaimed one of its own, Tihomir (Greek, Teichomeros), as tsar. So there were now two claimants to that title. Deljan invited Tihomir to a meeting, where he suborned his forces and had him stoned to death.[68]

The rebels now advanced directly on Thessalonike, where the emperor resided, albeit with a tiny bodyguard. Michael fled in haste to Constantinople, abandoning even the imperial tent. He ordered Manouel Ibatzes to bring it along, but Ibatzes, likely the son of the Bulgarian general who fought against Basil II, joined the rebels. Deljan now sent an army under a former general of

Samuil to secure Dyrrachion and another force into southern Greece, where it defeated the governor at Thebes. Deljan also sent a governor, one Litovoj, to Demetrias in Greece, who fortified the citadel, but the inhabitants contacted Konstantinos, the *doux* at Thessalonike, who dispatched a fleet. Litovoj and his men were captured. As it happened, the theme of Nikopolis in western Greece was in the midst of its own local rebellion against an oppressive tax collector, whom they killed—just as had Naupaktos in 1026 and Antioch in 1034. The theme now joined the Bulgarians.[69]

Tax issues were certainly a factor behind all this instability. Skylitzes says that Basil II had allowed the Bulgarians to pay taxes in kind, just as they had under Samuil, but Ioannes the *orphanotrophos*, out of greed, required payment in coin. The monetization of the Bulgarian economy definitely increased during the Byzantine period, and Ioannes was probably looking for ways to better supply the Danube armies against Pecheneg aggression.[70] This may have contributed to the uprising, but we should not underestimate national loyalties. The Romans and the Bulgarians viewed each other as distinct people, and many among the latter, especially the former ruling class, desired freedom from "Greek oppression."[71] We should not imagine anything like a modern nationalistic yearning for independence—otherwise we could not explain the mostly peaceful Roman occupation, which lasted two centuries. But there was something to which the likes of Deljan, Tihomir, and Ibatzes could appeal, or which appealed to them. Unfortunately, we do not know what it looked like as there are no contemporary sources. Later medieval Bulgarians called the Byzantine period "the Greek slavery."[72] And Deljan likely chose the dynastic name Petar because Petar I was venerated as a saint among the Bulgarians, his reign regarded as an age of milk and honey.[73]

Just when Deljan seemed to have reconstituted Samuil's empire, a new player appeared in September 1040. Alusian was a son of Ivan Vladislav who had become a Roman army officer in the east, but had been cashiered, fined, and placed under home arrest by Ioannes for unnamed offenses. He too escaped from the east disguised as an Armenian servant and joined Deljan, who gave him a large army with which to attack Thessalonike. The city was ably defended by the *doux* Konstantinos, the emperor's nephew, who, after withstanding a six-day siege, defeated Alusian in battle, and the latter returned to Deljan. The two Bulgarians now regarded each other with suspicion. Alusian invited Deljan to a banquet, blinded him, and took his place as tsar. Michael in Constantinople was meanwhile facing his own difficulties. He had summoned the eastern armies (whatever mobile units, that is, had not followed Maniakes to Italy), and the Varangians from Sicily. But plots were brewing against him in both the City and in Asia Minor. The one in the City was centered on Michael Keroularios (the future patriarch) and possibly had wider support: although the emperor was popular, his relatives were not. But the conspirators were arrested and exiled. The other was a coup planned by officers at the mustering grounds of Mesanakta. The *doux* of Antioch Konstantinos, the emperor's brother, arrested and blinded the ringleaders.[74] We do not know if these plots were linked, but they revived the destructive Roman habit of attacking a sitting emperor just when he was facing a major military threat. This habit would later turn mere difficulties into major disasters.

In mid-1041, Michael was ready to take the field in person, despite his deteriorating physical condition, due to dropsy. He had with him new armies from the east and units withdrawn from Sicily, including Harald's Varangians. At this point, Alusian at Mosynopolis entered into secret negotiations with the emperor: he would betray the Bulgarian cause in exchange for money and titles. The defection was arranged so as to cause the maximum confusion among the Bulgarians. It has been suspected that Alusian was a Byzantine agent from the start,[75] but that seems unlikely. Michael was able to advance through Bulgaria, from Serdica to Prilep (where he captured Ibatzes), putting out the embers of the resistance. He then returned to Constantinople with Deljan in tow to celebrate a triumph and games in the hippodrome.

In the triumphal parade, Michael was visibly at his last, his limbs and face swollen. Before he died, he was tonsured and became a monk at the monastery of the Anargyroi saints that he had rebuilt. When Zoe came to visit him, he refused to see her.[76] He died on December 10, and was buried there. He had governed well and his brothers were capable organizers and generals. The same would not be true of his nephew, Michael V.

The dramatic fall of Michael V (1041–1042)

Emperors were inherently vulnerable. No divine, dynastic, social, or legal right guaranteed their hold on the throne. Emperors instead had to work to maintain their popularity, which blocked rivals from mustering support for a coup. But potential usurpers were always watching, waiting, and weighing their chances. Emperors also had to be seen as strong, to intimidate domestic rivals as much as foreign ones, but not so terrifying that they became unpopular. Basil II had walked along that fine line carefully. Since his death, however, the incidence of plots among members of the political and military elite had steadily increased. Basil's successors had targeted—whether fairly or not—the likes of Diogenes, Komnenos, Dalassenos, Doukas, Monomachos, and Keroularios, in whose names we see written the subsequent history of the eleventh century. Between 1025 and 1041 the throne had become increasingly vulnerable, but there still had been no outbreak of open civil war. The last real one had been in the 980s (the attempt of 1022 was aborted too fast). It was inevitable that there would be another one, and indeed it would not take long. But disaffection from a different direction broke out first. The Paphlagonian regime would be destroyed by its own heir, Michael V, and then he in turn would be destroyed by the people of Constantinople.

Michael had long held the rank of *kaisar* and was adopted by Zoe, but had been barred from exercising any power under his uncle Michael IV. He was now summoned to the palace by his uncles. As the City waited in suspense, a deal was struck with Zoe: she would proclaim him emperor and he would swear to respect and obey her. Three days after the death of his uncle, he was acclaimed emperor of the Romans by the people, and crowned.[77] Like the two previous emperors, Michael bestowed honors and titles on senators and freed prisoners such as Dalassenos and Maniakes, whom he reappointed *katepano* of Italy. But then either Zoe (according to Skylitzes) or Michael himself (Psellos), acting on pent-up resentments, turned against the Paphlagonians' mastermind Ioannes, who was arrested and sent into distant exile along with his brothers Georgios and Konstantinos, though the latter was soon recalled and promoted to the high rank of *nobelissimos*. Michael took the extraordinary move of castrating all his living male relatives, regardless of their age, which presumably included Konstantinos, the savior of Thessalonike. Michael then tried to win over the people, through channels that we cannot precisely identify (our sources mention merchants and craftsmen). Michael was trying to build up a popular power base in order to move against Zoe, his next target.

Before putting his plan into motion, Michael tested his popularity during the Easter festivities of 1042. On Sunday, an exuberant procession to the church of the Holy Apostles—with massive chanting crowds and the streets lined in silk and covered in carpets lest his horse's hooves touch the ground—emboldened him. That night he arrested the empress and exiled her to one of the nearby islands, where she was tonsured. He also arrested the patriarch Alexios. The next morning (on April 20), he announced to the senate and the people that he had been the intended victim of a coup, but had managed to prevail against his enemies. But when the prefect of the City read this proclamation to the people in the forum of Constantine, their mood soured. Someone shouted, "We don't want the caulker Michael, but our mother Zoe," and the crowd erupted in violence. Chanting slogans against the emperor, which canceled out their previous acclamations, the people moved to Hagia Sophia. Every age group, gender, and social class joined in, as the news spread quickly in Constantinople. The patriarch had, meanwhile, escaped by bribing his guards, and was now compelled by a group of protesters to support the uprising. The senate convened with Zoe's eunuchs and moved, with popular consent, to fetch her sister Theodora from the Petrion monastery—where Zoe herself had once imprisoned her! At first she refused, but they threatened her and used force to drag her out and invest her with imperial regalia. On the next day, Theodora the unwilling nun was acclaimed in Hagia Sophia as co-empress along with Zoe. She declared Michael deposed and began to appoint her own magistrates. The Varangian guard declared for her and against "the tyrant."

The popular uprising followed traditional patterns. The people broke into the prefect's headquarters and freed the prisoners, plundered the mansions of the emperor's relatives and supporters, and gathered in the hippodrome. Psellos, a young imperial secretary at the time, was just inside the main palace gate and heard the roar of the angry crowd. He rode his horse into the City to observe the chaos. As for the emperor, he placed archers on the walls to shoot into the crowd and recalled Zoe, who was now terrified, producing her before the masses in the hippodrome; but they would not listen to him, and hurled insults and missiles at the imperial box. It was to be decided by force. The people assaulted the palace from three directions, and the emperor fought back with whatever men he had left. By Tuesday, April 21, three thousand had died; the people prevailed and entered the palace, which they pillaged, tearing up the tax rolls too. The emperor and his uncle Konstantinos, the former *doux* of Antioch, fled by ship to the monastery of Stoudios, where they sought refuge, accepting tonsure as monks.

The people now cheered and celebrated, but Zoe quickly tried to displace her sister, whom she hated. The crowd, however, demanded that the two reign together. There was a brief standoff, with Theodora in Hagia Sophia and Zoe in the palace. The people were clamoring for Michael to be executed, and Theodora sent guards to secure him. Psellos accompanied them, as, in his inimitable ability to be everywhere and know everyone important, he was a friend of the captain. Stoudios was surrounded by a crowd railing against the two suppliants, and Psellos recounts a tearful exchange between himself and the deposed emperor and his uncle, who were clinging to the altar. In the end, they were pulled out, paraded in a brief humiliating procession, and blinded in a tight circle of people, the uncle with stoic dignity and the nephew kicking and screaming. This is one of Psellos' most dramatically effective passages. The Scandinavian poets later claimed that the deed was done by Harald himself.[78] Meanwhile, Zoe invited Theodora to join her in the palace, and Theodora ceded to Zoe the higher status. Ruled by two sisters, the empire found itself in an unprecedented situation.

Michael's spectacular fall awed contemporaries. Three historians (Psellos, Attaleiates, and Skylitzes) devoted major set pieces to it, the first claiming that it was the most important event in his work. A poet wrote verses on Zoe's travails and Michael's blinding, and the fallen emperor figured in school exercises on the theme: "What would Michael say as he was being deposed?"[79]

Politically, the Paphlagonian regime is interesting for many reasons. First, it reveals the authority of impersonal institutions in Romanía. This family had humble origins and seized power through obscure and sideways means. Yet once these nobodies occupied state offices, without having any socioeconomic faction to back them up, they commanded loyalty from the empire, even if grudging in some quarters. Second, that loyalty evaporated when the balance of popularity shifted too far against them— but this was a danger to which all emperors were vulnerable. Among the sharks circling the throne in the early eleventh century, including successful generals and plotting political elites, it is interesting that it was the people of Constantinople who first destroyed an emperor, opening the floodgates of political instability. Of course, in their view it was Michael V who had made the first move by deposing Zoe. The people liked to defend the rights of dynastic heirs, which, as we saw, largely explains how the underage emperors Basil II and Konstantinos VII survived their childhood. Defending women and children gave the people leverage to control the ambitions of generals and courtiers. In fact, they used this leverage against Zoe herself when they insisted that she share the throne with Theodora. There was little that a regime could do against the collective power of the people. The Paphlagonians revealed not only that almost anyone could become emperor, but that an emperor could be destroyed by almost anyone—or, in this case, everyone. The events of 1042 were a pivot between the Macedonian dynasty and the leading men who had recently been exiled and were now brought back.

|

"No Less Laws than Arms"

Konstantinos IX Monomachos
(1042–1055), Part I

F OR THE FIRST time the Roman empire was ruled by two sisters, Zoe and
   Theodora. The usual costly promotions were given to senators and gifts
to the people. To pay for them the sisters temporarily recalled from exile the
recently blinded Konstantinos (the brother of Michael IV) and forced him
to divulge the loot from his time in power. Terrified, he revealed where he
had hidden 5,300 pounds of gold, i.e., 381,600 coins, which nicely covered
present needs, as the empresses were determined to buy everyone's support
with lavish gifts; he was then returned to exile. The sisters issued a proclamation throughout the empire that offices would no longer be sold, as presumably they had been under the regime of Ioannes the *orphanotrophos*. They
also appointed their father's eunuch Nikolaos as *domestikos* of the *scholai*, and
dispatched Maniakes back to Italy, for the situation there was already critical. Finally, they decided that a male emperor was needed, whom Zoe would
(again) marry.[1] The most esteemed man on the scene was Dalassenos, despite
his defeat in the Aleppo campaign of 1030. Ioannes the *orphanotrophos* had
not dared to blind or kill him. Dalassenos was, moreover, connected by marriage to Konstantinos Doukas and would be soon be connected to Ioannes
Komnenos. After the long suppression by Basil II and the violent repression
by his successors, a viable faction was finally taking shape.

In past centuries, the court would host bride shows to select a suitably
beautiful and pious wife for a young male heir. In 1042, the gender roles
were reversed: Zoe, who was over sixty but blond and still youthful-looking,
had her pick from among the best-looking and most distinguished men in
the empire. She began to interview candidates. The first was Dalassenos,

FIGURE 10 Mosaic in the gallery of Hagia Sophia depicting Konstantinos IX Monomachos (1042–1055) and the empress Zoe on either side of Christ. The heads of all three figures replaced earlier versions. The circumstances of this alteration cannot be recovered, but the face and name of Monomachos almost certainly took the place of one of Zoe's earlier husbands, either Romanos III Argyros or Michael IV (and his longer name had to be scrunched into a smaller space). Emperors were traditionally expected to bring gifts of gold to the church when they visited Hagia Sophia, which is why Monomachos is holding a bag. Source: Shutterstock, ID 48413917.

but he spoke rather arrogantly about imperial affairs to her and was ruled out. The second was the handsome Konstantinos Artoklines, a secretary of Romanos III with whom Zoe was rumored to have had an affair. He was selected, but died suddenly of an illness (some said poisoned by his wife, who would be required to join a convent "voluntarily"). After excluding other candidates, Zoe settled on Konstantinos Monomachos, from a family of civil officials (Figure 10). His father Theodosios had been implicated in a plot against Basil II, and he himself was exiled by Michael IV to Mytilene (on the island of Lesbos) for almost seven years. Monomachos had already lost two wives (the second a daughter of Skleros and Romanos III's sister). He was received by the City with an outpouring of public celebration, wedded to Zoe on June 11, 1042, and crowned by the patriarch Alexios the next day. Thus the dynasty was extended through her and his third marriage, which was again irregular. The patriarch made another exception, but did not perform the ceremony himself.[2]

Monomachos is described as a graceful and charming gentleman, likely in his forties, eager to have a good time and make friends. He had no experience of war or even high office. It was this man who was elevated to the throne at a most pivotal moment in imperial history. He set the tone with a round of senatorial promotions and handouts to potential supporters, and he sent a proclamation to all the provinces pledging prosperity for all and an end to evil. He intended to rule through generosity and indulgence.[3] As Psellos put it in an address to the emperor in 1043, the spigots of the treasury were opened and stayed there.[4] Monomachos made sure the empresses had all the money that they wanted, and throughout his reign he made generous gifts of money, land, and exemptions to churches and monasteries.[5] He took liberties for himself too. After the death of his second wife, he had fallen for her cousin, Maria Skleraina, who had followed him to Mytilene and supported him financially. Once in the palace, he brought her to the capital with Zoe's permission; eventually, he introduced her to the palace and began to treat her as a wife, a third empress with the title *sebaste* ("Augusta") and a third expense account for her own good works and favors. She and Zoe actually hit it off—Zoe was beyond jealousy at this point. The four of them, Psellos claims, settled in to relax, pursue their hobbies, and have a good time.[6]

This image was fashioned by Psellos to diminish an emperor who, at the last minute, had abandoned him to his enemies. It has since been perpetuated by Psellos' readers, both Byzantine and modern. As we will see, it is a great distortion of eleventh-century history. Monomachos was a capable, energetic, resourceful, and conscientious ruler, one of the best the empire ever had. It was not his fault that the empire found itself threatened by three dangerous foes all at once: the Normans, Pechenegs, and Seljuks.

Enter the Normans

The geostrategic position of Romanía was altered irrevocably in the eleventh century by the coming of the Normans to southern Italy and the Seljuks to the east, developments that impressed themselves urgently on Roman awareness during the reign of Monomachos. Two regions on opposite ends of the world that had been either a power vacuum (Italy) or in prolonged decline (the east) were suddenly occupied by dynamic new arrivals. The Romans had perhaps grown complacent, used to mastering every threat in those regions if only they paid attention. They were in for multiple, simultaneous shocks.

The history, fighting style, and sociopolitical organization and ambitions of the Normans made them a distinctively new threat to the empire. By the early eleventh century, the Normans were the Frenchified descendants of Vikings who had settled in Normandy ca. 900. Their ruling class practiced horsemanship and trained in a ruthless form of heavy-cavalry fighting. The dukes of Normandy were efficient organizers and tax collectors and, with armies of such knights, ably defended their realm and even conquered England in 1066. There was also intense competition and fighting within Norman society, in part because there was not enough land to provide for all who would be knights, or offices in the state to satisfy their ambitions. This resulted in the export of mercenaries and exiles, trained in violence and opportunism. What Norman leaders needed above all, both at home and abroad, were taxable properties to support themselves and their followers. In the eleventh century, they became experts at state takeovers: they would identify a weak or ailing state (England, Muslim Sicily, Byzantium in the 1080s), attack its army and aim to take over its government, subject the local population, enrich themselves, and fund further expansionism.

What they did in southern Italy was slightly different. Here they sought employ as mercenaries, as the land was especially inviting to Norman ambitions. Large powers here were either distant or weak. The *katepano* Boioannes had reestablished Byzantine control, but the region was ranked third or below in the priorities of imperial planners and contained a large Lombard, Latin-speaking population that was known to periodically resist imperial authority. The adjacent Lombard duchies were military weak and typically in conflict with each other, while the maritime cities had money but virtually no armies, making them all perfect buyers for the services of (expensive) Norman mercenaries. And the use of these mercenaries led to—in fact required—an intensification of conflict. This necessarily changed the rules of the game, and the Normans famously did not play by any rules but those of their own relentless and cynical opportunism: whenever their patrons or employers made a mistake, they would exploit it and leverage the ensuing confusion to their advantage. Eventually they established their own domains, which, in Italy and Sicily, coalesced into states. By switching sides repeatedly to obtain even greater rewards, one of these mercenary captains, Rainulf (whose brother had died fighting for Melo against Boioannes), obtained from Naples the lordship of Aversa in 1030. This provided the nucleus of settled Norman power and inspired others to pursue similar tactics of destabilization. There was no grand plan behind the Norman takeover of southern Italy, only a relentless exploitation of weakness and the errors of others by men who had little to lose and were loyal to no polity—until they had one of their own.

The men who would take the lead in destabilizing Byzantine Apulia were the numerous sons of one Tancred of Hauteville, especially Guillaume

(William) Iron-Arm and Drogon. They and their brothers Robert and Roger, the founders of the duchy of Apulia and the kingdom of Sicily, were celebrated by Norman partisans toward the end of the century (especially Amatus of Montecassino, Geoffrey Malaterra, and William of Apulia), whom we must read skeptically for both inaccuracy and bias. Guillaume and Drogon had served in Maniakes' Sicilian campaign among the Norman auxiliaries contributed by duke Guaimar IV of Salerno, an ally/vassal of the empire, and they had returned to the mainland in 1040 after their dispute with Maniakes, whatever that had been about. In 1040, possibly as a reaction to the impositions associated with the Sicilian campaign, Apulia was experiencing one of its anti-imperial convulsions, with officials being murdered and the governor, Michael Dokeianos, taking reprisals. Unfortunately, it is impossible to understand the factions involved, as we have only brief annalistic entries.[7]

One mistake that Dokeianos made was to place Arduin, who had led Maniakes' Normans in Sicily, in charge of Melfi, on the border with Benevento. Arduin now invited his former comrades, the Normans from Salerno, including Guillaume and Drogon, into Melfi, and from there into Apulia. This was a predatory move. In 1041, the Normans defeated Dokeianos in two battles (in March and May), relying on their cavalry charges, whereupon Constantinople replaced him with another Boioannes, likely the son of the previous *katepano* of that name. He too was defeated, and captured, in September. Effective Byzantine control was now limited to Brindisi, Otranto, and Taranto, the heel of Italy; even Bari was lost.[8] It had never been this bad since the reconquest of the province in the ninth century. The Norman sources elaborate these victories with impressive feats of strength and daring, such as punching out a Byzantine envoy's horse, fighting with a high fever, and impossible odds against the winners. In reality, these were battles between two thousand or three thousand men on either side.[9]

We do not know how the population of Apulia reacted to these events, whether they complied with the Normans out of fear or joined them. Arduin would have provided a Lombard face to the invasion, but he disappears in 1041. In February 1042, the people of Bari and the Normans agreed on a new leader: Argyrus, the son of the rebel Melo who had grown up in Constantinople as an honored guest/hostage after the defeat of his father. He was to have one of the most interesting careers of the mideleventh century. At the moment, he seems to have provided a local political face for a Norman military project. Just then, in April 1042, Maniakes returned to Italy as *katepano*, landing at Taranto; he had been released from prison by Michael V and dispatched there by Zoe. Our sources for subsequent events are poor. It seems that the two sides avoided direct battle. Maniakes stayed in the south, terrorizing the population with severe reprisals for defection, while the Normans and Argyrus besieged Trani in the north. By then Monomachos had come to the throne, and wanted to resolve the crisis differently. He basically hired Argyrus to be his man in Italy, offering him titles and authority. Argyrus accepted, ended the siege of Trani, and returned to Bari, which now declared for the emperor. Argyrus too, just like the Bulgarian rebel Alusian in 1041, has been suspected of playing a double game all along. At the same time, Monomachos sent a replacement for Maniakes, one Pardos, but this did not go well. The fearsome general's rage took over again and he had Pardos killed (October 1042). Skylitzes explains that Maniakes was on bad terms with Skleros, the brother of Monomachos' mistress, and that he expected to be mistreated. Psellos alleges that Maniakes was planning to revolt before Pardos arrived, and that this was known at the court.[10]

Maniakes, the conqueror of Edessa and Sicily, had enough of being recalled and imprisoned by emperors of the palace. He rebelled and began collecting an army to lead back home—another rebellion in the midst of foreign invasion. Apparently, he failed to have himself recognized at Bari, but some Normans did take up service with him. He staked everything, as indeed he must, on a strike against Constantinople. By February 1043 he had crossed the Adriatic. Italy, however, with the Normans still on the loose, remained unsettled.

1043: Trial by fire

In the year 1043–1044, Monomachos faced a rebellion by the empire's best general, a surprise foreign attack on the capital, multiple plots against him, and a popular uprising. The first had not happened in more than fifty years and the second in more than a century. Monomachos managed to survive, in part by chance and in part by skill, but the fissures in imperial authority were spreading and widening.

Maniakes landed at Dyrrachion in February 1043. A recent Roman defeat in the region had left that outpost undefended. Specifically, the Serb principality of Duklja (modern Montenegro) under Stefan Vojislav had sought to throw off its subordinate status. When Roman armies approached, the Serbs would withdraw into the mountains and practice guerrilla warfare. The general of Dyrrachion had accordingly been upgraded to a *katepano*. But in the fall or winter before Maniakes arrived, this situation had resulted in the ambush and defeat of a huge army under Michael, the *katepano*, though his army may have consisted mostly of south Slav auxiliaries contributed by the local lords (*župans*). Fortunately for the empire, Stefan Vojislav died later in 1043 and his heirs fought among themselves. His son would eventually become a "friend and ally of the Roman people" again.[11]

When he reached Bulgaria, Maniakes defeated an unnamed "general of the west" who confronted him. He rejected an offer of amnesty and marched toward Thessalonike, the terror of his advance preceding him. In March 1043, at Ostrovo (modern Arnissa), he was challenged by a large imperial army under the command of Stephanos, a eunuch. Maniakes personally led the charge that broke through the loyalist army, causing many of its soldiers to acclaim him emperor, but in the melee he received a mortal wound, likely from a stray arrow, and fell dead from his horse. His army surrendered. Stephanos celebrated a triumph in the City with the rebel's head paraded on the tip of a spear; it was later strung up on display in the hippodrome.[12] Monomachos also discovered that one of his court secretaries, Konstantinos (later Michael) Psellos, had a talent for oratory, and together they revived the performance of orations in honor of the emperor, a custom that had lapsed four centuries earlier. Psellos' first extant oration surveyed the history of empire since Basil II, concluding with the defeat of Maniakes.[13]

With the hindsight of the empire's later decline, some Byzantine writers lamented the loss of such a formidable warrior. His prowess in battle was played up by Byzantine and foreign authors in an age when Norman knights were setting new standards for battlefield carnage. Maniakes redeemed the valor of Byzantine arms. But he was not cut out to lead the empire as a politician. He had just as great a talent for making enemies as defeating them.

Monomachos was desperate to show that he was in charge. Emperors basically had three options: lead the army in person (Basil II), entrust major command positions to eunuchs (Konstantinos VIII, Romanos III), or entrust them to relatives (Michael IV). Monomachos had no choice but to rely on eunuchs, imperial authority was becoming progressively weaker, and there was greater need for spectacle and propaganda. The general of Cyprus Theophilos Erotikos also rebelled, inciting people there to murder a tax collector (which was turning into one of the most dangerous jobs). The rebellion was quickly suppressed by the fleet, and the rebel was paraded in women's clothes during the games in the hippodrome. Another plot was then discovered, still in 1043, which implicated the general of Melitene and the eunuch Stephanos, the recent victor over Maniakes. Stephanos was tonsured and exiled, whereas the general was tortured, blinded, and paraded through the forum. Just to be sure, Monomachos (some said Theodora) ordered the blinding of Ioannes the *orphanotrophos* too, and he died soon after.[14] Eunuchs, it turns out, could scheme on someone *else's* behalf.

There was to be no rest that year. Even as these domestic rivals were being suppressed, news arrived that the Rus' king Jaroslav was gathering a huge fleet to attack Constantinople. Jaroslav I the Wise (1015–1018, 1019–1054) was the son of Vladimir. Allegedly, some Rus' traders had quarreled with locals in Constantinople, it got heated, and one of their noblemen was killed. This so enraged Jaroslav that he decided to retaliate. Monomachos sent envoys pleading that there was no reason to disrupt long-standing good relations over something so trivial—but the king was determined. The Rus' fleet, consisting of hundreds of longships under the command of the prince Vladimir, arrived at the mouth of the Bosporos in July, but Monomachos was well prepared.[15] Rus' in the capital were arrested and dispersed to the themes. The Roman fleet had been assembled, land forces had been brought up to flank them, and the emperor had sailed up in the imperial barge, and stood on a hill overlooking operations, with the ubiquitous Psellos at his side. Another plea was rebuffed, whereupon Monomachos ordered his admiral, Basileios Theodorokanos, a veteran of Maniakes' Sicilian campaign, to engage with three ships. He sailed right into the Rus' fleet, incinerated seven ships with Greek fire, sank three, and captured one by boarding it in person and slaying its crew. The rest of the Roman fleet now moved to engage, and many of the Rus', retreating, foundered in shallow waters, where they were slaughtered by the land forces. Thousands of corpses littered the coast. However, a Roman squadron of twenty-four ships pursuing the fleeing enemy was surrounded and destroyed. Yet many Rus' had to return home overland, as they had lost their ships. They were attacked and defeated at Varna by Katakalon Kekaumenos, the *doux* of Paristrion and hero of Messina. He sent eight hundred captives to the emperor, who probably staged another public celebration.

Jaroslav's decision remains difficult to explain. There is no evidence that he was colluding with Maniakes through the intermediacy of Harald, who in fact did escape from Constantinople at around this time against the emperor's wishes and married Jaroslav's daughter. The attack was likely a traditional expedition for plunder that, moreover, consolidated Jaroslav's authority over his unruly subjects; it would have given him control over his most important trade route and also established his prestige vis-à-vis a culture he was eagerly imitating in building up Kiev.[16] On the Roman side, the devastating, coordinated, and well-organized response to the attack on short notice reveals that the imperial war machine was very much intact. There is no sign here of a "decline of Byzantine naval power."[17] A few years later relations were restored. Rus' sources claimed that the emperor gave a kinswoman in marriage to Jaroslav's son Vsevolod, whose son would be Vladimir Monomakh, king of Rus' (1113–1125).[18]

Monomachos had already survived more challenges than any emperor in living memory. Psellos presents him as affable if bumbling, but Monomachos was not at all reluctant to use force against his enemies, even preemptive force against only suspected enemies. Psellos claims that after surviving this year the emperor, encouraged by prophesies, came to believe that he was invulnerable.[19] And another court intellectual, Ioannes Mauropous, wrote epigrams thanking the Virgin for shuttling between east and west to defeat the two threats against the emperor.[20] Yet Monomachos came to within an inch of his life again on March 9, 1044. Just as he was leaving the palace in a religious procession, the crowd rose up against him, shouting that they did not want his girlfriend to be empress and for Zoe and Theodora to be harmed on her account. The two sisters had to appear on a balcony to calm them down.[21] This was a reminder that, just as he was the beneficiary of a popular uprising, Monomachos could become its next victim.

Domestic initiatives (phase I)

Among the emperors of our period, Monomachos is the only one to whom we may attribute if not a "policy" in cultural, social, and economic matters then at least a series of initiatives or preferences that were noted by contemporaries. Partly responsible for them was the eloquent Konstantinos Leichoudes (probably not a eunuch), whom Monomachos employed from the beginning of his reign as *mesazon*, a kind of "chief of staff." Leichoudes promoted the careers of a circle of scholars with whom he had prior educational links: Psellos (twenty-five in 1043, an imperial secretary), Ioannes Xiphilinos (a somewhat older judge), and Ioannes Mauropous (a generation older, and a teacher of Psellos). Our main source are the orations that Psellos wrote for his three friends, which, however, focus on their virtues in the abstract, offering little concrete information. Psellos presents Leichoudes as a learned orator and model politician, able to please everyone, handle any situation, and settle disputes. But specific actions or policies remain opaque.[22]

Psellos and Mauropous did not at first hold high office but produced propaganda for the regime through speeches and poems, giving it an aura of learning and culture. They revived the art of the panegyrical oration, praising the emperor and marshaling support among the elite for his decisions. This was to have a significant impact on the future of Byzantine literature and court life. The speech in praise of an emperor before an audience of leading courtiers was an earlier Roman practice that seems to have lapsed between the seventh and the eleventh centuries, but after its revival under

Monomachos it grew in importance under Komnenoi. It was probably Psellos who revived the custom in his role as court impresario, as it played to his strengths. Others courtiers were important because of their position in the army, the Church, and the civilian administration, but Psellos contrived to take center stage as the star performer of rhetorical skills of which he was the teacher and arbiter.

At the same time, Psellos and Xiphilinos ran private schools, in philosophy and law respectively. When a dispute broke out between their students, the emperor intervened and granted some kind of official recognition to both schools. The event is opaque, as we know it through the moralizing rhetoric of Psellos' funeral oration for Xiphilinos, written thirty years later. Psellos assumed the lofty title Consul (or President) of Philosophers and exercised some kind of supervision over higher education in the capital, though the institutional aspects of his position are unclear. Xiphilinos was made "Guardian and Teacher of the Laws" (*nomophylax didaskalos*) and placed in charge of a new law school instituted by an imperial edict authored probably by Mauropous. Anyone was allowed to study there, regardless of background, and it seems that the school granted certificates. Its purpose was to systematize legal training and eliminate confusion. These positions, created probably between late 1043 and early 1047, were given court titles and salaries.[23] The law school seems to have operated in a vast complex of new constructions built by the emperor at Mangana, at the City's eastern tip. This also included a monastery and church of St. George, a home for the elderly and poor, and a palace with a reception hall.[24]

From the standpoint of intellectual history, the work of Psellos represents one of the great accomplishments of Byzantine culture of this period— indeed of the whole of Byzantine history. Psellos sought to master all knowledge and, without necessarily providing a new philosophy or a new science, to draw the attention of his contemporaries to areas of learning and ways of approaching the world and human life that had been in abeyance for centuries. Specifically, he invested heavily in ancient philosophy, especially Neoplatonism, and sought to fuse it with Christian theology in a way that makes it hard to know which side of the partnership was truly in control. He denied that he was pushing pagan ideas, but of course he would do that, and he knew that he was being watched closely. Later there would be trouble over this. He also sought to revive ancient scientific ways of explaining the world and complained that his fellow Romans tended to ascribe everything to God and leave it at that. Moreover, he rebelled against the valorization of extreme Christian asceticism—he never missed a chance to mock monks—and he tried to rehabilitate the needs of the body as an essential aspect of human life. As Consul of Philosophers, a teacher, and an intimate of many emperors, Psellos was the most famous intellectual of his time—which, of course, also made him many enemies. He wrote in most genres of literature known to his culture and decisively shaped the future course of Byzantine intellectual life.[25] Interestingly, he seems to have come from the more middling social classes and was, therefore, a direct beneficiary of Monomachos' policies.

In terms of social policy, Monomachos liberally granted titles, benefits, and prestige to men from classes that lay just below the traditional court elite. Court titles used to be purchased from the state through a large payment and yielded a salary (*roga*). The latter rarely recouped the initial investment, though it conferred social prestige and political advantages that were presumably worth the cost. Monomachos now allowed groups vaguely described as "merchants," "middle class," "working class," and "the people" to receive court titles. Psellos praised the emperor's meritocratic promotion policy, from which of course he had benefited.[26] The expanding economy of this period lifted certain classes of the capital (guild leaders, merchants, and such) above a threshold where they had to be recognized politically. The Paphlagonian dynasty, who were former money changers, may have come from these classes, and Monomachos now opened the doors of the court system to them.[27]

What we might loosely call the "upper middle classes" now become visible in our sources, and do so in significant numbers for the first time. It may even be possible to recapture something of their cultural profile. They sent their sons to the schools of Psellos and Xiphilinos, hoping to secure posts in the lower levels of the now-enlarged imperial administration. Whereas the social horizon of literature in Byzantium was previously confined to a fairly small circle, we now observe, in the letters of Psellos and the poems of Christophoros Mytilenaios, a much wider group of contacts participating in previously elite cultural exchanges and asking for classical knowledge and epigrams to adorn their religious dedications. Their wealth was likely behind a building boom in the provinces, though it is mainly the churches from it that survive today. Future research would do well to consider whether these classes, along with the influence of Psellos, were linked to changes that began to take place now in Byzantine tastes and aesthetics, which included a turn toward the human and even all-too-human aspects of daily life, an openness to the erotic, and a willingness to criticize established values. The wealthier elite of the eleventh century, drawn from more diversified provincial elements, seems to have been more open to experimenting with additional aspects of human life than had the narrower and more conservative and pious court and Church of the tenth century.[28]

Monomachos' court had every reason to seek out the support of these new constituencies. But there was a cost. Most title holders probably purchased their rights in the usual way, which benefited the state, but an expanded constituency of men who had to be won over by each new regime with promotions and "gifts" could lead to fiscal trouble. It is not clear whether Monomachos merely lowered the social bar for admission to that exclusive club *in order to generate revenue for the court*—that is, to allow more people to invest in titles— or also lowered (or in some cases even waived) the initial investment that the beneficiary had to pay for the title *in order to buy political support at the treasury's expense*. There are later instances of this happening: when Romanos IV, upon his accession in 1068, wanted to buy a family's favor, he "increased the *roga*" of one son and promoted the other to a higher rank with a higher *roga*.[29] If this had been happening all along, emperors had been effectively buying political support at the treasury's expense. In the long run this burdened the treasury and reduced the relative value of titles: the eleventh century did witness title inflation,[30] and the senate swelled in numbers. One poem of the late 1040s praises Monomachos for providing "a golden flow of *rogai*," and another praised him for being a river of gold.[31] But the bill would later have to be paid. In fact, it seems that *roga* salaries had been reduced by one-seventh already in the first half of the century.[32]

In addition to the schools, Monomachos reformed aspects of the civilian administration too. Leichoudes' legal background may explain the bureaucratic-civilian nature of the regime's initiatives. Monomachos instituted a new bureau under a "Verdict Inspector" (*epi ton kriseon*). Provincial judges were required to send their trial transcripts in order to counter suspicions of corruption.[33] The civilian aspect of provincial administration had in fact steadily grown since the reign of Basil II. Most themes now had a dual hierarchy, with a judge (*krites*) or other civilian magistrate (*praitor*) in charge of the legal and fiscal administration, leaving local military matters to the general (*strategos*).[34] The creation of the new bureau centralized control over the emerging civilian administration of the provinces.

The regime of the mid-to-late 1040s has been called the government of the philosophers, but Psellos' later narratives are full of vague allusions to enemies plotting against them and slandering them to the emperor. He and Mauropous had to respond to multiple attacks from anonymous critics, for example that they were selling out for power and money,[35] and Leichoudes had enemies who would eventually bring him and the whole group down. Xiphilinos was also targeted, and Psellos rallied to his friend's defense by responding to an old judge who questioned the appointment as *nomophylax* of one so young and socially undistinguished.[36] But it may not have been enough. If Xiphilinos was retained it was not for long, and the *nomophylax* eventually became another secretarial position. To show his confidence, the emperor offered Psellos the position of *protasekretis* (head of the secretariat), but he had to decline it, probably realizing that he lacked support.[37] As we will see, he was also coming under religious scrutiny for the philosophical implications of his teaching. If it ever existed, the "philosophers' regime" unraveled quickly.

The annexation of Ani

As we saw, in the Georgian war of 1022 the Armenian king Smbat III pledged his realm of Ani to Rome upon his death, which took place probably in 1041.[38] Michael IV was in no position to claim it in 1041, and it is unclear whether he tried. Monomachos too was beleaguered until mid-1043, but then insisted on his legal claim. The Armenians had, however, elected a successor in the meantime, Smbat's nephew Gagik II, who suppressed a rival and fought the Muslim emir of Dvin. Gagik was willing to recognize the emperor but not to surrender Ani, so in 1044 Monomachos ordered the *doux* of Iberia, Michael Iassites, to take it by force. The war went badly, so the emperor dispatched that old standby, Konstantinos VIII's *parakoimomenos* and *domestikos* of the *scholai*, the eunuch Nikolaos, who had campaigned there almost twenty years earlier. Monomachos also invited the emir of Dvin, Abu al-Aswar, to attack Ani, allegedly ceding to him any forts that he captured. Another attack on Ani, which lay in a strong location, may have also failed, but imperial inducements prevailed in the end. Gagik traveled to Constantinople, where he exchanged his title for rich properties and titles. We should not accept the Armenian version that he had to be tricked in Constantinople to surrender; he would not have gone there if he did not intend to cede his claim. Ani may have resisted after his departure, but by early 1045 it too had surrendered to Iassites. It was made a *doukaton*, often united with Iberia in practice.

Unfortunately we know little about Roman rule in Armenia. It had never extended this far east and would not last for long, so it left little evidence of itself. Chalcedonian sees were certainly favored, and the Armenian *katholikos* Petros I was removed, first to Artze, then to Constantinople, and finally to Asia Minor. But his movements may not have been forced (unlike the Jacobite patriarch Yuhannan in 1029).[39] The nobleman and scholar Grigor of the leading family of the Pahlavuni also surrendered his lands to the empire at this time, was made *magistros*, and given lands near Edessa. He did not accept Chalcedon, but was made *doux* of Vaspurakan in the early 1050s.[40]

So far, then, and contrary to his image as an irenic and civilian emperor, Monomachos had decisively suppressed internal challenges, firmly repulsed the Rus', and expanded the empire's control in Armenia, enforcing Roman claims. Ani was recognized at the time as "a major bulwark, defending against barbarians who intended to invade Iberia through that region."[41] Then, immediately in 1045 the emperor sent Iassites against the emir of Dvin to recover the lost forts of Ani, allegedly reneging on his promise to cede them. This was not a complacent emperor. But Abu al-Aswar led the Romans into a trap by flooding the plain, and massacred them. Iassites was replaced as *doux* by Kekaumenos and Nikolaos by one Konstantinos, an Arab eunuch from the emperor's retinue, and they began reducing the forts individually. Yet this campaign was interrupted by news of Tornikios' revolt in 1047. Abu al-Aswar gladly agreed to a peace, which allowed Konstantinos to rush off to save the emperor.[42] The empire was entering a phase of war on multiple fronts, and the armies would often shuttle back and forth from east to west. At least between the summer of 1043 (the Rus') and early 1047 (the Pechenegs), the empire was at peace.

Having Muslim clients continued to pay off. A preacher named al-Asfar had begun to lead jihadist raids into Roman territory from Ra's al-'Ayn in 1047/8. Monomachos instructed the emir of Diyar Bakr, Nasr al-Dawla, to contain the problem. He summoned some of his tribesmen and told them to "get him to stop, or he will bring the Romans down on us." They arrested the preacher.[43]

The Pecheneg invasions and the Revolt of Tornikios

In the ninth and tenth centuries, the Pechenegs, who spoke a Turkic language and were cast in Byzantine ethnography as uncivilized nomadic "Skythians," were a major power in the steppes north of the Black Sea. Their actual political and social organization and cultural profile are difficult to recover through the rhetoric of the sources. Pecheneg khans were able to muster large armies and made both alliances and wars with their neighbors, including the Romans and Rus'. Within their territory they were basically pastoralists who controlled trade routes. By the mideleventh century, they were losing badly at the hands of the Rus' and large numbers of them were being pushed westward, to the Danube region, by the Oghuz (another Turkic confederation moving in from Central Asia). By the 1040s, this once-great territorial power was in terminal decline but could still disrupt Roman frontier defenses and even defeat imperial armies. Eleventh-century sources depict them as bestial: nomads who drank blood, lived like animals, and lacked organization. But even these texts give us glimpses of Pechenegs with infantry, discipline, and agriculture.[44]

Probably in 1046, two tribes of Pechenegs led by one Kegen fell out with the rest of their people and sought refuge in the empire. They went to Dorystolon and informed Michael, the *doux* of Paristrion, that twenty thousand of them wished to become imperial subjects. The emperor gladly consented, sent them provisions, and invited Kegen to the capital, where he was given a title and command over three forts, and named a friend and ally of the Roman people. The monk Euthymios was sent to baptize the whole group, and Kegen took the name Ioannes. This was standard policy for barbarian refugees. Kegen began to raid across the Danube against his enemy, Tyrach, selling his captives to the Romans—an irony, to see Pecheneg raids going in *that* direction. Tyrach protested to the emperor, who strengthened the watch along the river and dispatched a fleet. But in December 1046 or January 1047, the river froze, enabling Tyrach to cross over and begin to devastate Roman territory. This, at least, is the narrative in Skylitzes. In reality, Tyrach may have been driven to cross by pressures that remain opaque. At any rate, Monomachos responded with alacrity by ordering Kegen and three *doukes*—Michael (Paristrion), Konstantinos Arianites (Adrianople), and the former monk Basileios (Bulgaria)—to converge on Tyrach's Pechenegs. The latter were already suffering from dysentery; they were surrounded and surrendered. Kegen wanted to kill them, but the Romans had better plans. They were disarmed and settled in Bulgaria, by Serdica and Niš, where they would pay taxes and furnish recruits. Tyrach himself and 140 of his men were taken to Constantinople and baptized in public ceremonies.[45]

Monomachos had repeatedly proven himself an able defender of Romanía and promoter of its interests abroad, and had responded quickly and decisively to crises. Yet something then caused the *tagmata* in Macedonia to turn against him in the spring of 1047. This stemmed somehow from their demobilization at the end of the Pecheneg crisis, and the fact that they were idle and not receiving campaign pay while the eastern armies were active at Dvin. The plot centered on Leon Tornikios, an officer from Adrianople (the capital of Macedonia) who was a second cousin of Monomachos and close with the emperor's sister Euprepeia. At that time he held an eastern command, possibly of Melitene, so it is unclear how he was coordinating with the Macedonians. The emperor defused this crisis gently, by winning over the other officers, but it clearly caused disruption. Mauropous had composed a panegyrical speech for the feast of St. George (April 23, 1047), with a section on the Pecheneg settlement that was to be delivered at the new church of St. George built by Monomachos (the emperor's banner depicted that saint mounted and chasing the barbarians with a spear). At the last minute, however, Mauropous had to omit this section from the speech. The Pecheneg situation was controversial in some way we cannot recover. Tornikios himself was removed from command, tonsured, and moved to Constantinople.[46]

Tornikios was subsequently approached by Macedonian officers,[47] and on September 14 he escaped with them to Adrianople, where they began to canvass among the officers and soldiers. They quickly obtained the support of the *tagmata* of Macedonia and Thrace, the most powerful western field armies. Tornikios was proclaimed emperor, becoming a "sword-bearing monk," and established his own countercourt (there is no sign of Arianites, *doux* of Adrianople, at this time). The rebels' strategy was to take the capital quickly, before Monomachos could summon the other Balkan and eastern armies.

The City lacked an adequate defense force, but Monomachos was quick to act: he immediately summoned his eunuch Konstantinos from Dvin, mounted catapults on the walls, armed the citizenry, and took his stand in a conspicuous position at Blachernai (Figure 11). With the City gazing at his ranked files and siege engines, Tornikios was acclaimed as emperor and hurled insults at Monomachos, trying to win the people over. Monomachos

FIGURE 11 WALLS OF CONSTANTINOPLE. Heavily restored section of the triple land walls of Constantinople. Source: Shutterstock, ID 29415577.

was unsure of their loyalty, but this was where his general liberality, and bold presence on the walls, paid off: the people booed the rebel. Leichoudes advised that a force be sent outside, protected by a moat. It was a foolish plan: Tornikios' soldiers easily routed this makeshift force, causing the people to desert the walls and flee, even leaving a gate open. The City would have been taken had Tornikios not "miraculously" refrained from pressing his advantage. No one knew why he lost his nerve and recalled his men. Monomachos quickly reoccupied the walls, and hurled rocks at Tornikios for a few days, as the rebel's supporters melted away. After a weeklong siege, Tornikios withdrew and attacked Raidestos, the only Thracian city that had not joined him, but he failed there too. This now became a broader Balkan war, where the emperor had the advantage. Tornikios' lieutenant Ioannes Batatzes defeated the Roman army of Bulgaria that came up from the west, but the rebels were surrounded by the eastern armies that had just arrived under Iassites (and Monomachos possibly called on his Pecheneg allies as well).[48] Rebel soldiers defected until Tornikios and Batatzes fled to a church near Adrianople, where they were arrested and dragged before Monomachos. He blinded them on the spot, on Christmas day. Four days later Mauropous celebrated the victory in a panegyrical speech.

It had been a close call, but Monomachos' leadership was again swift and decisive, in spite of his deteriorating health (arthritis and diarrhea, allegedly). For a civil war, it had caused little damage. It was, however, the first appearance of a faction of seditious officers that could subvert the Balkan armies. And another, far more momentous development was taking place at the eastern ends of the empire that would alter its history entirely.

CHAPTER 9

"Squaring the Circle"
Konstantinos IX Monomachos (1042–1055),
Part II

The Seljuk invasions and the Pecheneg wars

The Seljuk conquests represented the most pivotal moment in the history of the Near East since the Arab conquests of the seventh century. They created a new Muslim world and unleashed forces that, among many other peripheral effects, struck Roman Asia Minor at the worst time and place. The Seljuks were an extended family of Turkoman (Turkish) nomads in Central Asia, who fought as mercenaries in the service of various powers east of the Caspian Sea. In striking ways, the rise of the Seljuks mirrored that of the Normans, only on the vaster scale afforded by Central Asia. They were cunning opportunists who preyed on weakness and switched employers to secure further advantage; successful raids (on eastern Iran) attracted more followers, which enabled them to rise to the level of armed invasion, exponential conquest, and state takeover. A myth of common origin was invented to unify this military confederation of Turks whose founders, just like the sons of Tancred of Hauteville in Italy, were endowed with religious and dynastic legitimacy by later panegyrists.

The creation of the Seljuk empire was accompanied by mass migrations of Turkoman nomads toward the west: Iran, Azerbaijan, the Caucasus, and Anatolia. A central dynamic of this story was the tense relation between the "tribes," searching for plunder and pasturage, and the sultans Tughril Beg (d. 1063) and his nephew Alp Arslan (1063–1072). A successful leader provided his followers with plunder from raids and good pasturage, and Roman

Caucasia beckoned with both. The *Georgian Chronicles* offers a fascinating description. The nomads would settle in areas

> where in winter, as in spring, grass is mowed and wood and water are found in abundance. A multitude of all kinds of game exists there, and there is every sort of recreation. In those regions they would settle with their tents; of their horses, mules, sheep, and camels there was no reckoning. They led a blessed existence; they would hunt, relax, take their pleasure. . . . They would engage in commerce in their cities, but would invade our borders for their fill of captives and plunder.[1]

Turkish attacks on Caucasia targeted precisely such regions and bypassed the forts that controlled the mountainous areas in which they were not interested. Surrounding settlements were attacked to eliminate threats to the pasture-land.[2] Attaleiates also understood that the Turks' goal was to turn Roman land into pasturage for sheep.[3] But the first inroads were for plunder, not settlement. And here Seljuk leadership was hotly contested: the sultans spent almost as much time fighting the established powers of the Near East (such as the Buyids) as they did their own cousins (e.g., Ibrahim Inal and Qutlumush) for control of the tribes. Thus, the erratic pattern of raids into Caucasia and Anatolia before the floodgates opened after 1071 is difficult to understand as it included armies led by the sultans or their supporters, rivals, and losers in internal conflicts, as well as by independent parties.[4] Tughril posed as the nominal lord of most groups, but also encouraged them to move westward so as not to destabilize the sedentary territories he was trying to consolidate.[5]

In the 1040s, Tughril had conquered eastern Iran and was moving west, against the Buyids and other dynasties. His goal was to consolidate control over Iran and Iraq, not to attack Christian powers. There are confused reports of a raid led by his cousin Qutlumush that detoured into Vaspurakan and defeated and captured its commander Stephanos Leichoudes, nephew of the *mesazon*, possibly in 1045.[6] Tughril regularly sent his relatives (i.e., potential rivals) on such raids, including his nephew Hasan to Azerbaijan, in 1048. From Tabriz, Hasan raided as far as Tbilisi and returned laden with booty by way of Vaspurakan. The *doux* was now Aaron, a son of the Bulgarian tsar Ivan Vladislav, who called for help from the *doux* of Ani and Vaspurakan, Kekaumenos. They laid a trap for the Turks by abandoning their camp, waiting for the enemy to start sacking it, and then fell on them by surprise. The Turks were slaughtered, Hasan included.[7]

Word now came of a more massive Turkish invasion, which the Romans naturally viewed as a response to Hasan's defeat. But there were other dynamics at play in the Seljuk world. Tughril had previously dispatched his half-brother and ally-cum-rival Ibrahim Inal to Hamadan. In 1048, a large group of Oghuz joined Ibrahim from Transoxania. Unable to support them, he led them into the Caucasus. Disagreeing about how to respond, Aaron and Kekaumenos pulled back all the way to Theodosioupolis, to the valley Outrou, where they were instructed by the emperor to wait for the arrival of their Georgian ally Liparit. Ibrahim meanwhile attacked and sacked the nearby trading town of Artze. When Liparit arrived, the armies fought a fierce battle by the fort of Kapetrou on September 18, 1048, but its outcome is uncertain. In most sources it is a Turkish victory, though Skylitzes, relying possibly on Kekaumenos himself, describes the results as mixed. But whether Kekaumenos broke through in the center or not, Ibrahim departed with all of his massive loot, and Liparit himself was captured and taken to the sultan.[8]

Such were the first encounters between the Roman armies and Turkish raiders. Turkoman raids basically tested for weakness, and the Roman response was not weak. This led to the first official diplomatic contacts between the two empires. Monomachos refused to pay "tribute" to the sultan but allowed him to sponsor the restoration of the mosque in Constantinople and to have his name honored in the prayers instead of the Fatimid caliph. The emperor's priority was the release of Liparit, who upheld Roman interests in Georgia, in his on-and-off conflict with king Bagrat IV. After one or two years, Tughril magnanimously released Liparit, possibly in order to destabilize Georgia. But Monomachos had already acted with his usual alacrity to defend Roman interests. Skylitzes' phrasing should be quoted, as it will become relevant later: "from that moment the emperor anticipated war with the sultan and, to the best of his ability, sent agents to fortify the regions bordering on Persia."[9] The threat came not only from the "official" armies of the sultan but from bands of Turks operating more or less outside any structure of authority. Even though Tughril told the Romans that he had no power over them, he was advising other Muslim rulers harassed by them to send them on against the Romans.[10]

Monomachos moved immediately. Already in late 1048 he dispatched the eunuch Nikephoros, a former monk whom he appointed to an ad hoc military post of "rector" (*raiktor*) and sent against the emir of Dvin, Abu al-Aswar. The latter, under pressure, had changed his allegiance from the emperor to the sultan and was raiding the Roman territory of Ani. Aided by king Bagrat, Nikephoros first frightened off a Turkoman raiding party from Ganja and then reduced Dvin to obedience. Abu al-Aswar picked up and moved to Ganja soon after that.[11] It is worth noting that the emir had in his retinue the Ziyarid prince, Kai Kawus b. Iskandar, later the ruler of his ancestral domains in northern Iran and author of the famous book of maxims, the

Qabusnama. In it he says that he had fought holy wars in India and then against Rome under Abu al-Aswar.[12]

Monomachos, far from being a civilian neglectful of the army, emerges as acutely sensitive to the empire's military needs. Again in the words of Skylitzes, "he hastened to respond to the enemy by armed force."[13] Probably in early 1049, he decided to sent fifteen thousand Pechenegs to the east, to reinforce local defenses. He armed them, gave them horses, and rewarded them—proving that they had been demilitarized in 1047—and ferried them to Asia Minor. But they had advanced only a few miles when they decided to return, allegedly by swimming across the Bosporos. When they reached Serdica, they summoned the rest of their people—presumably the former followers of Tyrach—who came armed with axes and scythes. The host crossed the Haimos mountains and settled in a fertile place called Hundred Mountains, likely near Preslav. There follows a perplexing story in Skylitzes: Monomachos summons Kegen and his army to Constantinople, Kegen is almost assassinated by some Pechenegs, Monomachos imprisons Kegen and his sons, and his Pecheneg army sneaks away to join their compatriots in revolt. We have no way to penetrate the background here, or assess the historicity of this tale. The emperor seems to have mistrusted Kegen and wanted to separate him from the other Pechenegs, but the result was a general uprising.

The united Pecheneg army recrossed the Haimos and began to plunder the territory of Adrianople. According to Skylitzes, they were met at Diampolis (Jambol) by Arianites, the local *doux*, but they beat him soundly.[14] According to Attaleiates, it was a standoff. Monomachos then decided to release Tyrach, who had been detained in the capital since 1047, on condition that he pacify his people. Tyrach predictably joined them instead. The emperor also summoned the eastern armies, probably regular tagmatic units stationed in northwestern Asia Minor, and placed them under the *raiktor* Konstantinos, aided by Kekaumenos and Latin knights under Hervé Frangopoulos ("Frankson"). Meanwhile, the Pechenegs had recrossed the Haimos again. The Roman army followed them to Diakene, near Hundred Mountains, before September 1049. According to Attaleiates, the Romans charged at the Pechenegs in a disorderly way, without establishing a camp first, and were massacred. He hints also that there was tension between the western and the eastern field armies, possibly poison oozing still from the civil war of 1047. Skylitzes recounts that story along with a contradictory one, involving a Roman camp and palisade, and drawn battle lines. Either way, it was a disaster. The Pechenegs were now plundering with impunity.

To meet this crisis, Monomachos placed his Arab eunuch Konstantinos in charge of yet another army consisting of the western survivors and more eastern units, whom he placed in winter quarters by Adrianople. In June, 1050, the Pechenegs crossed the Haimos and advanced against the camp. Samouel Bourtzes, grandson of Michael, led a reckless charge against them without Konstantinos' permission, which drew the rest of the Roman army into precipitous battle and, again, defeat. Arianites was killed and Michael Dokeianos (the veteran of Italy) was captured. When he was led before a Pecheneg chief, he grabbed a sword and killed him, whereupon he was torn apart by the rest. This defeat was at least not as costly in manpower, as the Romans managed to fall back on their camp and defend it. The Pechenegs withdrew when the *scholai* were brought up from Adrianople and the forces of Bulgaria arrived with their *doux*, the former monk Basileios.

The Pecheneg war had already become the worst string of Roman defeats in more than a century. The situation was completely unacceptable and Monomachos was furious at his generals for bungling it so badly. By this point the emperor's gout was so severe that he could not walk. To his credit, he realized that he had to change his strategy. Open battle was not working, and when he sent Kegen to pacify the Pechenegs, they killed him. Ever ready to adjust, Monomachos now assembled barbarian auxiliary units, Franks, Varangians, and mounted archers from the east, placing them under Bryennios and Michael, the Varangian captain, possibly a Latin. They began to mount guerrilla attacks against bands of Pechenegs in Thrace. Moving at night, they fell on a sizable contingent by Charioupolis (Hayrabolu) and annihilated it. Bryennios and Michael carried on this war apparently for three years (1050–1053), until the emperor in 1053 was ready to muster another regular army. By this point, the land south of the Haimos had been secured, but there was fear that the lower Danube would slip out of Roman control if left in Pecheneg hands for too long.

The assembled army, under the joint command of Michael and the long-serving *doux* of Bulgaria, Basileios, crossed the Haimos and reached Preslav. The Pechenegs successfully withstood them behind a palisade there, where-upon the Romans, running out of supplies, were divided: Michael was for fighting and Basileios for withdrawing, citing the emperor's orders not to engage in pitched battle.[15] The Romans accordingly began to withdraw at night. But Tyrach was prepared and attacked the Roman column, dispersing and slaughtering them, including Basileios. Despite this disaster, Monomachos would still not give up. He assembled the survivors and mustered more forces at Adrianople, planning another assault. By now the Pechenegs themselves had had enough, and sued for peace. It was agreed for thirty years, and held, though we do not know its exact terms. Certainly the Pechenegs had to recognize the emperor's sovereignty over their lands, but there was now a quasi-autonomous Pecheneg presence south of the Danube, within imperial territory.[16]

More troublingly, the Roman armies had performed poorly against the Pechenegs. It was only by repeatedly tapping Romanía's ability to mobilize manpower and resources that Monomachos had eventually worn them down. Even then it was a draw, and those capacities could not be taken for granted if they were put under additional strain. There was another major enemy now active in the east whose intentions and capabilities were unknown, and the Romans were lucky that the Seljuks were busy with the conquest of Mesopotamia during the Pecheneg war. And there were also the Normans, disrupting Italy. What if all three attacked at once?

Domestic initiatives (phase II)

At the beginning of his reign, Monomachos had an irregular "domestic" life, to be sure, featuring one official empress-wife, one unofficial empress-wife-mistress (Skleraina), and one empress-sister-in-law. He was criticized by a monk at the Stoudios monastery for his "affair" with Skleraina.[17] When she died in ca. 1046, he was heartbroken, and his court poets, including Psellos, duly wrote funerary poems.[18] She was buried in the emperor's newly constructed church of St. George of Mangana, where the law school was operating. The fund associated with that church was transferred from her to the *mesazon* Leichoudes, a sign of great favor.[19] But around 1050 Leichoudes was replaced and the "regime of the philosophers" was brought to an end. Around that time, Zoe died too. There is no proof that she had been the power behind the philosophers, though that is often asserted.

Zoe's death, which passed with hardly a notice,[20] was important for dynastic continuity; only Theodora now remained. Monomachos' own condition was visibly deteriorating already in 1047. His arthritis rendered him incapable of walking, and he had to be held up and then carried, in excruciating pain.[21] Yet his sex drive was undiminished. He acquired a new mistress, through diplomatic channels no less. Psellos claims that she was the daughter of an Alan king kept in Constantinople as an honored hostage. In the eleventh century, "Alan" was one way to call the Georgians, but it is unlikely that she was the daughter of Bagrat IV (born 1018). It could have been any Caucasian lord, even an actual Alan. After Zoe's death, this mistress too was elevated to the rank of *sebaste* and installed in the Mangana palace, with guards and expense accounts.[22] Monomachos had grandly received the Georgian lord Liparit in Constantinople after his release by Tughril, probably in 1050, and sent him to Georgia to promote Roman interests. Liparit was always warring against Bagrat, which is perhaps why Tughril had released him. He now forced Bagrat to go to Constantinople, where the king and his retinue were detained for three years (ca. 1050–1053)—Bagrat's second stay in Constantinople as a hostage—while Liparit governed most of Kartli-Abkhazia.[23]

Leichoudes was replaced by the young eunuch Ioannes the *logothetes* (a type of finance minister).[24] Leichoudes became a monk; Mauropous was made bishop of Euchaïta in Asia Minor, where he was not happy; and Psellos and Xiphilinos made a pact to leave the court by becoming monks, though the latter was more sincere in this choice and did so first.[25] Psellos stayed on as Consul of Philosophers and continued to write panegyrical orations for Monomachos until the end. The regime remained ever vigilant in suppressing potential plots against the throne, a number of which are attested in the later years, though no more armed rebellions.[26] It is possible that the associates or relatives of court plotters were resettled in eastern regions affected by the wars, which removed them from the court while strengthening the Roman presence there.[27]

Attaleiates does not mention Ioannes the *logothetes* but claims that in his final two years (1053–1055) Monomachos became an oppressive tax collector, targeting the rich and lands set aside for religious purposes. Skylitzes offers a jumbled summary instead: Monomachos imposed high taxes to build his church of St. George (a ridiculous notion), and was trying to make money through various nefarious means, but was also so generous that he began the ruin of the Roman state. Psellos strongly endorses the latter accusation, which is an argument from hindsight about a decline that appeared later.[28] The regime seems to have been generous throughout (which, of course, is compatible with strict tax collecting), and there were no more tax-related uprisings.[29] In 1044, Monomachos sent an assessor to impose taxes in Macedonia on towns and villages that had somehow slipped through the state's fiscal net, including those belonging to monasteries.[30] But such censuses were routine.

Two measures have been taken by historians as signaling a narrative of imperial decline, the first as a cause, the second as a symptom, though both are hard to interpret. The first is Monomachos' alleged demobilization, defunding, or overtaxation of the army in "Iberia," which is supposed to have exposed the empire to Seljuk attack through that corridor. This is placed by the sources in the context of the emperor's "greed," and will be discussed below. The second was Monomachos' broader use of Phokas' *tetarteron*, the lighter-weight gold coin, albeit now in a more devalued form and coupled with a partial devaluation of the standard gold coin (i.e., a reduction in the gold content of the coins). This had begun under his predecessors, but to a far lesser degree. The change enabled the mint to generate more coins than it had bullion (maybe by 10 percent). It used to be taken as proof of a budget deficit, until C. Morrisson ingeniously proposed that it was an effort to provide currency for an expanding and coin-starved economy. This has gained wide currency, though not without pushback.[31] Having considered the arguments, I would cautiously revert to the traditional view. Devaluing the coinage was a risky move that could damage imperial credibility, and it seems unlikely that an emperor would make it to facilitate private transactions. Also, we do not know that the devaluation resulted in a larger production of coins in absolute terms to service an expanding economy, rather than merely in a larger production relative to available bullion.

The regime was under more military stress than any of its predecessors, in Italy, the Balkans, and the east, and an artificial bump in revenue would have been handy, because its expenses had suddenly increased. Moreover, I will argue below that these expenses did not stem exclusively from military needs but also from the likely multiplication of state salaries that emperors had been awarding for almost three decades to curry favor with political constituencies. This was a function of imperial vulnerability, which had now become a fiscal issue. And before 1050, *roga* payments had been reduced by one-seventh, which is more consistent with fiscal constraints than a desire to put more cash into circulation. Only two years after Monomachos, Isaakios was forced to make drastic budget cuts, suggesting that the devaluation was an initial form of a budget problem.

Italy on the brink and the Schism of 1054

The decade after 1043 was the turning point between a viable imperial presence in southern Italy and its imminent extinction at the hands of Norman aggressors. The entire structure of power there changed in ways that had an impact on the empire's relations with the Latin west, especially the popes. There followed, in 1054, the visit of the papal legates in Constantinople, which has been discussed more than any other event of Monomachos' reign, because it allegedly shaped the future of Catholic-Orthodox relations, or at least revealed tensions that were liable to burst out at any moment. The Byzantine sources barely mention either events, and the so-called Schism of

1054 has been downgraded to the status of a "non-event."[32] But there may have been more to it, and the loss of Italy was certainly real.

In 1042 at occupied Melfi, the Normans had elected Guillaume Iron-Arm as their leader, and his position as count was recognized by Guaimar V of Capua, the Normans' nominal lord. The chief knights divided up both the conquered and the not-yet-conquered lands into fiefdoms (just as the Crusaders would do before the walls of Constantinople in 1204). But despite these formal structures of authority and aspirational legality, the Normans were, like the Turks, unruly bands of marauders preying on the weak. They were active on two fronts: first, toward the Lombard principalities, Capua and Benevento and, by extension, the popes and German emperors; and second, more aggressively, toward Byzantine Apulia and Calabria, where their advance is unfortunately known only through terse Latin annals and later partisan narratives. Here they inserted themselves through terrorism (murder, rape, kidnapping, the burning of crops), forcing the population to pay protection money and then establishing strongholds from which to enforce their now "legalized" claims and commit more aggression. One of the most successful of these bandits was another son of Tancred, Robert, who arrived around 1048 and was assigned to a remote fort in Calabria (Scribla, in the Val di Crati). He proved to be especially good at terrorism, earning the name Guiscard ("Cunning").[33]

A narrative of warfare in Apulia is beyond our grasp; Norman gains seem to have been slow and concentrated along the margins.[34] The commander of the Byzantine forces, Argyrus (not yet a *katepano*), was more often than not defeated by Guillaume, and was recalled to Constantinople in 1045 or 1046. Guillaume died and was succeeded by his brother Drogon in 1046. Argyrus' successors again both won and lost, but Byzantine control was gradually being restricted to the coast, and sometimes even Bari would not admit the *katepano*. The Byzantines do not appear to have had much of a plan during these years, which was when they were preoccupied with the Pechenegs, Tornikios, and Seljuks in the east. Argyrus returned in 1051 as *katepano*—the first and last time a local was appointed to that position—and this time there was a plan. He effected entry into Bari by suppressing the local resistance, which served interests unknown to us. He then inserted himself into a growing anti-Norman coalition taking shape around the reformist pope Leo IX (1049–1054). Argyrus may have been complicit in Drogon's assassination in 1051.

The Normans had made too many enemies in southern Italy, including of course the Byzantine authorities, many of the Lombards of Apulia, the duchy of Benevento, which they were threatening, and the pope, because of their attacks on Church interests and properties in the south and the obstacles that they were creating for reform. Broadly speaking, the reformists around Leo wanted the Roman Church to be more centralized, set apart from society, and self-governing, rather than a field for the exercise of secular interests. They insisted on clerical celibacy and papal supremacy and opposed the purchase of ecclesiastical offices. By declaring that the Church of Rome stood in a monarchical relationship to all other churches of the Christian world, they created the very idea of the "papacy," but this required an ideological framework that could not be accepted by the "Ecumenical Patriarchs" of Constantinople (as they had been called since the fifth century).[35] The two Churches had largely been willing to live with their differences, which were minor in the grand scheme of things, but papal reform sharpened and hardened them.

Still, in 1050 the reformers were also pragmatists and not ready to take on the entire world. One place to start was southern Italy. Leo certainly wanted to reimpose papal control over the Latin churches of Apulia, which Constantinople would have opposed, but containing Norman disruption was more pressing, and Benevento had appealed to him for help. Leo had asked Drogon, and Drogon had promised, to curtail Norman aggression, but when it continued the count gave the same answer that Tughril Beg did at the same time in the east: he could not control the separate bands.[36] So Leo and his advisors were willing to collaborate with the Byzantines in order to tame the common foe. However, the Normans—who now had a new count, another son of Tancred named Onfroi, or Humphrey—defeated Argyrus at Taranto in 1052 and 1053, and then defeated Leo's coalition army at Civitate in 1053, before Leo could join up with Argyrus. Belying Drogon's excuse, the Normans did rally together; even Robert Guiscard came up from Calabria for Civitate. The victors captured Leo and, although famously treating him with honor, pressured him to recognize their presence in Italy.

Leo's alliance had been the best chance to save southern Italy, and it had failed. But the game was not over. Though the Normans kept Leo under guard, in January 1054 he sent two of his closest advisors, cardinal Humbert and the chancellor Friedrich, to Constantinople. In letters to the emperor and patriarch Michael Keroularios, Leo defended papal supremacy but also tried to lay the groundwork for an alliance against the Normans.[37] Keroularios, we recall, was a failed conspirator under Michael IV who had been in exile for years. But so had Monomachos, who took a liking to Keroularios in 1042, when he recalled his predecessor's exiles,[38] and appointed him patriarch the next year. Contrary to his image after 1054, which highlighted his arrogance, Keroularios does not seem to have given Monomachos any grief,[39] though by 1050 he was taking issues of doctrinal and ritual correctness seriously. He (or clerics around him) scrutinized Psellos' teachings and promotion of non-Christian thought; they even conducted synodal inquiries about the matter. Psellos was being slandered to the emperor and had to sign a confession of faith to clear his name.[40] A more important issue for the Church was a by-product of imperial expansion: many Armenians had been brought under imperial rule who did not recognize Chalcedon and, among other differences, used unleavened bread (*azyma*), i.e., wafers, in the Eucharist, like the Latins. Polemical orthodox literature that implicated the Latins in these question-able practices ("Is it even bread?") had come to pope Leo's attention under Keroularios' name (but in reality written by Leon, archbishop of Ohrid, and sent to colleagues in Apulia).[41] Argyrus himself, during his five-year stay in Constantinople (1046–1051), had quarreled with Keroularios over the *azyma* and was even refused communion.[42] Moreover, the Normans had been suppressing orthodox services in conquered Apulia, and it was alleged that Keroularios had shut down Latin churches in Constantinople, which affected visiting westerners, especially Amalfitan and Venetian traders (though it is debated whether that actually happened).[43] For these reasons, Leo raised both religious and military issues in his letters.

Those letters were delivered by the pope's legates, who, after conferring with Argyrus, arrived in Constantinople around the same time the pope himself was dying (April 1054), which technically invalidated everything that they did afterward. They held conferences in the palace, presumably about the strategic situation in Italy, but our documentation concerns reli-gious matters exclusively. Modern narratives, however, are problematic. They allege that Humbert and Keroularios clashed and that the patriarch thereby undermined and eventually ruined the emperor's foreign policy. In reality, Keroularios and the legates never discussed religious matters; indeed they never met after the legates delivered the papal letters. The legates were given every assurance by the emperor that their view of papal supremacy would be upheld, and Keroularios stayed out of it entirely, probably on orders by the palace.[44] Then, on Saturday, July 16, the legates entered Hagia Sophia right before the liturgy and placed on the altar a formal "bull" of excommunica-tion directed against the patriarch and his associates, detailing their heresies. These included the rejection of Catholic practices regarding baptism and the Eucharist and doctrines regarding the procession of the Holy Spirit, i.e., the now-notorious *filioque*. By contrast, the legates were careful to praise the emperor and people of Constantinople.

Keroularios had the document translated and brought to the emperor, who recalled the legates. Humbert claims that the patriarch also stirred up a popular protest against the emperor, to force his hand, but this is suspect.[45]

The legates refused to present themselves before the synod, and so the emperor let them go and informed Keroularios that the excommunication had to be answered. The patriarch, for his part, blamed the translators and Argyrus. A synod met on July 24, which condemned Humbert, exposed Argyrus' plots, and made a record of the transactions.[46] The synod carefully did not condemn the pope or the Church of Rome, but it listed Humbert's errors in ways that would have implicated most Catholics. But when Humbert returned to Italy, he continued to believe that the emperor was on his side.

There is a "traditional" view about these events, which is that they led to a schism between the two Churches and that Keroularios was mostly to blame (as most old views are pro-western and anti-Byzantine). There is now also a "new traditional" view, which is that these events had almost no immediate impact, even on Church relations; were hardly noticed by contemporaries; and were caused by two misbehaving individuals (Humbert and Keroularios). But it is probably time to revisit the new orthodoxy too, as it ameliorates the past by downplaying the significance of conflict, probably to cater to modern feelings. To do so, it focuses on the limited immediate effects of "1054" and steers attention away from what made it possible in the first place. The two sides could not have excommunicated each other, or disseminated treatises against each other, just because they had pugnacious prelates. Rather, they did so because they were committed to mutually exclusive theological-eccle-siastical positions, and they were perfectly aware that this was the case. The reformers' emphasis on papal supremacy was not negotiable and would have led to a schism with the east sooner or later. Schism could have been avoided only if the eastern Romans had simply accepted papal claims, i.e., had surrendered their Orthodoxy to some conceited German in Rome.

In contrast to Humbert, Keroularios was discreet and does not deserve the odium heaped on him. His letter to Leo in 1053 was conciliatory,[47] for all that the pope pounced on it. Even after Humbert's scene in Hagia Sophia, Keroularios cleared his every move with the emperor, and the Synod's decision echoed the emperor's directives. Keroularios' negative image rests on Humbert's caricature and Psellos' later polemic, which had to do with completely different issues.[48] Keroularios is routinely accused of sabotaging the negotiations with the emperor, but there is no proof for that. We have no idea what agreement was reached in the palace, and the project may have fizzled for now only because the pope died. Still, Keroularios did hold that some Latin beliefs and practices were wrong, and so did many other Byzantines, and he may have acted on those beliefs by closing down Latin churches and barring Argyrus from communion. Therefore 1054 was possible only because key Byzantines too held inflexible positions. Some believed that those differences were nonessential and could be accommodated,[49] but this view lost in both the short and long run, and was likely already in the minority.

Schism does not mean only that two Churches are in open war against each other. It is not necessarily a legal fact created by official documents. It may also be a sense or belief that there is no community between two Churches. The situation in 1054 showed that this was already the case for many at Rome and Constantinople, and not among fringe elements either. "New traditional" historians like to point out that Humbert and Keroularios excommunicated each other and not their respective Churches, and yet both knowingly justified their excommunications in ways that defined each other's Church, polemically and with many distortions, to be sure, but recognizably so. Schism was already there. The only question was how it would play out. Would it be ignored to forge alliances on other common projects, e.g., against the Normans, or would it be used to justify wars? Before the decade's end, the Church of Rome would recognize the Normans as its own warriors and within a couple of decades it would endow them with the right to conquer Byzantium in the name of God.

Coping with new challenges

History sped up during the reign of Monomachos. He was the first emperor since the 980s to face a viable military revolt—two of them in fact. There were few Romans alive who would have remembered those against Basil II. Monomachos also came to power after a popular uprising, and faced its sequel in 1044. He uncovered numerous plots by both army officers and courtiers. As the link to the previous dynasty was becoming increasingly attenuated and there were no plans for a succession, more vultures began to circle around the throne. Yet Monomachos handled all these challenges successfully, with a minimum of disruption to the political sphere. He did not become a paranoid executioner, and the civil wars were over quickly, with few casualties. He promoted intellectuals at the court, men such as Mauropous, Psellos, and Christophoros Mytilenaios, who left their mark on the history of Byzantine literature and thought. He made access to education and the court and senate more feasible for many, though we cannot gauge the social consequences of his policies. He was "generous," though again we cannot gauge its economic effect. Did he squander money? We cannot know.

As for imperial defense, Monomachos must be rehabilitated immediately. The worn narrative that he was a "civilian" emperor who did not care much for the army and allowed the empire's strategic situation to deteriorate is completely false. Even modern rehabilitations of him stress his visionary *civilian* agenda.[50] He must also be rehabilitated as a military emperor: every crisis—and he faced more than the usual—found him alert, informed, usually prepared, and instantly responsive. He never let a situation slide, except in Italy, which had always been a low priority. Monomachos used both eunuch-generals from his household and the "bearded" officer class.[51] The military setbacks of his reign were theirs, not his. During his reign, the Roman armies had trouble taking Ani, and were defeated by the Serbs of Duklja, the emir of Dvin, the Pechenegs (too often), the Seljuks, and the Normans. There is no indication that these Roman armies were smaller than usual, or underpaid, or demoralized. But the cliché about Romans is that they often lost the battle only to win the war. In the end Monomachos did take Ani, subdued the emir of Dvin (twice), held the line against the Seljuks, made a settlement with the Pechenegs, and annihilated the Rus' invasion. It had been a rough ride, but he did well. The only true loss was in Italy, and it would prove irrevocable. Otherwise, the empire continued to expand in the east as well as economically and intellectually.

In terms of geostrategy, the reign of Monomachos was pivotal. It was the first time in centuries that the empire had simultaneously faced challengers on three fronts: the Normans in Italy, the Pechenegs on the lower Danube, and the Seljuks in Armenia. As we have seen, it was usually difficult for the empire to cope with two at a time. Three was just too much, and this explains the effective loss of Italy. There was only so much any emperor could do. The typical strategy was to deal with the more pressing dangers first and, with that accomplished, mount an expedition to Italy. However, the challenges facing Monomachos were not typical. All three enemies were "new," sometimes with unfamiliar fighting styles (especially the Normans), but more importantly with new objectives. The Normans were not just a Lombard uprising or yet another pathetic incursion by a German emperor. They were mercilessly filling a power vacuum in southern Italy. The Pechenegs intended to stay on the lower Danube, south of it if possible, away from the Oghuz. And the Seljuks were creating a vast and powerful new state in the Near East the likes of which had not existed there since the early ninth century. By 1055, they were still acquiring new territories and sorting out their internal differences to have a coherent policy toward the empire, but their rise unleashed a Turkoman population movement that did serious damage to its eastern territories. Apart from scattered bands, the sultan was not above the occasional raid for plunder, and possibly conquest. Monomachos was lucky that the Pecheneg wars occurred during a lull in Seljuk hostilities, when Tughril was busy in Iraq and Iran.

The Seljuk advance overshadows a controversial fiscal reform of the Iberian army (or army in Iberia) attributed to Monomachos by three Roman writers. Many historians view this measure as a main cause of the collapse of the eastern front later on, so it requires close attention. One pillar of that belief can be demolished right now: it is impossible that in ca. 1050, when the reform is usually dated, Monomachos thought that all would be peaceful henceforth. Lurching from crisis to crisis, Monomachos could not have taken peace for granted. Before we look at the sources for the reform, let us review the response to an incursion by Tughril at the end of the reign, presumably after the reform had taken place.[52]

In 1054, Tughril moved northwest to confirm the loyalty of Tabriz, Ganja (under Abu al-Aswar), and the Marwanid emir of Diyar Bakr. The last two were former Roman clients, so we observe that Seljuk expansion had already stripped the empire of its Muslim buffer states. He then raided as far as Theodosioupolis, which is deep in Roman Armenia.[53] According to Skylitzes, he accomplished nothing because the inhabitants had secured themselves in forts, and he turned back when he heard that the Roman army was mustering at Kaisareia—a classic defense-in-depth strategy, though using *Kaisareia* in this way takes us back to the geostrategic situation of Nikephoros Phokas. Tughril then focused on capturing Mantzikert. According to Aristakes, Tughril did not go far past Mantzikert, but sent raiders north. Aristakes laments the damage that they did, but reveals that a unit of Varangians annihilated one of the main raiding parties (and a confused notice in Skylitzes reveals that units of Frankish mercenaries and Varangians had been posted throughout Chaldia and Iberia at precisely this time).[54] Moreover, Tughril accomplished nothing in his monthlong siege of Mantzikert, thanks to the heroism of the Roman governor, Basileios Apokapes, who is praised in all the Christian sources. One of his Latin soldiers rode out to destroy a siege engine by hurling a hand grenade of Greek fire at it. Overall, then, a good showing.

So what had Monomachos done to the Iberian army? The response of the 1054 raid is not by itself suggestive, though it reveals that forts were maintained and Varangian units stationed far in the east. Attaleiates says that the formidable army in Iberia was supported by public lands, which the emperor took away because of his "greed." Thus he not only lost those men as resources but caused them to be added to the empire's enemies. Skylitzes says that in his avarice he used a certain Leon Serblias to disband the Iberian army, some fifty thousand strong, so that from those regions he raised not soldiers but taxes. Kekaumenos says that the tax collector Serblias went to Iberia and Mesopotamia and made registries in order to impose taxes that had never been seen in those parts, which caused the locals to go over to the Seljuks and lead them against the Romans.[55]

What are we to make of this? First, we can dismiss the rhetoric of "greed." That is just a way of saying a tax was imposed, which we can infer anyway. Monomachos had a specific goal, not just to make money (which he could have done in easier ways). Also, the tale of people so overtaxed that they leave their country was (and is) a conventional trope that sounds dramatic but whose exact impact is hard to assess. It may have happened to some degree, but none of our sources tell us who these people were or when they defected; nor was the Seljuk advance facilitated by deserters. Possibly a single anecdote lies behind this.[56] We may also distrust Skylitzes' number of fifty thousand; his figures are impossible as often as not. Finally, we can reject explanations that make Monomachos act foolishly, such as demilitarizing the eastern frontier at precisely a time when it was rapidly becoming threatening again.[57] We have seen that he was consistently attentive to matters of defense and was no fool. In 1051, he was using Argyrus in Italy to recruit more Normans for the struggle with the "Persians."[58] Nor was he disbanding an Iberian army that had threatened his throne (the Balkan armies had been far more dangerous to him).

The core information provided by our sources is this: new taxes were imposed on certain groups in "Iberia," taxes were extracted from them (or a different group) instead of military service, and material support provided to soldiers from "public" lands was terminated. Although the sources are not precise enough for us to identify specific arrangements—not that historians have not tried[59]—the general idea makes sense in a Byzantine fiscal context. There were soldiers—the standard "thematic" type established in tenth-century legislation—who were defined by their relationship to a specific category of land. To simplify, that land paid fewer taxes and, in exchange, its owner provided military service (*strateia*). But it was possible to cancel this arrangement: the land would pay full taxes, military service was no longer owed, and the state (presumably) used the cash to hire professional soldiers. This is called "fiscalization of *strateia*," wherein a service obligation is commuted to cash. This could be an option or it could be made mandatory, as seems to be the case here. Fiscalization could be an efficient arrangement, so long as the state actually used the cash to defend the province. Full-time soldiers (e.g., the *tagmata*) were better, but fiscalization entailed the risk that the money could be used elsewhere, e.g., for churches or political favors, leaving provinces undefended. This might be what Aristakes was complaining about, albeit with the benefit of hindsight and a propensity to lament everything. He accuses Monomachos of not spending his taxes on cavalry but on whores—lots and lots of whores—thereby allowing the Turks to win.[60] Or this may be a generic complaint unrelated to fiscalization.

Unfortunately, we cannot assess the impact of Monomachos' reform. We do not know what percentage of the armies commanded by, say, Iassites and Kekaumenos consisted of local, "land-supported," soldiers as opposed to mobile tagmatic forces. If high, then the reform was far-reaching, even revolutionary; if low, then the state was canceling a tax exemption for which it was gaining little in return. We also do not know the scale on which fiscalization was applied, as "Iberia" and "Mesopotamia" could be used loosely. Current thinking has it that fiscalization of *strateia* was by now more or less the norm throughout the core territories of Romanía, at least as an option ("pay or serve"), which is certainly plausible if difficult to prove.[61] If this were the norm everywhere, why was it controversial to apply it to Iberia? Perhaps the Iberian reform had to do with a specific fiscal aspect of the relatively recent incorporation of Tao and Ani. Those realms used to have their own, non-Roman armed forces. How had they, and the royal lands of those realms, been absorbed? This fellow Serblias may have been extending regular taxation to Tao and Ani,[62] as the Romans had previously done to Bulgaria, and thus his reforms changed an aspect of the relation between land and service dating back to when those lands were first annexed.

At any rate, it is not likely that Monomachos was just looking for money; his goal was to improve imperial defenses, not abolish them. We will keep our eye on these provinces for hints. In the response to Tughril's 1054 raid, we see a strategy of withdrawing the population to forts, not bringing out a local army to face the invader; we also see Frankish and Varangian units posted in those very provinces; and imperial armies mustering further west, at Kaisareia. Always dispatching armies to hot zones, soon before his death Monomachos sent the Macedonian *tagmata*—his old foes—to the east.[63] A few years later, in 1056 and again in 1057, we hear of Franks stationed full-time in the Armeniakon theme, possibly with their own estates. Were these the professionals who were hired with the Iberian money?[64]

We should also not overlook Syria, which was at peace after the Fatimid treaty. Monomachos realized the dream of finishing the rebuilding of the church of the Holy Sepulcher, by sending an architect and funds from Constantinople (the project may have begun under Michael IV). Byzantine interest in this church may have stemmed from the rising tide of mostly western pilgrimage in the eleventh century.[65] Antioch is described as a prosperous city by the Baghdadi physician ibn Butlan, who passed through in ca. 1050. The walls, he says, were held by four thousand soldiers sent from Constantinople in shifts of two years, and the land between the city and Aleppo was populous and peaceful.[66] Spectacular gifts were exchanged between Cairo and Constantinople, including an elephant and giraffe to the latter, and in 1054 the emperor promised to send grain to Egypt to alleviate a famine. There were flare-ups, due mostly to third parties, but no major problems. An embarrassment occurred when the emperor agreed that Tughril should be recognized in the Muslim prayers in Constantinople, just when the Fatimid envoy happened to be in the City.[67]

We can glimpse the final days of Monomachos only through the self-serving account of Psellos' decision to flee the court and become a monk, involuntarily and temporarily, in Bithynia. The philosopher's enemies (Keroularios?) had finally make the court too hot for him,[68] and the emperor's lack of support may have contributed to the negative portrait that he painted of Monomachos later in his history. As he lay dying at the Mangana palace, the emperor and his eunuch advisors decided to designate Nikephoros Proteuon, the governor of Bulgaria, as his successor. But Theodora's people learned this and brought her swiftly to the palace, where she was reacclaimed empress—a coup by a sitting empress. She and Monomachos had not gotten along for some reason "and even at the time of his death she was not reconciled to him."[69] Proteuon was arrested and sent to a monastery in Asia Minor. Monomachos died on January 7/8 or 11, 1055, and was buried at St. George, with Skleraina.[70]

CHAPTER 10	"With Sword Drawn"
	It All Comes to a Head, 1055–1059

Theodora (1055–1056)

For the second time in its history the Roman empire came into the hands of a woman who decided to rule on her own. Theodora was now the last of her dynasty, the greatest that the empire had ever known. She was in her early seventies, and had an interesting story. Placed in a convent by her sister for conspiring with Konstantinos Diogenes, she twice came to power via coups: first when the people rose up against Michael V in 1042 and (against Zoe's wishes) elevated Theodora to imperial rank; and again in 1055, when she and her household eunuchs scuttled Monomachos' succession plans. Her career thus combined most of the avenues to imperial power that could be traveled in the eleventh century: military plots, dynastic continuity, a popular uprising, and a palace coup. It was assumed by all that Theodora's prime order of business in 1055 would be to find a man capable of running the empire, but she decided to rule in her own name. She did a good job, was accepted by her subjects and praised by later historians. The patriarch Keroularios, however, seems to have insisted, apparently to her face, that the state had to be run by a *man*.[1] It is noteworthy that Theodora decided against a new round of promotions and gifts, as, she claimed, this was not a new reign but the extension of an existing one.[2] The last emperor who had gotten away with this was her father, in 1025. But possibly now there were budgetary constraints too.

Theodora's first move was to exile Monomachos' eunuchs, who had tried to elevate Proteuon, and confiscate their property. She replaced them with her own household eunuchs, whom she placed in top army posts too. Her main advisor was Leon Paraspondylos, a priest (and former assistant to the patriarch). Psellos came out of his (monthlong?) monastic retreat and ingratiated himself with the new regime. The biggest threat facing the late Macedonian dynasty was men who could seize the throne and found dynasties of their own. Theodora's regime—a woman and a few eunuchs— represented the ultimate response to this threat, both the most extreme and the last. Something had to give, and soon would. Roman officers had a thousand-year history of obeying the court, and they knew the difference between the people in power and the majesty of the Roman state, but ambitions could be pent up only for so long. A succession crisis was inevitable. The first peacock to spread his plumes was Bryennios, an officer from Adrianople, who had fought the Pechenegs under Monomachos and had been sent by him to the east with the Macedonian *tagmata*. He now marched to Chrysopolis, on the other side of the Bosporos, but was arrested and exiled for leaving his post, and his armies were sent back east.[3] What was he thinking? Probably not to fight but bully the regime when it was still thought that Theodora was looking for a man.

Theodora exchanged embassies with Tughril Beg, who took Baghdad in December 1055, but raids by quasi-independent bands of Turks and the emir of Dvin against Roman Armenia continued. The governor of Taron, one Theodoros Aaron, had enough soldiers to fight them off a few times before he was killed in battle. Theodora sent another Theodoros, her *domestikos* of the eastern *scholai*, to check these inroads, but we do not know what he did.[4] Also, the Egyptian historian al-Maqrizi reports that Theodora decided not to send the grain shipment that her predecessor had promised to the Fatimids, provoking the latter to take over Laodikeia and the coast south of Antioch. The following year, 1056, the Roman forces of Antioch retook this territory with the assistance of eighty ships sent from Constantinople.[5] The fleet was, then, still in good order. Attaleiates and Psellos remembered the reign for good governance and lack of foreign and domestic troubles.[6]

Theodora died on August 31, 1056, after intestinal complications. As she lay dying, Paraspondylos and the other eunuchs pressured her to designate as her successor one Michael Bringas, a native of Constantinople, who was himself very old (he signed his name as "Michael the Younger," to distinguish himself from his predecessors named Michael, and so his subjects reactively called him "the Old Man").[7] Michael was also known as *stratiotikos*, because he had spent his career in the military bureaucracy (there is no evidence that he had been a soldier). He was allegedly naïve and docile, and they believed, correctly, that he would do what they told him. Before crowning him, the patriarch Keroularios insisted that Theodora, who was too weak to speak, personally assent to this decision, at least with a nod.[8]

Michael VI (1056–1057)

The regime of Michael VI was as similar to the regime of Theodora as her eunuchs could make it, except it lacked the fig leaf of dynastic continuity. Instead of an empress ruling through eunuchs, eunuchs now ruled through a weak emperor. The late Macedonian "solution" had attained its ultimate devolution. Michael's age and lack of children meant that this arrangement was temporary, so the race was on. His brief reign was nothing but a stage on which the other elements of the republic—the people, the patriarch, politicians, and army officers—forcefully reclaimed the political sphere.

The first to make a bid was Monomachos' cousin Theodosios. He and his clients paraded down the Mese, mimicking a popular uprising by protesting and freeing the prisoners from the prefect's headquarters. But the streets emptied out. Theodosios found the palace barred against him, and also Hagia Sophia, where he had hoped the patriarch, clergy, and people would proclaim him emperor. In the end, he was abandoned there with his son, to beg for mercy. He and his associates were exiled to Pergamos. It was too soon, or he was just not popular. This feeble attempt only bolstered the Old Man,[9] who indulged in a new round of gifts and promotions, especially to the senate. He recalled Bryennios from exile and placed him again in command of the Macedonian armies sent to fight the Turks in east, but he did not restore his property; "deeds first, rewards later," he said. This alienated a known insubordinate. The Norman mercenary Hervé Frangopoulos, in Roman service since the time of Maniakes, asked for a promotion (to *magistros*), but was denied and insulted. He now returned to his post in the east—either in Koloneia or the Armenian themes—where he persuaded three hundred Franks to desert. They joined the Turkish raider Samuk, but then fell out with him, and at Khliat (ruled by the Marwanid emir Nasr al-Dawla) most of them were killed and Hervé was imprisoned.[10]

Worse was to come at Easter, 1057, when title holders came to be paid by the emperor. A group of officers hoped for promotions, but instead they were rebuffed by Michael during a solemn public ceremony. They included the *magistros* Isaakios Komnenos, who had just been removed by Theodora from the office of *stratopedarches* (army commander of the east). Isaakios was the son of Basil II's officer Manouel Komnenos, had served as *doux* of Vaspurakan and Iberia, and was married to Aikaterine, the daughter of the tsar Ivan Vladislav. His brother Ioannes was married to Anna Dalassene. There was also the *magistros* Katakalon Kekaumenos, who had just been stripped of his command of Antioch, probably because of the temporary loss of Laodikeia in the brief war with the Fatimids. Michael VI reproached him for almost losing Antioch too. With them were the *vestarches* Michael Bourtzes, the grandson of the conqueror of Antioch; the *vestarches* Konstantinos Doukas, who was married to Eudokia, niece of the patriarch Michael Keroularios; his brother Ioannes Doukas, a friend of Psellos; a Skleros; a couple of Argyroi; and others. In this group we see the future of the empire for the next thirty years, indeed for the next century and more. Looking back—as these men would have been in their fifties—we see a generation who matured in the aftermath of Basil's long reign, and led the families whom he had promoted.

The officers approached Leon Paraspondylos to intercede, but received the same negative response. They now decided to rebel, with Komnenos as their leader, and went back to Asia Minor.[11] Their grievances may have run deeper than Michael's refusal to promote them. The army probably disliked the regime of eunuchs and civilian politicians that had held power for so long. As Psellos explained a few years later:

> For a long time the soldiers had found the situation of the state to be intolerable ... because the emperor was always chosen from among the other side, I mean the civil servants. Even when a decision was to be made concerning the head of the army or the commander of a unit, leadership was entrusted to men inexperienced in war. Those who lived inside the cities received greater offices than those who endured the hardships of war. When the need arose for some to conduct hard battles and resist adverse fortunes, those who lived in Constantinople could sit back and relax as if in a great castle, while those who lived far away from the City in the countryside suffered terribly. For these reasons they were ready to protest against this situation in a most violent manner, and they lacked only a spark to set off their explosion. And then it happened. No one asked them their advice concerning the appointment of the new emperor and they were held in contempt.[12]

The conspirators needed armies, so they approached the disgruntled Bryennios, who quickly agreed to join them. With his Macedonian *tagmata*, they controlled a large part of the armies of both the east and the west. Yet Bryennios moved too fast. He arrested his paymaster and gave bonuses to soldiers of the Anatolikon theme. But the commander of the Pisidian and Lykaonian units of the Anatolikon theme—it is unclear whether these were tagmatic or thematic armies, for all that they are called *tagmata* by Skylitzes—realized that this was a usurpation and quickly attacked Bryennios. He captured him and turned him over to the paymaster, who blinded him. The conspirators were now afraid of being exposed, so they hastily convened at Isaakios' estate in Paphlagonia and proclaimed him emperor on June 8. The rebel armies assembled there, though it is unclear which of the conspirators other than Bryennios held command positions; it seems that they had to canvass for support among the officers and soldiers and forge orders of imperial appointment for themselves.[13]

The Roman army now split between loyalists and rebels. The Old Man still had some support in the east, including the Macedonians, and he moved other western armies over to Asia Minor too. *Now* he showered his officers with honors and titles, and placed in command of his armies Theodoros, Theodora's eunuch, as *domestikos* of the eastern *scholai*, and Aaron, Isaakios' brother-in-law. The loyalists held Nikomedeia and the rebels took Nikaia. A drawn battle was eventually fought at a place called Hades. Aaron defeated Skleros on the rebels' right, but Kekaumenos defeated Basileios Trachaneiotes and the Macedonians on the loyalists' right, and took their camp. This enabled Isaakios to defeat Aaron in the center, and the eunuch Theodoros went over to Isaakios. The battle was said to be bloody with great casualties on both sides—almost entirely Roman.

The Old Man now tried to shore up support in the capital, handing out more gifts and honors and circulating a document pledging nonrecognition of Isaakios, which all senators had to sign.[14] But he also sent envoys to treat with the rebel, who had advanced to Nikomedeia; these were Monomachos' *mesazon* Konstantinos Leichoudes, Leon Alopos, and Psellos, who wrote an account of the embassy, highlighting his own role. The first proposal was that Isaakios should become *kaisar* and thus Michael's heir, but this was rejected, and it was alleged that the envoys met secretly with Isaakios and exposed the emperor's weakness in the capital to him. The envoys came back with a new deal: Komnenos would be proclaimed co-emperor, adopted as Michael's son, his appointments would be confirmed, and Paraspondylos removed from power. This was accepted. But events were already spinning out of control in Constantinople, when a crowd assembled at Hagia Sophia and began to cheer for Komnenos. "Their voice was calling out to cut the emperor into pieces and give the throne to the one who had won the battle."[15] They were protesting that, by making a deal, Michael VI was forcing them to break their own oaths, and so *he* was the perjurer. It was also suspected that the patriarch Keroularios was behind them, as his niece was married to Doukas, although others believed that the protesters forced him to join them.[16] Eventually, on August 30, the clergy joined in the acclamations of Isaakios, and Keroularios advised Michael to abdicate; it was what the people were demanding. Michael wanted no more bloodshed, and asked what he would get in return. "The kingdom of heaven," he was told. So he stepped down and was tonsured. When Keroularios embraced him with a kiss, Michael said, "May God reward you fittingly for this embrace."

Kekaumenos hurried to secure the palace on August 31. As Psellos put it, "rebellion had been transformed into lawful power."[17] On September 1, Isaakios was crowned emperor in Hagia Sophia.[18] He had already bestowed on his close followers the higher ranks for which they had fought the war.[19] This, then, was the first military rebellion that successfully toppled a regime in the City since Nikephoros Phokas in 963, a century before. Both had played out similarly, with a military advance followed by popular protests. Interestingly, both had toppled an old man from the Bringas family.

Isaakios I Komnenos (1057–1059): Fiscal reforms and the fall of Keroularios

Isaakios was about fifty when he became emperor. In his public appearances he was intimidating, fierce, and laconic; in Psellos' account, it was as if a dark cloud followed him around.[20] He depicted himself on his coins, unusually, with a drawn sword (Figure 12). Although this probably signaled nothing more than the return of capable military rule, it was misinterpreted as a boast that his accomplishments came not from God but from his own prowess (this coin type was imitated by William the Conqueror in England).[21] His top officers were his fellow conspirators, and he made his brother Ioannes

FIGURE 12 Gold coin of Isaakios I Komnenos (1057–1059) showing the emperor with drawn sword. Intended probably as a declaration of military might and determination, this posture drew criticism for its arrogance. © Dumbarton Oaks, Byzantine Collection, Washington, DC (accession no.: BZC.1948.17.2961).

domestikos of the west.[22] The two brothers had lived in the Stoudios monastery when they were growing up after the death of their father Manouel.[23] Isaakios' son Manouel had already died. Ioannes' son, Alexios, was a toddler. Isaakios' wife, Aikaterine, who began life as a Bulgarian princess and was enslaved by Basil II, now became empress of the Romans. Isaakios rewarded his soldiers handsomely but quickly sent them back east, to forestall trouble in the City, for which everyone was grateful. He rewarded the patriarch for his support by giving him the authority to decide on personnel, promotion, and fiscal oversight within the Church, and he bestowed high court titles on the patriarch's nephews.[24] That was the emperor's endearing side, and it lasted for a few days.

Isaakios was the first emperor in our period who certainly faced a deficit in the budget, and had to take drastic measures. This strengthens the traditional view that Monomachos' devaluation of the coinage had been an initial reaction to deficits. Isaakios specifically wanted to reallocate money to the army, knowing that trouble was brewing on all fronts. But what was causing the deficits? Psellos has left us a graphic image of a bloated body politic, to whose monstrous form most emperors since Basil had added more limbs and fat with their lavish spending. Isaakios now cut away at it, with surgery, cauterization, dieting, and trimming. He became a strict tax collector, raising revenue. But what expenses did he cut? First, he canceled all of his predecessor's gifts and awards, and then took aim at those of past emperors too. He canceled or reduced the *rogai* (state salaries) they had awarded to their favorites. As we have seen, political weakness had driven most emperors after Basil to buy favor and support. I suspect (though this cannot be proven) that they had handed out the rights to a *roga* either for free or at a discount. Because of the systemic insecurity of the throne, the budget had thereby been shaped by political concerns, not economic or administrative needs. Isaakios, we hear, quickly became unpopular with some people, but the way in which he had come to the throne gave him a position of strength from which to implement reforms.[25] A later historian believed that the image on his coins signaled how he would cut through political problems.[26]

Isaakios canceled grants of public land to private interests, but above all he seems to have targeted grants made by prior emperors to monasteries and churches, including regular payments, lands, and tax exemptions. Some religious houses had grown rich, turning into landowning-trading businesses to which emperors had given legal privileges too. Psellos and Attaleiates cheered Isaakios' reforms in this sector, ironically noting that it was all in the monks' best interest, as now, without having all these material distractions around, they could devote themselves to self-denial!

Of course, these reforms made him unpopular with some in the Church, as had similar measures by Nikephoros Phokas a century before. Their objections were not immediately threatening (and modern scholars generally overestimate the Church's political power and influence). Unfortunately, we cannot quantify these measures fiscally.[27]

It is not clear whether the patriarch Keroularios opposed these measures specifically, but relations between him and the emperor deteriorated quickly. He had tasted the power of a king maker, in 1057, and now he developed a lofty conception of the "imperial" dignity of his office. He spoke abruptly to Isaakios, admonishing, reproaching, and ordering him about, reminding him how much the emperor owed him, and even threatened him, saying "I made you, and I can unmake you." It was alleged that he began to wear purple footwear, an imperial prerogative. Possibly Keroularios was influenced by papal theories about the relationship between the *imperium* and the *sacerdotium*, or was taking literally some Byzantine rhetorical pronouncements about their parity. Unfortunately, we are not told any of the particular matters on which the patriarch expressed strong views. We have only character sketches of an imperious prelate (an image that modern scholars have projected back onto the events of 1054). Isaakios had had enough. He waited for the patriarch to visit a church outside the walls, on November 8, 1058, and sent the Varangians to arrest him and take him to an island exile. It was done this way to prevent his followers from resisting. Yet whatever the dynamics of popularity at the time, Keroularios was not then and did not later become an inspirational figure for the orthodox laity.[28]

There was nothing unusual about Keroularios' deposition. In the Roman empire, patriarchs always served at the emperor's pleasure and many had been removed from office, or resigned, for failing to follow imperial orders. Isaakios pressured Keroularios to resign, but he would not budge, so a synod had to be convened to go through the motions of finding him guilty of a whole range of trumped-up charges. It was set to be convened in Thrace, away from the City. Psellos took pleasure in composing a long speech against his nemesis, accusing him of wildly improbable religious offenses, including satanic rituals. This was payback for the inquisition to which Keroularios had earlier subjected him (and it is likely that his speech was not actually going to be delivered but was merely a fun exercise for Psellos). However, Keroularios was gracious enough to die on his own, on January 21, 1059, before the trial took place, which solved everything nicely. In February, Isaakios made Psellos' old friend and patron Konstantinos Leichoudes patriarch, and matters returned to normal.[29] Even here, however, the emperor made money: in exchange for becoming patriarch, Leichoudes had to surrender the St. George of Mangana fund that Monomachos had given him after the death of Skleraina.[30]

Barbarians of the east and west

So how did this martial emperor fare in war? Psellos claims that the barbarians of the east caused trouble at first, but when they realized who was in charge, they stopped altogether, so that Isaakios turned his attention to the west.[31] But this is not accurate.

The Roman civil war had left the east exposed. We learn from Aristakes that Ivane, son of the Georgian lord Liparit, took over two forts on the frontier without violence, captured the tax collector, and then besieged Theodosioupolis. Its commander called for help from the general at Ani, who chased Ivane away. But Ivane then called in some Turks, who allegedly raided as far as Chaldia. On a second raid, they reached Keltzene (Erzincan) and then sacked the fort of Blurs by Theodosioupolis; another division went south to Chorzane. Aristakes has it that these raiders gruesomely killed everyone they could find, and even had fun with the bodies afterward.[32] This was before Isaakios took power. A month after his coronation, the raiders reached Melitene. It seems that the population was allowed to evacuate under the cover of a Roman unit before the Turks entered and sacked the city for many days. The sack itself is not mentioned in the Greek sources, but it was a major loss. Yet the sequel was interesting: local forces seized the passes and forced the Turks to spend the winter in Chorzane, until March 1058. When they besieged the fort of Mormrans, they were ambushed and fled, and many of their captives were rescued. The Romans did not offer battle, but ambushed them again. And when the Turks entered Taron, an army came down and destroyed them.[33] In sum, the empire was no longer inviolate, as it had been for decades, but it had also reverted successfully to the guerrilla tactics of the past century: minimizing or absorbing losses, while wearing down and destroying invaders. There is no evidence that Monomachos' reforms had downgraded the local defenses of the eastern frontier. Melitene was upgraded to a *doukaton* after this and its walls repaired.[34]

Isaakios led only one campaign in person, against the Pechenegs and Hungarians, who had made some kind of pact. Unfortunately, this campaign is recounted vaguely. In late summer of 1059, the emperor went to Serdica, where he made a treaty with the Hungarians, which is opaque to us. He then turned on the Pechenegs by the Danube, presumably the same ones with whom Monomachos had made a treaty in 1053. Most of their leaders now submitted to Isaakios, except for one Selte, who was defeated and his stronghold on a high rock was captured. It sounds like a minor affair. However, the army suffered a catastrophe on the return march, on September 24. By the foot of a mountain it was caught in a downpour of rain and hail. Many soldiers were lost in the flooding, freezing, and loss of supplies. The emperor was nearly crushed by a tree that was struck by lightning right next to him. He hastened back to Constantinople because of a false rumor that an imperial tax assessor in the east was plotting rebellion.[35]

Later that year, Isaakios was hunting by the Bosporos when he fell ill with a fever. Sensing his imminent death, and surrounded by his family in the palace, he designated his fellow rebel Konstantinos Doukas as his successor, in late November. Psellos, writing the first installment of his history under Doukas, insinuates that he himself orchestrated this regime change, even against the wishes of Isaakios' wife Aikaterine, but this may just be self-promotion and favor currying. Extending the work during the reign of Doukas' son, Michael VII (1071–1078), Psellos complicates the narrative: Isaakios recovered enough to have second thoughts, but then Psellos seized the initiative by proclaiming Doukas, leaving Isaakios no choice but to accept the deed. Still, no source presents this transition as a coup; nor is there any evidence for a conflict between military and civilian factions, as much modern scholarship imagines. Isaakios became a monk in the Stoudios monastery, where he had been raised, and lived on for another six months, humbly performing his duties, including that of doorman. His wife and daughter also joined convents but remained visible in Constantinopolitan life.[36] Had there been a coup, Komnenian tradition would have remembered it, especially in the later anti-Doukas climate.

General Considerations
The Return of Multipolarity

MANY MODERN ACCOUNTS of the mideleventh century present it nega-tively. This was when the Byzantines allegedly lost the peace by fail-ing to prepare for a host of emerging new challenges, and when imperial defenses atrophied at the hands of "civilian" emperors more interested in mistresses and building churches. This follows Psellos' criticisms of Basil's successors, especially Monomachos. Some historians have then superimposed on it a story of feudalization, proposing that "great families," defined as landowners, struggled against the Macedonian state in an effort to impose their class interests on it. Others have seen the rot set in under Basil II, sug-gesting that he undermined the empire's traditional defenses, the thematic armies, in ways that his incapable heirs could not fix to respond to new ene-mies. Although the eleventh century has been rehabilitated economically and intellectually, the shadow of political and military decline hangs over it.

Let us sort out what we know and what is modern imagination. The most striking development, absent from most modern surveys, is the return of multipolarity to the political sphere. For thirty-five years, Basil II had concen-trated power into his own hands. During that time he did not face challenges from rival politicians, other elements of the court, the people of the City, or the clergy, and faced only one mutiny in the army (quickly over). Perhaps *this* was the deviant development in the history of the empire, whose political sphere was normally defined by contestation and imperial vulnerability. All those elements, whether individually or in combination, traditionally tested the regime for weakness or set limits to its power. In the thirty-five years after Basil, the situation had gradually returned to normalcy: the political sphere was turbulent again. Power was dispersed and up for grabs. The first to actually topple an emperor was the populace of Constantinople (in 1042). Army officers tried in 1043 and 1047, but the first to succeed was late, in 1057 (Isaakios). Even the patriarch was involved in that one, whether voluntarily or not. It is also possible that the successions of 1034 and 1055 were court coups (by a eunuch and a nominal co-emperor). Thus, by 1057 we again have a political scene in which the people, patriarch, armies, courtiers, and senators were active in claiming and reassigning power. It takes us full circle back to 963, when claims by all those elements shaped the rise to power of Nikephoros Phokas.

What we do not find any evidence for, by contrast, is the idea that these political developments reflected a socioeconomic struggle between the imperial state and large landowners, called Anatolian magnates or the like in modern literature. The existence of this class is debatable, as the Introduction explained, and the idea that they had some kind of political agenda—much less that it was aimed against the state—finds no support in the evidence or the events. Imperial representatives of this alleged class, Nikephoros Phokas and Isaakios Komnenos, pursued the same "statist" agenda as the Macedonians and, in some ways they increased its potential impact on what modern historians take to be their own "class," especially if Isaakios' budget cuts affected title holders and landowners, as they must have. There is no evidence that the independent peasantry declined, that large estates were growing,[1] or that the officer class had any socioeconomic class consciousness.

The revolts of 1043, 1047, and 1057 were perpetrated by army officers pure and simple, not the putative military wing of a landowning class.[2] Maniakes, who rose through the ranks, has not been cast as a "landowner," even though we are told that by 1042 he had estates in Asia Minor (and why not?).[3] Moreover, all our sources are explicit that the revolt of 1047 was the work of disgruntled army officers in the Macedonian *tagmata*, not of some new class of Balkan landowners (though no doubt there were rich landowners in the recently pacified provinces, and these officers were likely among them). Skylitzes' account of 1057 reflects the viewpoint of one of the leaders, Kekaumenos, and both he and our other sources present the revolt as driven by the grievances of army officers fighting on behalf of the army, not an (alleged) socioeconomic class. These events also generated no socioeconomic propaganda, though Kekaumenos would surely have alluded to such issues had they existed, seeing as he would have been addressing his own class. Thus the idea that Maniakes' revolt was the work of a "lone gun" whereas those of 1047 and 1057 reflected deeper economic interests has no basis.[4] Moreover, rebel leaders had no ability to deploy "personal" forces from outside the army. They did not have private armies; in other words, they did not have the ability to challenge the state independently of its own infrastructure. In 1047 and 1057, the rebels had to canvass among other officers and soldiers in order to have a shot at rebelling.[5] Whatever lands they owned did not give them the resources with which to challenge the Roman state. And when they finally did "take over the state," in 1081, they had lost most of their lands in Asia Minor.

This is the place to address the distinction between the political wing of the state and the military, or, in the sources' language, between the *politikon* and the *stratiotikon*. Older views that these represented two competing "parties" in the state have been laid to rest, as has the view that the careers of families and individuals divided neatly between the civilian bureaucracy or the military. Still, a loose structural distinction can be allowed between soldiers and career officers on the one hand and civil officials and bureaucrats on the other.[6] The terms are used by the sources loosely, so *politikon* can be the bureaucracy but also the people of the City (*polis*), or various interest groups therein. Military and civilian institutions obviously interfaced broadly, as neither could function without the other. During this period, however, the army was under strong civilian control. Michael IV's brothers, who had no military background, took over command positions as *doukes* and the armies obeyed them. Monomachos, whom Psellos and many modern historians depict as the archetypical "civilian" emperor, was fully engaged in military planning. Apart from two rebellions, he was also fully in control of the armies and put them through complex maneuvers.

The terms *politikon* and *stratiotikon* are used by the sources in a sharpened sense only in connection with the military rebellions, especially those of 1047 and 1057, which were instigated by disgruntled and ambitious officers.[7] Officers felt left out of decision making and rewards. The passage of Psellos quoted in Chapter 10 formulates this discontent nicely. But such tensions were old. Nikephoros Phokas had complained that tax collectors oppressed soldiers—as if the army could be paid without them.[8] But there is no evidence that any emperor was trying to "starve" the army. In 1047, the officers were upset that they were not on campaign (and thus not receiving campaign pay), while in 1057 they felt left out of the system of honors and distribution of titles. Let us not forget that the years 1055–1057 witnessed an extreme form of rule by eunuchs with a woman and then an Old Man on the throne; these regimes were naturally terrified of the bearded officer class. The generals' rebellion was an inevitable reaction to this lopsided situation. There is no sign that the armies were being degraded or downsized. Soldiers supported (or did not support) their commanders' ambitions for the same reasons they had done so throughout Roman history, since the late Republic.

The emperors did begin to face budget shortfalls around 1050, and this is likely the reason they devalued the coinage. They had been spending too much to maintain the loyalty of their subjects, which was a function of the systemic weakness of the throne, especially as dynastic continuity was becoming more attenuated with every succession. Also, Monomachos had to deal with multiple active fronts (Italy, Danube, the east) and had to make up losses of manpower to the Pechenegs, the emir of Dvin, and the raiders of Ibrahim Inal. Multiple active armies and losses cost money, and Monomachos probably also had to pay off the Pechenegs to secure his treaty with them. Isaakios made budget cuts, probably targeting court salaries, but we cannot calculate how much, from where exactly, or whether he increased military expenditures. It was getting tight, but there is no reason to talk about "decline."

This must be stressed on the level of imperial defense and control too: there was no decline here in the period 1025–1059. Historians have assumed that because everything fell apart visibly after 1071, internal factors must have been rotting the empire on the inside all along, and some have wanted to trace that rot back to Basil II. What we have instead was a series of systemic problems that were endemic to the Roman empire and came to a head in this period. First, there was the problem of weak imperial legitimacy, especially as the Macedonian dynasty was winding down. Emperors had to devise ways to protect themselves against the bearded officer class, which sometimes led to policies that alienated the latter (as in 1057). Second, emperors resorted to wide-scale political bribery, which, when combined with the appearance of new external foes, resulted in a budgetary crisis. And, third, there was the catalyst for the crisis itself: the coincidence of three major opponents (Normans, Pechenegs, Seljuks), an external problem, not the product of systemic failure. The Roman empire had never been able to cope with such a situation without difficulty. Predictably, Italy was put on the back burner. A full imperial expedition would have crushed the Norman upstarts, but there were more pressing dangers closer to home, which allowed the Normans to advance. The Balkan situation was stabilized, even after many major defeats.

The problem in the east was the return of predatory raiding, which the empire had not faced on a large scale since the ninth century and not at all since the midtenth. Predatory raiding was the norm for Byzantine history. The sacking of a city or two in Armenia does not point to a systemic problem (the oddity was rather the relative *absence* of such events during the past century). Whatever exactly Monomachos did to the Iberian army in ca. 1050, the responses to the raids of 1054 and 1057–1058 show that local defenses had adapted to the new situation and were more or less adequate. The empire had successfully fallen back on ambush-and-recover tactics. In light of this, and the multiple active fronts of the 1040s and early 1050s, I reject the idea that the emperors were lulled into thinking that eternal peace had come at last, demobilized the army, and so "lost the peace."[9] This is especially implausible for Monomachos (though Konstantinos X Doukas is a mystery, as we will see).

This was not a decline within Byzantium but a change in the international scene itself, which was also becoming more multipolar. The power vacuum of southern Italy was being filled by the Normans, and the Seljuks possessed an as-yet-unknown potential to transform the strategic situation in the east. But just because new enemies appear, costing the empire more money, does not mean that we must postulate some kind of internal rot. The strategic situation was more ominous, yet none of the emperors in this period failed Romanía, least of all Monomachos. Domestic spending was a problem, and Isaakios took measures to rein it in. For most of the inhabitants of the empire, especially for Romans in the core territories, this period would have been one of prosperity, and imperial largess would have made many rich too. In the provinces we witness a boom in construction, though it is mostly churches that survive today. Yet measures were also taken against the non-Orthodox: the Jacobites in 1029 and afterward; the Armenian *katholikos* after the fall of Ani and the *azyma* question, which affected both Armenians and Latins; the alleged closing of Latin churches in Constantinople; and the pressure brought to bear on the philosopher Psellos. None of these quite became an all-out persecution, but taken together they represent a resumption of legal harassment by the imperial authorities and an insistence on Orthodoxy. This intolerant turn has not yet been studied, so any explanation would be premature.

PART III | Collapse

CHAPTER 11

"The Agony of a Virulent Poison"
The Road to Mantzikert, 1059–1071

Konstantinos X Doukas (1059–1067): Domestic mispriorities

Upon his acclamation, Konstantinos X Doukas circulated throughout the empire a brief narrative written by Psellos of Isaakios' abdication and his own elevation, promising to promote justice. He also spoke to the representatives of the people, pledging compassion and prosperity for all.[1] He was just over fifty years old. He had been imprisoned by Ioannes the *orphanotrophos* in the 1030s for speaking on behalf of his first father-in-law, Dalassenos, but beyond that Doukas' career is a mystery. He appears among the supporters of Isaakios Komnenos in 1057 and presented himself as a "military person" to a visiting Georgian monk,[2] but there is no evidence of him holding a military post or of doing anything notable (or anything at all) before his accession in 1059. Nor is there evidence that he did much after his accession either.

If Byzantium experienced any decline before the collapse of the 1070s, it happened during Doukas' reign. Unfortunately, it is poorly documented in the Byzantine sources. The detailed narrative of Skylitzes ends in 1057; Attaleiates is still giving only summaries; Psellos, an honored guest at the Doukas court, is expanding his history by writing a panegyric of the dynasty, though it is laced with sarcasm; and the continuer of Skylitzes is mostly summarizing Attaleiates. A push against Robert in Italy is occluded in the Greek sources, as is most of the Turkish advance, except the sack of Ani in 1064. Eastern and western sources fill in some of the gaps, but do not give a coherent picture of the regime.

Psellos and Attaleiates generally agree on Doukas' domestic priorities and image, though we have only their general statements to go by. He was concerned to restore justice, presided over many cases himself, and cultivated a reputation for piety. On the fiscal side, he restored the honors to those from whom Isaakios had removed them, and presumably their salaries. Like most of his predecessors, he gave a round of gifts to the senate and people upon his accession, yet found the treasury empty, so he was also keen to raise revenue.[3] It would seem, then, that Isaakios' austerity was reversed. Worse, Doukas raised (or saved) money by cutting the military budget. Psellos says that he preferred diplomacy over war because the latter was more costly and, in an allusive passage, hints that Doukas followed bad advice in downsizing the armies at a time when enemies were growing stronger. Psellos supported strong armies; in fact, one of the purposes of the first version of his history from Basil to Isaakios was to convince Doukas of that.[4] Attaleiates is less discreet. Doukas, he says bluntly, neglected the army and the frontier defenses. Specifically, the soldiers were not properly equipped or supplied, and the more costly, high-quality soldiers were discharged, leaving the worse ones behind.[5] Unfortunately, we cannot translate this into precise or institutional terms; nor do we have hard data to gauge the extent of the problem. What is baffling is that anyone would think, in 1059, that this was sound policy. No one in the recent history of Byzantium had advocated such a terrible idea.

Doukas was the first emperor in a century, since Romanos II (d. 963), to have a surviving son. In fact, in 1059 he had two, Michael and Andronikos, and he had one more after his accession, Konstantios. Like the Paphlagonians in the 1030s, he tried to create a family-based regime. He crowned both Michael and Konstantios co-emperors, though oddly he did not do the same with his middle son Andronikos; nor do the sources say much about him.[6] Doukas also made his brother Ioannes *kaisar*. It seems that Ioannes had been in Antioch at the time of the succession, possibly as *doux*, and stayed there during the first year of the regime.[7] Ioannes was a friend of Psellos, liked hunting, and had some scholarly interests. Our manuscript of Konstantinos VII's *De administrando imperio* was prepared for him and possibly arranged by him.[8] He was a formidable figure, but often fell short at critical moments. Having heirs presaged dynastic stability, but nothing was guaranteed in Byzantine politics. The children were too young to play an active role. The regime is otherwise opaque. Except for Ioannes, we do not know the names of Doukas' circle, nor who served as his financial advisors.

Within months of his accession, in April 1060, Doukas became the target of an elaborate assassination plot, and was saved by chance.[9] The conspirators included the prefect of the City and other officials, including elements in the imperial fleet, but we do not know whom they intended to place on the throne. The plan was to attack the guards and make a commotion while the emperor was visiting the shrine of St. George; he would then rush to the docks and escape by ship; and the crew would then throw him into the sea. And so it happened, but the emperor got on a different ship to return to the palace, and would not climb aboard the conspirators' vessel when it rowed up to him on the way and offered him swifter passage. The *kaisar* Ioannes then marched through the City restoring order. The investigation implicated many, who were exiled and their property was confiscated, but no one was executed.[10] It was a close call, but Doukas ruled securely afterward. The conspirators do not seem to have championed different policies; their coup was just a power grab.

The emperor's celebrated piety also entailed an intensification of hostilities against the Monophysites. According to Syriac sources, the patriarch Leichoudes ordered the eviction of all non-Chalcedonians from Melitene (something that was impossible to do) and the burning of their books. The Jacobite patriarch was arrested and hauled to Constantinople for another "debate," but died en route. When Leichoudes died, he was replaced by Psellos' other friend, the former *nomophylax* Xiphilinos (1063–1075), who pursued the same policies, exiling the Jacobite bishop of Melitene.[11] There was more to come against the Armenians.

Frayed frontiers: Seljuks and Oghuz

Our information about Turkish raids before and after the conquest of Ani (1064) is poor. Psellos refers in a letter to barbarian dangers not far from the theme of Thrakesion, in western Asia Minor, which was not yet overrun.[12] Unfortunately, we have to rely mostly on the highly unreliable Matthew of Edessa. He says that in 1059/60, a Seljuk army sacked Sebasteia, which was deep in imperial territory, and returned home without encountering resistance, and that the city was unwalled. But the tale features Matthew's typical novelizations, and is likely misplaced and garbled. He uses it to complain about how the Romans left Armenia defenseless, and only two chapters later he recounts how the Romans tortured Armenians in Sebasteia to get their hands on the treasure of the *katholikos* Petros. Why did the Turks not take it during their eight-day sack?[13] Aristakes, writing soon after 1072, does not mention a sack of Sebasteia. Matthew recounts a more plausible (if still novelized) raid in 1062. Tughril's generals attacked Pałin and Tilkum in Mesopotamia, not far from the border with Mayyafariqin. But this time there was a response: Diabatenos, the *doux* of Edessa, and Hervé Frangopoulos—the latter freed from captivity and promoted to *stratelates* of the east—together attacked Amida in reprisal. The *doux* was killed, but Hervé found the raiders, who had reached Theodosioupolis, massacred them, and recovered the plunder. Matthew then has it that Hervé was denounced to the emperor for taking bribes from the Muslims or allowing Diabatenos' death. He was taken to Constantinople and executed.[14] The political background in Constantinople is extremely opaque to us.

In 1064, the new sultan, Tughril's nephew Alp Arslan (or "Heroic Lion"), conquered Ani, an event celebrated (or lamented) widely in eastern and western sources. Actually, the sultan did much more than that. He had just settled a succession struggle against his father's cousin Qutlumush and had to impose his will on the Seljuk northwest through raids and conquest. It was also an opportunity to showcase his new regime, so he brought his son and heir Malik Shah and his vizier, the great Nizam al-Mulk. In the summer of 1064, he marched up the Araxes valley from Azerbaijan, reducing Roman forts and installing his own garrisons. He moved around Ani to Georgia, subjecting its lords, including king Bagrat. His army then converged on Ani, which, as the Romans had found, was highly defensible. But it so happened that one Bagrat (Pankratios) had persuaded Konstantinos X to make him *doux* and in exchange he would make Ani self-sufficient; the Romans would not have to supply its garrison or pay his salary. Thereupon he skimped on expenses to make a profit, downgrading defenses. We have an inscription from the wall of the Ani cathedral detailing some of Bagrat's fiscal measures (Figure 13). During the siege, dissension broke out between Bagrat and the emperor's representative, almost certainly the nobleman Gregorios Pakourianos. At a critical moment, on August 16, the city's defenders abandoned the walls, and the Seljuks poured in and slaughtered everyone who had not made for the citadel. The sources describe the massacre quite graphically.[15]

Ani, the royal and economic hub of Armenia, had been in Roman hands for just twenty years. What is missing from our accounts of its fall is any reaction by the emperor. Monomachos would have instantly sent field armies under one of his eunuchs. Doukas did nothing at all. Did he figure it was not worth the cost to recover such a remote outpost? "And thus," Attaleiates bitterly pointed out, "such a city was taken along with all its villages and their lands on account of greed and an untimely economizing."[16] Ani's fall marked the start of a new phase because the Seljuks now first decided to hold conquered territory, if through client rulers, rather than depart after the plunder. Alp Arslan placed Ani under Abu al-Aswar, the emir of Ganja (whom we remember as the former Roman client-emir of Dvin). The sultan would

FIGURE 13 Cathedral of Ani: carved on the outside wall is an inscription listing the fiscal measures implemented by the imperial governor Pankratios, who lost the city to the Seljuks. Source: Shutterstock, ID 351638243.

return to the Caucasus in 1067 to confirm his hold over Ganja and Georgia. The empire was beginning to lose territory, and Armenia was being flipped.

It was this loss that, paradoxically, brought to the empire its final gain, the Armenian kingdom of Vanand centered on the city of Kars, to the west of Ani. It too had been raided and its Bagratid king Gagik-Abas (since 1029) had to submit to Alp Arslan. Immediately after that, in 1064/5, he surrendered his kingdom to the emperor in exchange for estates in Cappadocia for his family. This was an eleventh-hour acquisition, and it is often assumed that Constantinople did not have time to install an administration, but seals of the *katepano* (plural) of Kars prove otherwise.[17] There is something sadly ironic about this transaction, for all parties. Moreover, Doukas was cracking down on the Armenian Church as well, though we have poor documentation for this, the fanciful and partisan tales in Matthew of Edessa, which cannot be retold with a straight face. If they contain a "kernel" of truth, it would be that the *katholikos* Xač'ik was brought to Constantinople, detained for three years, and released only after the petitions of the former rulers of Ani and Vaspurakan; some Church properties were confiscated; there were doctrinal "debates" in Constantinople with the former kings; and Gagik, the former king of Ani, killed the bishop of Kaisareia for naming his dog "Armen."[18]

No sooner had Alp Arslan left Ani than a new threat appeared on the Danube. A large number of Oghuz Turks crossed the river in the fall of 1064, defeated the Bulgarian army of the Roman governors Basileios Apokapes (the hero of Mantzikert in 1054) and Nikephoros Botaneiates, and began to plunder the Balkan provinces. Allegedly they went as far as Greece, but this may be an exaggeration. The archaeology of their destruction seems limited to the lower Danube, by the Black Sea. Doukas at first did nothing, either out of stinginess or more likely because he knew there was little he could do. Pitched battles with these types had not gone well. But political pressure mounted for him to do *something*, so he took 150 guardsmen and marched out of the City, going a few miles. This image is probably a caricature; field armies were not stationed in the City but collected along the way. Anyway, the emperor got lucky. News arrived that some of the Oghuz had recrossed the Danube, while those who stayed had been destroyed by disease, famine, and attacks by the Bulgarian and Pecheneg forces. The problem was solved. Doukas returned to Constantinople to celebrate his victory in church, and settled the survivors on public lands in Macedonia.[19]

Greece was disturbed by a tax rebellion in the summer of 1066, after the widely noted passage of Halley's comet. Discontents from Larissa and the Vlachs of that region appointed as their leader a local notable, Nikoloutzas Delphinas, and their makeshift army seized some forts, including Servia, before an imperial amnesty and tax forgiveness, presented by the *katepano* of Bulgaria, broke up the party. Nikoloutzas was exiled to the Armeniakon theme, where he wrote a self-exculpatory account of the rebellion, according to which he was trying to foil it before it even started. It is full of fascinating observations about the dynamics of provincial society. We have a summary of it made by a relative, a moralizing author of maxims Kekaumenos.[20] This rebellion did not differ from others of its kind, except for the role of the Vlachs, a transhumant people about whom Kekaumenos added a hostile ethnography. This is not the place to enter the controversial question of their origin. They were part of the Bulgarian empire conquered by Basil II, were expanding their presence in Greece and Bulgaria, and would play important roles in later Balkan history.[21]

The end of Byzantine Italy

Byzantine Italy disappeared during the 1050s and 1060s. The empire's gravitational pull weakened and the region was fully absorbed into a different political world, that of the Normans, the papacy, and Lombard duchies. This is not the place to tell that story in full, beyond major events that affected future Byzantine-Norman relations. Besides, we have poor information about the Norman conquest of Calabria and Apulia.[22]

After their victory over pope Leo IX in 1053, the Normans continued to attack towns in Apulia, and the balance shifted from extracting tribute through terrorism to making permanent conquests, especially in Calabria, where Robert Guiscard was active. In ca. 1057, Robert succeeded his brother Onfroi as leader of the Normans in Apulia and was joined by his young brother Roger (with whom he would periodically feud for years). By 1060, the two brothers had effectively completed the conquest of Calabria, including Reggio. But just before that, a revolution had occurred in the affairs of southern Italy. The reformist party at St. Peter's, who had elected pope Nicholas II, was hard pressed by the opposition at Rome, which had elected its own, rival pope. In 1059, at a council at Melfi, the reformers, having no other viable allies, recognized the Normans as vassals of the Church in exchange for assistance against their enemies. In the typical way in which legalism meets imperialism, Robert was awarded the aspirational title of duke of Apulia, Calabria, and even Sicily, which was still under Muslim rule. In papal eyes, Robert was henceforth the legitimate ruler of southern Italy and a defender of the Church. His very title also contained an invitation to conquer the infidels "by the Grace of God and St. Peter,"[23] which could be turned against any who did not submit to Rome. The papal-Norman alliance would be unstable in coming decades, but when its interests aligned against Byzantium it would pose a potent threat. The Normans, moreover, were never content; they were already eyeing Sicily and would soon regard the empire itself as a weak and so tempting target. For its part the papacy had reason to think of the Orthodox as schismatics or worse. Although these options were latent in 1059, the pope had already awarded all of Apulia to Robert, as if it were his to give.

According to Skylitzes, after the fall of Reggio the Romans still held Bari, Otranto, Taranto, Brindisi, and other towns. The governors posted there from Constantinople never had sufficient forces to defeat the Normans, though they did resist them and some cities changed hands multiple times.[24] The Norman advance was slowed by local resistance and uprisings, by their ventures into Sicily, and by internal disunion, such as the fighting between Robert and Roger. In 1066, Geoffrey, count of Taranto (taken in 1063), assembled a fleet to attack Byzantium across the Adriatic. In Constantinople, this was understood as an imminent attack by Robert himself, and possibly news of the fall of England to William the Conqueror had arrived, showing what Normans could do to large kingdoms, not just imperial outposts such as southern Italy. But Geoffrey was defeated by the admiral Michael Maurix, who transported a Varangian unit to Bari. This counts as a miniresurgence by the Byzantines before the very end. Robert's own followers in Apulia rebelled against him in 1067–1068, financed by the *doux* of Dyrrachion, Perenos. The rebels were defeated, however, and fled to Constantinople.[25] In August 1068, Robert began the siege of Bari, which would last for almost three years. Its conclusion in 1071 ended the Byzantine presence in southern Italy.

Doukas was ill, and possibly incapacitated, between October 1066 and his death on May 22 or 23, 1067. He was buried at the monastery of St. Nikolaos outside the Golden Gate.[26] His reign is frustratingly opaque. He seems to have been a good man, but lacking Monomachos' energy and sense of responsibility. Our sources claim that he defunded and downgraded the army, but it is difficult to know what that meant. If I could have the budget figures for one reign, it would be his. Psellos' panegyrics stress Doukas' victories over barbarians who "are constantly pouring in against us," revealing a defensive anxiety about this issue that is absent from his previous orations.[27] The nonreaction to the fall of Ani is hard to understand. Attaleiates hints at a possible explanation: Seljuk advances had so far targeted mostly the "heretics," such as Armenian non-Chalcedonians, and the Byzantines, including the pious emperor, may have thought it served them right. But soon the trouble would come to the Orthodox as well.[28] Can we attribute such puerile thinking to Rome's imperial planners? That was fit for sermons, not strategy. There must have been money to raise armies; the emperors had not yet resorted to "borrowing" it from churches, though they would eventually. Why had Doukas not sent army after army, as Monomachos had done? The frontier did not collapse during his reign, but its defenses seem to have been weakened at a time when they should have been strengthened.

Eudokia and the succession: Romanos IV Diogenes (1068–1071)

When he died, leaving behind a wife and children, Doukas was in the situation of Romanos II in 963. To protect the succession of his sons from interlopers—the equivalent of a Nikephoros Phokas—he bound Eudokia with an oath that she would never remarry. She had to swear and sign it before the patriarch, *kaisar*, her children, and the senate; and the senators and patriarch then had to sign it themselves. By a curious chance, we have the text of this oath. In it the empress promises to remain faithful to Doukas by invoking the sky, earth, and all the elements, calling on the Trinity, Theotokos, Cherubim, Seraphim, and all other orders of angels, prophets, apostles, martyrs, and saints, and agrees to be torn apart, burned, and thrown into the sea if she even thinks about remarrying.[29] Michael VII (about nineteen years old) and Konstantios (about seven) were now the emperors. Ironically, the one person against whom the oath did not protect them was Eudokia herself. She decided to exercise power herself, and Michael, Psellos' student, was so docile that he gladly let her take over. It was said of Michael that he was so naïve and incapable that he was good only for being a bishop.[30] The reign of Theodora was a recent precedent for Eudokia. She released the exiled Syrian bishops.[31]

But the empire was in trouble, and Seljuk raids were intensifying. Matthew recounts many against the territory of Edessa in ca. 1066, but it is difficult to take them all at face value, given their novelistic qualities and goal to show that Romans are bad and Armenians good. Overall, the imperial forces seem to have put up a credible defense. But the *doux* of Edessa, Leon Arbantenos, was defeated in 1067 by the sultah's general Gümüştegin, and had to be ransomed.[32] In that year, Alp Arslan also returned to Georgia to enforce his suzerainty over Bagrat, and the Romans feared that he might invade Asia Minor from there.[33] That was done instead by raiders from Mesopotamia, led probably by one Afshin, who penetrated to Kaisareia, sacked and burned the city, and also plundered the church and tomb of St. Basil. Then he crossed into Cilicia, killing and looting, stopped at Aleppo for reinforcements, and returned to plunder the territory of Antioch. According to Attaleiates, Roman defenses were crippled by inadequate pay and provisioning; the soldiers were simply unwilling to fight.[34] Asia Minor was now exposed and open. Eudokia realized that "our empire is withering and regressing," as she put it to Psellos.[35]

This was the shock that the Romans needed to awake from their slumber. The empress and others realized that a general had to be placed on the throne, but inevitably there would be a dispute over who and there was also the matter of the oath. Unfortunately, we cannot reconstruct the factions precisely. The man whom Eudokia chose was the handsome Romanos Diogenes, a son of Konstantinos Diogenes, who had been imprisoned by Romanos III and had hung himself. Romanos Diogenes, *doux* at Serdica, was caught in a plot that involved the Hungarians. Yet at his trial, where he was sentenced to death (commuted to exile), the empress and some of the judges (among them Attaleiates) thought that they had found their man, and it was even suspected that Eudokia had fallen for the tall, muscled, and good-looking general. He was recalled from exile and, on December 25, 1067, made *magistros* and *stratelates*. According to Attaleiates, who was probably present, the empress, the senators, and the patriarch deliberated and decided that the common good had to be placed over the jealous wishes of a dying husband: the oath "would harm the common good and contribute to the destruction of the Roman empire." She chose Diogenes and the others fell in line, except for the *kaisar* Ioannes Doukas, who opposed the choice.[36] The elevation of a Diogenes was full of danger for the Doukas dynasty—and the reverse (Figure 14).

Skylitzes Continuatus tells a funny story. It was feared that the patriarch Xiphilinos would enforce the oath. A eunuch was therefore sent to him, offering that if he annulled it publicly the empress would marry his brother (or cousin) Bardas. The patriarch eagerly went around to the senators who had signed it, explaining its invalidity, whereupon Diogenes was brought into the palace. It is possible that this story was invented later by the Doukai to delegitimate Diogenes. At any rate, Diogenes had to promise to uphold the rights of Eudokia's children. On January 1, 1068, he married the empress and was made emperor. The Varangians objected to his acclamation, defending the rights of Doukas' sons, but Michael VII himself announced that it was all done according to his wishes. Yet Psellos reveals that Michael had been told only the night before![37] Diogenes elevated Doukas' other son, Andronikos, as co-emperor, and took him with him.[38] War was at hand.

FIGURE 14 Imperial seal showing Romanos IV Diogenes and Eudokia Markembolitissa being crowned by Christ on the obverse, and Michael VII Doukas, Andronikos Doukas, and Konstantinos Doukas on the reverse. It nicely illustrates how surrounded Romanos was by the Doukai, and how crowded the throne. © Dumbarton Oaks, Byzantine Collection, Washington, DC (accession no.: BZS.1958.106.539).

In 1067, the Romans seem to have come to their senses. The eastern frontier was collapsing and they were about to lose the heartland of their empire. Nor was it clear why this had happened. Twenty years had passed since large imperial armies had operated in the east (against Ani, Dvin, and Ibrahim Inal). Why had it been so long? For ten years after that they had credibly defended against attacks. But now everything was in shambles. Diogenes knew exactly what he had to do: massively reassert the imperial presence on the frontier and, if possible, inflict a devastating defeat on the enemy. Ideally, this should have been done ten years earlier; it was, per-haps, what Isaakios Komnenos wanted. Perhaps it was not too late. Yet the political context was far less favorable. Isaakios had ruled alone after the end of a dynasty. He had no domestic rivals other than those he created. But Diogenes had to contend with the entrenched clan of the Doukai, which required political finesse at home (literally!) on top of the military force he had to project abroad. He failed at both, of course, and the Doukai tarred him with it afterward. Psellos seems to have supported Diogenes during his reign, but criticized him later, under Michael VII; however, we need not assume he was always hostile.[39] A more sympathetic image emerges from Attaleiates, one of Diogenes' military judges and advisors. According to him, Diogenes made a valiant effort and was more a tragic hero than a failure. If only he had listened more to ... Attaleiates. It is this constant second-guessing that vitiates the judge's history.

Chasing Turks

In early 1068, Diogenes left the capital, sent off by an oration by Psellos,[40] and began mustering the *tagmata* in the Anatolikon theme. Attaleiates later wrote a famous description of their pitiful state, which should be quoted because much Byzantine military history has been written on its basis. We should remember, however, that it is rhetorical and meant to shift blame for what happened onto the previous Doukas regime.

> It was something to see the famous units and their commanders now composed of just a few men, and these bent over by poverty and lacking proper weapons and war horses. For long they had been neglected, since no emperor had gone on an expedition to the east in many years, and they had not received their allotted money for supplies; little-by-little they were being defeated and routed by the enemy because they were in a miserable condition and unprepared. . . . They had been driven to the

absolute depths of misery and appeared cowardly, feeble, and absolutely useless for anything brave. Their very standards silently proclaimed this, for they looked filthy as if exposed to smoke, and those who marched under them were few and pitiful. It was depressing to those who considered from what source and by what means the army might be restored to its ancient condition ... given that the men remaining in their units now were few and at a loss when it came to using weapons or maneuvering with their horses, and the young men had no combat experience. Opposed to them and advancing against them was a foe accustomed to the dangers of battle and warlike to the extreme.[41]

Romanos needed to recruit and train more soldiers. He had reports of two groups of marauders, one in the north, probably in Chaldia, and the other in Syria.[42] Diogenes chose to go south and pass the summer in Lykandos, but the northern raiders meanwhile sacked Neokaisareia in Pontos. Diogenes rushed north and, leaving the infantry and baggage at Sebasteia, pursued them with his cavalry for eight days. He took them by surprise, killed many, and recovered their plunder. In October, he returned to Sebasteia, then Syria, where he invaded the territory of Aleppo. The Mirdasid dynasty there was in its death throes, its rulers fighting among themselves for decades. Its current ruler was Mahmud, but Turkish bands had injected themselves as power brokers in local disputes, and were using Aleppo as a staging ground for devastating raids into the territory of Antioch, from where they had removed thousands of cattle and captives for the slave market. Notable among their leaders was Afshin, who was besieging Antioch itself in early 1068, when he was recalled to Iraq by the sultan. Another was ibn Khan, who captured the key fort of 'Artah in July.[43] The Roman hold on Syria was failing. Diogenes was right to go there. He understood that northern Syria was now more important to the Seljuks than the Caucasus.

The emperor marched straight for Manbij (Hierapolis) and captured it at once, except for the citadel, which soon surrendered on terms. Attaleiates says that most of the inhabitants had left the city in advance, though the army found supplies there. The Arab sources by contrast say that Romans killed everyone.[44] Meanwhile the forces of Aleppo and the Turks defeated the *tagmata* of the *scholai* and *stratelatai*, which Diogenes had placed in protective cover around the city, first by shooting at them from a distance and then charging into their midst. The Romans were blockaded inside the city for the night. The next morning—November 20—the two armies fought again and the Romans prevailed. Diogenes prudently restrained his soldiers from chasing the retreating Arabs and Turks, though Attaleiates criticizes him for not pressing the advantage all the way to the walls of Aleppo itself. Diogenes instead placed a Roman and Armenian force in the citadel of Manbij. Shadowed by enemy riders, he then marched to ʿAzaz, where Romanos III had been defeated in 1030, but realized that it was too strong to take by assault. He did not encamp nearby because there was no water—the mistake that Romanos III had made—so he returned to Roman territory, intending to retake the fort of ʿArtah across from Antioch. Its Arab garrison abandoned it instead, so Diogenes manned it with his own. The emperor avoided Antioch, because his army would strain its depleted resources, and he returned instead through Cilicia. Here he learned that Afshin's raiders had, meanwhile, slipped through the defenses of Melitene and sacked the city of Amorion. As there was nothing he could do about this now, he went back to Constantinople, arriving in January 1069.

The expedition of 1068 was a great success. It attained its primary strategic objective, which was to plug the hole in the defense of Syria, and began to impose costs on raiding. Moreover, it restored Roman morale. It was now that "Romans began to stand up to their enemies and organize their resistance."[45] Psellos, who was to all appearances a supporter of Diogenes during the reign, could imagine that the main blaze had been put out, and only smaller fires remained.[46]

The emperor was eager to return to the field in 1069. But first he had to deal with a different kind of crisis, the importation of Norman-style troubles to the imperial heartland. Roger Crépin (Crispin) was a Norman who had fought the Muslims in Spain, had joined his countrymen in southern Italy (which may have entailed fighting the Byzantines), and was then hired by the emperors to fight the Muslims in Asia Minor.[47] His company was stationed in the Armenian themes and now, just as Diogenes was setting out, he rebelled and seized the taxes. Diogenes sent five western *tagmata* against him, but he defeated these too. When the emperor reached Dorylaion and began to muster the full army, Crépin submitted, but was arrested. In retaliation, his company, which had not followed him, began to plunder Mesopotamia. This episode should be flagged. We do not know exactly what Crépin was aiming for in his "rebellion," and possibly he was only claiming back pay to which he felt entitled. But that was precisely how the Normans operated: postulate a legal claim, real or invented, cause a disturbance, and see if something shakes loose. Crépin was the first of these Latin crusader types who tried to seize a piece of Byzantium for himself—and not in Italy. That was the problem with hiring Franks: they quickly turned on you, even as they were fighting the Turks on your behalf. Franks and Turks would fight it out over the corpse of Romanía for centuries to come, and this was when it started.

Diogenes now started to chase Turks around Asia Minor. He caught and destroyed a group in the mountainous terrain around Larissa (between Sebasteia and Mesopotamia); then he chased another group, probably under Afshin, from the territory of Melitene back over the Euphrates.[48] He left a portion of the army there with Philaretos Brachamios and crossed the Tauros mountains from Hanzit to Keltzene (Erzincan), where he was soon joined, however, by the remnants of . . . Philaretos' force. They had been defeated by Afshin, who made straight for Ikonion, and sacked it. Afshin was methodically picking off the unspoiled and rich cities of Roman Asia Minor. Diogenes set off in pursuit but also sent units to his *doux* of Antioch, Chatatourios (an Armenian name), to block their escape through Cilicia. Evading the emperor, the raiders did cross to Cilicia but were attacked by Armenians—this probably means the soldiers of the Armenian themes—and had to abandon their booty; however, Chatatourios and his reinforcements failed to engage them and they made it safely back to Aleppo. The emperor posted soldiers to block further raids, and returned to Constantinople in the autumn of 1069. This, then, was not a decisive win, and every year another city was sacked. The territory of Melitene was by now so ravaged that it could not sustain the presence of a large army. The Turks were doing to it what the Romans had done a century before, when they conquered it. But the emperor's overall strategy was sound, even if it required frantic pursuits. Had Chatatourios sprung the trap on Afshin, it would have given the empire a much-needed reprieve. Attaleiates criticizes many of Diogenes' decisions, but his own recommendations are not necessarily better. The emperor knew what he had to do: hunt down the chief raiding parties. But Attaleiates is simultaneously distancing himself from a strategy that led to an infamous defeat. He presents himself as trying vainly to correct Diogenes, even as he also has to defend him because he was associated with his regime (Figure 15).[49]

Diogenes decided to spend the next year in Constantinople. One son had already been born to him and Eudokia, and another would follow (Leon and Nikephoros). This posed obvious dynastic complications. Diogenes sent out Manouel Komnenos to lead that year's campaign, the young nephew of Isaakios I (and older brother of the future Alexios I, who was in his teens).[50] The emperor was forging closer ties with the Komnenoi, likely to counterbalance the Doukai. He married his grown son Konstantinos (from a previous marriage) to Theodora, Manouel's sister.[51] The *kaisar* Ioannes prudently or involuntarily withdrew to his estates in Bithynia.[52] The expeditionary army in 1070 was split in two. One part went to Manbij, which was hard pressed

FIGURE 15 ATTALEIATES RING. Ring of the high official and historian Michael Attaleiates with an image of the Virgin and the inscription "Mother of God, help your servant Michael Attaleiates." © Dumbarton Oaks, Byzantine Collection, Washington, DC (accession no.: BZ.1947.19).

by a siege. We learn nothing more about this, but apparently the siege was ended, as the Romans held the city until 1075. Manouel went to Sebasteia, where he engaged with a Turkish army and was defeated by the age-old stratagem of the feigned retreat. The general was among the captured, though the city harbored the survivors. At the same time, news came that Chonai had been sacked, including its famous shrine of the archangel Michael. This was the farthest west that Turks had yet penetrated. In a surprising turn of events, the Turkish leader who had defeated Manouel now defected to the emperor, bringing Manouel with him to the capital. The Romans were delighted. He was Erisgen (or Arisighi, Greek Chrysoskoulos), one of the sultan's brothers-in-law.[53] He rebelled against Alp Arslan and was being pursued by Afshin (who went on to attack Chonai, as stated above). Once in Constantinople, Arisighi willingly provided information about Seljuk tactics and politics. But that year's campaign had been a failure.

In 1070, Diogenes also funded the construction of forts inside Asia Minor. Two which are known epigraphically guard passes between the center and the coastal lands, indicating that strategically all of Asia Minor was now believed to be a potential war zone.[54] It was a premonition of the Komnenian empire. The annual campaigns had become progressively less impressive. It was time for another major push by the emperor himself.

Mantzikert

The campaign of 1068 had more or less plugged the gap in the Syrian frontier, and added a new conquest, Manbij. The campaigns of 1069–1070 had targeted raiding parties inside the empire, with mixed results. Diogenes now aimed to plug the gap in the Armenian east, and possibly add a conquest to reinforce it: Khliat. The southeast was safe for now, but in early 1070 Alp Arslan had taken Mantzikert and manned it with Turks and Daylami.[55] Then, in late 1070, he had marched into Roman Mesopotamia and taken some smaller forts, but failed to take Edessa despite a determined siege; the city was defended by the *doux* Basileios Alousianos, another descendant of the Bulgarian tsars. The sultan moved on to Aleppo in the spring of 1071, but failed to take that too.[56] He was at Aleppo, Azerbaijan, or Mosul when he heard the news of the emperor's advance to Armenia.[57] Our uncertainty about the sultan's movements, as well as the lack of a proper modern biography, illustrate the problems of writing about the battle of Mantzikert, the most famous in Byzantine history, excepting the siege of 1453. The tale of a warrior-emperor defeated and held captive by a sultan for eight days, treated generously, and let go, excited the moral imagination of many cultures. Moreover, the battle was long held to have shifted the balance of power between Christians and Muslims in the east. There are dozens of sources in many languages about it, especially Arabic and Persian, but the latter are so novelized and distant that, except for specific details, they are useful mostly for the study of reception.[58] The Seljuk perspective has been lost to legend. In the end, we have one firsthand account, that of Attaleiates. It is also likely that distinct firsthand information about the battle was passed by general Bryennios to his grandson, the historian Bryennios, writing in the early twelfth century.

The emperor set out from Constantinople on March 13 after distributing the annual *rogai*. Allegedly he could not pay them all in gold, and did so partly in silk.[59] He traversed Asia Minor to Kaisareia, mustering the army along the way. One early casualty—to illness—was Manouel Komnenos.[60] The emperor passed by Sebasteia, Koloneia, and came to Theodosioupolis. As the territory ahead had been thoroughly ravaged, like that of Melitene, Diogenes ordered his soldiers to take two months of rations with them. We do not have reliable figures for the size of his army; around forty thousand is the best modern estimate.[61] He sent his Pechenegs and Franks—the latter under Roussel de Bailleul—ahead to Khliat to forage and pillage. The emperor came to Mantzikert and assessed that he would be able to take it with only a fraction of his army. He therefore sent the larger and better part to Khliat, under Ioseph Trachaneiotes, who was to secure the fields around the city for provisions. Diogenes did indeed reduce Mantzikert easily, but just then it was reported that Turks were near. It was in fact the sultan, but Diogenes apparently believed it was only a minor force. He sent Nikephoros Bryennios, the *doux* of the western *tagmata*,[62] to deal with them, but he ran into determined resistance: not only shooting from afar, in the Turkish manner, but hand-to-hand combat as well. Alp Arslan had, over the previous years, added mercenary units to his army.[63] Diogenes now dispatched the *doux* of Theodosioupolis, Nikephoros Basilakes, with "local" soldiers, as the rest were with Trachaneiotes. Basilakes pursued the enemy too far, all the way to their camp, and was captured. As the wounded were brought back to the Roman camp, Diogenes himself sallied forth but did not encounter anyone. When he returned, some Turks shot at the Pechenegs and supply personnel, which forced everyone inside in a near stampede.

The Romans spent the night in fear, being shot at by the howling Turks, who, in the morning, blocked off their access to the river. The situation was now similar to that of Romanos III at ʿAzaz in 1030. A group of Oghuz defected to the Turks[64]—their way of life was so similar anyway, Attaleiates comments—but the Roman infantry returned fire at the Turks and got them to back off. Diogenes now grasped the miscalculation in dividing up the army. He had planned to link up with the other contingents quickly, or recall them in a pinch, but now he was simply cut off. Believing that they would not arrive in time, he wanted to settle the issue by battle. The arrival of envoys from the sultan opened the possibility of a negotiated peace, but Diogenes ultimately decided against that and marched out, on August 26. We now have two versions of events. According to Attaleiates, the Turks retreated before the emperor, who pursued them for a long while but stopped when he realized he had left the camp unguarded and feared an ambush. He gave the signal to turn around, but this was misinterpreted in the rear as a signal to retreat because the emperor had fallen, which caused a panic. Some claimed that Andronikos Doukas, son of the *kaisar* Ioannes and general of some *tagmata*, started this rumor and treacherously ordered his soldiers back to camp. Seeing that the emperor was alone, the Turks now wheeled around and attacked his men. Attaleiates was with the camp,[65] where there was commotion and confusion. Stragglers returned, followed by mounted pursuers cutting them down. No one knew where Diogenes was because, after a fierce fight, he had been captured.

Attaleiates' account may be the best that we have, but it was written in a context of heated recriminations and a contest over memory. In his account, the main Roman and Turkish armies never really engaged; there was no "battle of Mantzikert." Most of the Roman army was with Trachaneiotes, and the emperor was ahead of his own forces when he was captured, almost alone with his bodyguard. The takeaway image here is that only Diogenes actually fought, ahead of the Romans, and unsupported by them. This image stands for the reign as a whole, and even the entire period: one Roman fought while the rest fled. The tradition in Bryennios-the-grandson, by contrast, which is *possibly* based on the recollections of his grandfather the *doux*, agrees on the outcome but recounts a more formal battle in which the Turks defeat the Roman right wing, Andronikos in the rear retreats (for no apparent reason), and the emperor is surrounded and taken.[66] In this version, it is not clear that most of the army was with Trachaneiotes. It *was* a formal battle: the same elements, but tweaked differently.

In the end, splitting the army proved catastrophic, as contemporaries realized.[67] Diogenes also failed to gather intelligence effectively. He had no idea the sultan was coming to Mantzikert, prepared to fight. Attaleiates' defense hinges on Diogenes' ability to recall Trachaneiotes and Roussel if there was need, but it is unlikely such a need was foreseen. If it was, the emperor was being extremely optimistic about how quickly they could be recalled, in hostile mountainous terrain across 45 kilometers. As a result of these miscalculations, a Roman emperor was captured in battle for the first time in nine hundred years, and held for eight days. The Turkish victory was celebrated throughout the Seljuk world. The eastern sources preserve authentic accounts of the two rulers' conversations, Diogenes himself sent an account to the empress on his release,[68] and he later spoke to his support-ers too. A common motif is this exchange: "What would you have done to me if our positions were reversed?" the sultan asked. "I would have killed you cruelly." Impressed with the candid answer, Alp Arslan wondered, "So what should I do with you now?" In the end, the two worked out an agree-ment. Its terms are difficult to reconstruct from the hints and variants in the sources, and it was never implemented anyway. It included the cession of territory, certainly Vaspurakan (and Mantzikert) and probably more, annual payments to the sultan, a release of prisoners, and a marriage alliance.[69] Alp Arslan released the captured Romans, including the emperor, who was wear-ing Turkish clothes. Diogenes traveled to Theodosioupolis to rest and piece together the tatters of his reign. First, he changed back into Roman clothes.

Civil war

The battle of Mantzikert was not costly in terms of casualties, but the sur-vivors had scattered and were leaderless.[70] The most high-ranking officers on site who could have rallied them, such as Andronikos Doukas, rushed back to the capital to play politics. Moreover, there was no money. Diogenes himself had admitted to the sultan that "I have used up the monies of the Romans ... in the reorganization of the armies and in wars, and I have impoverished the nation."[71] The biggest challenge the emperor faced was the blow to his prestige. He had been brought in to provide much-needed military leadership, and it had led to this. His credibility was gone. He had also told the sultan that "if you kill me, they will put another in my place."[72] But he knew that could happen anyway; this was the basic challenge of imperial legitimacy in Romanía. And this time it would not require a revolution: there already were three other emperors in the capital, one empress, and one *kaisar* nearby.

In Constantinople, only confusion reigned at first as survivors trickled in with conflicting reports about the battle and the emperor's fate. Once a coherent picture emerged, the gaggle of crowned heads and their attendants convened and decided to declare Diogenes deposed. An order was sent throughout the provinces that he was no longer to be recognized. At first Eudokia and Michael VII were acting together, but in October Diogenes' letter arrived. The Doukai—meaning the *kaisar* Ioannes and his sons Andronikos and Konstantinos—used the Varangian guard to proclaim Michael VII sole emperor and to depose Eudokia and tonsure her in a convent on the Bosporos.[73] After all, it was she who had brought Diogenes in and was the mother of his children. The Doukai acted as if a new regime had taken over, distributing honors and promises to the senate and people, though they had no money. They also sent out an army against Diogenes under the command of Konstantinos Doukas, who began to recruit in northwest Asia Minor. Meanwhile, Diogenes had been collecting taxes in the Armeniakon and had reached Dokeia (modern Tokat). The two armies engaged in skirmishes. Diogenes entrusted operations to his supporter Theodoros Alyates, the general of Cappadocia, whereas Konstantinos had been reinforced by the mercenary Crépin, whom Diogenes had imprisoned and the Doukai now set loose. Crépin defeated Alyates, who was captured and cruelly blinded with tent pegs.[74]

Diogenes fell back on Cappadocia, where he was joined by his *doux* of Antioch, the Armenian Chatatourios. With the onset of winter, they fell back again, on Cilicia. The mini-state that they formed there in the winter of 1071/2 presaged others to come in this region during the great breakup of Romanía, but this first version was not to last (its potential would later be realized by Philaretos and the Crusaders). In Constantinople, Anna Dalassene and her sons the Komnenoi were exiled to the island of Prinkipo on suspicion of plotting with Diogenes, their in-law.[75] Direct negotiations with Diogenes came to nothing as he insisted on keeping his title while the Doukai were offering only an amnesty. In the spring, they sent out Andronikos as *domestikos* of the eastern *scholai*, again with Crépin. It seems that the latter was conducting the war for the Doukai, the first time that a Norman played such a role. They crossed to Tarsos through mountain passes, which had apparently been left unguarded, and defeated Chatatourios in battle. Diogenes, we note, was not leading operations in person. It seems that he had switched to the role of the emperor who reigns while others do the fighting. But Chatatourios was captured and Diogenes blockaded at Adana. Psellos now sent an enthusiastic letter to Andronikos, congratulating him on his victory and mastery of military science: "The dragon has been defeated, but his teeth still have venom. Don't let that basilisk Chatatourios slip through your grasp. You have given new life to the Roman empire, which was dying!"[76]

Diogenes appealed for Seljuk help and even tried to subvert Crépin, but in vain. In the end, a lack of supplies and hope forced his surrender, and a deal was struck. He would abdicate and become a monk, but no harm would come to him. Three bishops guaranteed his safety. Diogenes was conveyed by mule to Kotyaeion (modern Kütahya), but there the order arrived that he should be blinded. It was done cruelly, allegedly by an inexperienced Jew, on June 29, as the bishops stood by helplessly and Diogenes begged for mercy. (The detail about the Jew may be Attaleiates' attempt to blacken the regime.) Psellos, who defended the deed as absolutely necessary to preserve the state, wrote a consolatory letter to Diogenes explaining that everything happens for a reason and that the Sleepless Eye of divine justice sees all. Now that he has lost his sight, Diogenes can enjoy the divine light that God will ignite in his soul. Psellos denies that Michael was behind the decision.[77] The one responsible was probably the *kaisar*, but no one came out of this war looking good. The regime was tarnished and weak, at the worst possible time for the empire. There would be a reckoning.

Diogenes was conveyed to the island of Prote, where he died on August 4, 1072. Eudokia was allowed to arrange his burial. Emperors in the past had been murdered (Michael III) and even blinded (e.g., Michael V), but Diogenes became a tragic figure in Byzantine imagination. He had made a valiant effort to save the state and had done no harm to his political opponents. On top of his own failure, he was dealt multiple betrayals. The image of his ghost, broad-chested and eyes gouged out, is a somber moment in the underworld satire *Timarion*.[78]

The "traditional" view was that the battle of Mantzikert sealed the fate of Asia Minor, which would now become "Turkey." The "new traditional" view is that the battle itself was not a disaster, as only a small part of the army was lost. It was the civil war that opened the floodgates to Turkish settlement. The real problem was the systemic weakness of the Byzantine political sphere.[79] But in reality, there is no way to separate foreign warfare from domestic politics in Romanía. The civil war was caused by the battle, which, in turn, was shaped by decades of political and military history. The significance of Mantzikert cannot moreover be weighed solely by its casualties; it dispersed the imperial armies in full view of the Seljuks, opened the eastern frontier, and sent a signal of Roman weakness. Contemporary authors preferred moralizing interpretations. Aristakes attributed the loss of the east to divine justice for the blinding of Diogenes. "The princes dealt treacherously with one another and ... the Lord became filled with rage and sent many [foreign] peoples for vengeance."[80] And Skylitzes claimed that the Turks turned from raiding to conquering when the Doukas regime failed to uphold the treaty Diogenes had made.[81] But Aristakes wants to link disaster theologically to immorality, not to tactical errors. And we cannot believe that prospective Turkish settlers were so bound by the formal aspects of international legal relations, especially after Alp Arslan left the area. In late 1071 eastern Anatolia was vulnerable, and no treaty made in captivity could protect it.

CHAPTER 12

"Squeezed by the Pangs of Death"
The Empire on the Verge, 1071–1081

Michael VII Doukas (1071–1078): The new regime

This last reign by a Doukas was when the empire lost Asia Minor, so it was bound to elicit negative verdicts. Many lost their lands and homes at this time. But our sources had additional reasons to be hostile. Attaleiates was a partisan of Diogenes, the victim of the Doukai, and was offering his history to the emperor, Nikephoros III Botaneiates, who had deposed Michael VII. Bryennios was writing in part to praise his grandfather, Nikephoros Bryennios, who had also rebelled against Michael VII, and Anna Komnene was writing to praise her father Alexios, who was loyal to Michael VII at the time but, as emperor, cast himself as the solution to the problems created by the Doukas dynasty.

No one hated Michael Doukas personally. He seems to have been a decent enough young man, except he was completely unfit to be emperor, especially in a time of crisis. (The only two times that dynastic succession actually worked in the eleventh century produced bad rulers: Michael V and VII.) Michael was said to be fit only to be a bishop. Others complained that he wasted his time "on the useless study of letters, trying to compose iambic verses … led astray in this by the Consul of the Philosophers [Psellos]."[1] Also, no one thought that Michael was really in charge. At first it was his mother, then the *kaisar* Ioannes. Early on, in 1072, another Ioannes, the eunuch-bishop of Side, was placed in charge of the civilian administration, but he was soon replaced by the eunuch Nikephoros, called by the diminutive Nikephoritzes. He would be the last of the great eunuch ministers of Byzantium. He had served as *doux* of Antioch under Konstantinos X, but was arrested and imprisoned by Eudokia. Later he became the governor of Greece, and, being skilled in administration—which probably means that he was good at finding money—he was now brought in to head the government as its finance minister (*logothetes*). Needless to say, this is who later writers hate. He plays the necessary role of the crafty eunuch, imposing taxes on everyone to enrich himself and allegedly alienating Michael from his own relatives, including the *kaisar* Ioannes, who had supported Nikephoritzes in the first place. Ioannes again retired to his estates with his son Andronikos. But we should be careful: both Attaleiates and Bryennios may have wanted to shield Ioannes from the odium heaped on Nikephoritzes. As we will see, Ioannes and Nikephoritzes were not necessarily enemies.[2] Moreover, it is not true, as many assert, that Nikephoritzes elbowed out Psellos. They appear to have been on good terms.[3]

By 1071, Michael had married an Abkhazian-Kartvelian princess whom the Greek sources call Maria of Alania. This was Martha, the daughter of Bagrat IV and sister of his successor Giorgi II (1072–1089). She was said to be extremely beautiful, and would play a crucial role in imperial politics.[4] Already she was used to forge a link between the Doukai and the Komnenoi: her cousin Helene was now married to Isaakios Komnenos (Alexios' older brother).[5] In addition to the Komnenoi connection, the regime kept in place most of Diogenes' generals. Botaneiates remained general of the Anatolikon theme, but with the rank of *doux* (possibly because it was now a war zone); Basilakes was posted to Paphlagonia and then Dyrrachion; Ioseph Trachaneiotes to Antioch and his son Katakalon to Adrianople; Diabatenos to Edessa; and Bryennios to Bulgaria and Dyrrachion.[6] Most of them had served the dynasty already under Konstantinos X, and his son wanted to keep them onside. Unfortunately we do not know the exact state of the army in 1072. Parts of it had been mauled and dispersed at Mantzikert, but the army sent to Khliat under Trachaneiotes and Roussel returned to Mesopotamia, albeit under unclear circumstances; they too may have been attacked.[7] The civil war would have reconstituted the armies—for another two maulings. Unfortunately, we do not know the numbers that fought for either side.

These were hard times. In his funeral oration for Xiphilinos (d. 1075), Psellos refers to the general poverty that had struck both rich and poor in the patriarch's final years. There simply was no money, and the demand for charity was greater.[8] Something was drying up the wealth in the capital, and it was almost certainly the loss of revenues from the lands in Asia Minor being overrun by Turks and deserted by Romans. The gradual debasement of the currency by previous emperors now became a precipitous decline, to a low point of 10 percent gold content (down from a previous low in the 1060s).[9] This was a devaluation born of fiscal desperation. It naturally led to inflation, which earned the emperor the nickname "Parapinakios" (from a system of measuring grain).[10] It is possible that the state now began to make "payments" in the form of tax exemptions and of imperial properties granted to individuals from which they might draw income. One of the earliest known, involving properties in Miletos, was given in 1073 to Andronikos Doukas, the *kaisar's* son, possibly as a reward for destroying Diogenes.[11]

The year 1071–1072 was a global turning point. The Romans lost their last Italian possession, Bari, to the Normans. They had already lost much of Armenia, certainly Vaspurakan, before Mantzikert, and now they lost the remainder. There was a new regime in the palace after a civil war, and a new king in Abkhazia-Kartli, Giorgi II. Even Alp Arslan had gotten himself killed in a silly way off in Central Asia, and was succeeded by his son Malik Shah (1072–1092), a teenager. The situation was grim, but hardly hopeless. The empire still had resources and determined defenders. Let us survey the frontier.

The state of the provinces

The Balkan provinces remained generally stable and were probably providing most of state revenue. There were some losses along the edges. Specifically, in ca. 1071, the Hungarian king Salamon (1063–1074, d. 1087) attacked Belgrade in retaliation for a Pecheneg raid that apparently violated the terms of a treaty (the Romans were vouching for Pecheneg behavior this far to the northwest?). The Belgrade fleet resisted with Greek fire, but then the city was besieged for months until a fire forced the *doux* Niketas to surrender. The Hungarians moved on to Niš, from which they extracted ransom. But the Hungarians did not keep these cities, and left. It does, however, seem that Sirmium came into their possession at this time, at the northwest extreme of the empire.[12]

Despite that loss, the empire's defenses in the west were not crumbling, and they appear strong in their response to yet another attempt at Bulgarian independence (most likely in 1072, possibly 1073). A Georgi Vojteh at Skopje took advantage of the multiple crises to invite the ruler of Duklja, Mihailo I, to support a rebellion against Rome. Skylitzes claims that the rebels objected to the oppressive fiscal measures introduced by Nikephoritzes, which is exactly what he had said about the rebellion of 1040 and Ioannes the *orphanotrophos*.[13] Be that as it may, Mihailo was descended from Samuil of Bulgaria, which made him and his son Konstantin Bodin suitable claimants for the Bulgarian crown. Mihailo dispatched his son with three hundred men, and at Prizren he was proclaimed Bulgarian tsar by the Skopje rebels, taking the royal name Petar III. The *doux* at Skopje, Nikephoros Karantenos, and his replacement who had just arrived, Damianos Dalassenos, marched out to suppress this revolt with a mixed Roman-Bulgarian army, which was defeated. The rebels must have been augmented by pro-independence sympathizers. Their army now split into two. One contingent, under Petrilos, took Ohrid (which had remained unwalled) and Diabolis but was defeated at Kastoria by the pro-Roman element who had fled there in fear of the "Bulgarian natives." By this point Petrilos is said to have had a "vast" Bulgarian army. He now returned to his lord in Duklja. The other contingent, under Bodin himself, captured Niš. The emperor was concerned to nip this in the bud and sent out the general Michael Saronites with "a large army of Macedonians, Romans, and Franks." Saronites took Skopje and, when Bodin came down through the snow to meet him in December, Saronites defeated, captured, and sent him to the emperor, who passed him on to be held in Antioch. The Germans and Varangians of the imperial army pillaged the region around Prespa, including the churches.

The Roman response in the western Balkans immediately after the civil war of 1072 reveals no systemic weakness. But what about the east? The situation there was chaotic, in part because of the nature of Turkish movements. There are no contemporary Turkish sources, and the Greek ones focus on the careers of specific individuals (Roussel, Ioannes Doukas, Alexios Komnenos), noting the existence of Turkish bands here and there (and everywhere . . .) only in passing. They were disrupting Anatolia's agriculture and tax base; cutting off trade, exchange between town and countryside, and communication with Constantinople; and driving Romans off their lands to make pasturage. They were also behaving like Normans, extorting payments from communities for "protection." All this was causing famine and scarcity.[14]

Let us start in the northeast. Trebizond or its hinterland was taken by the Turks at some point, but they were driven off by the officer Theodoros Gabras, a vehement warrior of local origin who ruled the region as a Roman but more or less autonomously. This cannot be dated precisely but was in the 1070s.[15] Theodosioupolis remained under the command of a *doux*, in this case Gregorios Pakourianos, the Armenian-Kartvelian lord who had lost Ani in 1064, and it is possible that he held Kars too. In that case, the *doukaton* of Iberia still held on.[16] Much of Taron passed under the control of an Armenian dynasty at Muš, whose first ruler was Tʻorʻnik of Sasun.[17] The *doukaton* of

Mesopotamia was the main artery for Turkish raids, and control here was likely breaking down. Still, a *doux*, Nikephoros Palaiologos, was in position in 1077.[18] Edessa remained under the *doux* Leon Diabatenos, who had defended it against Alp Arslan in 1070. The city was difficult to govern at this point, but there is no reason to see Diabatenos as anything other than an imperial officer.[19] An extensive swath of territory in the southeast was held by Diogenes' Chalcedonian-Armenian general Philaretos Brachamios, who controlled Melitene, Germanikeia, Samosata, and later Edessa and Antioch. He refused to recognize Michael VII after the civil war (though later he did recognize Nikephoros III).[20] The empire still retained Antioch and its environs. During and after the civil war, its *doux* conducted successful operations against the Mirdasid Mahmud of Aleppo, which resulted in a truce in 1073, requiring Mahmud to send his son to Constantinople as a hostage. It was not until 1075 that the Romans lost Manbij (acquired in 1068), after a long siege to Mahmud's successor Nasr.[21] This cut Antioch off from Edessa.

Thus, the imperial periphery did not collapse after Mantzikert and the civil war. Paradoxically, it was the center of Asia Minor that collapsed first, and eventually dragged down the periphery with it. So many Turkish bands had entered in search of fresh plunder and land that communication, taxation, and control became tenuous. Within a generation, the majority of Asia Minor, which had been Roman for a thousand years, would be split between three powers: the Seljuk sultanate of Rum in the center (around Ikonion), the Danishmends in the center-east (around Sebasteia), and the Armenian Rubenid dynasty in Cilicia and the Tauros mountains. The Romans would regain many of the coastal areas. But the loss of Asia Minor was not inevitable in 1072. The rise of the aforementioned dynasties was still in an embryonic state, and shrouded from us by later legends (e.g., the Turkish epic *Danishmendname*). In 1072, it was possible to reverse their gains or block their advance. In that year the Romans had, at the corners of their empire, successfully defeated a Bulgarian uprising and aggression from Aleppo. They could in theory do the same in the heartland. But, as it turned out, it was not only the Turks that they had to fight in the mid-1070s; it was also another act of Norman self-aggrandizement. This broke the back of Roman Asia Minor.

A Norman statelet in Asia Minor

Roussel de Bailleul's attempt to create a realm for himself in central Asia Minor closely followed the Norman playbook for interlopers, importing to Romanía the strategies that he and his countrymen had been practicing in southern Italy. It went like this. First, they took up mercenary service. If they saw that their employer needed them more than they needed him, that their forces were roughly balanced, or that he was facing a crisis (why else would he have hired them, after all?), they looked for some legalistic pretext to turn on him and seize his assets. Then they murdered some people in the countryside and offered to protect the population from marauders in exchange for cash, which effectively became a tax in their budding new realm. Then they would invent a title for themselves, or concoct a puppet regime, or obtain papal sanction, all authorizing them to make additional conquests. At this point the playbook for interlopers became that for conquerors (see Sicily, England), where they instigated a direct attack on a foreign society with the aim of taking it over and replacing its ruling class with their own followers, all in the name of a legalistic or religious pretext. Roussel did this in Asia Minor exactly as his former comrades Robert and Roger were finishing up in Italy and Sicily and casting their gaze eastward to the Roman empire, which was looking weak and tasty at the moment.[22]

It was from traumatic experience and not prejudice that Byzantine writers constantly call the Franks "treacherous," "greedy," and "violent." Three out of three captains of the Frankish mercenary unit had rebelled or attacked Roman interests in some way (Hervé, Crépin, and Roussel). Skylitzes put it well: from small pretexts they make big accusations, disturbances, and rebellions. One of their own called them "a shrewd people . . . avid for profit and domination, ready to feign or conceal anything."[23] Still, when tamed— which meant in all cases after spending time in prison—they were a tremendous asset. A rehabilitated Crépin won the war against Diogenes. In 1073 he died and was succeeded by Roussel, who had not yet spent time in prison. He would later, bringing him to his senses, but for now he was dreaming Norman dreams. His rebellion is described in detail (if without exact dates) in a number of contemporary sources, including Attaleiates and Bryennios, the latter likely using memoirs by the *kaisar* Ioannes Doukas.[24] The events themselves are easy to follow, but rather than recount them in detail we will identify the stages in the deterioration of Asia Minor, as whatever chance the Romans had to reconstitute it in 1073 was lost by a Norman misadventure.

A new expeditionary force was assembled in 1073 to pacify Asia Minor and placed under Isaakios Komnenos as *domestikos* of the east, accompanied by his brother Alexios. The army is called substantial, and must have included the units that defeated Diogenes, but it was unlikely to have included more than four thousand men. It also included four hundred Franks under Roussel. When the army reached Ikonion (or Kaisareia), Roussel protested when one of his men was arraigned for harming a local, and so he marched off to seek his fortune further east. He reached Melitene (or Sebasteia) and defeated some Turks there. Isaakios was not as successful. At Kaisareia he was badly defeated by the Turks and captured. His soldiers dispersed and their smaller bands were scattered further by raiders who overran the country. Cities would not open their gates to other Romans at night out of fear. This defeat suggests that the Romans may not have been able to salvage Asia Minor after all—but had Roussel not betrayed his employers, Isaakios might not have been defeated in the first place. Isaakios was ransomed, but *his was the last Roman army that would march across Asia Minor to Kaisareia*. That would be done again only by the Crusaders.

Meanwhile, Roussel had decided to establish his power in central Asia Minor, extracting money from the cities, probably selling protection from the Turks. Unfortunately, we know almost nothing about his mode of "governance." In early 1074, the emperor and Nikephoritzes decided to send out another army, this time against Roussel under the command of the *kaisar* Ioannes. The idea that Nikephoritzes wanted in this way to get rid of Ioannes was likely propaganda invented later by Ioannes himself.[25] He had Varangians, Frankish mercenaries under one Papas, his own son Andronikos as *domestikos*, and also Nikephoros Botaneiates with the last native units of Asia Minor. We do not know the size of this army, but as the Franks made up its right wing during the battle, the whole force cannot have had more than two thousand men. It marched past Dorylaion and came to the Zombou bridge over the Sangarios river. Roussel had come in haste and appeared on the other side. The imperial Franks defected to Roussel before the battle, and Botaneiates withdrew when he saw that it would not go well (he thus did to the Doukai what Andronikos was rumored to have done to Diogenes at Mantzikert, three years previously). Ioannes and Andronikos were overwhelmed and captured, the latter with serious wounds. *Theirs was to be the last Roman army in Asia Minor* making any progress inland before the First Crusade. There would be no more *tagmata* in the east. At this point Asia Minor was effectively lost.

Roussel now marched on Constantinople, reaching Chrysopolis, which he burned in full sight of the City to demonstrate the regime's impotence. Almost all the Franks had joined him, to the number of about three thousand. But if he thought that the Roman people would join him, or depose Michael VII, he was disappointed. So Roussel made a fascinating and almost unprecedented decision: he created his own puppet emperor and Roman court. He had his prisoner the *kaisar* Ioannes proclaimed emperor and took on a political advisor, Basileios Maleses, another prisoner but one who hated Michael. The Norman adventurer was creating a shadow Roman government to provide political cover to his aggression. This policy would be repeated by Robert Guiscard only a few years later and by the Crusaders in 1203. Nikephoritzes now took a fateful step of his own, which would foreshadow the future course of Byzantine history: he hired a Turkish marauder in Bithynia, one Artuk (founder of the Artukid dynasty), to defeat Roussel. Artuk, with an army about twice the size of Roussel's, easily defeated him by a feigned retreat and then picking off the Franks from afar with arrows. Artuk captured Roussel and Ioannes, and proceeded to auction them. However, before the emperor's gold could arrive the Norman was bought back by his wife, who was in a nearby fort, and let loose to resume his state building. Ioannes returned to Constantinople, but first he was tonsured and appeared chastened at the court as a monk.

In some ways, these events marked an important transition: henceforth, and for the rest of their history, the Romans would hire Franks to fight Turks and Turks to fight Franks, depending on who was threatening them more. This was when Franks and Turks began to fight between themselves over the corpse of Romanía, which they would do hotly for another five hundred years.

Roussel now resumed his ambitions in the Armeniakon theme, selling protection from the Turks and from himself to the locals, so the Romans had gained nothing from hiring Artuk. The court, probably in 1075, decided to call on Giorgi II of Georgia, the emperor's brother-in-law. Nikephoros Palaiologos was dispatched and, in the tradition of the civil wars of the late tenth century, received an army of six thousand men from Giorgi. Palaiologos went to the Pontos and began operations against Roussel, but he could not pay his men for long and most deserted him. Roussel defeated the small remnant easily. It is likely that the deal with Giorgi involved the transfer of Tao, Kars, and Vanand back to Georgia, which was done by the last *doux* at Theodosioupolis, Gregorios Pakourianos; the Georgians also reclaimed Anakopia on the Black Sea.[26] *The Roman empire now lost all its holdings in the Caucasus.* It could not have defended them anyway.

There was now no way to save Roman Asia Minor. The court had given the Turks a huge boost in its single-minded determination to eliminate Roussel. He may have made matters worse for himself when he appointed Ioannes emperor because that created a political threat to the regime that exacerbated dynastic rifts rather than pose only a military threat to the empire. Attaleiates, a friend of Maleses, seems to have preferred a political settlement with Roussel and a joint fight against the Turks; in later Byzantine terms he would be a Latinophile.[27] But we have seen repeatedly that emperors made decisions based on their political, and not military, vulnerability. The court now gave the task of capturing Roussel to Alexios Komnenos, the future emperor, who was not yet twenty. He had no money and hardly any men, but was likely loyal. We note that only men with the names Doukas, Palaiologos, or Komnenos were put in charge of these missions in Asia Minor, regardless of their military experience, and not Bryennios, Basilakes, or Botaneiates, though they were more experienced generals. It is also striking that we do not hear of the participation of western units in the wars in Asia Minor, even though armies did survive there and were used against the Bulgarians in 1072/3 and later, in the rebellion of Bryennios. It is possible, though it cannot be proven, that the western generals refused to participate in the salvage operations in Asia Minor. During the Mantzikert campaign, Bryennios and Trachaneiotes (both from Adrianople) had advised falling back.[28]

The Komnenian writers dramatize Alexios' capture of Roussel, probably in 1076. He allegedly waged guerrilla warfare against the Franks with 150 Alan soldiers. In reality, the court put out another warrant for Roussel's arrest among the local Turks, and one Tutak (possibly the same as Artuk), who was on good terms with him before, now treacherously arrested him at a feast and delivered him to Amaseia. Alexios seems to have been there only to accept the captive; possibly he had to raise the money in Amaseia, and Bryennios interestingly reveals that some locals preferred to have Roussel protecting them, rather than any alternative at hand. This is interesting in itself, and Alexios had to resort to a trick: he pretended to blind Roussel, which dissipated his support.[29] Whether any of this happened is debatable. The truth was that when Alexios left for the capital with his prisoner, whatever was left of Roman rule in the Armeniakon theme went with him. An interesting story is told about the return journey. Alexios wished to see his grandfather's estate at Kastamone, but found it deserted.[30] He then had to evade Turkish bands to get to the City, where Roussel, "that Frankish dog,"[31] was tortured and imprisoned.

The Romans were able to suppress the little Normandy that was being carved out of their territory, but at the cost of losing Asia Minor to the Turks. There was local resistance to the new conquerors at Sebasteia and by Theodoros Gabras in the northeast.[32] But theirs was in many ways a post-Roman order. Unfortunately we have no sources for what was happening in the interior. Few of the cities seem to have fallen by 1078, and provincial officials were appointed throughout the decade, yet the countryside seems to have been overrun. Many provincial Romans fled to the coastal towns and from there to the islands, including abbots who otherwise confessed that they had a duty to stay at their posts no matter what. The fleet may have helped the evacuation from Pontos. Kastamone had been abandoned. Even Chrysopolis, across from Constantinople, had become a Turkish lair before

1078.[33] We should remember, however, that the Franks had reached it first, just as they would destroy Constantinople first, in 1204, before the Turks could do so in 1453.

Breakdown

The regime of Michael VII did not lack initiative. It had sent many armies to retake Asia Minor, albeit none under a proven commander, and hunted down Roussel tenaciously, albeit at a huge cost. It was also active diplomatically. An embassy was sent to the Seljuk sultan Malik Shah in 1074, probably to Baghdad. An exposition of Christian belief by Psellos, written on the emperor's behalf, has been seen as a follow-up communication, and refers to a religious debate at the sultan's court involving the original embassy. We do not know if any agreement was reached, but it may explain why the Turkish generals in Asia Minor were so cooperative in apprehending Roussel.[34] It is possible that an alliance was now made with king Géza I of Hungary (1074–1077); he married the daughter of one Synadenos and she was sent with a crown that bore enamel images of Géza, Michael, and Michael's son Konstantinos. These were later incorporated into the Holy Crown of Hungary (Figure 16).[35]

After Robert Guiscard's foiled naval attack on the Balkans in 1066, there was always fear that he would invade again.[36] After 1073, that would squeeze the empire between him and his former henchman Roussel in Asia Minor. Thus in that year the regime of Michael VII approached pope Gregory VII, who was in conflict with Robert, and they planned what to all appearances was a Crusade: an army drawn from all over the west would clear Asia Minor of Turks before going to Jerusalem. The plan was put into motion, but then fizzled.[37] Nor could the pope provide effective protection against Robert. Meanwhile, Constantinople was making direct overtures to that most dangerous man. With the chaos raging in the east, an attack by him might prove fatal to the empire as a whole. After a preliminary proposal was rejected, they agreed that Robert's daughter Olympias (or Olimpia, renamed Helene in Constantinople) would marry Michael's newly-born-in-the-purple son Konstantinos and thereby possibly become the next empress. In exchange, Robert would defend the empire and have the same friends and enemies. He received the right to distribute forty-four Byzantine court titles to his followers with their salaries paid by Constantinople, to a total of 14,400 gold coins per year. The terms are spelled out in a document drafted by Psellos and preserved among his works.[38] In effect, Robert was being paid to do no

FIGURE 16 The Holy Crown of Hungary, used to crown the kings of Hungary since the twelfth century. It contains enamel images of Michael VII Doukas and Konstantinos Doukas (either his brother or son). Source: Shutterstock, ID 1698277.

harm. This was protection money on an imperial scale. The plan worked for Michael VII, but the court should have known better: any agreement or even contact with a Norman created actionable precedents and legalistic pretexts for future aggression.

The Norman conquest of southern Italy had already dislocated families that moved to Greece.[39] Interestingly, the Norman conquest of England also produced a flood of Anglo-Saxon refugees who were dislocated by the racist regime of William the Conqueror, and many of them trekked to Constantinople and took up service in the Varangian guard. There, they would soon have the chance to fight Normans again, in a different theater.[40] And of course many fled the Turkish depredations in Asia Minor. The 1070s were an era of mass flight that we can barely glimpse in the sources, which fixate on a few individuals.

Nikephoritzes is credited with two initiatives. He gathered up refugees from Asia Minor, armed them, and trained them to fight as cavalry lancers, thus imitating the Normans. From the best among them he reconstituted the *tagma* of the Immortals.[41] He also centralized the grain market of Raidestos, one of the major transit markets for the capital. This reform was and is controversial. He did not create a state monopoly, as is often claimed. Rather, he required buyers and sellers to use one clearing house, or *phoundax*, increasing the state's take in fees, which were farmed out to private contractors. Moreover, prices previously remained low through multiple venues and competition, but now a few buyers could purchase in bulk, which drove prices down and so hurt producers, and then the buyers could resell at higher prices in the capital, which hurt consumers. Attaleiates, our source for this, understood the underlying economics, especially how higher grain prices led to higher costs in other sectors and caused scarcity.[42]

Nikephoritzes' fiscal reforms caused disaffection in the lower Danube too. At an uncertain date, he canceled the annual subsidies to the multilingual cities there (the nature of these subsidies is unclear), and the soldiers were unhappy at being excluded from the local administration (whatever that means). The cities, especially Dorystolon (Dristra), turned to the Pecheneg leader Tatous to help them rebel, and he garrisoned their city. In response, the emperor sent out one Nestor as *katepano* of Dorystolon (i.e., Paradounabon). He was an "Illyrian" who had served Konstantinos X, possibly a Serb. Nestor now joined the rebels, possibly because his property had meanwhile been confiscated by Nikephoritzes or else he sympathized with their cause. After an uncertain time, he led the Pechenegs into Macedonia. This is not dated precisely, but Attaleiates places it around the time of Roussel's arrest, so ca. 1076. The Roman army of Adrianople did not dare resist them, so the Pechenegs plundered freely all the way to the City, causing a famine and demands for Nikephoritzes' surrender. The emperor was feeling the pressure to dismiss the unpopular minister, but he resisted, and yet Nestor and the Pechenegs inexplicably returned home.[43] Paradounabon remained partially outside of imperial control, and the regime had become dangerously unpopular. Soldiers from Adrianople came to the capital to protest that they were not being paid. In the winter of 1076–1077, Constantinople was filling up with refugees that could not be fed.[44]

Antioch was also becoming unstable. As always Antiochene society remains opaque to us, but there seems to have been a faction led by the patriarch Aimilianos that supported Philaretos Brachamios and another that supported the "lords" in the city, either imperial officials or the rich. In 1074, Constantinople sent Isaakios Komnenos to be the new *doux*, a year after his release from Turkish captivity. Isaakios managed to send Aimilianos to Constantinople through a ruse, but Antioch was in turmoil and Isaakios had to use the army to suppress the rioters. Ironically, he was subsequently captured in a Turkish raid and his backers in Antioch had to ransom him—again.

A lot of money had changed hands over this man, so it is no wonder that he henceforth deferred to his younger brother Alexios, the Romans' ransomer-in-chief. Isaakios held on to Antioch until the end of the reign, when it passed to Philaretos, who recognized Nikephoros III Botaneiates but was de facto independent.[45]

By October 1077, the second Doukas regime had finally lost credibility. Its two most prominent generals, men who had commanded in every part of the empire and had been present at the most decisive campaigns of the past twenty years, proclaimed themselves emperors. They were Nikephoros Botaneiates, *doux* of Anatolikon at Lampe, and Nikephoros Bryennios, *doux* of Dyrrachion (who had been "adopted" by Romanos IV Diogenes as his brother). They were both natives of the provinces they governed. Curiously, the regime of Michael VII had broken with a long-standing policy of not appointing locals for long terms in command of their native provinces.[46] Maybe it calculated that native appointees would energetically defend their own properties, but it also enabled them to raise local allies. The real threat was Bryennios, not Botaneiates, who was almost eighty years old and had only three hundred soldiers. He had to hire Turks for his rebellion, and the emperor counted on his own Turkish allies to eliminate him.[47] These two rebellions are interesting because they reveal the deep crisis of the military-political system. They were also the first to occur simultaneously in east and west.

The historian Bryennios models the origin of his grandfather's rebellion against Michael VII on that of Isaakios against Michael VI: a group of generals are disgruntled at their shabby treatment by the court and rebel. Addressing Alexios' court, the historian seems to be implying that "what justified your uncle justified my grandfather too." It was Ioannes Bryennios—the rebel's brother—who suborned the *doux* of Adrianople, Katakalon Trachaneiotes, and his army, the only substantial force that seems to have been left in the Balkans, and even it had not resisted the Pechenegs the previous year. Nikephoros Bryennios did not bring an army from Dyrrachion when he joined his brother, but he did win over Basilakes at Thessalonike. All these were names from the Mantzikert campaign. By force and persuasion they took over many cities in Thrace, and Bryennios was acclaimed emperor at Traïanoupolis before being greeted in triumph at his home city of Adrianople. This was another distinctly "Macedonian" revolt, like that of Tornikios thirty years earlier, and there was an Ioannes Batatzes on board this time too. The people of Raidestos tore down the hated *phoundax* and Bryennios distributed offices and honors as an emperor, appointing Ioannes *domestikos* of the *scholai*—though what *scholai* survived is unclear. They had many Franks, Varangians, and Roman Pechenegs on their side. Ioannes now marched ahead and encamped before the City, acclaiming his brother and trying to win over the people, albeit with no success. When he (or some of his men) set fire to a suburb, he lost the contest for public opinion. Not knowing what else to do, he retreated to Thrace and went into winter quarters.[48] Oddly, it had turned out much like Tornikios' rebellion in 1047. But the empire was now in disarray. The Pechenegs took advantage of the civil war, raided Macedonia, and besieged Bryennios in Adrianople. He had to pay them to go away.[49]

Michael VII and Nikephoritzes were desperate. They held little territory and had no money. They began to confiscate church treasures, and their only supporter who counted was Alexios. Actually, they had one more asset: Roussel. He had been caught trying to escape to Botaneiates (which is interesting, seeing how Botaneiates had backed out of fighting him at Zombou a few years earlier). The emperor now made up with Roussel and placed him and Alexios in charge of defeating the western rebel. At this time, over the objections of his mother Anna Dalassene, who hated the Doukai, Alexios married Eirene Doukaina, the daughter of Andronikos and granddaughter of the *kaisar*.[50]

Meanwhile, Botaneiates was on the move toward Phrygia. He had lost the support of two officers, Nikephoros Melissenos and Georgios Palaiologos, who were connected by marriage to the Komnenoi. Botaneiates began canvassing for support in the capital while the emperor hired Sulayman, the son of Qutlumush, Alp Arslan's old enemy. Sulayman and his brothers had sought refuge in Asia Minor and now agreed to block Botaneiates, but were won over by him through the intermediacy of Arisighi (Chrysoskoulos), the emir who had defected to Manouel Komnenos in 1070. Botaneiates promised him Nikaia. Roman politics in Asia Minor had become a game of aligning Turkish interests, and every civil war resulted in more gains for them. Botaneiates and his three hundred were admitted into Nikaia and acclaimed. His rebellion resembled that of Isaakios in 1057, with people in the capital working to overthrow Michael VII and prepare the ground for the rebel general, whose forces, however, were now miniscule. Leading the conspirators in the capital were churchmen—angry, perhaps, at the confiscation of Church wealth—especially Aimilianos, the patriarch of Antioch arrested by Isaakios Komnenos. In late March 1078, the rebels caused the usual commotion in Hagia Sophia, freed the prisoners, and stormed the palace. Replaying 1057, the emperor stepped down and Botaneiates sent men to take control of the palace. Michael became a monk at the monastery of Stoudios (and later bishop of Ephesos), and Nikephoritzes was caught trying to escape; he was imprisoned and tortured cruelly to surrender his treasure, but he died in the interrogation. Botaneiates entered Constantinople triumphantly in early April and was acclaimed emperor. He had been born in the first decade of the century, under Basil II. He now found the palace thoroughly plundered.[51]

Nikephoros III Botaneiates (1078–1081)

Botaneiates' extremely distinguished career had been in the military, but his name is associated with no victories. When he took the throne, Attaleiates wrote him heroically back into his account of past battles, but only the defeats. It was a powerful symbolic choice.[52] In a thousand years, no Roman emperor had taken hold of a more diminished state. Asia Minor was effectively lost, the Balkans in the throes of a major rebellion and periodically overrun by Pechenegs, and imperial revenues severely diminished. The state had begun to appropriate Church gold to cover expenses. Yet Botaneiates began by liberally distributing offices, promotions, and titles, and forgiving debts, debasing the coinage further to fund this generosity.[53] He was following the policies that he had observed emperors follow his whole life, those which had broken the fisc.

Botaneiates' regime was basically an extension of the Doukas dynasty. The new emperor sought to marry into it, even though he had married twice already, and considered first Eudokia Makrembolitissa but was dissuaded from this choice by the *kaisar* Ioannes; Eudokia and her daughters were at least brought back from exile to the City. Botaneiates married Maria of Alania instead (Figure 17), who was beautiful and brought foreign connections, but this marriage was so uncanonical that the priest who performed it was defrocked.[54] Maria's four-year-old son by Michael VII, Konstantinos, remained in the palace, though not as the heir-apparent, and so did the previous emperor's brother Konstantios (who was confusingly called Konstantinos sometimes).[55] Alexios was also retained as the leading general, and seems to have been "adopted" by the empress Maria. In the place of Nikephoritzes, Botaneiates relied on two of his own household "slaves" of Skythian origin, Borilas and Germanos, and also on Ioannes, the eunuch-bishop of Side who had been elbowed out by Nikephoritzes and was brought back to head the civilian administration. Not much changed.

Roman rivals always took precedence over foreign invaders. Bryennios refused to accept the rank of *kaisar* and the status of heir, and began to march on the City again, so Alexios was appointed *domestikos* of the western *scholai*, only there were no *scholai* left. What was left of the western armies marched

FIGURE 17 Image of Nikephoros III Botaneiates and Maria of Alania (formerly the empress of Michael VII Doukas) being crowned by Christ from a manuscript of the *Homilies* of John Chrysostom (Bibliothèque Nationale, Coislin 79). Source: Snark, Art Resource NY.

with the rebel. An army of two thousand was thus sought from Botaneiates' Turkish friends at Nikaia, Mansur and Sulayman, the sons of Qutlumush, to which were added Frankish mercenaries, the remainder of Nikephoritzes' Immortals, and other surviving Roman units.[56] Whereas Franks and Turks had previously been used against each other, they were now both being used together against rebel Roman armies. If we are to believe his grandson, Bryennios had ten thousand soldiers or more, led by the western Roman officer class. A fierce battle was fought at Kalabrye by the Halmyros river in Thrace, and many fell on both sides. We have two accounts of the battle that are impossible to reconcile. Bryennios may have been winning but the tide was turned by the sudden appearance of a Turkish army over a hill—either late arrivals or Alexios' stratagem. Bryennios was defeated, captured, blinded on orders by Borilas, and brought before Botaneiates, who pardoned him. The war was over quickly, if bloodily, in 1078. Bryennios' brother Ioannes, however, was murdered in Constantinople by a Varangian whose nose he had cut off during the rebellion. Botaneiates probably had the guardsman executed, which caused the rest of the Varangians to rise up and try to murder him in the palace. There was fighting in the halls and stairways, but the Roman guardsmen prevailed.[57]

Alexios was barred from entering Constantinople and immediately sent out, with the rank of *doux* of the west, to put down another rebel, Nikephoros Basilakes, the *doux* of Dyrrachion and veteran of Mantzikert. The western officer class had taken no part in the effort to reclaim Asia Minor in the 1070s and now seemed determined to oppose Botaneiates.[58] Basilakes brought up the armies of Dyrrachion and Bulgaria and some Franks from Italy, allegedly some ten thousand in total, and made Thessalonike his headquarters. He attacked Alexios at night as the latter approached the city, hoping to take him by surprise, but the plan had been betrayed. Alexios left his monk-attendant to greet the enemy in the camp, while he ambushed the attackers from a forest. Basilakes fled to the citadel of Thessalonike, which was taken by assault. He too was now sent to Botaneiates and blinded.

The west was pacified, at least for now. Its armies were mauled but still sufficed for basic defense. After defeating Basilakes, Alexios marched from Adrianople against some Pecheneg raiders in Bulgaria and chased them away.[59] So in 1079, Botaneiates turned his attention to Asia Minor. Imperial control seems to have collapsed in the interior, except for pockets. Philaretos Brachamios had created his own statelet in Cilicia and Syria, including Melitene, Germanikeia, Samosata, and Edessa (governed for him since 1077 by the former Roman general Basileios Apokapes). Alexios' brother Isaakios had governed Antioch until 1078. After a brief disturbance, this city too was taken over by Philaretos, who sought and obtained recognition from the emperor Botaneiates. In name he was now an imperial official, but in practice he was autonomous. These were former Roman officials of Armenian origin creating a postimperial future for the region.[60] In early 1079, Botaneiates gathered an army, said to be substantial and including the Immortals. But when these soldiers, some of whom were reluctant to face Turks, were ferried over to Chrysopolis, Konstantios Doukas (the brother of Michael VII) incited some to a rebellion against the emperor.[61] This dysfunction was now the norm for the Roman polity. But the expeditionary force was divided and persuaded by the emperor's agents to surrender the rebel, who was tonsured and exiled. It was over with no bloodshed, but this expedition had been unable to even leave the coast.

Every rebellion in those years had a sequel. Just as Basilakes had followed upon Bryennios in the west, in 1080 Nikephoros Melissenos raised a rebellion in Asia Minor, having refused to join that of Botaneiates in 1078.[62] The story that we are told is odd. He was living on the island of Kos, yet somehow crossed over to western Asia Minor, gathered a Turkish army and went from city to city. They surrendered to him as emperor and he "unwillingly" installed Turkish garrisons in them, including at Nikaia (this is strange because Nikaia was already ruled by the sons of Qutlumush). Botaneiates ordered Alexios to campaign against him, but Alexios refused; his forces were simply insufficient and, moreover, the rebel was married to his sister, so that a failure by Alexios could easily be interpreted as sedition. The emperor then gave the command to the *protovestiarios* Ioannes, a eunuch from his household. He marched the army to Nikaia, but accomplished nothing and withdrew to the City rather than face the Turks.[63] It is unclear, then, what kind of regime "emperor" Melissenos had in northwestern Asia Minor. He seems to have been an "emperor of opportunity" for the Turks, just as the *kaisar* Ioannes Doukas had been for Roussel a few years earlier.

Botaneiates was running out of options, resources, and support. In the east his support had come from the Seljuks, but now apparently that was lost. In the west, he had put down two rebellions and pushed back the Pechenegs, but this was accomplished by his general Alexios Komnenos, whose army included many Turks. Botaneiates was almost eighty, and had no sons. All eyes would be on the succession, and specifically on Alexios. The emperor now made a fatal mistake: he designated as his heir his nephew Nikephoros Synadenos.[64] This sidelined his wife's son Konstantinos and alienated the Doukas faction. It also put Alexios in an awkward and perilous situation, the outcome of which could not long have been in doubt. Anna Komnene, the future emperor's daughter and biographer, presents us with a dramatized account of the Komnenian revolt and capture of the City and throne. We need not rehearse here all its twists and turns, moments of danger, narrow escapes, the sinister plotting of Borilas and Germanos, the solidarity of the Komnenoi brothers and their pro forma reluctance to rebel, which was overcome by their noble devotion to the common good. Anna's tale, self-serving as it is and often questionable, cannot be improved in the retelling here.

What merits attention is the extraordinary kinship structure of the rebels' group, which laid the foundation for the distinctively Komnenian style of rule. Isaakios Komnenos was married to the empress Maria's cousin. Alexios was, in some way, adopted by Maria—but there was talk that he intended to marry her also. At the time he was married to Eirene Doukaina, whose grandfather, the *kaisar* Ioannes, was angered by Botaneiates' passing over Konstantinos Doukas as heir in favor of Synadenos. So the Doukas family joined the Komnenoi, and in return Alexios promised to safeguard Konstantinos' dynastic stake (eventually he betrothed his daughter Anna to him). Alexios' sister was married to the rebel Melissenos, with whom the Komnenoi reached an accommodation. A main supporter was Georgios Palaiologos, married to Anna Doukaina, the sister of Alexios' wife Eirene. Alexios was also supported by Gregorios Pakourianos (Grigor Bakuran), the Armenian-Georgian noble who was promised the position of *domestikos*, and by Oumbertopoulos, possibly a nephew of Robert Guiscard.

The City was betrayed to Alexios on April 1, 1081, by the German guard of one section of the walls. The rebel's forces plundered it violently before an expanding wave of acclamations confirmed that he would be the next emperor. Botaneiates was forced to abdicate and was made a monk. It was a critical moment for the empire, as Robert Guiscard was preparing a major invasion of the Byzantine Balkans. Alexios may well have found support because more people believed that he, rather than Botaneiates, could defeat the Normans. They were correct, but the war lasted many years, was close-run, and required many innovations and desperate measures on the part of Alexios and his supporters. With Asia Minor mostly lost and the western Balkans overrun by Normans, contemporaries felt that the empire was almost lost. According to one bishop, it held sway only between the Golden Gate and the palace, i.e., over Constantinople alone.[65] "We were pressed on all sides *by the bonds of death*," noted a contemporary.[66] Yet Alexios inaugurated a new dynasty and a new era for the Roman empire. The Romans mustered the resources and the will to pull through and rebuild. When the Crusaders arrived in 1096, they encountered a Komnenian Roman empire.

General Considerations
Imperial Collapse

BYZANTINISTS ARE UNDERSTANDABLY reluctant to admit the reality of decline and fall, especially after struggling for decades to banish those terms, but we cannot deny that something went catastrophically wrong in the third quarter of the eleventh century. Its nature and causes have been discussed often, but most explanations are guesses. We cannot anchor them in *data* about armies, economies, or imperial decisions. The present section will summarize what the events suggest and then examine some of the key concepts around which explanations have been built.

Something seems to have gone wrong in the defense of Asia Minor in the reign of Konstantinos X Doukas, though its nature remains opaque. We hear of cutbacks to military spending, though we do not know exactly what form they took, how they were implemented, or why. There is no reason to suppose that the state was generating less revenue than before, and Isaakios had already cut back on some apparently wasteful civilian expenses (though, again, we have no figures). Doukas does not seem to have *used* his armies much, at least compared to Monomachos and Isaakios, and seems to have prioritized political spending over military spending. At the end of his frustratingly opaque reign, the Roman armies appear demoralized, underfunded, and disorganized. Major cities of Asia Minor were sacked. Yet the vigorous campaigns of Diogenes show that numbers, organization, discipline, and strategic sense were still there, albeit also a shortage of cash. Diogenes closed the Syrian gap, chased down marauders (with mixed results, though that would have been a long-term effort in any case), and, but for the battle of Mantzikert, would have closed the Armenian gap. Some historians have tried to argue that Mantzikert was not the disaster that it has been made out to be, and it is certainly true that it did not cause a huge loss of life. But that is not why it was a disaster. Diogenes' defeat and capture put enormous stress on the emperor's already fragile legitimacy, a perennial problem in the Roman system that was now ever more acutely felt (political rivalries may have contributed to the defeat, if we believe the accusations against Andronikos Doukas). The defeat enabled Diogenes' enemies to move against him. It also signaled to the Seljuks that Asia Minor was open for conquest and settlement. A victory at Mantzikert, by contrast, would have secured Diogenes against his rivals and possibly secured Asia Minor against the Seljuks (though we cannot know that, given how little we know about them). The consequences of the defeat cannot be separated from the chaos that it precipitated.

Mantzikert ushered in the civil war of 1071–1072, the three-year war with Roussel (1073–1076), and the multiple civil wars of 1077–1081. Those wars were the logical outcome of Rome's systemic weakness when it came to succession and legitimacy, a weakness that had been growing for decades as emperors tried to protect themselves against rivals and generally keep everyone happy, often by bribing them, but the system exploded when it was placed under such stress. It has also been proposed that the empire's theological ideology contributed to this spiral: emperors who were losing in foreign wars were perceived as having lost God's favor, which then inspired rivals to become God's chosen, leading to a proliferation of civil wars exactly when the empire was most in need of unity and cooperation.[1] This was an aspect of the empire's competitive politics and its lack of absolute standards of legitimacy.[2] Thus, every civil war after 1071 fueled a death spiral of imperial collapse. At the end of those wars, there were hardly any Roman armies left in the east. The process was incredibly swift. Diogenes was able to muster a field army forty thousand strong or more, in 1071. By the mid-1070s, the armies being led by the Doukai and Komnenoi could not have topped four thousand. Asia Minor was being overrun by multiple, apparently large Turkish armies that were preventing the state from accessing taxes and manpower. Precisely as both civil and foreign wars were destroying the Roman armies, the empire was losing the resources necessary to rebuild them.

The political problem was systemic. Was there also a systemic problem in the army? Historians have searched for and proposed underlying changes that made Byzantine defenses vulnerable to Seljuk attack. Before we discuss them, we must consider the possibility that structural weakening, even if it can be proven, was immaterial, i.e., that the Seljuks posed a threat of such magnitude that Byzantium would not have withstood it either before or after the alleged changes to its defenses. Perhaps we have jumped to reverse-engineer explanations for the loss of Asia Minor that are based entirely on Roman factors, mostly because they are somewhat recoverable. But we know little about the Turks, especially their numbers (probably large), goals, coordination, tactics (beyond the feigned retreat), weapons (beyond the bow), leaders, economies, and relationship with the Seljuk dynasty. We even lack a reliable, accurate history of the early Seljuks giving dates, politics, and names. Were the raiders decentralized bands looking for plunder and pasturage? Or were most of them organized by a relatively coherent plan for conquest? We do not know the basics, so we deem Romanía weak largely on the basis of the outcome. But that is endogenic analysis by default.

What factors supposedly weakened the Roman army so that it could not keep out the Turks? The most commonly cited is the "decline of the thematic armies." According to this theory, thematic armies were primarily defensive, located in the affected frontier regions, bound to the lands that supported them, and geared more toward harassing raiders in passes than conquering foreign lands. The armies of conquest relied instead on the more professional, mobile *tagmata*, which gradually eclipsed and replaced the thematic forces. The transition from one type to the other was enabled by the fiscalization of *strateia*, by which someone who owned thematic land could, instead of serving in person or providing a recruit, pay the tax difference between thematic lands and other kinds of land. The state would then take that money and hire tagmatic soldiers, who were more expensive and so there were fewer of them, but they were better and more mobile. Of course, instead of hiring soldiers emperors could use that money to build churches or enrich their supporters. Since Psellos and Aristakes, that very charge has often been leveled against the "civilian" emperors of the eleventh century, but without budget sheets we cannot know for sure. Historians have argued instead that the tagmatic armies stationed in the provinces were not as good as the thematic ones had been at defending Asia Minor. The empire had eroded its own defenses when it switched to a more offensive mode.

Maybe this did happen, but it is impossible to prove. First, we do not know the extent to which the *strateia* (military obligation) was fiscalized. It was *possible* to do this in the tenth century already, but we do not know the extent to which it was done at any time.[3] What was the state of the thematic army of the Anatolikon in, say, 1000, 1050, or 1070? We do not know because we cannot track the individual history of those armies after ca. 980.[4] We hear of armies stationed in the themes of Asia Minor throughout our period, but we do not know what kind of units are meant. The *doukes* would have been in charge of both kinds. The sources, however, do not use technical terms and can refer to *tagmata* under the name of the theme in which they were recruited or stationed (thus making them seem like thematic forces)[5]; and the term *tagma* could have the generic meaning of "military force."

Consider Attaleiates' description of the decrepit soldiers whom Diogenes tried to muster in 1068 (p. 242). Historians like to see these as thematic soldiers, which validates the theory of the "thematic decline," but Attaleiates explicitly calls them *tagmata*. It does not matter that they were stationed in a theme (here Anatolikon), because most armies were stationed in themes by this point. In fact, if we follow the logic of Attaleiates' rhetorical argument, he *must* be referring to the *tagmata*, for he wants to argue that neglect under the Doukai had degraded the best parts of the army, so he would have to showcase the bad shape of the *tagmata*. And the fact that the image is rhetorical allows us to doubt it. Diogenes put this army through complex maneuvers, and they kept up. In any case, we do not know how many soldiers at any time were tagmatic and how many thematic. It is also possible that adjustments had been made to the fiscal-service relationship between soldiers and the state that eroded the thematic-tagmatic distinction. But we lack the sources that would allow us to track this.[6] My hunch is that in, say, 1050 most of the armies were tagmatic.

But, even so, how can we know that the old thematic armies would have been more effective against the Seljuks than the *tagmata*? Here the field has to come clean about the moralizing and politicized way in which it has discussed thematic armies, who are valorized as patriot "farmer-soldiers" as opposed to the professional or "mercenary" armies of the eleventh century that were led by the incipient forces of Byzantine feudalism. The idealization of thematic armies was political from the outset. It was an integral component of an argument according to which a freer society of soldier-farmers was "feudalized" when their smaller properties were gobbled up by the estates of aristocrats; at the same time, the impersonal state (represented by the Macedonians) lost its struggle against "the families" (represented by the rise of the Doukai and the Komnenoi). Historians following Ostrogorsky wanted to link imperial decline to this socioeconomic transformation, which they viewed negatively.[7] Although few still uphold this model, its fetishization of the thematic armies lives on independently. Yet that too needs to be laid to rest along with the feudalization narrative.

Just because the thematic armies had defended Asia Minor from the Arabs does not mean they could have done so against the Seljuks. These were different enemies in different contexts. My suspicion is that Seljuks had larger armies and were backed by sources of migrant manpower that surpassed anything the Arabs deployed against Rome. After 1071, the Turks began to settle in large numbers, transforming the human and natural landscape, which the Arabs did not. After 1100, "the palaeoenvironmental as well as the archaeological and historical data" indicate "a sudden downturn in rural agrarian activities" and cereal production in the central Anatolian plateau.[8] Also, the Turks fought differently. The old thematic armies had never faced large armies that could use archery so efficiently; in fact, neither had the *tagmata*, not until they faced the Pechenegs and Seljuks in the late 1040s, and began to lose to them. Fighting styles might have been a crucial factor here.[9] Monomachos immediately tried to adapt by sending fifteen thousand Pechenegs to the east, but they rebelled. My hunch, if I may be permitted another, is that the *tagmata* stood a better chance against the new enemy than the *themata*. Harassing them was no longer enough, and the *tagmata* were better, more mobile, and (by now) locally based. Six *doukes* posted along the frontier from Antioch to Iberia with armies of professionals were just as responsive as the old thematic generals. They were not, as we saw, fixated on "preclusive" defense that could do nothing once the line was breached.[10] The *doukes* were capable of receiving the Seljuks on ground of their choosing well inside the frontier (in fact, in their first encounter in 1048), ambushing them, or chasing them down (as in the 1050s). There was no Maginot Line mentality.

Another key term is "mercenary." We have to be careful with this word and to distinguish between mercenaries and professional soldiers. Byzantinists rarely do this, but it is crucial.[11] The *tagmata* consisted largely of professional Roman soldiers paid to fight for their country. In our period they almost never attacked civilians. They participated in civil wars, but that is because, as Romans, they had a stake in the polity. Mercenaries, by contrast, were hired foreigners who could and did switch allegiance, which is usually how they came into the emperors' employ, as the latter had more money. An intermediate category were foreign units provided by allied rulers (imperial "vassals") or hired with their permission by the emperors. But in the era of collapse, mercenaries were usually Franks and the like. The *tagmata* after Basil II did not consist of mercenaries, far less foreign ones, though that is often assumed.[12] They were augmented by mercenaries in the hundreds, perhaps a couple thousand at most. As stated in the Introduction, when sources list the ethnicities that made up a given Roman army (Franks, Rus', Pechenegs, etc.), we should not assume that the whole was divided equally into those groups. Rather, those units added color on the flanks to a Roman tagmatic core. They draw the sources' attention so often because they were exotic and distinctive, not because they made up the majority of the army.

Their soldiers were probably not even registered and paid in the same way as the tagmatic armies.[13] "Total numbers of foreign mercenaries were never large, yet they fulfilled extremely effective service."[14]

It was only in the 1070s, after the destruction of the native armies, that mercenaries made up a greater (relative) percentage. And then they proved to be disastrous, especially the Normans, but they had always been unreliable, even the Pechenegs and Oghuz.[15] It is true that foreign mercenaries posed less of a threat to emperors, as they generally did not participate in political contests.[16] But this was a fringe benefit. Most of the armies were Roman and emperors had to keep them under control in other ways, for example by paying them on time, placing them under eunuchs of their household, dividing commands, and not allowing generals to command them for too long or in their native province. In sum, the armies of Rome had not yet been replaced by (unreliable) mercenaries because of a cost-benefit analysis or political calculation. However, the reliance on mercenaries after 1071 becomes problematic in light of another factor. In the 1070s, we begin to see a split between the Balkan and Anatolian officer class. This is not mentioned as such in the sources, but, while Asia Minor was being lost, the likes of Bryennios, Basilakes, and Trachaneiotes—and their Roman armies—did little to help in the east, and were (apparently) not asked to do so by the Doukas regimes. Their western armies seem to have survived to fight multiple civil and foreign wars in 1078–1085, and they are sometimes described as substantial. This cleavage is mysterious, as is the bifurcation in Roman fortunes (the Balkans vs. Asia Minor) during this decade. Usually emperors (witness Monomachos) were able to transfer armies from east to west and vice versa to meet pressing needs. Where were the westerners when the east was being lost?

Another argument for imperial decline that can be dismissed is the case for "buffer states," which goes back to Matthew of Edessa. This is the notion that conquest deprived the empire of crucial buffer states that would have protected it against enemies. But there is no proof that these realms would have withstood the Seljuks better than the empire did in control of their territories. In fact, some of the local kings gave up their realms because they could not cope with the new threat. Hamdanid Aleppo was an active threat that the Romans reduced to, and successfully used as, a buffer state. Antioch and Bulgaria were profitable and strategically advantageous acquisitions. Antioch had been marginal in the Muslim world, but central again under Roman rule. Bulgaria had not been able in the past to fend off the Magyars, or had been unwilling to do so; it had failed to defeat the Rus' under Svjatoslav and had joined them afterward in fighting against Byzantium. There is therefore no reason to suppose that it would have done a better job of protecting the empire against the Pechenegs later. The "buffer" argument does not work here.

Another factor that should probably also be discounted is the increasing intolerance shown toward the Armenian and Jacobite churches after 1029. Our Enlightenment bias predisposes us to see religious intolerance as wrong, futile, and ultimately harmful to the perpetrator, but in reality it often induces people to accept the dominant religion. Romanía offered tremendous social, political, and economic advantages that were appealing to non-Chalcedonians. We should not be misled by the true believers who later wrote histories (e.g., Matthew of Edessa). Non-Chalcedonians had no incentive to side with the Seljuks, who were attacking them too. No great acts of spiteful collaboration are recorded on their part, despite the occasional suspicion of the Roman writers.[17]

Finally, the civil wars of the eleventh century also had nothing to do with a putative process of feudalization. Quite the contrary, the Komnenoi came to power at a time when all lands, whether belonging to peasants or "magnates," were being lost to the Turks. The Komnenoi rose on the basis not of their socioeconomic power but of their military-political careers. Anna says of her father at the time of his usurpation that he was "not by any means seriously rich."[18] Let us not forget the image of a young Alexios visiting his ancestral lands in Kastamone—abandoned because of Turkish raids. Psellos talks in the 1070s about how the rich had lost their lands and revenues—at the very moment when modern historians claim that they were "taking over" the state. The patriarch Xiphilinos was spending more on charity because "the situation had taken a turn for the worse, the rich could not get by on their patrimony, on the fortunes they had amassed, or on the imperial gifts they received, while poor people had no income at all."[19] Far from being taken over by the landed aristocracy, under the Komnenoi it was the state that had to financially support its ruling class.[20] Far from landowners using their socioeconomic power to leverage political standing, they were banking on their military careers to gain power within the state precisely in order to ensure their socioeconomic survival.

Until the Komnenoi, emperors did not rule through extended families. The only emperor of the eleventh century to did so was Michael IV, who came from the opposite of what historians consider an aristocratic family. He did so likely because he had little choice in supporters and, lacking prestige, leaned tremendously on the impersonal authority of the state, Zoe's endorsement, and his family. Other emperors deliberately chose not to rule through their families, in the traditional Byzantine manner,[21] even when they had adult relatives or in-laws whom they could have brought onside. Even in the case of Konstantinos X Doukas it is not clear that we are dealing with a "family regime," as we know so little about his cabinet. He does not seem to have used his brother Ioannes for much. It is only with Michael VII that we observe a preference for using Doukai and Komnenoi in the east, possibly a response to an extraordinary situation of east-west disaffection among the generals. It is with Alexios Komnenos that we get "family rule," but only because he developed that option, probably for purely contingent reasons. We should not project it back onto the previous century, as if there had been an underlying "aristocratic" dynamic favoring family rule. Again, the reason some historians see "family" as the norm is that they see the period as driven by incipient "feudalization," a now-useless concept. The idea that there were families struggling to entrench themselves against "the state" has to be abandoned.

In the end, the main cause of the imperial collapse was likely exogenous. In the late tenth century, the Romans were waging offensive warfare, enjoyed crushing advantages, and succeeded in conquering territories lost to the empire for more than three centuries. By 1081, they were fighting for their survival and had lost the east. One way to understand this comparison is by realizing that in 955 Byzantium had to deal with only one active front, that in southeast Asia Minor, and was fighting weaker enemies than itself (the Cilician towns and the emirate of Aleppo). After 1050, however, there were three active fronts (the west, north, and east) and new enemies: the Normans, Pechenegs, and Seljuk Turks, some of whom were backed by substantial resources. Even without postulating internal decline, we can automatically understand why Byzantium would not fare as well in the eleventh century. No Roman empire—ancient or Byzantine, with *themata* or *tagmata*—could cope with three new enemies simultaneously. It did not adapt to them fast enough, and was distracted by its systemic political crisis. It lost Italy, then the lower Danube, then Asia Minor. One *might* argue that even Asia Minor was a lost cause from the start, regardless of the outcome of any one battle. The Turks were raiding deeply into it before Mantzikert, even during Diogenes' campaigns.[22] This underscores how little we know about the imbalance of power between Romans and Turks.

And so, in the course of a decade or less, Roman Asia Minor went from the oblivion of peace and prosperity to the oblivion of foreign occupation. Our narrative sources tend to focus on unusual, dramatic, or extraordinary episodes, and so, for the century after 962, their coverage of Asia Minor is limited to the occasional civil war or to emperors passing through. For scenes of daily life we turn to the *Life of Saint Lazaros*, though these are largely generic. After the 1060s, by contrast, Asia Minor was lost, an embarrassing failure politely veiled, until its partial redemption with the unexpected help of allies from the west.

Epilogue

A Byzantine History of the First Crusade

The so-called First Crusade presents itself in almost perfect narrative form. Its flawless pace and trajectory (through beginning, middle, and end) betray the hand of a master dramatist. In Act I (1095), a spiritual leader (pope Urban II) calls upon high and low alike to right an injustice being done in faraway lands by vicious heathens. The call is answered by grand lords who, in dramatic displays, take up the cross and vow to march east. They include Adhémar, bishop of Puy-en-Velay; Raymond of Saint-Gilles, count of Toulouse; Robert II, count of Flanders; Robert II, duke of Normandy; Godfrey, duke of Lower Lorraine (and Bouillon); the latter's brother Baldwin of Boulogne; and Bohemond, prince of Taranto, the largely disinherited son of Robert Guiscard. They are joined by thousands of knights, ordinary soldiers, and common folk, who begin the long trek across central and eastern Europe, or who cross the Adriatic, to converge on Constantinople. In Act II (1096–1097), our protagonists enter the Christian but foreign land of Byzantium, a once-supreme but now distressed empire, and reach its magnificent capital. Its ruler, Alexios I Komnenos, is outwardly supportive but has goals of his own and wants to use the crusaders to advance them. Minor dramas ensue as our lords try, but fail, to avoid swearing an oath of submission; they promise to restore to the Byzantines any of their former territory taken back from the Muslims. This part of the story should ideally be staged with a backdrop of golden halls, decadent sophistication, and a whiff of intrigue. Our heroes are true at heart and hard of purpose, but may be getting in over their heads. Still, they and Alexios capture the city of Nikaia from the Turks. Actually, they do the fighting while Alexios manages to take the city through negotiation with those inside (Turks and Byzantines, it turns out, can reach an agreement).

In Act III (1097–1098), the crusaders march out into the unknown, passing through hills, mountains, and deserts. They are attacked en route by the Turks, who do not yet understand what they are up against. Our heroes win a glorious victory at Dorylaion on July 1, and their journey to Syria is thereafter unopposed. They capture some cities in Cilicia, and Baldwin leaves the crusade to establish a principality at Edessa. The rest settle down to besiege Antioch, a brilliant move by the dramatist. It pauses the story's momentum to introduce other elements of dramatic tension: cold, hunger, patient endurance, and the outbreak of rivalries among the leaders. Meanwhile, their military moves and countermoves play out against the spectacular backdrop of the ancient capital of Roman Syria, which eventually we come to know well. The city is taken by treachery right before our patience is exhausted. And just as the crusaders take the city, they are besieged in it by a relief Muslim army from Mosul. This could not have been done better in a work of fiction. But our famished heroes sally forth and defeat the enemy Kerbogha in battle. Then, there is an (appropriate) lull between Acts III and IV, as the crusaders seem to lose sight of their goal, and become disorganized and disunited. Bohemond is angling to take over the lordship of Antioch by himself. But this lull is necessary to heighten the climax. In Act IV (1099), some of the survivors finally get their act together and march on Jerusalem, which they capture after a fierce siege. They massacre the population and defeat a Fatimid army. Godfrey is chosen as the ruler of the new realm. The story thus ends by achieving exactly the lofty goals set out at the beginning, which rarely happens in history, and our heroes do so against the odds and after many adventures in foreign lands.

As a tale of adventure, high drama, and conquest, the First Crusade easily rises above its mundane historical context. Granted, it lacks women and strips the men down to single-minded bearers of religious devotion and a craving for violent acquisition. It is a deceptively easy story to tell, which is why it was retold so often in the years to come. But this spectacular singularity also makes it hard to integrate into its context—which is inevitably humdrum by comparison. Similar events that happened before (and elsewhere) are excluded when we label this the *First* Crusade. Moreover, the Crusade did not end with the conquest of Jerusalem; more waves continued to arrive, only they were far less spectacular in their accomplishments and have been played down accordingly. Historians have struggled to find the most relevant context for this story anyway. Generally, they have settled on the religious, social, and martial landscape of northern Europe, from where most of the crusaders came, rather than southern Europe, where some of them had been most active previously; or Byzantium, whose recent history and territories set the stage for most of its narrative trajectory; or the Muslim Near East, where it culminated. Those other contexts have certainly received attention in the crush of crusading scholarship that has appeared in recent decades, but it is difficult for experts to master each other's fields enough to do them justice, and the Byzantine matrix of the First Crusade has been particularly understudied. "We have lost the sense of Byzantium as something integral to the crusading movement."[1] The concern of this chapter is not with Byzantine "views" of the crusade. We really have only one, by Anna Komnene, which serves a personal (rather than a "Byzantine") agenda, was written more than fifty years later, and was shaped by subsequent events.[2] Nor am I referring to an intriguing theory according to which Alexios was the prime planner of the First Crusade even before 1096, with some help by pope Urban, a theory that can be neither proven nor disproven.[3]

Instead, this chapter will survey the crucial Byzantine contribution to the making of the First Crusade and its course, as one of its many matrices. The crusade was only a dramatic combination of preexisting elements, which its own brightness later cast into permanent shadow, and then it progressed according to patterns that are best revealed by the history of Byzantium that is recounted in the present book, including the strategic choices of the Byzantine leadership. To give an analogy, among the many streams that came together to form the torrent of 1095–1099, some had previously flowed in Byzantine channels while others were forced to do so when the crusade reached territories marked profoundly by the Byzantine experience. These were facets of the crusade that neither the Latin chronicles nor Anna wanted to dwell on, but we can identify and reconstruct some them on the basis of the history we have surveyed.

Crusading in broader perspective

The First Crusade was only a dramatic combination of preexisting ideals and behaviors. In its aftermath, crusading was an established and even routine part of the cultural repertoire of medieval Europe, recognized through a more or less stable system of signs, practices, and conventions. Among them, the focus of much recent scholarship has been on the penitential, devotional, ecclesiastical, and military culture of the west. This is because the crusaders came from there, but also because a mighty effort has been made to rehabilitate their motives and religious sincerity, in ways that come across as apologetic. This chapter will not reopen those debates but instead aims to highlight the imperial interests and strategies of Byzantium in the central part of the story, that is between 1096 and the siege of Antioch. During that time, the crusaders were forged into an army serving imperial interests, a fact that does not sit well with its modern devotional apologists. We will begin by looking at developments in Mediterranean history that came together in the First Crusade and, where appropriate, at the Byzantine context specifically. This chapter will argue that, as the crusade later worked its way across post-Roman Asia Minor, it marched under imperial direction, replayed experiences from the recent Byzantine past, and poured itself into the old flasks that the empire had left behind in the east.

One constitutive element of the crusade was the overland pilgrimage to Jerusalem, which had increased substantially during the eleventh century, and had often followed the same route.[4] The crusaders regarded themselves as pilgrims, and the Byzantines had extensive experience of such groups and their logistical and diplomatic needs from the moment they entered Romanía, crossed to Asia at Constantinople, and ventured into Muslim lands. In 1064–1065, for example, thousands of pilgrims led by bishops set out on what is called the Great German Pilgrimage. They were harassed by the Pechenegs, who were ravaging the Balkans that year, and their leaders were received by Konstantinos X in Constantinople. (Important pilgrims were typically charmed by gifts and such receptions.) The Germans passed through Asia Minor without incident and left imperial territory at Laodikeia. Of the 3,500 kilometers between Bamberg and Jerusalem, 2,000 lay in Byzantine territory. In this sense, a pilgrimage journey was a mostly Byzantine experience. After Laodikeia they encountered danger and violence on the way to Jerusalem, in that destabilized region.[5] The ease or difficulty with which pilgrims crossed the relatively short distance from Laodikeia to Jerusalem was governed in the eleventh century by the entente between the empire and the Fatimids over Syria, a major theme of the present narrative.[6] The pilgrims (along with most medieval historians of the crusades and some modern ones) were largely unaware of the late-tenth-century wars that had resulted in that status quo. After spending some days in the Holy Land, pilgrims would then repeat the whole journey on the way back. Therefore, the Seljuk conquest of Asia Minor had dramatic consequences for the pilgrimage route. It meant that a far larger portion of their journey (in both directions) took place in Muslim-controlled territory. This would have been apparent already by the mid-1070s.

Enough westerners traveled to the east in the eleventh century that their experiences and tales made the journey a familiar form of Christian devotion.

But specific prosopographical links can also be made. Some of the leaders of the First Crusade were personally connected to Byzantium through family traditions of such pilgrimage. Robert I, the duke of Normandy (nicknamed "the Devil"), had died and was buried at Nikaia on the way back from Jerusalem in 1035; he too had probably been received by the emperor (Michael IV). Robert was the father of William the Conqueror and grandfather of Robert II, who took the cross in 1096. His tomb was significant for the Normans, and in ca. 1086 his body was moved to Apulia on William's orders. It was also under Robert I that the Normans, including the sons of Tancred of Hauteville (Bohemond's grandfather), began to move to southern Italy.[7] Stephen of Blois, another leader in the First Crusade, was married to William's daughter, Adela of Normandy, and wrote her letters during the expedition. Robert I, count of Flanders and father of the crusader Robert II, had made the pilgrimage as recently as ca. 1089, and swore some sort of oath to Alexios on the way back.[8]

Likewise, Raymond of Toulouse's brother and predecessor William IV of Toulouse had also gone on pilgrimage to Jerusalem in 1088 and died there. Thus, travel to Byzantium was close to these men's family experience, not unimaginably exotic. Bohemond too had his own experience of "travel" to Byzantium, when he joined his father's invasion of it in 1081. These lords traveled with retinues (if not small armies), while the emperors for their part provided them with passports of permission to enter, traverse, and leave Romanía.[9] Pilgrim security was an imperial priority. In 1055 the Byzantine governor of Latakia "refused an exit-visa" to bishop Lietbert of Cambrai for his own protection, saying that it was unsafe for Christians to enter Muslim territory.[10] The emperors sometimes even assigned soldiers to escort pilgrims to Jerusalem.[11] Alexios' handling of the crusaders—the way his administration processed their entry and provided them with a military escort—drew on these protocols and prior experiences on both sides, even if events were unfolding on a vaster scale.

The second aspiration that propelled the First Crusade was religious war against Muslims. On a certain level, war is war: killing people to take their land and stuff and citing a pretext that the aggressors call, and usually believe *is*, a just cause. But the way a religious war plays out, the contours of its violence, and the impact on religious-political history are also dependent on the cultural specifics of its justification and motivation. Violence and faith were generally entwined in medieval Christianity, but two theaters in which the ideology of religious war against Muslims had been pioneered and deployed to justify conquest and the expansion of Christianity (i.e., the realm of the Church of Rome) were Spain and Sicily. In 1087, the king of France had called on his subjects to help their fellow Christians against the Moors in Spain, "a testing ground for crusading ideology," and among those who took up the call were knights who later joined the First Crusade. In 1089, pope Urban II, the initiator of the First Crusade, had promised remission of sins for those who helped him rebuild Tarragona.[12] Proto-crusading ideologies became increasingly prevalent in the later eleventh century, especially when adventurers from the European north were involved.[13]

As for Sicily, a pope had proclaimed Robert Guiscard its duke in 1059, before the island had even been conquered, and in 1063 another pope granted "absolution for their sins" to the Norman warriors "who were helping him to win Sicily from the pagans and to hold it forever in the faith of Christ," thereby anticipating the crusading indulgence (this absolution was possibly renewed in 1076 by pope Gregory VII).[14] A case can be made that "in Sicily, the fundamental concepts of crusading were born."[15] Urban II had himself visited Sicily in 1089 to organize the ecclesiastical administration of this newly conquered land. There was a wave, then, rolling across the Mediterranean of religious war against the Muslims that aimed to subject their lands to the Church. It was only a matter of time until it set its sights on the east. This export of war to Europe's Muslim ring is exemplified by Crépin, a Norman who fought against Muslims in Spain, Italy, and Byzantium in the 1060s. From the Muslim standpoint, there was no sudden "First Crusade," but rather a series of Frankish attacks across the Mediterranean that culminated in Syria and Palestine.[16] The Byzantine perspective would likely not have been different, had it been put in writing. Urban II too had been active consolidating gains in Spain and Sicily before he turned his attention to the east: he seems to have viewed all these early crusades as a "triptych: . . . three fronts in a single war to recover from Islam the lost lands of Christendom."[17]

The Byzantines (dangerously) tried to exploit this momentum and give it an outlet that would serve their interests. This brings us to the third constituent element of the First Crusade: the appeal for military aid from the eastern empire. The spark that set Urban's mind aflame with dreams of conquest (or liberation) in the east was allegedly an embassy from Alexios that reached him in 1095 at the Council of Piacenza and begged him to bring assistance against the pagans. This is reported only in the chronicle of Bernold of Constance, a contemporary and, it seems, reliable source (but not present at the council in person).[18] Even if this is accurate, we still do not know what Alexios wanted exactly or the details of the embassy's discussions with the pope. A (Latin) letter from Alexios to Robert of Flanders calling for help against the Turks is a later forgery that does not reveal plans and mentalities before the First Crusade.[19] We need to make a distinction between job advertisements for mercenaries, whom the Byzantines were hiring increasingly in the eleventh century, and plans for a massive western campaign against the Turks. The latter made sense only after 1072, when stories began to circulate in the west about alleged Muslim atrocities and attacks on pilgrims. It was well known among western courts that Byzantium wanted warriors and could pay for them, and Alexios seems to have "adopted a kind of 'scatter-gun' approach, sending off messengers with 'letters . . . full of tears' everywhere."[20] The fall of Asia Minor had affected vital Christian pilgrimage routes for both Latins and Byzantines, and it created a strategic situation in which the empire required more western soldiers. There is evidence that Alexios was hiring more and more of them to use in Asia Minor before the Crusade.[21]

Muslim conquests inflamed the Christian imagination. The antipapal writer Benzo of Alba concocted a letter allegedly from Konstantinos X Doukas inviting the German emperor Heinrich IV to destroy "those turds" the Normans and then free the Christians all the way to Jerusalem; Byzantium would quietly surrender to him, apparently.[22] A plan for what is to all appearances a crusade to liberate eastern Christians was hatched between Michael VII Doukas and pope Gregory VII in 1073. This was when Constantinople was trying to bribe Robert Guiscard to cancel his anticipated attack on Byzantium after his capture of Bari. In 1073, Gregory received envoys from Michael offering Church Union—which for Gregory meant the subordination of Constantinople to Rome—in exchange for an unspecified but ambitious plan. During the next year and a half, Gregory tried to mobilize western armies to march out against the Saracens who were attacking the eastern empire. He specifically invited Raymond of Toulouse (later of the First Crusade). Gregory claimed that fifty thousand had answered his call and were ready to set sail with him personally as leader, but, for reasons that are unknown, this plan fizzled.[23] It is not clear how involved the Byzantines were in its inception and planning. Nor do we know whether anyone in the west or in Byzantium remembered it when Urban preached crusade in 1095—though he had been Gregory VII's right-hand man. It was, moreover, the first time in its history that Byzantium sought military assistance against the Turks in exchange for Church Union, a dynamic that would define the later history of the empire.

Gregory was willing to plan an expedition to save Byzantium, but only if it enabled him to conquer the eastern empire ecclesiastically, by subordinating its Church to his. When that prospect receded, he was just as willing to authorize Robert Guiscard to conquer Byzantium on the most specious of pretexts, in 1081, when the pope and the duke made up.

Gregory made it clear that the planned war *against* Byzantium was a Just War, in religious terms, and excommunicated Alexios.[24] And unlike the more helpful expedition planned in 1073, this one was actually launched and nearly destroyed the empire in the early 1080s. Church Union was already both carrot and stick: East-West relations teetered on a razor's edge and could tip either way, depending on the plans of the emperor and pope in a given year.

To conclude, many leaders of the First Crusade had personal or family histories of travel through Byzantium that shaped their perception later, in 1095, of what a Crusade might be and what it might accomplish. Some of them had prior knowledge of Byzantium's troubles and had already been involved in attempts to defend it. On the other side of the ledger, Bohemond and many other Normans from Italy had made war against the empire, especially in 1081–1085. They knew the empire better than any of the other leaders of the Crusade, and their prominent participation would complicate matters. In fact, Bohemond and his Normans were likely not thinking of Jerusalem but of existing Byzantine provinces: the horizons of their ambitions did not extend past Romanía, which reveals Byzantium again as an integral part of the Crusade's inception. And the Crusade's reception by the empire once it was underway steered it inevitably in Byzantine directions. Without always knowing it, the Crusaders would reenact typical Byzantine experiences from the past century as they marched across the empire.

The making of a surrogate Byzantine army

Historians interested in Byzantine perceptions of the First Crusade have only Anna Komnene's panegyrical history of her father, the *Alexiad*. This work was written almost fifty years later, is extremely biased, and is influenced by later events (including the Second Crusade), and its narrative is propelled less by accurate chronology and reporting than by a brilliantly crafted (if historically doubtful) moral drama of Alexios' struggles and triumph. Anna suggests that news of the crusaders' imminent arrival took her father by surprise, and she suppresses his role in soliciting their services. For her they were basically a barbarian invasion. In the overarching drama of the *Alexiad*, they form the second act of a "triptych" between Robert Guiscard's invasion of 1081 and Bohemond's later invasion of 1107.[25] Her choice to structure the narrative around these episodes (instead of what was happening, say, in Asia Minor) is explained by the fact that Alexios decisively beat the Normans every time. The *Alexiad*, then, does not necessarily represent all Byzantine views of the

Crusade, or even Alexios' policies toward it. To reconstruct those, we must draw conclusions from all the sources.

First, a quick look back at the preceding fifteen years is necessary. This is a chapter on the First Crusade viewed against the background of the rise and fall of the Byzantine empire in 955–1081, and not on the reign of Alexios Komnenos. Facing a dramatic crisis, Alexios in many ways had to reboot the imperial state, both by implementing new policies and by taking ad hoc measures that over time became fixed.[26] This revolution—the introduction of the distinctive Komnenian system of governance—is still poorly understood. A number of attempts to sort it out have been abandoned. The sources—chiefly the *Alexiad*—are problematic and still not well understood. Historians are therefore not in a position to write the history of the reign in a manner that would extend the narrative approach of this book through Alexios' first fifteen years. But we can give a general outline that will set the stage for the irruptions of western attention in 1096–1097.

The immediate threat facing the new emperor when he usurped power in 1081 was Robert Guiscard's invasion of the Balkans, whose flimsy pretext was the restoration of Michael VII Doukas. This led to a five-year war ending with Robert's death, but it was closely fought with major losses on the Byzantine side. These required emergency measures for the gathering of funds and rebuilding the armies, multiple times. Alexios also had to make a major trade deal with the Venetians, granting them tax concessions in exchange for military help in the Adriatic. Meanwhile, Turkish emirs established themselves in western Asia Minor, and one of them, Tzachas (Çaka), created a fleet to capture Aegean islands and terrorize the seas. No sooner had the Norman war ended than the Pechenegs too began to ravage the western Balkans in turn, resulting in many more years of fighting, with heavy Byzantine losses, until Alexios finally defeated them at the battle of Lebounion in 1091. The Pechenegs would thereafter serve the emperor.

Alexios had thus finally tamed two of the major threats that had emerged under Monomachos, forty years earlier. Only the Seljuks now remained, in Asia Minor, and some small efforts to push them back came to nothing. On the domestic front, Alexios faced a severe shortage of funds. He had to appropriate Church funds, stirring up a great deal of religious opposition, and he abolished the old system of state salaries. In the early 1090s, he also overhauled the coinage, as the system that had been in place since Nikephoros II Phokas was exhausted. Also, more than any other emperor before him, Alexios relied on his extended family to rule the empire, especially at first his mother and brothers. Over time, the Komnenoi became more like a true aristocracy than Byzantium had ever known, which also aroused opposition. And there were old contenders to worry about. In 1094 Alexios survived major plots by the sons of Romanos IV Diogenes. By 1095, he had largely secured the Balkans, and more or less tamed the domestic scene, and was ready to take on the Turks in Asia Minor. It was for this reason that he sought western assistance. The Crusade was well timed to serve Alexios' needs.

In 1096–1097, right on cue, the crusader armies began to pour in: "like tributaries joining a river from all directions, they streamed toward us in full force," wrote Anna.[27] The empire had never seen anything like it: seventy thousand violent people intent on helping it and then passing through to a more distant goal. Yet their reception by the imperial authorities indicates that plans had methodically been made for them, with provisions stored up.[28] No one starved, which means that Alexios was not surprised at the size of the turnout. Premodern economies could not support so many people so efficiently on a mere moment's notice. The administration had either laid its plans in 1095 or moved with awesome dispatch to requisition the harvest of 1096 in anticipation of the crusaders' arrival later in that year and in the next. A composite picture of Alexios' arrangements can be assembled from the reports in the various sources, each of which gives only part of the overall picture. When the system failed it was because some crusaders were intent on violence, at any rate for political and not administrative reasons.

Specifically, each army was met at its point of entry by the resident official or special envoy and given written authorization to traverse imperial territory to Constantinople. It was also authorized to access special stores of provisions near the major cities, sold to them at fair prices. The authors who were not unduly biased against the Byzantines reveal that the Latins were not gouged, and they should be believed over the others, though occasionally the crusaders were likely ripped off.[29] At times, the emperor restricted access or raised prices to discipline misbehaving crusaders. He took the precaution of shadowing them with his Pechenegs, to keep them from plundering, which some wanted to do. He also sent interpreters who knew "Latin" (probably French).[30] The plan worked well along both Balkan routes.[31] These were, first, the via Egnatia (Dyrrachion, Thessalonike, and then Constantinople) for the majority of the crusaders, and, second, the overland route from central Europe via Belgrade, Niš, Serdica, Philippopolis, and Adrianople, which was followed by Godfrey of Lorraine and Stephen of Blois. And on the coast of the gulf of Nikomedeia, in Asia, Alexios had built the fort of Kibotos, which he had ready, stockpiled with provisions, when the first armies arrived.[32]

This was a remarkable accomplishment of Byzantine logistics. What precedents did imperial administrators follow to pull it off? They had experience escorting and issuing "passports" to groups of pilgrims, but never quite so large. They also had experience with foreign armies that had to be conveyed through imperial territory, but we have little or no information about how this was done (e.g., the Varangians sent by Vladimir in 988; the fifteen thousand Pechenegs sent from the lower Danube to Asia in 1049; the Anglo-Saxons who arrived in large numbers after 1066). Our sources love battles, not logistics and paperwork. But even those groups were small compared to these armies. Ultimately, only one sector of the administration could rise to this demand, namely the supply network of the Byzantine armies themselves. The crusaders were probably plugged into that system of supply and requisition, which means they were being treated as a nominal Roman army from the start. The cost would have been prodigious for the Byzantine state and refutes any claim that Alexios did not "support" the crusaders. The latter were traveling with large amounts of funds, yet they were not gouged. To the contrary, the emperor showered their leaders with gold and expensive gifts from beginning to end. This was not how emperors reacted to invasions but rather how they treated potential clients, recruits to the imperial system. To judge from their behavior when they reached the capital, the dukes and counts understood this perfectly and largely consented to it.

But the failures of the reception system are also worth discussing. Let us consider them in (roughly) chronological order. The first groups to arrive— the so-called People's Crusade with Walter Sansavoir and then Peter the Hermit—occasioned the most violence and breakdown of order, in the summer of 1096. They were, at the very least, ahead of schedule and not good at liaising with state authorities. Even so, our main source, Albert of Aachen, does not support the notion that the Byzantines were unprepared to receive armies from this direction. These first groups of pilgrims came with a reputation for violence and pillaging, and they were refused help when they behaved badly. When they came to their senses, Niketas, the *doux* of "Bulgaria" at Niš, had both the resources to provision them and the authorizations for them to travel to Constantinople. Alexios was ready to receive them there graciously.[33] At one point, this Niketas, who seems to have been an able officer, had to maul some of Peter's followers who were bent on violence and had wreaked havoc in allied Hungary too. The fact that he then sent to Alexios for instructions indicates, however, that he did not view them as unknown hostiles, whom he could and should have destroyed on his own, but as a warped version of the pilgrim army he was expecting. When Godfrey arrived later that autumn, everything was ready for him all the way to Constantinople.[34] Arrivals from the northern route were not, then, unforeseen.

The other armies took a southern route. The first to arrive, probably in October 1096, was Hugh of Vermandois, the brother of the king of France.

He had sent messengers ahead to Alexios long before he crossed the Adriatic, so here too there were no surprises. The *doux* of Dyrrachion, Alexios' nephew Ioannes Komnenos, and the fleet commander were prepared to greet him. But Hugh's fleet was destroyed by a storm. He was shipwrecked on the coast, but spotted, entertained lavishly by the *doux*, and sent to Constantinople, where he swore an oath of loyalty to Alexios. For some reason, he is reported as being "not entirely free" in Byzantine hands, though we do not know why. Possibly he was kept under detention until he swore the oath.[35] Whatever this detention was, when Godfrey passed Philippopolis in December he demanded that Hugh be "released" and started plundering to force the issue, which worked.[36] It is likely that Hugh's "captivity" was misunderstood.

Bohemond crossed soon afterward, in October 1096. For the Byzantines, this was the tensest part of the operation, for Bohemond and the Normans had visited these parts before, in the 1080s, as conquerors. His new pretext—crusade—did not persuade everyone to see this Norman army differently from the last one. Anna claims that his ulterior motive was to manipulate events in order to seize the capital; pilgrimage was just a pretext.[37] Bohemond had been sidelined in his father's inheritance. Robert Guiscard had left most of his realm to his younger son Roger Borsa, squeezing Bohemond at Taranto and Bari (both former Byzantine territories). His ambitions had little breathing room in Italy. Geoffrey Malaterra admits that Bohemond was "always looking for a way to subject that region [*Romania*] to his authority," so when he saw that Normans serving under his brother (the duke) and his uncle (the count of Sicily) were taking up the cross, he did so as well to become their leader.[38] Thus, not only did opportunities in the east now open up; he also shifted the balance of military power in southern Italy.

The Norman contingent would likely have been under strict instructions about where to cross, specifically to enter at the district of Dyrrachion. When Richard of the Principate, Bohemond's cousin, tried to avoid the Roman fleet, it attacked him and brought him to heel.[39] But Bohemond's itinerary is a problem. Instead of marching via Ohrid, he went to Kastoria, where his army celebrated Christmas. The inhabitants apparently would not sell them provisions, so the Normans plundered the region for what they needed. They then destroyed a community of Paulician heretics at Pelagonia—killing them all—before reaching the via Egnatia at the Axios. At that point, they were plugged into the supply system, albeit not without initial battles with the emperor's Pechenegs.[40] How are we to understand the first leg of their journey, which seems to have taken longer than it should have? It was unlikely to have been an imperial plan to relieve pressure on the food supply elsewhere.[41] In that case, there would have been supplies at Kastoria. Bohemond was also probably without an escort, who would not have allowed the murders at Pelagonia. Heretics or not, those were imperial subjects. And the people at Kastoria had good reason to flee. Their city had been occupied by Bohemond during the last Norman-Byzantine war.[42] He was, then, revisiting his old stomping grounds in 1096, but what he hoped to accomplish exactly is opaque. To test imperial defenses and see if his old dream of a Balkan principality could be realized? It is possible that he did more damage to the Balkans than the whitewash in the *Gesta* reveals. No wonder, then, that he was attacked by the Pechenegs when he appeared: he had, for months, been disobeying imperial orders. Two independent sources imply that he later sent messages to Godfrey, inviting him to attack Alexios.[43] Nothing came of this, and he came to Constantinople as a pious crusader, around April 1097.

The journeys from Dyrrachion to Constantinople of Robert of Flanders, Raymond of Toulouse, and Robert of Normandy were uneventful, apart from skirmishes involving Raymond's group, the single largest contingent, which required delicate negotiations afterward.[44]

Alexios also had a realistic and smart plan for handling these armies and their proud leaders as they converged on Constantinople. The sources more or less tell the same story. The armies themselves were excluded from the City, which made sense for its protection and to prevent temptation. They were amply provisioned outside the walls at fair prices. Soldiers were allowed inside only in small groups, who could be more easily intimidated by Constantinople's marvels and security.[45] Alexios was also eager to bring the crusade's leaders into the City and persuade or pressure them, mostly through extravagant gifts and flattering solicitations, to swear an oath of loyalty to him. His gifts, which were probably beyond the means of any western ruler at this time, dazzled the crusaders, and our sources pay considerable attention to them. But they disguised the emperor's strategy, which was to bring the leaders into the City in advance of their armies and separate from each other, so that each might be won over, piecemeal, from a weaker bargaining position. The emperor wanted to prevent them from coming together and forming plans of their own, which may not have agreed with his, before he had the chance to put his own framework of patronage and supreme leadership in place. But once a few leaders had sworn, he could then admit new arrivals to their company, for they would naturally exert peer pressure on them to do the same.[46] Then, Alexios could ask them to move their armies across the sea to Kibotos, where they would pose even less of a threat to Constantinople. His fleet controlled the sea.

By and large this strategy worked. After Hugh, there was initial resistance from Godfrey, who seemed to understand exactly what the emperor was doing. Godfrey refused to enter, whereupon Alexios pressured him by withholding supplies. Godfrey's men began to ravage the outskirts of the City, and this led to battles with imperial forces. But in the end Godfrey submitted and went to the palace. Albert's description is worth quoting.

> The emperor was seated, as was his custom, looking powerful on the throne of his sovereignty, and he did not get up to offer kisses to the duke nor to anyone, but the duke bowed down with bended knee, and his men also bowed down to kiss the exceedingly glorious and powerful emperor [who spoke] "I have heard about you that you are a very powerful knight and prince in your land, and a very wise man and completely honest. Because of this I am taking you as my adopted son, and I am putting everything I possess in your power, so that my empire and land can be freed and saved. . . ." The duke was pleased and beguiled by the emperor's peaceful and affectionate words, and he not only gave himself to him as a son, as is the custom of that land, but even as a vassal with hands joined, along with all the nobles who were there then. . . . And without any delay priceless gifts were taken from the emperor's treasury for the duke and all who had gathered there.[47]

With this precedent it was hard, if not impossible, for Bohemond to avoid doing the same, escorted to the City as he was without his army. A critical mass was thereby built up, as the lords who swore were rewarded with money and gifts. Bohemond, in fact, became a champion of the emperor's cause among the other leaders—at least for now.[48] Only Raymond of Toulouse resisted, though finally he swore a watered-down version of the oath promising nonaggression.[49] Indeed, he became a staunch upholder of imperial interests and ally of Alexios. Tancred, Bohemond's nephew, bypassed the City to avoid the whole business. Stephen of Blois, by contrast, was so impressed that he wrote to his wife Adela, the daughter of William the Conqueror, that Alexios "has no equal alive on earth today. He showers gifts on all our leaders. . . . Your father, my love, gave many great presents, but he was almost nothing in comparison with this man."[50]

The nature and contents of the oaths sworn to Alexios have been much debated. The Latin chroniclers and many modern historians of the Crusade, being medievalists by training, view it instinctively within a western "feudal" framework. Alexios intended the oath to be comprehensible to the western lords, so it was likely pitched in their cultural idiom, but not exclusively. It is probably more correct to view the oath in the long Byzantine tradition of securing foreign armies and lords for imperial service, which flexibly accommodated their values. Anna says that it was the oath customarily sworn in Byzantium by the Latins, i.e., mercenaries and others in imperial service,[51]

and Albert (quoted above) notes that Godfrey's "adoption" was done according to Byzantine tradition (wherein the emperor was the "father" of other
client-rulers). As for its clauses, the most specific was the obligation to surrender to Alexios any former Byzantine cities and territory that the crusade
recovered from the enemy. It also made the emperor the nominal commander
of the entire expedition. It is impossible to ascertain what exactly the crusaders expected Alexios to do from this position in practice, as many of the key
texts are contaminated by the later bias that arose against him, especially
after Bohemond seized Antioch and later again invaded Byzantium. And
Alexios himself was notoriously secretive about his intentions. But what he
had accomplished through his reception of the crusading armies was impressive. When they arrived, they had no overall leader and no definite strategy.
They certainly intended to reach Jerusalem and do . . . something there, and
freeing the Christians of the east, including of Asia Minor, was part of their
original purpose.[52] Yet now they had an overall leader and at least a proxi-
mate set of goals before entering Syria: to defeat the Turks in Asia Minor, as
Alexios directed, and to restore his empire there, after which they could move
on (whether with or without him probably remained unclear).

In fact, the decentralized origin of the First Crusade and convergence
on Constantinople had left it with little choice but to accept Alexios as its
leader. It was because of him that they had reached Constantinople more
or less intact in the first place, and they realized that "without his aid and
counsel we could not easily make the journey, nor could those who were
to follow us by the same route."[53] Moreover, "they were about to enter a
deserted and trackless land, one completely without goods of any kind," in
which they would require the "daily rations" he could provide.[54] Also, as the
emperor of Romanía, Alexios outranked them by far, sat on the most prestigious throne in the Christian world, had a solid military reputation—as
the victor of Robert Guiscard—and overwhelmed the leaders of the Crusade
personally with money, gifts, flattery, and piety. This was how Byzantine
diplomacy had always worked, at its best. These counts and dukes never
really stood a chance; even the stiff-necked among them were won over or
brought to heel.

Alexios had probably gone as far as he could toward turning the crusade into an official imperial army. There were no Romans in it, but the
empire had relied increasingly on foreign units after 1071, especially after
the mauling of its remaining native units in the Norman war of the early
1080s. Most of its leaders had accepted him as their lord, they were probably
being supplied by the central requisition system, and they were effectively
being paid. One Latin writer even noted that "everything which the duke

[Godfrey] distributed to the soldiers out of the emperor's gift went back straight to the royal treasury in buying food . . . to no one's advantage except the emperor's"[55] (the Roman monetary economy, in a nutshell). But one crucial element is missing from the picture. Alexios seems to have distributed no court titles or offices to the crusaders, which had typically been the chief way of bringing outsiders onside. Even Frankish mercenaries had been given governorships and command positions in the Roman army. Not this time, however. Bohemond apparently asked to be appointed *domestikos* of the east, but the request was deflected.[56] And, according to the oath, captured towns were to be turned over to the officers sent by Alexios, implying that his new "sons" did not formally count as officers of the Roman empire.[57] This fact proves that the arrangement was understood, at least by Alexios and likely also by Bohemond, to be temporary.

Restoring the Roman east

The last Roman army to march across Asia Minor as far as Armenia was led by Romanos IV in 1071. The expedition against the Turks of 1073 reached Kaisareia before being mauled, and that of 1074 barely made it past Dorylaion. After that, Alexios had to conduct guerrilla warfare against Roussel, and in 1076 he had to evade Turkish raiders just to leave Asia Minor. The expedition of 1080 reached Nikaia, only to withdraw, as did another one later, under Tatikios. Turkish fleets had meanwhile begun to operate in the Aegean sea and Sea of Marmara, harassing the City itself, and the Seljuks of Rum picked off the post-Byzantine realms in the east, removing Antioch from Philaretos in 1084/5. This was the low point in the retrenchment of Roman Asia Minor. It was confirmed when the undisciplined first wave of the crusade (that associated with Peter the Hermit) was massacred, not far from Nikaia, by the Seljuks under Kilij Arslan, the son of Sulayman (the son of Qutlumush). The imperial fleet rescued the survivors, and Alexios bought up their weapons, for everyone's safety.[58] Only then did the pendulum start to swing in the opposite direction. The restoration of Roman Asia Minor was begun by the second wave of the crusade under Alexios, twenty years after he was last there as a general serving the Doukas regime. The events of the crusade are well known,[59] but it is worth highlighting how its march across Asia Minor and into Syria reversed and redeemed recent Byzantine history. Moreover, the crusade has largely been viewed as something separate from Byzantium, as only passing through. In fact, it was functioning largely as a Byzantine imperial army, and the role of Alexios himself needs to be rethought.

The campaign began with a poignant image of how the crusade was there to reopen Byzantine blockages. When the first part of the army set out for Nikaia, in May 1097, the old Roman road was overgrown, so Godfrey sent three thousand men ahead to clear it and set up crosses marking the route.[60] This was likely done under the direction of the Byzantine officer who accompanied this part of the army, Manouel Boutoumites, who is mentioned in none of the Latin chronicles. The latter want to present events in the black-and-white terms of Latin-Muslim conflict, but as the emperor's representative Boutoumites stressed negotiation, backed by force only when necessary. Anna reveals that he entered Nikaia to negotiate its surrender, but the defenders preferred to wait for their sultan.[61] The army was meanwhile supplied generously by Alexios: "On imperial orders, sailing merchants were striving to race across the sea with ships full of rations, corn, meat, wine, barley, and oil; they dropped anchor at the port of Kibotos, where crowds of the faithful procured [them]."[62] Alexios stayed behind near Nikomedeia, but provided the crusaders with abundant materials for siege warfare. All in all, he was correct to say, when he wrote soon after to the abbot of Monte Cassino, "we have spent more on them than anyone can count."[63] Historians like to distance him from the crusade by pointing out that he did not bring an army of his own to Nikaia, but in fact there would have been no point in that. More manpower would not have made a difference, and he had to guard against dangers in the west (see below).[64] Alexios did give the crusaders his veteran officers Boutoumites and also Tatikios, whose nose had once been cut off and now commanded a contingent of a few thousand. This was appropriate, as Tatikios was the last to have reached Nikaia with an imperial army.[65] The Roman restoration was picking up precisely where it had left off—with extra Latin muscle.

The crusaders (predictably) failed to capture Nikaia by storm, but they did defeat a relief army brought in haste by Kilij Arslan from Melitene. The victors sent a thousand heads of slain Turks to the emperor.[66] This is usually passed over without commentary in modern accounts but, as we have seen, it was a standard way in Byzantium for a general to announce his victory to the emperor, so that the latter could, in turn, parade it before the City. The crusaders were behaving as an imperial army, and were supplied and maintained as one too. The garrison in Nikaia eventually surrendered to Alexios (only to him), when he had ships hauled overland into the lake before the city, thus cutting it off from forage. The Latin accounts present this as a crusader idea, but Anna says it was her father's (who owned the ships and the crews, and had often shown himself an inventive strategist).[67] The surrender went smoothly: the city was turned over to Tatikios and Boutoumites, who was appointed its *doux*;

the Turkish garrison was spared; and the crusaders were allowed inside in small groups, just as at Constantinople, to pray.[68] To appease their frustrated desire for plunder, Alexios gave generous gifts to the host, which were noted and remembered. So how should we tell the story of Nikaia? The Latin accounts, and some modern ones, tell it as a military conflict between Latins and Turks whose climax is interrupted by Byzantine secret deals. But it turns out that the dominant story was probably an ongoing Byzantine-Turkish negotiation, in which crusader violence was but a new chip brought to the table. We are still in Byzantine history; the crusaders were not yet writing their own story, and they knew it. They were following (and clearing) Roman roads, military and diplomatic.

According to the traditional narrative, the army then split into two parts to march across Asia Minor, "with the emperor's permission."[69] We will see that this is a partial view of its history, but let us stay with it for now. Beyond Nikaia, Alexios could no longer provide the crusaders with food, building equipment, fleets on demand, and diplomatic settlements. They were on their own, although he had given them detailed advice on how to fight the Turks and navigate the complex world of Muslim diplomacy; and they were accompanied by Tatikios, Alexios' representative who would, according to the oath, receive any cities they took.[70] We will see, moreover, that the crusade's march east belies the belief that Jerusalem was its singular objective; in fact, it implemented a project of Roman imperial restoration that could have come only from Alexios. And in marching through Asia Minor it not only followed Byzantine military routes; its story fell into patterns familiar from recent Byzantine history.

The last Roman army to march past Nikaia had, under the *kaisar* Ioannes, been defeated in 1074 not far from Dorylaion, a great military camp. It was now in that area that the crusaders defeated a joint Seljuk-Danishmend army under Kilij Arslan.[71] The Turks surprised the contingent under Bohemond and Robert of Normandy, surrounded them, riding, howling, and unleashing swarms of arrows. The crusaders found themselves in the same situation as Romanos III near Aleppo in 1030 and Romanos IV at Mantzikert. The Turks used the same tactics, and the crusaders reacted with the same horror. Bohemond and Robert held their men together, just as those emperors had, and would probably have been destroyed had the rest of the army, the larger part, not come to their rescue at the critical moment. This was precisely what Romanos IV had been hoping for before Mantzikert, namely that the larger part of his army, which he had placed under Trachaneiotes, would return to rescue him. As a defeat of the Seljuks, Dorylaion symbolically (and tactically) "reversed" Mantzikert. In fact, it would prove to be exceptional. Not only had the People's Crusade been scattered by the Turks in 1096, the same fate would befall the crusaders of 1101 (Ankyra) and the German crusaders of 1147/8 in various places but chiefly at Dorylaion. It was the First Crusade alone that created the fiction that a Christian army could march through what was quickly becoming a Turkish heartland. The pendulum would swing back only this one time.

The army then marched to Ikonion and Kaisareia, setting the clock back to 1073. The reason they marched south, rather than east to Ankyra, surely reflected Byzantine strategic considerations: Alexios was planning his own parallel moves in Asia Minor (see below).[72] This part of their journey is the most interesting for the Byzantine historian, but the least well covered in the sources. We hear little about the arrangements that were made between the army and the cities they passed, or whether Tatikios left imperial officials in them, as he was charged. When the main part of the army reached Cappadocia, the crusaders encountered the ruins of empire in the east, all those Byzantine, Syrian, and Armenian elements that had experienced the breakup of Philaretos' realm in the 1080s and the breakup now of Seljuk power. It is likely that the crusaders went to Kaisareia precisely in order to reestablish links between the empire and its former territories,[73] and to this degree they were following Alexios' strategy.

They attacked a Seljuk emir in Cappadocia named Hasan, "leaving one of our princes with several thousand soldiers of Christ in charge of all his territory to continue fighting him."[74] This replacement was likely appointed by Tatikios. Beyond Kaisareia, a local, Simeon, was placed in charge of a strong place, again likely on Tatikios' authority,[75] and a Latin, Peter d'Aups, was placed in charge of another city (possibly Komana in Cappadocia). The Latin sources pretend that he was a crusader like any other, but unlike them he had long been in imperial service and probably received his new post from Tatikios.[76] At Germanikeia (Maraş), the Latin sources say only that the army was fed by a local lord who took over after the Turkish garrison fled; they do not reveal that he (Tatul) recognized Alexios, was the Roman *doux* of the city (and held other court titles), and was regarded in Armenian sources as a "Roman" (he later fought against the Latins for Alexios).[77] Gabriel, the de facto independent and Chalcedonian ruler of Melitene, had, like Philaretos before him, recognized the emperor and also received court titles.[78] Edessa was ruled by the "Roman" Toros (i.e., Theodoros), who was married to Gabriel's daughter and presented himself as a "Roman official," specifically a *kouropalates*.[79] Likely he was exactly that. These were pro-Roman elements waiting to be plugged back into contact with Constantinople.

In sum, the fact the army did not head directly for Antioch, but went on this long detour to restore the empire's clients in Cappadocia-Armenia, suggests that its goal at this point was still a broader restoration of Christianity in the east under imperial direction, and not just Jerusalem. That is likely why its chronicles say so little about this phase of the journey. The Armenian world of Cappadocia, Cilicia, and northern Syria that the crusaders encountered had been created by Byzantine imperial expansion in this region as well as by its subsequent collapse and the chaos caused by the Turkish invasions. Far from universally hating the empire, some of these local lords were former imperial officials who identified with the imperial order and sought to reconnect with it. In this longer-standing relationship, the crusaders were only middlemen; they hardly "wiped away the old order."[80] The periphery was being rebuilt in traditional Byzantine ways, by enticing local Roman elites to Alexios' patronage. That is probably what Anna meant when she said that he had restored Roman authority to the Tigris and Euphrates.[81] The crusade's aims as an *imperial* army extended far beyond providing a distraction for Alexios to restore western Asia Minor only.

While the main part of the crusader army marched to Kaisareia, Baldwin of Boulogne (Godfrey's brother) and Tancred (Bohemond's nephew) crossed the Cilician Gates and reduced Tarsos, Adana, and Mopsouestia. As a strategy, the two-pronged approach to Antioch (via Cilicia and Kaisareia) replayed that of Nikephoros Phokas and was surely recommended by the Byzantines. The Latin sources make it seem as if Baldwin and Tancred were seizing the Cilician cities in their own name, without even paying lip service to the emperor, but this is probably a distortion of omission. A stray reference in one of them reveals that Cilicia was immediately turned over to Tatikios, for when he pulled back from Antioch the next year he entrusted it to Bohemond.[82] Modern narratives give the impression that the oath to return captured cities to Byzantine control basically petered out after Nikaia, but it seems to have held straight through Asia Minor, all the way to Cilicia and Cappadocia-Armenia.

In early 1098, Baldwin had moved on and retained no control over the Cilician cities he had reduced; if he had taken them in his own name, he would have stayed there or appointed his own men to consolidate his rule. He was subsequently invited to Edessa by its ruler, the *kouropalates* Toros, as hired muscle. To make a long story short, Toros was murdered and Baldwin took his place as "duke" of Edessa (or *doux*).[83] The initial nature of Baldwin's rule at Edessa is ambiguous, including elements of sheer opportunism, continuation of local patterns of authority, implied acceptance of the Byzantine framework, and planned geostrategic assistance to the crusade. Eventually, Edessa became a more distinctly Frankish county, as did the Latin principality of Antioch, which emerged out of the same mixed background when Bohemond seized it at the end of the siege.[84] These two were the first crusader states, but basically they only replicated the old Byzantine *doukata* of

Antioch and Edessa. In fact, Bohemond's entire career, from beginning to end, consisted of nothing but attempts to carve pieces out of the empire's current or former provinces, in Italy, the Balkans, and finally Antioch. His ambitions never looked past the boundaries of Romanía. Even when breaking with the empire, the crusaders were still inhabiting its old framework.

But what had Alexios and the Byzantines been doing while the crusaders marched on Antioch? One of the driving dynamics in the drama of the crusade is the alleged absence of the Byzantines. After Nikaia they drop out of the story—as it is told in the Latin chronicles and many modern histories. Alexios' failure to assist in the siege of Antioch led to the debacle of its seizure by Bohemond, and the tangled and partisan story of their claims and counterclaims to it, which we will not review here. Did Alexios simply abandon the crusaders to their fate, as implied by his "absence," while he consolidated his recent gains in Asia Minor? According to his bitter critic Raymond of Aguilers, Alexios claimed that he could not go east with them because he feared the Hungarians and Cumans in his rear.[85]

In fact, we know exactly what Alexios was doing in the meantime, and whether we see it as an "abandonment" of the crusade or not depends on how we view the crusade in 1097. In that year the crusade was not driven by a single-minded determination to reach Jerusalem, if it ever was. It fulfilled the original terms laid out by Urban, namely, to help the Christian communities of the east under Turkish rule and "to liberate the Churches of the East," as the pope put it[86]—a broader conception. Also, it followed the instructions of Alexios in laying the foundations of an imperial restoration in the east. For his part, in 1097–1098, the emperor entrusted his army and fleet to his brother-in-law Ioannes Doukas, who ended the Turkish emirates of Smyrna and Ephesos and then marched inland to retake Sardeis, Philadelpheia, and Lampe.[87] This operation revived Romanía in western Asia Minor. It is sometimes presented as a "selfish" imperial operation—Alexios looking to his own interests while abandoning the crusade. But it is more likely that it was coordinated in advance as part of the same plan: the imperial armies would retake the west while the crusaders would strike south, likely in *support* of the imperial operation,[88] and then they would move east to restore imperial connections in Cappadocia, Cilicia, and Syria. Finally, the emperor would meet up with them at Antioch, which we know was the plan.

The Byzantine operations in the west in 1097–1098, therefore, were entirely in keeping with the spirit and intent of the crusade—to rescue eastern Christians under Turkish rule—and should be reintegrated into its history (or it should be integrated into Byzantine history). The emirates of Smyrna and Ephesos were not merely "local" Byzantine concerns either.

They had been building fleets and terrorizing both the Aegean and the Sea of Marmara for a decade. So restoring the safety of the pilgrim route, even for westerners, required that they be eliminated. This is exactly what Alexios promised the crusaders, "that he would not permit anyone to trouble or vex our pilgrims on the way to the Holy Sepulcher."[89] Such pilgrims would have included future reinforcements for the crusade. Clearing western Asia Minor and the seas had to be part of the plan.

In other words, the crusade did not leave Alexios behind at Nikaia and "strike out on its own." Rather, it performed one part of a two-part operation across Asia Minor. Alexios did not "disappear," as he does from some modern accounts. He also seems to have delivered on his promise to continue to supply the crusaders by sea. The empire did not yet control the southern coast of Asia Minor, so supplies would have to be shipped either from the Aegean or (more likely) from Cyprus. A military historian has observed that "this great maritime endeavor, led and supported by the Byzantines, was one of the key factors which enabled the crusader army to survive the bitter nine-month siege of Antioch and to triumph over their enemies."[90] And finally, in the summer of 1098 the emperor arrived in person at Philomelion, intending to join up with the crusade, as he had said he would. Most of the crusader lords still intended to give up to him all the cities that had formerly belonged to his empire, including Antioch. But it was at Philomelion that things went wrong, when crusaders fleeing from Antioch told Alexios that all was lost and persuaded him to turn back. Coupled with Bohemond's cynical seizure of Antioch, which "spoiled the crusade for Alexios," its history diverged at this point from that of an imperially managed operation.[91] We do not know, nor can we easily imagine, what the crusade would have looked like and what end it would have reached had it remained, as it was heretofore, under imperial command.

The crusade did not merely pass through Byzantium. It was Alexios who turned it into a single force and directed its movements and strategy all the way to Antioch; the crusading army, let us not forget, assembled only at Nikaia. And once it passed outside Byzantine direction, after Antioch, it immediately fell into pieces. It was quite a feat for some of its leaders to gather a part of the original force for one last march to Jerusalem. As for Byzantium, the crusade marked the moment after which it could no longer treat the west as a distant backwater. This was when Byzantium realized that the west had become quite a separate world of its own, propelled by novel tensions that it could not control. For the rest of its history, Byzantium would be surrounded and colonized, inspired and repulsed, engaged and destroyed by the west.

GUIDE TO THE TEN MOST IMPORTANT
NARRATIVE SOURCES

Yahya of Antioch (Arabic): A Christian Arab, he was forced to move from Fatimid
  Egypt to Byzantine Antioch toward the end of Basil II's reign. The extant part
  of his history covers the years 937–1034, focusing on what we would call the
  Middle East, including the Byzantine east. Yahya is accurate, sober, and usually
  impartial.

Ioannes Skylitzes (Greek): A high official under Alexios I Komnenos, Skylitzes
  produced a history of the years 813–1057 by condensing and rewriting previous
  works, probably in the early 1090s. He is an invaluable source, but often garbles
  chronology and mixes facts, literary invention, and propaganda indiscriminately.
  His work was later continued down to 1079 by Skylitzes Continuatus (possibly
  the same man), relying on Attaleiates.

Leon the deacon (Greek): Around 995, Leon wrote a heroic account of the careers
  and reigns of Nikephoros II Phokas and Ioannes I Tzimiskes, based on part on
  his own experience and in part on the rhetorical and classicizing elaboration of a
  small kernel of actual facts.

Stepʿanos of Taron, aka Asołik (Armenian): Sometime after 1000, he wrote a
  world history whose third (and last) book covers the tenth century. He provides
  valuable information about Byzantium and the Caucasus, but exaggerates (and
  likely invents) the prominent roles that Armenians played in events throughout
  the world.

Michael Psellos (Greek): In ca. 1060, Psellos wrote this highly literary account
  of court life from Basil II to the abdication of Isaakios I Komnenos, an account
  that, in the 1070s, he continued down to the regime of Michael VII Doukas,
  albeit in a more overtly panegyrical mode. Psellos witnessed much that he
  records, especially after 1041, but the work is in many ways a justification of

his own intellectual career; his omissions and characterizations are politically motivated.

Michael Attaleiates (Greek): In ca. 1080, Attaleiates, who had served in various high positions at the court, dedicated to Nikephoros III Botaneiates an original history of the years 1034–1079, which aimed to explain the Byzantine decline. It focuses on the reigns of Romanos IV Diogenes (whom Attaleiates served closely) and Michael VII Doukas. Attaleiates was present at the battle of Mantzikert and is usually reliable—which makes him dangerous to use because he often distorts for political reasons.

Aristakes of Lastivert (Armenian): A churchman writing in the 1070s, Aristakes covers the history of Armenia and its neighbors during the eleventh century. He provides useful information that is not always fictionalized or garbled, but it is marred by the purpose of his work, namely to lament; its title is *History Regarding the Sufferings Caused by the Foreign Peoples Living Around Us*.

Nikephoros Bryennios (Greek): Grandson of the general and rebel Nikephoros Bryennios, and husband of Anna Komnene, Bryennios (early twelfth century) wrote a heroic (but at times ambiguous) account of the rise of his father-in-law, Alexios I Komnenos, providing valuable information about the 1070s.

Anna Komnene (Greek): Daughter of the emperor Alexios I Komnenos, Anna wrote a panegyrical history of her father's reign, the *Alexiad*, in the 1140s. It is an indispensible source for Alexios but is biased, takes liberties with the sequence and significance of events, and omits uncomfortable facts.

Matthew of Edessa (Armenian: Mattʿeos): An Armenian monk who lived between the late eleventh century and the midtwelfth, he wrote a chronicle of events from the later tenth century to his own times. He is extremely unreliable regarding our period, offering romantic tales, garbled chronology, and fictitious letters and events, and is heavily biased against the Byzantines, especially in their dealings with Armenians. Unfortunately, he is sometimes our only source.

NOTES

Preface

1. Attaleiates, *History* 274.
2. Ibid. 55.
3. Ibid. 82.
4. Kaldellis, "Manufacture."
5. Specifically, 1: Theodosios the Deacon, *Capture of Crete*, pr. 1; 2: Liudprand of Cremona, *Embassy to Constantinople* 10; 3: Leon the Deacon, *History* 6.1–5, 10.11; 4: Psellos, *Chronographia* 1.3; 5 & 6: Basil II's epitaph (see the end of Chap. 6); 7: Anna Komnene, *Alexiad* 3.8; 8: Konstantinos IX Monomachos, *Novel on the Nomophylax*; 9: Psellos, *Orationes Panegyricae* p. 95; 10: Attaleiates 60; 11: *Timarion* 22; 12: Attaleiates 198.

Introduction

1. Basil II, *Novel* of 996, pr. 3–4; another case in an imperial act in Psellos, *Orationes forenses* 7.
2. Neville, *Heroes*, 109; Cheynet, *Aristocracy*, I; for its origins, see Haldon and Brubaker, *Byzantium*, chap. 8.
3. Kaldellis, *Republic*.
4. Konstantinos of Rhodes, *On Constantinople* 319–349.
5. Oikonomides, *Fiscalité.*
6. Liudprand, *Antapodosis* 6.10; Oikonomides, "Title." Some were paid directly from local contributions.
7. See the story of a priest in Konstantinos VII, *De administrando imperio* 50.235–256.
8. Vlysidou, *Οἰκογένειες*, 80–101.

9. Konstantinos VII, *Book of Ceremonies* 2.15; cf. Liudprand, *Antapodosis* 6.5.

10. Oikonomides, "Recruits" (the system was probably old by the eighth century); Górecki, *"Strateia"*; Haldon, "Service." For fiscalization, see also pp. 211, 273 below.

11. Already in Tacitus, *Agricola* 32; Prokopios, *Wars* 8.28.2, 8.30.17–18; Larkin, *Al-Mutanabbi*, 54–55 (for Sayf al-Dawla).

12. Konstantinos VII, *Military Speech* 6, 8 (cf. 2); see McGeer, "Two Military Orations."

13. Nikephoros II, *Praecepta militaria* 1–2.

14. Dagron and Mihăescu, *Le traité*; McGeer, *Sowing*, esp. 179.

15. Krsmanović, *The Byzantine Province*.

16. Harvey, *Expansion*; Laiou and Morrisson, *Economy*.

17. Lefort, "Economy," 282.

18. Cheynet, *Aristocracy*, I; Holmes, "Elites."

19. Cheynet, *Aristocracy*, I, 31–38. The most effective "private" force I know was assembled by a curator of imperial estates to defeat "bandits" attacking the local peasantry (not *dynatoi* who wanted their lands), and he was punished for this presumption of authority: *Life of Paulos the Younger* 30.

20. Skylitzes 340 (Maleïnos): see p. 117 below.

21. Cheynet, *Aristocracy*, I, 24–27; Frankopan, "Land," 123–124, 129; Haldon, "Élites," 183, and "Service," 29 n. 75; for estates, see Kaplan, "Proprietaires," 137–153, esp. 148 (office preceded wealth).

22. Krallis, *Attaleiates*, 15–27.

23. Whittow, "East," 62.

24. Kaplan, *Hommes*, 331, admitting ignorance: 331–338.

25. E.g., Kaplan, *Hommes*, 327, 359; see the caution of Magdalino, "Court Society," and others.

26. For the legislation, see Svoronos, *Novelles* (text); McGeer, *Legislation* (tr.).

27. Cf. Kaplan, *Hommes*, 359, with Oikonomides, "Structure"; Magdalino, *Empire*, 160–162.

28. Saradi, *"Archontike."* She shows that property transfers in the early eleventh century took place within the framework of the land legislation, which means it was working; for Justinian, Kaplan, *Hommes*, 170–173. The problem and its solution go back to the Gracchi.

29. Morris, "Powerful."

I *"Avengers of Rome"*

1. Vlysidou, *Οικογένειες*, 80–101.

2. Liudprand, *Antapodosis* 5.21.

3. Brokkaar, "Basil"; Wander, *Joshua*, 93–132.

4. Theophanes Continuatus, 445, 459; Skylitzes 238; Cheynet, *Société*, 473–497.

5. Theophanes Continuatus, 468; Pseudo-Symeon 756; Toynbee, *Constantine*, 24–25, for additional sources.

6. Pro-contra in Skylitzes 237–238. Theophanes Continuatus is panegyrical.

7. Haldon and Kennedy, "Frontier"; Bosworth, *Arabs*, XII; and Decker, "Settlement," 253–266; 238–249 for its meager archaeological record.

8. Haldon, *Warfare*, 42; Dagron, "Minorités," 180.

9. Ouranos, *Taktika* 65.

10. Dagron, "Minorités," 181–184; Kennedy, *Prophet*, 278; Melitene: Leveniotis, *Κατάρρευση*, 255–261.

11. Banu Habib: ibn Hawqal in Vasiliev, *Byzance*, v. 2.2, 419–421 (discussion: v. 2.1, 270–273); Treadgold, *Army*, 34, 78; for population transfers, see Charanis, *Studies*, III; Toynbee, *Constantine*, 70–107 (here 84–85); Ditten, *Ethnische Verschiebungen*. For Armenian colonists, see the career of Melias (Mleh) in *PmbZ* 25041 (mainly from Konstantinos VII, *De administrando imperio* 50); in general, Dédéyan, "Arméniens," 75–87 (use with caution); Oikonomides, "Organisation," 295–297. The challenge was in getting Armenian military colonists to stay: McGeer, "Decree." Policy of conversion of expulsion: ibid. 290 n. 31, 295; Bosworth, *Arabs*, XIII, 12, 15. For Melitene, see Tinnefeld, "Melitene"; Vest, *Geschichte*.

12. Dagron, "Minorités"; Holmes, " 'How the East'," 42–46.

13. El Cheikh, *Byzantium*, 165–166.

14. Haldon and Kennedy, "Frontier," 106–115; Bosworth, *Arabs,* XIII.10–11, esp. XIV; Pryor and Jeffreys, *ΔΡΟΜΩΝ*, 62–63, 72; McGeer, *Sowing*, 230–232, 245.

15. Bikhazi, *Hamdanid*, 636–638, 737.

16. Overviews: Canard, "Hamdanids"; Bianquis, "Sayf al-Dawla." Detailed accounts: Canard, *Histoire*; Bikhazi, *Hamdanid*; for Sayf al-Dawla's armies, see McGeer, *Sowing*, 232–246; for the context, see Kennedy, *Prophet*, 198–209, 265–282.

17. Canard, *Histoire*, 763–770; Bikhazi, *Hamdanid*, 716–722.

18. El Cheikh, *Byzantium*, 167.

19. Canard, *Histoire*, 776, 778; different reports in *PmbZ* 23841 (Konstantinos).

20. Theophanes Continuatus 459.

21. Bikhazi, *Hamdanid*, 765–778.

22. Canard, *Histoire*, 787–792; Vasiliev, *Byzance*, v. 2.1, 356–358; Bikhazi, *Hamdanid*, 780–781; Vest, *Geschichte*, 995–1006.

23. Yahya I:773. He was Abu al-ʿAshaʾir.

24. Yahya I:774; Vasiliev, *Byzance*, v. 2.1, 359.

25. Theophanes Continuatus 452–453; Vasiliev, *Byzance*, v. 2.1, 360; Bikhazi, *Hamdanid*, 783–784.

26. Yahya I:774–775; Vasiliev, *Byzance*, v. 2.1, 360.

27. Skylitzes 241.

28. McCormick, *Victory*, 159–166.

29. Konstantinos VII, *Book of Ceremonies* 2.19; McCormick, *Victory*, 161–165.

30. Yahya I:774; Bikhazi, *Hamdanid*, 786–787.

31. Yahya I:774–775.

32. Bikhazi, *Hamdanid*, 785–786, evaluates rival theories.

33. Yahya I:775; Theophanes Continuatus 461–462; *Chronicle of Vat. gr. 163*, 95; Konstantinos VII, *Military Speech*; triumph: McCormick, *Victory*, 166.

34. Theophanes Continuatus 460.

35. Canard, *Histoire*, 798–799; Bikhazi, *Hamdanid*, 843–844; date: Yahya I:779.

36. Falkenhausen, *Dominazione*, expands her fundamental *Untersuchungen*. Martin, *Pouille*, is a *longue durée* study of Apulia; see esp. 255–272, 292–301, 489–520, and 693–714. A survey in idem, "Thèmes italiens"; and Lambakis et al., Στρατεύματα; Kreutz, *Before the Normans*, 11, 14–15 for demography. The foundational book, Gay, *L'Italie*, is still useful.

37. The *New Cambridge Medieval History*, v. 3, offers introductions to Muslim Sicily, southern Italy, and the Ottonian empire.

38. Liudprand, *Embassy* 7.

39. Chiarelli, *History*, 82–100; Kennedy, "Sicily," 662–669. The caliph was al-Mansur.

40. Theophanes Continuatus 453–455; Vasiliev, *Byzance*, v. 2.1, 372 n. 1. The destruction of the Arab fleet by winds (mentioned later) is confirmed in Arabic sources, though placed later. Marianos is *PmbZ* 24962.

41. For different reconstructions, see Lev, "Navy," 235–235; Lambakis et al., Στρατεύματα, 376–380; Brett, *Fatimids*, 241; Chiarelli, *History*, 100–103; *PmbZ* 24962 (367). For a Fatimid source, see Stern, "Embassy."

42. Vasiliev, *Byzance et les Arabes*, v. 2.1, 375; Stern, "An Embassy," 245–246.

43. Bikhazi, *Hamdanid*, 820–822.

44. Skylitzes 242–244, 247. For Polyeuktos, see Lilie, "Caesaropapismus."

45. Theophanes Continuatus 472–473.

46. Romanos II, *Funeral Oration* 270 (ancestry: 269); also Konstantinos VII, *De administrando imperio* 26 (the name, and Charlemagne); Theophanes Continuatus 431; Liudprand, *Antapodosis* 5.14 (Greeks care only about the father's side), and 5.20. The sources call this a marriage, not just an engagement: Panagopoulou, Γάμοι, 143. Romanos was subsequently engaged to Hadwig, niece of Otto I, but this was scotched: ibid. 145–148.

47. Cutler, *Hand*, 235 (gift), 205 (date), 25 (kissing).

48. Leon 2.10; Skylitzes 240, 246–247.

49. Theophanes Continuatus 458 (a daughter of one Krateros); Cheynet, *Société*, 586–587.

50. Markopoulos, *History and Literature*, IV; Christou, Εξουσία, 227–239; *PmbZ* 23529.

51. Theophanes Continuatus 471.

52. Christides, *Conquest*, and "Raids"; Tsougarakis, *Crete*, 30–76, 209–213; failed attempts to retake Crete: Makrypoulias, "Expeditions."

53. Canard, "Ikritish"; Miles, "Byzantium," 16; Christides, *Conquest*, 114–136; for intellectuals, see idem, "Raid and Trade."

54. Konstantinos VII, *Book of Ceremonies* 2.44–45; Treadgold, "Army," 100–157; Haldon, "Theory"; Pryor and Jeffreys, *ΔΡΟΜΩΝ*, 547–570.

55. Mazzucchi, "Basilio," the poem at 302; Pryor and Jeffreys, *ΔΡΟΜΩΝ*, 183–186, 522–523.

56. Theophanes Continuatus 474–475; *Chronicle of Vat. gr. 163*, 98.

57. Tsougarakis, *Crete*, 62–63, rightly doubts the figure of seventy-two thousand infantry and five thousand cavalry given in Arabic sources. The number of ships in Byzantine sources (3,307) is impossible. Leon 1.7 mentions forty thousand Arabs on a hill outside Chandax, also impossible. Theodosios, *Capture of Crete* 1.183–249, gives to Nikephoros for one assault on Chandax fifty thousand cavalry and countless infantry—impossible; and so on.

58. Kaldellis, "Conquest," but often taken at face value, e.g., Tsougarakis, *Crete*, 61–74.

59. Kaldellis, "Byzantine Argument."

60. Foss, *Ephesus*, 123–124.

61. Leon 1.3; Skylitzes 249. Theophanes Continuatus 475–476 is based on Prokopios. Date: Yahya I:782.

62. Theodosios, *Capture of Crete* 1.101–131; Theophanes Continuatus 476.

63. Theodosios, *Capture of Crete* 1.183–249; Leon 1.8.

64. Leon 1.3–4 and Theodosios, *Capture of Crete* 4.75–111 (respectively); pacification: Theophanes Continuatus 476; Leon 1.7; Skylitzes 249; "fire and sword": Theodosios, ibid. 1.135–138. The general was Nikephoros Pastilas.

65. Theodosios, *Capture of Crete* 2.58–80; Leon 1.7–8.

66. Theodosios, *Capture of Crete* 3.173–194.

67. Canard, "Ikritish"; Tsougarakis, *Crete*, 68–70; tr. of the Arabic sources in Tibi, "Two Sources." The account of these envoys in Theophanes Continuatus 477 is not credible: Kaldellis, "Conquest."

68. Theophanes Continuatus 478–480.

69. Leon 2.7–8; date: Yahya I:782; Skylitzes 249.

70. Theodosios, *Capture of Crete* 5.85–106; Leon 2.8.

71. Leon 2.8; Pseudo-Symeon, *Chronicle*, 759–760; McCormick, *Victory*, 167–168; Kaldellis, "Conquest." Scholars correctly reject Skylitzes' testimony (252) that Nikephoros was not allowed into the City after his victory. Skylitzes' chronology is confused, and earlier (250) he said that Nikephoros was recalled to the capital after Crete.

72. *PmbZ* 20421.

73. Ibn Jubayr, *Travels*, 359.

74. Leon 2.8.

75. Tsougarakis, *Crete*, 179–180.

76. Yahya I:782–783. For a treasure associated with the capture, see Bonovas and Tzitzibassi, eds., *Byzantium*, 41.

77. *Life of Nikon* 20–21. The hagiographer exaggerates Nikon's importance. Other saints were endowed in retrospect with prophesies about the successful conquest: *Life of Loukas of Steiris* 60.

78. Herrin, *Margins*, 139–140.

79. Holo, "Genizah Letter."

80. Yahya I:781; Miskawayh, *Experiences*, 195–196. For Naja, see Bikhazi, *Hamdanid*, 845; *PmbZ* 25487. An excellent reconstruction of the 959–965 wars is Garrood, "Conquest."

81. Leon 2.1–2.

82. Leon 2.2 (n. 17 of the tr. for dates; Cheynet, *Société*, 485, accepts 960).

83. Theophanes Continuatus 479. Leon 2.3 implies that he brought forces from the West. For the expression *ek prosopou*, see Krsmanović, *Province*, 25 n. 50.

84. *On Skirmishing*; see McGeer, *Sowing*, 228.

85. Miskawayh, *Experiences*, 196.

86. Leon 2.5.

87. Theophanes Continuatus 480.

88. Bikhazi, *Hamdanid*, 848; *PmbZ* 25487. For ʿAbd Allah, see below.

89. Yahya I:783–784; Miskawayh, *Experiences*, 206–208 (fifty-four forts); Bikhazi, *Hamdanid*, 850–856. Leon 2.9 gives a rhetorical account of the fighting, 961–963, mentioning sixty forts taken.

90. McGeer, *Sowing*, 245 n. 56; Garrood, "Conquest," 133.

91. Canard, *Histoire*, 807–811; Bikhazi, *Hamdanid*, 859–860 (another raid by Naja from Mayyafariqin).

92. Abu Firas, *Les Byzantines*; Seyyedi, "Abu Firas"; Vasiliev, *Byzance*, v. 2.2, 349–370 (down to 959); Patoura, *Αἰχμάλωτοι*, 93–97.

93. Yahya I:784–787; Miskawayh, *Experiences*, 208–211; for the detailed account in a source used by Yahya, see Forsyth, *Chronicle*, 105–112; the best Greek source is the *Chronicle of Vat. gr. 163*, 99–100; Canard, *Histoire*, 811–817; Bikhazi, *Hamdanid*, 860–866; Garrood, "Conquest," 133–134.

94. Garrood, "Conquest," 132, 134–135; Muslim reactions: Bosworth, *Arabs*, XIII, 11.

95. Yahya I:794.

96. Theophanes Continuatus 471–472; Skylitzes 252 maliciously attributes this to Theophano.

97. Theophanes Continuatus 479; Skylitzes 250–251.

98. *Chronicle of Vat. gr. 163*, 100; Leon 2.10, and Polyeuktos in ibid. 2.12. For regencies, see Christophilopoulou, "Ἀντιβασιλεία," esp. 62–64.

99. Leon 2.11.

100. Skylitzes 254.

101. *Chronicle of Vat. gr. 163*, 100.

102. Tserebelakis, *Φωκᾶς*, 18–19.

103. Skylitzes 254.

104. Sullivan, "Siege Warfare."

105. Östenberg, *Staging*; Byzantine revivals: Kaldellis, "Original Source."

106. *Chronicle of Vat. gr. 163*, 100; Leon 2.12.

107. Leon 3.2–3; Skylitzes 256; Michael the Syrian III:128. The role of the officers is stressed by al-Rudhrawari, *Continuation*, 5.

108. Skylitzes 257; Yahya I:788.

109. Leon 3.6.

110. Leon 3.6; Konstantinos VII, *Book of Ceremonies* 1.96 (434). For a commentary on the latter, see Kresten, "Beobachtungen."

111. Leon 3.7; Konstantinos VII, *Book of Ceremonies* 1.96 (435).

112. Leon 3.2, 3.7 (Paschalios and the Tornikoi). Marianos is *PmbZ* 24962.

113. Skylitzes 257: biased, but borne out.

2 *"The White Death of the Saracens"*

1. Leon 3.8; Skylitzes 260; the ceremony for investing a *kaisar* is in Konstantinos VII, *Book of Ceremonies* 1.43; Guilland, *Recherches*, v. 2, 27.

2. Liudprand, *Embassy* 28.

3. Skylitzes 260.

4. The ceremony for investing a *proedros* was added, possibly by Basileios, to Konstantinos VII, *Book of Ceremonies* 1.97. As the acclamations refer to a *kaisar*, Basileios' promotion followed that of Bardas.

5. Leon 3.9; Skylitzes 260–261; cf. Liudprand, *Embassy* 41; Lilie, "Caesaropapismus," 389–393. Princes could have a crowd of godparents (e.g., Konstantinos VII): Macrides, "Godfather," 147, 159–160. There could be confusion about who was in that group and who just present; for spiritual relationships, see Patlagean, *Structure*, XII. I do not believe Skylitzes that Nikephoros initially expelled Theophano from the palace.

6. Leon 3.8; Skylitzes 281–282.

7. Liudprand, *Embassy* 3.

8. Morris, "Two Faces." It is hard to find pro-Phokas sources: Markopoulos, "History Writing," 188 n. 29; Holmes, *Basil*.

9. Chiarelli, *History*, 105–106.

10. Leon 4.7–8; Skylitzes 267.

11. E.g., al-Athir, *Annales*, 278–281.

12. Chiarelli, *History*, 107–110, here 107; Lev, "Navy," 236–237. For the two commanders, see Liudprand, *Embassy* 43 (graphically embellished).

13. Falkenhausen, "Nilo," 292–293; Cheynet, *Pouvoir*, 21, 386.

14. *PmbZ* 25608.

15. Leon 5.1.

16. *PmbZ* 25784 (Par. gr. 497).

17. Miskawayh, *Experiences*, 213–214; Canard, *Histoire*, 817–818; Bikhazi, *Hamdanid*, 878–879; Vest, *Geschichte*, 1021–1025.

18. Garrood, "Conquest," 135.

19. Skylitzes 267–268; Yahya I:793–794 (confuses Tzimiskes and Nikephoros); Miskawayh, *Experiences*, 216–217; Canard, *Histoire*, 818–820; famine: Bikhazi, *Hamdanid*, 893–894.

20. Yahya I:795; Miskawayh, *Experiences*, 222; Bikhazi, *Hamdanid*, 894–899, 917–920.

21. Leon 3.10, misdates the capture of Mopsouestia to 964; Skylitzes 268, is probably wrong that Tarsos was not attacked in the summer of 964; Miskawayh, *Experiences*, 222, confuses Tzimiskes and Nikephoros (at 224 confirms that Nikephoros brought the family); see Garrood, "Conquest," 136.

22. Yahya I:795–796; Bikhazi, *Hamdanid*, 897.

23. Metcalf, *Cyprus*, esp. 428–429 (condominium), 460–468 (administration).

24. Skylitzes 270, possibly 964.

25. Yahya I:794–795.

26. Metcalf, *Cyprus*, 485, 489.

27. Miskawayh, *Experiences*, 224.

28. Leon 3.10 (walls), 3.11 (misdates Mopsouestia to 964), 4.1–4 (fall of Tarsos; Leon offers only rhetorical elaboration and generic military information); Yahya I:796–797; Skylitzes 268–270 (Egyptian fleet); Miskawayh, *Experiences*, 225; Garrood, "Conquest," 138. For Arab accounts, see Bosworth, *Arabs*, XIII, 12; XIV, 278–279.

29. Miskawayh, *Experiences*, 225–226.

30. El Cheikh, *Byzantium*, 173.

31. Leon 4.4; Skylitzes 270.

32. Thierry, "Portrait."

33. Michael the Syrian III:130–131; Dagron, "Minorités," 187–188; Benner, *Kirche*, 25–34; Vest, *Geschichte*, 1077–1107.

34. Yahya I:803–804; Bikhazi, *Hamdanid*, 927.

35. Kennedy, "Antioch"; Todt, "Antioch."

36. Miskawayh, *Experiences*, 226–228; Yahya I:797–798, 804–805; Bikhazi, *Hamdanid*, 922–928; Todt, "Antioch," 173.

37. Miskawayh, *Experiences*, 228.

38. Leon 4.10–11; Skylitzes 270–273.

39. In addition to the Byzantine sources, see Yahya I:805–806; Bikhazi, *Hamdanid*, 931–935; Garrood, "Illusion," 23.

40. Halkin, "Translation," 259 (the date is when the tile was deposited).

41. Greenwood, "Patterns."

42. Garsoïan, "Integration"; Greenwood, "Patterns," 89.

43. Step'anos of Taron 3.8; Skylitzes 279; Yuzbashian, "L'administration," 140–148; Adontz, *Études*, 197–263. They were Grigor and Bagrat.

44. Konstantinos VII, *De administrando imperio* 43; Greenwood, "Patterns," 82–84, 89–92. Tornik is *PmbZ* 28364; the events probably date to the 930s.

45. Oikonomides, *Listes*, 264–265, 355–356; Krsmanović, *Province*, 93.

46. Konstantinos VII, *De administrando imperio* 44; Ter-Ghewondyan, *Emirates*, esp. 87–88; for previous raids against them by Kourkouas, see Greenwood, "Patterns," 96; for the position of *doux* of Chaldia, see Krsmanović, *Province*, 123–126.

47. Step῾anos of Taron 3.8; Yahya I:825.

48. Skylitzes 273–278; Morris, "Two Faces."

49. Skylitzes 274; Polyeuktos later demanded that Tzimiskes revoke imperial control of episcopal elections: Leon 6.4.

50. Svoronos, *Novelles*, 151–161 (text); McGeer, *Legislation*, 90–96 (tr.); Thomas, *Foundations*, 149–153; Morris, *Monks*, 166–199; only Charanis, "Properties," 59 rightly emphasizes state interests; for Nikephoros and Athanasios, see Morris, "Two Faces," 100–106. For monastic opposition, see Laiou, "General," 410–411 and n. 63.

51. Skylitzes 274–275; Riedel, "Nikephoros." Note that Theodosios, *Capture of Crete* 2.115–125, has the emir explain Muslim beliefs on this question. The poem was dedicated to Nikephoros in 963; could it have been a reminder of the infidel nature of such thinking?

52. Skylitzes 273–274.

53. McGeer, "Decree," 134–135.

54. Leon 4.6–7; Skylitzes 275–276; and Zonaras 16.26. The date 967 (March 31) is proposed also by the *PmbZ* 27115 (Sisinnios). For the wall, see Bardill, "Palace," 226.

55. Leon 4.6; Skylitzes 274; Zonaras 16.26 (distinctive information).

56. *On Skirmishing* 19 (216–217).

57. Kaldellis, *Republic*, 194–196.

58. Nikephoros made only minor modifications to Macedonian policy: Svoronos, *Novelles*, 177–181 (text); McGeer, *Legislation*, 97–101 (tr. with commentary). I omit a *Novel* attributed to an emperor Nikephoros that purports to raise fourfold the fiscal encumbrance of the highest grade of military lands: McGeer, *Legislation*, 104–108. This has been used to argue for the creation of new units of heavy cavalry. However, Kolias, *Φωκᾶς*, identified many problems with this text, making it effectively unusable. Magdalino, "Byzantine Army," 16–26, defended its authenticity, but offered *too many* possible interpretations, which are tenuous. McGeer sides with Magdalino, but corrects many of his interpretations too. This is a quagmire. In any case, Nikephoros' "new *kataphraktoi*" are a fiction.

59. Ibn Hawqal, *Configuration*, 193–194; for Arab views, see El Cheikh, *Byzantium*, 168–178.

60. Skylitzes 275; Zonaras 16.26; Hendy, *Studies*, 233, 507; and "Light Weight *Solidi*," 70–72; market: Laiou and Morrisson, *Economy*, 60. The inflation, however, may have been due to the food scarcity of 968; see below.

61. Liudprand, *Embassy* 10.

62. For Petar's Bulgaria, see Fine, *Balkans*, 160–171; Simeon's education: Shepard, "Manners"; for Byzantine views, see Kaldellis, *Ethnography*, 126–136. There is a confused notice in Skylitzes' coverage of mid-963 (255) stating that the treaty was renewed when Maria died (date unknown) and that Boris and Roman were sent to Constantinople as "hostages," to be released when their father Petar died (in 969, but not specified here) to face the Kometopouloi. This notice poses many problems that cannot be resolved; cf. Božilov and Gjuzelev, *Istorija*, 294–300 (I thank Ian Mladjov for this).

63. Leon 4.5–6.

64. Cf. Lauxtermann, *Poetry*, 233–236, for a similar text. The story appears to have been modeled on the *exact same* event in Theophanes the Confessor 429 (Konstantinos V and the Bulgarians). Simeonova, "Short Fuse," 60–62, knows that Nikephoros' treatment of the Bulgarian envoys was aberrant, but accepts it as reported.

65. Historians have assumed (on no basis of evidence) that the tribute was paid for the upkeep of Maria Lakapene, and in reality to keep the peace. There are no other references to it. We do not know when Maria died (*PmbZ* 24919 conjectures 963).

66. Skylitzes 276–277.

67. Shepard, "Bulgaria," 583; for Byzantine-Magyar relations, see Stephenson, *Frontier*, 38–45.

68. Zonaras 16.27. Liudprand, *Embassy* 45 records two Magyar raids in Macedonia in March 968 (but he wants to make the Byzantines look weak). See Mladjov, "Bulgarians," 68–70.

69. Historians follow Stokes, "Background," in dating the Thracian tour to 966 and the first Rus' invasion to 967, but Stokes took Leon's enraged Nikephoros at face value, undermining his reading of other sources. A date of 967 for the Thracian tour is supported by the fact that the western envoy Dominicus (*PmbZ* 21585) met Nikephoros "in Macedonia" that year: Liudprand, *Embassy* 31.

70. Stokes, "Balkan Campaigns," 468–469; Fine, *Balkans*, 181–182.

71. Liudprand, *Embassy* 19–21.

72. Bartlett, *Europe*.

73. Smith, *Europe*.

74. We do not have an account of what Otto I was acclaimed in 962. Possibly he did not use the modifier *Romanorum*: Müller-Mertens, "Ottonians," 251; but it was used for him by others, and for his heirs: Erdmann, "Reich"; Keller, "Kaisertum"; and Arnold, *Germany*, 75, 84. Otto's coronation imitated Charlemagne's, who had used the Roman modifier.

75. For various proposed ideas, see Erdmann, "Kaiseridee"; Folz, *Empire*; Arnold, *Germany*, 75–97.
76. Ohnsorge, *Konstantinopel*, 176–181, 199; Leyser, "*Theophanu*," 15. See the reception of the papal letter in Liudprand, *Embassy* 47.
77. Fögen, "Reanimation," 19–22; tr. and commentary in Folz, *Empire*, 181–184.
78. Lambakis et al., Στρατεύματα, 386–392; Kreutz, *Normans*, 102–106; Mayr-Harting, "Liudprand," for the importance of Pandulf.
79. Loud, "Southern Italy," 630–633.
80. Liudprand, *Embassy* 7; Mayr-Harting, "Liudprand," 551–552.
81. Patoura, Αἰχμάλωτοι, 93–97; El Cheikh, *Byzantium*, 169.
82. Skylitzes 277–278; Leon 4.6; Liudprand, *Embassy* 34, 44.
83. Liudprand, *Embassy* 15, 18 (a threat by Basileios *parakoimomenos*), 27, 36.
84. Liudprand, *Embassy* 29–30.
85. *PmbZ* 21772.
86. Loud, "Southern Italy," 630.
87. Falkenhausen, *Untersuchungen*, 83; Lambakis et al., Στρατεύματα, 396–398.
88. Skylitzes 278–279; Yahya I:799–802, 807–810; *PmbZ* 23099 and 21277 respectively. Sayf al-Dawla seems to have argued in a letter that Nikephoros' invasion was in response to the burning of the Holy Sepulcher, but this deflected responsibility away from himself: Bikhazi, *Hamdanid*, 929–930.
89. El Cheikh, *Byzantium*, 170, 173; Haldon, *Warfare*, 29 (301–302 n. 72 for the legendary nature of these claims).
90. Yahya I:807, 813–814.
91. Yahya I:814–816; Leon 4.10–11 (confused on the itinerary and *keramidion*); Skylitzes 271–272. Laodikeia: Miotto, Ἀνταγωνισμός, 81. Petros as *stratopedarches*: Krsmanović, *Province*, 33–35, 38, 40, 66–67.
92. Leon 5.1; Yahya I:826.
93. Michael the Syrian III:131; Benner, *Kirche*, 36–51, 137–144.
94. Leon 5.1–2, presumably referring to the initial Rus' invasion (Leon does not mention the interruption in the Rus' conquest); Skylitzes 288.
95. *Russian Primary Chronicle* 84–86 (erroneously dating Svjatoslav's initial attack on Bulgaria to 967).
96. Leon 5.3, 5.6; see n. 62 above for the problems with Boris' movements.
97. Stokes, "Balkan Campaigns," 480–481.
98. Skylitzes 272–273; Leon 5.4–5 (at 4.11 Nikephoros expresses a desire to take the city intact); Yahya I:822–823, 825 (fires made him angry).
99. Yahya I:825–826.
100. Guilland, *Études*, v. 1, 334–367.
101. Miskawayh, *Experiences*, 226.
102. The sources give different reasons for the tension between Theophano and Nikephoros: Leon 5.5–9; Skylitzes 279–280; Yahya I:827–829; Psellos, *Historia Syntomos* 105; Zonaras 16.28. For the topography of the murder,

see Guilland, *Recherches*, v. 1, 334–367; burial: Morris, "Two Faces," 93–94 n. 37.

103. Geometres, *Poems*, 283, 290; Lauxtermann, "Geometres," 367 n. 48 for a list. Most of these poems refer to the emperor's death.

104. Quoted in El Cheikh, *Byzantium*, 172.

3 "A Mind Full of Cares, Brave in Danger"

1. Tzimiskes' speech in Leon 8.3 is illuminating.

2. Leon 5.9–6.1; Skylitzes 284. Prior agreement with the *parakoimomenos* is suspected by Cheynet, *Pouvoir*, 327; Christou, *Ἐξουσία*, 245–247.

3. Leon 6.2; Skylitzes 284 (Nikephoros went to Imbros).

4. Leon 4.3, 6.3; Skylitzes 312 (in an interpolation), possibly a panegyrical description.

5. Leon 6.4; Skylitzes 285–286 (wrong that Tzimiskes went to the patriarch on the night of the murder). Two centuries later, the canonist Theodoros Balsamon claims to have seen a decree of the Holy Synod passed under Polyeuktos declaring that the unction of imperial investiture cleansed one of past sins: Rallis and Potlis, *Σύνταγμα*, v. 3, 44. This testimony is impeachable; moreover, "unction" must be understood metaphorically: Christophilopoulou, *Ἐκλογή*, 109–110; Dagron, *Emperor*, chap. 8.

6. Leon 7.9; Skylitzes 294; Yahya I:830 (rank).

7. Leon 6.3; and see below.

8. Morgan, "Satirical Song."

9. Leon 6.5.

10. Krsmanović, *Province*, 36–37, 69.

11. Michael the Syrian III:131; Benner, *Kirche*, 51–53; Vest, *Geschichte*, 1077–1107.

12. Leveniotis, *Κατάρρευση*, 35.

13. Lambakis et al., *Στρατεύματα*, 392.

14. Davids, ed., *The Empress Theophano*.

15. Kaldellis, "Original Source."

16. Leon 6.10; Skylitzes 288–289; Stokes, "Balkan Campaigns," 486.

17. Leon 6.11–13; Skylitzes 288–291. I suspect it is modeled on Prokopios' *Wars*; the diplomatic exchanges are fictitious as reported. Holmes, *Basil*, 272–273, suspects a pro-Skleros source.

18. Leon 7.1–8; Skylitzes 291–294, from the same source; cf. Yahya I:831–832.

19. Leon 7.9.

20. In Leon 8.4, the emperor's army has thirteen thousand cavalry, fifteen thousand infantry, and the Immortals; in Skylitzes 295, it has five thousand infantry and four thousand cavalry; these cannot be reconciled as easily as Treadgold, *History*, 949 n. 18, proposes.

21. Leon 8.2, has Tzimiskes (implausibly) suggest that the Rus' did not expect an attack before Easter. Stokes, "Balkan Campaigns," 493 argues that there was a truce, which the emperor was breaking.

22. Leon 9.3–4 (an island in a lake in Bithynia); Skylitzes 303 (Prote). Yahya I:830–831, says that the empress Theodora ordered the blinding.

23. Date: Kaldellis, "Original Source," 6; battle rhetoric: McGrath, "Battles."

24. Leon 9.11; Terras, "Leo"; Kaldellis, *Ethnography*, 102–106.

25. The text of the treaty in the *Russian Primary Chronicle* 89–90 conflicts with its narrative.

26. Leon 9.12; Skylitzes 310; *Russian Primary Chronicle* 90.

27. Oikonomides, *Listes*, 262–263, 344–346; Kühn, *Armee*, 163–168, 206–213, 221–222; western Mesopotamia: Madgearu, *Organization*, 39–43; Kühn attributes the first *doukata* to Nikephoros, but Treadgold, *Army*, 35–36, more plausibly to Tzimiskes; Krsmanović, *Province*, 133–145.

28. Holmes, "Eastern Frontier," 89–99; Cheynet, "Antioch," 2–3.

29. Oikonomides, "Recherches," "Occupation"; Stephenson, *Frontier*, 53, 56; Madgearu, *Organization*, chap. 2.

30. Stephenson, *Frontier*, 53, 55–58; Madgearu, *Organization*, 101–114.

31. Skylitzes 286, 311.

32. Yahya I:824–825; Canard, *Histoire*, 667–674, 832–837 (tr. of the terms); Bikhazi, *Hamdanid*, 949–953; Farag, *Byzantium*, 174–183 (discrepancies in the sources over the tribute); for the boundaries, see Miotto, *Ανταγωνισμός*, 80–81.

33. Farag, *Byzantium*, 167–168.

34. Yahya I:824; ibn Manik is *PmbZ* 22701.

35. Leon 6.6; Skylitzes 286; Yahya I:832; Grumel, "Patriarcat," 133–134. For the administration and demography of Antioch, see Forsyth, *Chronicle*, 26; Cheynet, "Antioch." For a contemporary report, see ibn Hawqal, *Configuration*, 176–177.

36. Cheynet, *Société*, 342–343. It is possible that Nikephoros sent his relative Eustathios Maleïnos to (briefly) govern Antioch when he deposed Bourtzes: Saunders, "Reliquary."

37. Walker, "Ismāʿīlī Daʿwa"; Kennedy, *Prophet*, 307–342.

38. Brett, *Fatimids*, 308.

39. Leon 5.1; see p. 46 above.

40. Skylitzes 287 (no date); mention in Leon 6.8; Walker, "Byzantine Victory."

41. Yahya II:350–351; Brett, *Fatimids*, 311–315; Bianquis, *Damas*, 37–64; Kennedy, *Prophet*, 318.

42. Miotto, *Ανταγωνισμός*, 183–184.

43. Canard, "Date," and *Histoire*, 841; Yahya II:354–356; Miskawayh, *Experiences*, 326–327.

44. Donohue, *Buwayhid Dynasty*, 268–270.

45. *PmbZ* 25042 (Melias); esp. Canard, "Date," 105–106, and *Histoire*, 842; for his captivity, see Miskawayh, *Experiences*, 335–336. The brother was Hibatallah.

46. Kaldellis, "Did Ioannes I Tzimiskes."

47. Matthew of Edessa 1.19–21.

48. Starr, "Byzantine Incursions"; Walker, "Crusade," 320–321. I do not believe the text is based on a letter by Tzimiskes; cf. MacEvitt, "*Chronicle*"; Kaldellis, "Did Ioannes I Tzimiskes."

49. Bianquis, *Damas*, 90–112.

50. In 974, a Roman ambassador arrived at Cairo, but died there: Walker, "Crusade," 313–314.

51. Leon 10.4, has Tzimiskes capture Manjib (it was not on the way) and then Apameia (which belonged to him by treaty). We should reject these claims. For Apameia, see Canard, *Histoire*, 833.

52. Walker, "Crusade," 315; date: Yahya II:368.

53. Walker, "Crusade," 316–319; Miotto, Ἀνταγωνισμός, 105–107; see Leon 10.4; Yahya II:368–369; and esp. ibn Qalanisi in Canard, "Sources arabes," 293–296.

54. Walker, "Crusade," 321–323; Miotto, Ἀνταγωνισμός, 108; see Leon 10.4–6; Yahya II:369.

55. Kennedy, *Prophet*, 321–322.

56. Oikonomides, *Listes*, 262–263, 344–346; Kühn, *Armee*, 170–187; Treadgold, *Army*, 35–36.

57. Holmes, "Eastern Frontier," 89–99.

58. Leon 10.11; Skylitzes 311–312; the tale reached al-Rudhrawari, *Continuation*, 6; date: Morris, "Two Faces," 114 n. 103.

59. Geometres, *Poems*, 267–269, 286; Lauxtermann, "Geometres," and *Poetry*, 311 (Ioannes the bishop of Melitene).

60. Baun, *Tales*, 15, 72, 222–225.

61. Leon 6.3.

62. Leon 10.2–3; Skylitzes 311; Cheynet, *Pouvoir*, 26.

63. Leon 6.8 (unspecified).

64. Skylitzes 311.

65. Morris, *Monks*, 141, 189, 231.

66. Leon 9.5.

4 *"From Spectator to Contestant"*

1. Skylitzes 314; Yahya I:831.

2. Al-Athir, *Annales*, 292; Lambakis et al., Στρατεύματα, 399–400; Chiarelli, *History*, 115.

3. Fine, *Balkans*, 191. See below for Armenian claims.

4. Skylitzes 255–256 (garbled), 328–329 (with likely interpolations); Yahya II:418. The castration, stated by Skylitzes, is confirmed by Step'anos of

Taron 3.22, whose account fueled Adontz's Armenian nationalism: *Études*, 347–407; but cf. Seibt, "Untersuchungen." Samuil's state: Fine, *Balkans*, 188–193.

5. Skylitzes 330; Holmes, *Basil,* 102–103.
6. Skylitzes 314–315.
7. Yahya II:372.
8. Yahya II:372, 398; Miskawayh, *Experiences*, 424; al-Rudhrawari, *Continuation*, 6; Skylitzes 315–316; Forsyth, *Chronicle*, 375–393; discussed by Holmes, *Basil*. Armenian support for Skleros: Dédéyan, "Arméniens," 85–86.
9. Skylitzes 317–319; Yahya II:373–374.
10. Skylitzes 319–320 (Michael Kourtikios).
11. Skylitzes 320–323.
12. Skylitzes 322 and Leon 10.7 report different naval battles: Holmes, *Basil,* 456 n. 27; *pace* 117, 451–452, I do not trust Leon's chronology, because he is giving a rhetorical list by type, not a narrative.
13. Yahya II:375–378.
14. Skylitzes 324; Yahya II:374; western armies: Step'anos of Taron 3.15.
15. Forsyth, *Chronicle*, 384–388; Holmes, *Basil,* 453–456. Essentially, they disagree about the battle of Pankaleia: Skylitzes places it last, by the Halys river (a Phokas win), whereas Yahya places it first (a Skleros win). Leon 10.7, agrees with Yahya, placing Pankaleia by Amorion, where Skylitzes says the first battle took place. Pankaleia cannot be located: Belke, *Galatien*, 212.
16. Yahya II:375; Skylitzes 324–325; Leon 10.7.
17. Skylitzes 326.
18. *Life of Ioane and Ep't'ime* 8–10 (pp. 88–91); he is *PmbZ* 22926; also Step'anos of Taron 3.15; cf. Cheynet, *Pouvoir*, 330–331.
19. Yahya II:399; Skylitzes 326–327; inscription: Forsyth, *Chronicle*, 386–387.
20. Skylitzes 327–328.
21. Panagopoulou, Θεοφανώ, 23–24.
22. Thietmar of Merseburg, *Chronicon* 3.20; cf. Gay, *L'Italie*, 328–330; Loud, "Southern Italy," 643.
23. Thietmar of Merseburg, *Chronicon* 3.20–23; in detail, Panagopoulou, Θεο φανώ, 118–134; in general, Kreutz, *Normans*, 122–123; Lambakis et al., Στρατεύματα, 402–405; Chiarelli, *History*, 116–117. Al-Athir, *Annales*, 300–301, is wrong that Otto invaded Sicily.
24. Falkenhausen, *Dominazione*, 183–184; Kreutz, *Normans*, 118–119.
25. *PmbZ* 23632; Falkenhausen, *Untersuchungen*, 168–169.
26. Vlysidou, "Πολιτική," 122.
27. Liudprand, *Embassy* 18 (referring to the emperor Phokas).
28. Toumanoff, "Armenia," 614; for genealogy, see Toumanoff, "Bagratids," esp. 6–7. Martin-Hisard, "Constantinople," 428–465 for Romano-Iberian relations.
29. *PmbZ* 21432.

30. *Georgian Chronicles* 274–275; Toumanoff, "Armenia," 617–618; for the adoption scheme, see Rapp, *Imagining History*, 548–549.

31. Stepʿanos of Taron 3.15; *Life of Ioane and Epʾtʾime* 11 (91); Forsyth, *Chronicle*, 388–392; Holmes, *Basil,* 320 n. 39; *PmbZ* 21432 (72 n. 18).

32. Kennedy, *Prophet*, 210–247; for ʿAdud al-Dawla, Donohue, *Buwayhid Dynasty*, 65–86.

33. Kennedy, *Prophet*, 222.

34. Miskawayh, *Experiences*, 419–430; Yahya II:398–399; Canard, *Histoire*, 561–571; Forsyth, *Chronicle*, 315–316, 394, 449.

35. Yahya II:398; Canard, *Histoire*, 674–681; Forsyth, *Chronicle*, 395–399.

36. Miskawayh, *Experiences*, 436; al-Rudhrawari, *Continuation*, 7–8; Yahya II:399–401; Skylitzes 327.

37. Yahya II:400–401; Skylitzes 327; Forsyth, *Chronicle*, 400–416; Farag, *Byzantium*, 79–99.

38. Embedded in al-Rudhrawari, *Continuation*, 23–34, previously published by Amedroz, "Embassy"; date: Forsyth, *Chronicle*, 410–411; Beihammer, "Sturz." The report is collaborated by a proclamation made by ʿAdud al-Dawla before any treaty was signed: Bürgel, *Hofkorrespondenz*, 152–156; Farag, *Byzantium*, 95–97.

39. Yahya II:407.

40. Ratification: al-Rudhrawari, *Continuation*, 39; Ouranos: Skylitzes 327; Yahya II:401, 420–421 (possibly a prior embassy: *PmbZ* 25617); nonimplementation: Forsyth, *Chronicle*, 411–416; Farag, *Byzantium*, 122–125.

41. Yahya II:412–413.

42. Yahya II:413; al-Qalanisi in Canard, "Sources arabes," 296–297; Canard, *Histoire*, 681–686, 849–851; Forsyth, *Chronicle*, 419.

43. Miotto, Ανταγωνισμός, 78–80.

44. Yahya II:415–418; Forsyth, *Chronicle*, 421–423; Farag, *Byzantium*, 185–187.

45. Forsyth, *Chronicle*, 420, oddly does not link this with the clashes of 985–986.

46. Yahya II:417.

47. Yahya II:417, rightly preferred, e.g., by Brokkaar, "Basil," 232; Skylitzes 335, dates it vaguely between 979 and 987; Psellos 1.19–21 wrongly places it between the defeat of Phokas and Skleros in 989, but his moral drama took liberties: he wanted to associate the emancipated Basil with total control.

48. Svoronos, *Novelles*, 214 (text); McGeer, *Legislation*, 128–130 (tr.). Psellos 1.20 refers to this.

49. Lambakis et al., Στρατεύματα, 405.

50. *PmbZ* 24531.

51. Lauxtermann, "Geometres," 357, 367–371, on Lakapenos: 373–378.

52. Skylitzes 330; Holmes, *Basil,* 103, 402, especially 489–491. Western sources refer to a Bulgarian embassy to Otto I in 973, though we do not know who sent it: Božilov and Gjuzelev, *Istorija*, 314. Leon 10.8 says that before 986

Samuil had been harassing "Macedonia," which may just refer to the lands already under his control (but which Romans regarded as Roman, so just by ruling them Samuil was unjust). Kekaumenos 73 refers to unsuccessful attacks against Larissa (Thessaly) in 976–983, but he wants to make his grandfather, the governor, look good. Under 986–987, before his account of Basil's attack of 986, Step'anos of Taron 3.22 tells a romantic tale in which Basil offers the hand of his sister Anna to one of the Kometopouloi in exchange for peace. They refuse the offer when they realize that the girl is an imposter and kill the bishop of Sebasteia, who brought her. I do not believe this story. It would have been mentioned in other sources; also princesses were not sent along with marriage offers, most of which were rejected anyway.

53. Leon 10.8; Skylitzes 330–331; Yahya II:419; Step'anos of Taron 3.23 (seeing Armenians everywhere, here saving the emperor).

54. Holmes, *Basil*, 225–228.

55. Skylitzes 330; starvation: Kekaumenos 73. Skylitzes says that the Romans recovered Preslav in 1000/1 (343–344), so 986 is regarded as its likely loss. Frankopan, "Workings," 87–89, questions the loss of Preslav but overlooks this dated passage.

56. Skylitzes 329 (an addition); Seibt, "Untersuchungen," 90–94; *PmbZ* 26983 (703).

57. Stephenson, *Legend*, 15–17; Holmes, *Basil*, 250–251, 493; Geometres, *Poems*, 296; Poppe, "Background," 217; in general, Fine, *Balkans*, 193.

58. Psellos 1.11–12; Skylitzes 332–334; Holmes, *Basil*, 276–278, 289, 290 n. 104; Beihammer, "Sturz," 33–34. Phokas' revolt also produced propaganda, e.g., the epitaph for Nikephoros by Ioannes of Melitene, in Skylitzes 282–283, on which see Lauxtermann, *Poetry*, 233–236; see also the tale of Nikephoros' treatment of the Bulgarian ambassadors (p. 55 above). A reconstruction of this war is in Forsyth, *Chronicle*, 423–462.

59. Al-Rudhrawari, *Continuation*, 116–117; Yahya II:419 dates and confirms the Arab version.

60. Al-Rudhrawari, *Continuation*, 115–116; al-Qalqashandi (handbook of diplomacy): Canard, "Deux documents," 60 and 65–68 (tr.); also Farag, *Byzantium*, 127–135.

61. Step'anos of Taron 3.24; Yahya II:420–421; al-Rudhrawari, *Continuation*, 117; for Bad, Ripper, *Marwaniden*, 109–116, 121–125.

62. Yahya II:420–421; Ziyad: al-Rudhrawari, *Continuation*, 135. Buyid support is established by correspondence in 989–900: Canard, "Deux documents," 63.

63. Yahya II:421; Skylitzes 332; dates: Forsyth, *Chronicle*, 429–432.

64. Al-Rudhrawari, *Continuation*, 117–118; Step'anos of Taron 3.25 (allies); Yahya II:421–423; Psellos 1.12; Skylitzes 334–336 (insurance).

65. Blockade: *Synopsis of the Miracles of Eugenios* 101–112, written in the fourteenth century by Ioannes Lazaropoulos; for this text, see Holmes, *Basil*, 97–99. I am skeptical about its account of the fighting near Trebizond.

66. Poppe, "Background"; Raffensperger, *Reimagining Europe*, 159–163. The better sources are Yahya II:423; Step'anos of Taron 3.43; al-Rudhrawari, *Continuation*, 118–119; cf. Skylitzes 336, who does not mention the conversion; cf. Kaldellis, *Ethnography*, 39–43, 131, 136. The most problematic is the *Russian Primary Chronicle* 96–119, with mostly legends. See Panagopoulou, Γάμοι, 172–178 for the embassies. For Hugh's request for Anna, see ibid. 170–172. "Unheard of": Liudprand, *Embassy* 15.

67. *Russian Primary Chronicle* 93; cf. Blöndal, *Varangians*, 42–43.

68. Leon 10.9; Yahya II:424; Step'anos of Taron 3.25; Psellos 1.13; Skylitzes 336.

69. Stethatos, *Life of Symeon the New Theologian* 95.

70. *PmbZ* 22428.

71. Yahya II:424–425.

72. Leon 10.9; Yahya II:425–426; Psellos 1.14–18; Skylitzes 337–338. Antioch: Yahya II:427–428.

73. Yahya II:426–427, 430–431; Psellos 1.23–29 (exaggerates this phase); Skylitzes 338–339. For Skleros' correspondence with Baghdad, see Canard, "Deux documents," 62–64 and 68–69.

74. Forsyth, *Chronicle*, 434; Farag, *Byzantium*, 236.

75. Respectively, Poppe, "Background" (202 for the date), and Raffensperger, *Reimagining Europe*, 172–173.

76. *Fornicator*: Thietmar of Merseburg, *Chronicon* 7.72; Cherson: *Russian Primary Chronicle* 111–113; retinue: Panagopoulou, Γάμοι, 175–176.

77. Blöndal, *Varangians*, 42–46.

78. *Georgian Chronicles* 276–277, covering up a genuine conflict (and hiding Roman involvement); Step'anos of Taron 3.28; Forsyth, *Chronicle*, 460–461 n. 141; Toumanoff, "Armenia," 618.

79. Yahya II:429–430; Step'anos of Taron 3.43; Skylitzes 339; Forsyth, *Chronicle*, 465–470, 517–518; for minor operations against Armenians and Georgians who supported Phokas, see ibid. 464–465 (posing insoluble prosopographical problems); Rapp, *Imagining History*, 546.

80. Yahya II:428.

81. Yahya II:430; Leon 10.10, dated securely to 989.

5 *"Guarding the Children of New Rome"*

1. Leon 10.10; Yahya II:428–429; Skylitzes 331–332. The lament is published among the works of Psellos, *Oratoria minora*, 35; Mango, "Collapse."

2. Step'anos of Taron 3.27; Maranci, "Trdat." The contemporary Armenian poet Grigor of Narek mentions the restoration, not Trdat: Mahé, "Basile," 560–561.

3. Psellos 1.22, 1.29; Kaldellis, *Argument*; no literary interests: Lauxtermann, "Byzantine Poetry."

4. Psellos 1.32–34.

5. Psellos, *Orationes panegyricae* 2.123–132 (23).

6. Psellos 1.35–36.

7. Yahya II:435; al-Rudhrawari, *Continuation*, 221–225; Canard, *Histoire*, 687–690; Forsyth, *Chronicle*, 481–483; Farag, *Byzantium*, 190–191; for Bakjur's career, see Bikhazi, *Hamdanid*, 991–992 n. 75.

8. For this report, cf. Forsyth, *Chronicle*, 270, 485, with Bikhazi, *Hamdanid*, 976, 988 n. 70; Miotto, *Ανταγωνισμός*, 115.

9. Yahya II:438–439; al-Rudhrawari, *Continuation*, 229–231; Forsyth, *Chronicle*, 124–136, 486–499; Bianquis, *Damas*, 193–201; Farag, *Byzantium*, 239–253; Miotto, *Ανταγωνισμός*, 115–119; cf. Canard, *Histoire*, 694–705, 855–858. There remain insoluble problems, stemming from the sources' disagreement.

10. Lev, "Navy," 241.

11. Yahya II:440–441.

12. Lev, "Navy," 241.

13. Yahya II:442–443; al-Rudhrawari, *Continuation*, 232–233.

14. Al-Rudhrawari, *Continuation*, 199.

15. Yahya II:443–444.

16. Forsyth, *Chronicle*, 496–497; Lev, "Navy," 242; Brett, *Fatimids*, 418–421; Miotto, *Ανταγωνισμός*, 119–120.

17. Yahya II:449–450.

18. Yahya II:451–452, 454–455; Farag, *Byzantium*, 255–256; Lev, "Navy," 242–243.

19. Miotto, *Ανταγωνισμός*, 75–76. For Tyre, see below.

20. Stepʿanos of Taron 3.37; Yahya II:455–456; al-Rudhrawari, *Continuation*, 238–241; ibn al-Qalanisi in Canard, "Sources arabes," 297–300 (Tyre and Apameia).

21. Al-Rudhrawari, *Continuation*, 241–243.

22. Yahya II:460–461.

23. Yahya II:457–460; Apameia: Stepʿanos of Taron 3.42; Forsyth, *Chronicle*, 529 n. 100.

24. Walker, *Caliph*, 228 (tr.).

25. Yahya II:460–462; al-Rudhrawari, *Continuation*, 243.

26. Forsyth, *Chronicle*, 514.

27. Ibid. 468–472. Farag, *Byzantium*, 146, argues that the 992 Roman attack on Mantzikert and Khliat reported in Arab sources (al-Rudhrawari, *Continuation*, 262) refers to attacks by Davitʿ; this would invalidate Forsyth, *Chronicle*, 478–481; various possibilities in Ripper, *Marwaniden*, 135–136.

28. Route and meetings: Stepʿanos of Taron 3.43; also Yahya II:460 (Ouranos); Smbat, *Bagratids* 53 (from the same source as the addendum to *Georgian Chronicles* 374); Aristakes 1.3–4; Skylitzes 339 (chronologically confused); Forsyth *Chronicle*, 471–478; Rapp, *Imagining History*, 546–551; for Mumahhid al-Dawla, see Rippert, *Marwaniden*, 139–141. Did Theodosioupolis became its own theme or was it incorporated into the theme or *doukaton* of Iberia? See Holmes, *Basil*, 360–363; Krsmanović, *Province*,

181–182; Leveniotis, *Κατάρρευση*, 65–67. Chauzizion: Oikonomides, "L'organisation," 293; Holmes, "Eastern Frontier," 97.

29. Grierson, *Catalogue*, v. 3.2, 606.

30. New sees: Greenwood, "Armenian Neighbours," 359; Arutjunova-Fidanjan, "Aspects," 312; population: ibid. 314–315; Leveniotis, *Κατάρρευση*, 62–64; for religious tensions, see Garsoïan, "Integration," 66–86.

31. Mahé, "Basile," 536, and 568–569 for the theological issues; tr. from Greenwood, "Armenian Neighbours," 359; for the positive image of Basil in Armenian literature, see Garsoïan, "Integration," 83–84.

32. Stepʿanos of Taron 3.44; Yahya II:460 (misdated, it seems).

33. Skylitzes 378.

34. Al-Rudhrawari, *Continuation*, 119; cf. 229, 232; Attaleiates 229; Yahya II:444; cf. 431; Skylitzes 348.

35. Holmes, *Basil*. Strässle, *Krieg*, is a bloated "modern" account of the war, with long digressions into military theory and practice; it has a useful survey of forts at 162–197.

36. Skylitzes 339 and 341 (Taronites); Yahya II:430–431; Stepʿanos of Taron 3.33.

37. E.g., *PmbZ* 22428; Krsmanović, *Province*, 149–150.

38. Krsmanović, *Province*, 150–152.

39. Al-Rudhrawari, *Continuation*, 229, 232; Yahya I:439.

40. Skylitzes 346 dates this after 1002, after the emperor took Vidin. But Yahya dates Roman's death to 997 (see below), so he cannot have been captured after 1002. Skylitzes was especially confused about the career of tsar Roman. Specifically, he says that in 1002/3—he gives a definite indiction date—Basil attacked Vidin while Samuil made a swift attack on Adrianople. The emperor then set out to return to Constantinople, arrived at Skopje, defeated Samuil at the Axios river, and received the surrender of Skopje by tsar Roman. I propose that there is a seam in this account between Vidin-Adrianople and Skopje-Axios: Skylitzes, as so often for this reign, has stitched together material from different years. Vidin-Adrianople took place in 1002/3, as dated, but the rest did not. Skopje is not on the return from Vidin to Constantinople, which is where Skylitzes explicitly says Basil was going. Operations by Skopje fit the first stage of the war, i.e., 991–994, which our sources place in "Macedonia," likely in 993–994 after the capture of Beroia. It was then that Aleppan envoys found Basil "in the heart of Bulgarian territory." Another problem is that the defeat of Samuil at the Axios is a doublet of his defeat at the Spercheios (see below). But this affects any dating. Past discussions of this whole issue: *PmbZ* 26848; V. Zlatarski in Fine, *Balkans*, 190, arguing for 991; Adontz, *Études*, 368–371, suspected Skylitzes' account of the Vidin-Skopje campaign.

41. Skylitzes 347; Stepʿanos of Taron 3.34. His capture can be dated from his release (Skylitzes 357) and the appointment of Ouranos.

42. Krsmanović, *Province*, 153–154; Cheynet, *Aristocracy*, VIII, 87.

43. Skylitzes 341–342, 364 (bones); Yahya II:446 (in ca. 996/7); Strässle, "Raum"; the victory is likely alluded to in the congratulatory letter that Leon of Synada (*Letters* 13) sent to Ouranos from Italy (see commentary, 102). This attack on the Peloponnese is probably the one in the *Life of Nikon* 40: the governor of the Peloponnese, Basileios Apokaukos (*PmbZ* 21006), was terrified to face Samuil.

44. Yahya II:446–447. Later Latin and Slavonic sources, starting ca. 1200, refer to Samuil as tsar or *imperator*, and some Greek sources call him *basileus* of Bulgaria (though this was not always a technical term). Yahya provides the best proof for Samuil's imperial title. The Bitola inscription of Samuil's nephew and successor Ivan Vladislav (1015–1018) calls both men emperors, using the technical Bulgarian terms (although the section on Samuil is partially reconstructed): Zaimov, *Bitolski nadpis* (I thank Ian Mladjov for his help). There is also the problem of Dyrrachion. Skylitzes 342–343, 363 says that Samuil married the captured Asotios Taronites to his daughter Miroslava and sent him to Dyrrachion, but Asotios persuaded his new wife to defect. The emperor sent Eustathios Daphnomeles to receive the town, but this ending to the story may belong to a later phase of the war, twenty years later in fact, when we know that Daphnomeles was active and (again?) appointed to Dyrrachion. See Holmes, *Basil*, 42, 104–105, 497–498; Fine, *Balkans*, 193–195 (a doublet of this story is in the chronicle of the priest of Dioclea). Dyrrachion may have changed hands many times during the war. The *Chronicle of Lupus Protospatharius* says that it returned to the emperor in 1004/5.

45. Skylitzes 343–345; Holmes, *Basil*, 105–109, 495–497 (at least one antedates 997). The *PmbZ* wants to date most of these episodes to 1001, assuming that the narrative is chronological. The traitor Malakenos is mentioned in the *Life of Nikon* 43. It has been proposed that one of Nikon's charges was to deal with potential Bulgarian sympathizers in the area: Anagnostakis, "Μονεμβασία-Λακεδαίμων," 128–129. For Samuil's military nobility, see Nikolov, "Aristocracy."

46. *PmbZ* 21386, puts this too in 1001.

47. Skylitzes 343–344; Holmes, *Basil*, 496.

48. Skylitzes 346; cf. Yahya II:461–462: after the treaty with the Fatimids, Basil went back to conquer and destroy Bulgaria.

49. The numismatic evidence for the Byzantine occupation of northeast Bulgaria is presented by Stephenson, *Legend*, 20; the sigillographic: Frankopan, "Workings."

50. Venice: Holmes, *Basil*, 49, 493; Serbs: Ostrogorsky, "Ambassade Serbe."

51. Holmes, *Basil*, 461–475.

52. Psellos 1.28; cf. Kekaumenos 82.

53. Yahya III:461 (on 1021).

54. Psellos 1.30.

55. Sifonas, "Basile"; Cheynet, *Pouvoir*, 329–336.

56. Holmes, "Elites," 50–51 n. 49; *Basil*, 465–466.

57. Cf. Bell, *Conflict*, for the sixth century.

58. Bobos: Holmes, *Basil*, 107–109; for the confiscations (called "massive") and the formation of imperial *episkepseis*, see Cheynet, *Aristocracy*, VIII, 77–78.

59. Skylitzes 340.

60. Svoronos, *Novelles*, 200–217 (text); and McGeer, *Legislation*, 114–132 (tr.). Readers should distinguish between the original version and the modified (in some places enhanced) version of the later eleventh century.

61. Kaplan, *Hommes*, 193, 440–441, for later uses of it.

62. Motivation: *Novel* of 996, pr. 2; investigated and discovered: pr. 1; travels: pr. 2 and 4; imperial tribunal: 2.1; petitions: 3.1, 6.1; demolition: pr. 4 (version 2 gives his name as Philokales).

63. Kelly, *Ruling*.

64. Augustus: *Novel* of 996, 4.1; fisc officials: 4.2; Lakapenos: 6.1.

65. Holmes, "Elites," 61, though I do not see Lakapenos as central to the law, which looked to the future.

66. Skylitzes 347, 365; Holmes, *Basil*, 535–536, and 189 n. 44 for Sergios' dates; communal liability: Górecki, "*Strateia*," 166; Lefort, "Economy," 281–283; Kaplan, *Hommes*, 212–214, 440–443.

67. Magdalino, "Preface," xiii; cf. Laiou, *Mariage*, 24–25, 58; for the *tomos*, see Burgmann, "Sisinnios," esp. 178 for the emperor's involvement.

6 "No One Ever Saw My Spear at Rest"

1. Skylitzes 348.

2. Stephenson, *Frontier*, 69–77, and *Legend*, 21–25; but see Holmes, *Basil*, 498–499. Matthew of Edessa has two dated entries on the Bulgarian war: 1.43 (= 1006/7) linked to the Easter controversy, which Yahya II:481–483, puts in that year too (without mentioning Bulgaria); and 1.46 (= 1011/2) when Basil conquers Bulgaria for good. No trust can be placed in these entries, or in the tales of the *Chronicle of the Priest of Dioclea (Duklja)*: Bujan, "Chronique"; Zivković, *Gesta Regum*, v. 1.

3. E.g., the renowned Ibatzes in Skylitzes 354; and the wall of Roupenios (364), built in the meantime.

4. Skylitzes 348–349; Kekaumenos 19 gives the same figure, but does not mention the blinding; Attaleiates 230.

5. Moutsopoulos, "Le tombeau."

6. Stephenson, *Frontier*, 72; Holmes, *Basil*, 154–155; at 211–212 she questions some dates.

7. Skylitzes 350–351; Attaleiates 230 calls the *doux* Nikephoros and has him die at the battle of Kleidion; the two historians agree that his son, the father of the later emperor, was named Michael, but Attaleiates transfers to him the

glory for the defeat of the Bulgarians at Thessalonike (230–234). It is not clear who is right. These were possibly different men.

8. Skylitzes 345.

9. Skylitzes 353–354; Yahya III:407. The interpolations in Skylitzes are usually ascribed to Michael, bishop of Diabolis in the early twelfth century, who had access to information about western Balkan and Bulgarian affairs; but see now Treadgold, *Middle Byzantine Historians*, 252–253. Plots against Gavril Radomir and Ivan Vladislav: *Chronicle of the Priest of Dioclea (Duklja)* 36, but we cannot accept its fanciful versions.

10. Skylitzes 355–356; Longos: Strässle, *Krieg*, 178; Krakras: Nikolov, "Aristocracy," 148–149.

11. Skylitzes 357–360 (the treasure was 100 *kentenaria*, i.e., 720,000 *nomismata*).

12. Skylitzes 364–365; Athens: Kaldellis, *Parthenon*, 81–91.

13. Skylitzes 365–366; he is *PmbZ* 24045 (also known as Philomas); Stephenson, *Legend*, 39 n. 26.

14. *Chronicle of the Priest of Dioclea (Duklja)* 38.

15. Krsmanović, *Province*, 196–197; Madgearu, *Organization*, 63–64.

16. Krsmanović, *Province*, 185–205; Kühn, *Armee*, 223–234; for Paristrion, see Stephenson, "Balkan Frontier," 114–115; for a table, see Strässle, *Krieg*, 220–221. Tzimiskes' *doukaton* of Mesopotamia of the West seems to have lapsed. For the walls, churches, and garrison at Sirmium and nearby sites, see Stephenson, *Frontier*, 65–66.

17. Cf. Ahrweiler, "Recherches," 48–49, 78–80.

18. Romans and Bulgarians: Kaldellis, *Ethnography*, 126–139; Nikolaou and Tsiknakis, eds., Βυζάντιο και Βούλγαροι.

19. Yahya III:407; Ohrid was apparently left unwalled after its capture: Skylitzes Continuatus 164.

20. Skylitzes Continuatus 162.

21. Skylitzes 412.

22. Ivan: *PmbZ* 23365 (= David?). Stephenson, *Frontier*, 64 claims that the first appointee was Georgios, on the basis of seals, but their publisher, Seibt, dated them to the reign of Tzimiskes.

23. *Sigillia*: Gelzer, "Bistumsverzeichnisse," 42–46; Stephenson, *Frontier*, 75.

24. Wasilewski, "Sirmium-Serbie."

25. Popović, "Fortresses"; Stephenson, *Legend*, 44.

26. For their seals, see Stephenson, *Frontier*, 29, 74–75; *Legend*, 42–44.

27. For surveys, see Forsyth, *Chronicle*, 532–557; Farag, *Byzantium*, 192–204, 264–281 (though I do not share his interpretation of Basil's policies); Felix, *Byzanz*, 48–78.

28. McGeer, "Tradition."

29. Skylitzes 345; Forsyth, *Chronicle*, 593–594 n. 6; Felix, *Byzanz*, 53 n. 29. It is unclear whether this was related to the al-Asfar incident (see below).

30. Yahya II:466–467, and III, 391 (escape); Miotto, Ἀνταγωνισμός, 228–230, for other versions.

31. Yahya III:391–393; conversion: Felix, *Byzanz*, 56 n. 40.

32. Yahya III:399.

33. Yahya III:401–403; for trade generally, see Farag, *Byzantium*, 275–279; citadel: Todt, "Antioch," 180. For the military basis of the embargo, see Ouranos, *Taktika* 65.

34. Yahya III:405.

35. Walker, *Caliph*.

36. Yahya II:506, 519; III: 417–419; *Life of Lazaros* 19–20 (not only the subjects of the caliph but traveling Romans too); Canard, "Destruction"; Forsyth, *Chronicle*, 216; Walker, *Caliph*, 85, 205–214; embassies: Farag, *Byzantium*, 272.

37. Yahya III:461.

38. Yahya III:433; the latter refortified in 1024 by Dalassenos, *doux* of Antioch: ibid. 471.

39. Yahya III:459.

40. Yahya III:473.

41. Yahya III:469; for the dating problems, see the tr., n. 69.

42. Aristakes 1.6. For the lands and their status, see Forsyth, *Chronicle*, 560.

43. Aristakes 2.11–13; Smbat, *Bagratids* 58–59; *Georgian Chronicles* 282–283; Yahya III:461–463.

44. Yahya III:463.

45. Skylitzes 352; Aristakes 1.5–6.

46. Cession: Yahya III:463; Aristakes 3.19; Skylitzes 354–355 (out of sequence); Kekaumenos 81; Matthew of Edessa 1.47–49 (fanciful); Seibt, "Eingliederung"; Holmes, *Basil*, 360–367, 483–484; Leveniotis, Κατάρρευση, 128–145; first Turkish raid: Kafesoğlu and Leiser, "Seljuk Raid"; crown lands: Howard-Johnston, "Crown Lands," 95–96. Yahya's chronology is preferable. Senekʿerim's vassals' lands are listed by Arutjunova-Fidanjan, "Aspects," 312.

47. Ter-Ghewondyan, *Emirates*, 106, 115–116.

48. Aristakes 2.16; Skylitzes 435.

49. *PmbZ* 25675 and 25661 respectively; Holmes, *Basil*, 515–525.

50. Skylitzes 366–367.

51. Yahya III:465.

52. Skylitzes 366–367 (lion); Yahya III:465–469; Aristakes 3.18–20 (I am skeptical that Basil shut himself in a fort in Basean when he learned of the rebellion); *Georgian Chronicles* 283; Matthew of Edessa 1.51 (garbled).

53. Yahya III:467.

54. Yahya III:467–469 (blaming a minister of Giorgi), 483 (release); Aristakes 3.20–4.23; Skylitzes 367 (garbled); Smbat, *Bagratids* 61–63 and *Georgian Chronicles* 283–284 (the same embellishment); a rhetorical account in Attaleiates 234–236.

55. Aristakes 4.25–27; Forsyth, *Chronicle*, 570–572; Felix, *Byzanz*, 137–140; and Holmes, *Basil*, 484. Matthew of Edessa 1.47–48 points to the Seljuks, but too soon.

56. Yahya III:471; Aristakes 5.30; Ter-Ghewondyan, *Emirates*, 105, 115–116; Ripper, *Marwaniden*, 37–38.

57. Surveys in Falkenhausen, "Two Empires"; Holmes, *Basil*, 429–447; basic information on administration and sources in Falkenhausen, *Untersuchungen*, esp. 83–87, 170–191.

58. Falkenhausen, "Two Empires," 143–144; Holmes, *Basil*, 437.

59. The text survives in a later version: Pozza and Ravegnani, *Trattati*, 21–25; Nicol, *Byzantium*, 40–42.

60. Ibn Hawqal, *Configuration*, 8, 61; Magyar factor: Leyser, *Germany*, 103.

61. Konstantinos VII, *De administrando imperio* 28.

62. Bari: Lambakis et al., *Στρατεύματα*, 409–410; marriage: Nicol, *Byzantium*, 45–46; Panagopoulou, *Γάμοι*, 184–188. The chronology of Skylitzes 343, is garbled. Romanos I: Yahya III:485.

63. Leon of Synada, esp. *Letters* 1, 6 (quotation), 8–11. Philagathos is *PmbZ* 23486.

64. Panagopoulou, *Γάμοι*, 178–184; Todt, "Frau," 141–142.

65. Kreutz, *Normans*, 151.

66. Lambakis et al., *Στρατεύματα*, 406–407; Falkenhausen, "Two Empires," 152–153.

67. *PmbZ* 25033; Martin, *Pouille*, 520.

68. Guillou, *Studies*, VIII; events in Lambakis et al., *Στρατεύματα*, 411–415; also *PmbZ* 21090; Falkenhausen, "Two Empires," 147; cf. Holmes, *Basil*, 190.

69. Lambakis et al., *Στρατεύματα*, 415–419; Normans: Joranson, "Inception"; France, "Occasion."

70. Adémar, *Chronicle* 3.55.

71. Boioannes: Lambakis et al., *Στρατεύματα*, 419–424; Falkenhausen, "Two Empires," 147–150; and *PmbZ* 21094. Up to Rome: Skylitzes 426 (a flashback). New towns: Martin, *Pouille*, 258–264.

72. See previous note and Skylitzes 368; al-Athir, *Annales*, 351. Adriatic: Fine, *Balkans*, 274–279.

73. Yahya III:480–483; Skylitzes 369; Schreiner, *Kleinchroniken*, v. 1, 158; *Necrologium*, tr. and discussed in Grierson, "Tombs," 58. For an attempt in the 1930s to identify his sarcophagus, see Stephenson, *Legend*, 126–128.

74. Lauxtermann, *Poetry*, 236–238 (tr. modified).

75. Stephenson, *Legend*, 92.

76. Psellos 1.36, 7.76 (collections of his sayings circulated in 1059).

77. Yahya III:483.

78. Psellos 1.29–30; in general, see Crostini, "Basil." Leon: Sykoutris, "Λέοντος." Sikeliotes, *Commentary on Hermogenes' Peri Ideon*, p. 447.

79. Stephenson, *Legend*, 51–62.

80. Lakonia in the *Life of Nikon*; Mt. Athos in the *Life of Ioane and Ep't'ime* and the *Lives of Athanasios of Athos*; Asia Minor (especially Ephesos and Magnesia) in Gregorios the Cellarer's *Life of Lazaros*; Constantinople in Stethatos' *Life of Saint Symeon the New Theologian*.

81. Yahya III:483.

82. Psellos 1.31. A modern critique is that hoarding starved the economy, but this overlooks the fiscal constraints of premodern states (which could not borrow from banks), fails to prove an economic slowdown or drag, and fails to explain how imperial spending might have stimulated structural growth in the economy.

General Considerations

1. Shepard, "Expansionism," 74.

2. E.g., Garsoïan, "Annexation." *Contra*: Forsyth, *Chronicle*, 573–576.

3. Kekaumenos 89–90.

4. Kennedy, "Antioch," 190–191; Todt, "Antioch," 182–186.

5. Haldon, "Service," 53, for the military context; in general, Kaldellis, *Hellenism*, chap. 2, esp. for the Greeks; the topic is little studied: Laiou, "Foreigner."

6. Haldon, "State Formation," 1113.

7. Howard-Johnston, "Crown Lands," 88–94; Holmes, *Basil*, 373–375. Little stress can be placed on the distinction between tax and tribute in literary sources.

8. Cheynet, *Sceaux*, 22–23. Holmes, "'How the East'," 48–50, presents Kulayb and ʿUbayd Allah as the norm, but they were exceptional.

9. Todt, "Antioch," 183–185; Cheynet, "Antioch."

10. Martin, "Thèmes italiens," 538.

11. Holmes, "Eastern Frontier"; Krsmanović, *Province*.

12. Ouranos, *Taktika* 57.1, 59.1, 65.3–12; McGeer, "Tradition." *Campaign Organization* assumes the same.

13. Skylitzes 367–368.

14. *Campaign Organization* 29.

15. It is mentioned in *Campaign Organization* 1.100, 1.161, which cannot be dated.

16. Haldon, "Service," 51; Howard-Johnston, "Crown Lands."

17. I plan to present this evidence in a separate study.

18. Psellos book 1, 5.22, 7.52, 7.76; Attaleiates 222–229; Bryennios 1.10.

7 "Intrigues of the Women's Quarters"

1. Psellos 1.16; Yahya II:425; Stepʿanos of Taron 3.26; Farag, "Aleppo," 53.

2. Yahya III:481; Aristakes 4.27–28; Holmes, *Basil*, 522–524.

3. Greek sources: Johnson, "Constantine VIII"; Lilie, "Realität"; a survey in Todt, "Herrscher."

4. Yahya III:483; Matthew of Edessa 1.56.

5. Yahya III:483; Skylitzes 373, 375.

6. Skylitzes 370–373 for Konstantinos' appointments.

7. Stephenson, *Frontier*, 123–125, and "Balkan Frontier," 122–126; Holmes, *Basil*, 425–427.

8. Balsamon, *Commentaries*, v. 3, 97, 103 (Gangra canon 3).

9. Skylitzes 371–372; Aristakes 5.29–30; Yahya III:483.

10. Respectively: Yahya III:485, and Smbat, *Bagratids* 66–69; *Georgian Chronicles* 286–287. Aristakes 5.30–31, complicates the story.

11. Yahya III:485–487; Psellos 2.9–10; Skylitzes 373–374; Laiou, "Marriages," 167–169.

12. Todt, "Herrscher," 102–103.

13. Psellos 2.3, 7.52–53.

14. *PmbZ* 26835.

15. Kaldellis, *Argument*, chap. 2.

16. Psellos 3.6, 7.53; Skylitzes 375–376.

17. Yahya III:489; *Georgian Chronicles* 287–288; Skylitzes 377.

18. Skylitzes 385; Vannier, *Familles*, 49.

19. Skylitzes 376–377, 384.

20. Grumel and Darrouzès, *Regestes*, nos. 838–840; Yahya III:489–491; Aristakes 6.32–33; Michael the Syrian III:140–145; Dagron, "Minorités," 199–204; Benner, *Kirche*, 80–91; Vest, *Geschichte*, 1196–1252. Ioannes of Melitene is praised in Psellos, *Orationes funebres* 5. Armenians: Garsoïan, "Integration," 79 n. 107.

21. Psellos 3.7; Yahya III:495; Skylitzes 379.

22. For the campaign, see Yahya III:493–503; Skylitzes 377–382; Psellos 3.7–11; Matthew of Edessa 1.57; also Zakkar, *Emirate*, 105–126; Felix, *Byzanz*, 81–91.

23. Skylitzes 381–382.

24. Yahya III:501, 507–509, Skylitzes 384–385.

25. Yahya III:501–515; Skylitzes 379, 382–383; Felix, *Byzanz*, 92–96.

26. For the problems of al-Hassan's visits to Constantinople, see Felix, *Byzanz*, 101 n. 174.

27. Matthew of Edessa 1.58–59; Skylitzes 387; Yahya III:515–519; Aristakes 7.34–36; Felix, *Byzanz*, 143–146; Ripper, *Marwaniden*, 297–304.

28. Cappel, "Response," 129.

29. Skylitzes 385; Psellos 7B.10.

30. Skylitzes 384; Psellos 3.12–16; Dark, "Byzantine Church."

31. Skylitzes 389.

32. Skylitzes 385–386; Matthew of Edessa 1.60.

33. Skylitzes 388.

34. Yahya III:521–535; Felix, *Byzanz*, 98–103.

35. Skylitzes 386–387 (probably a doublet, and Nauplion may be Naupaktos).

36. Yahya III:529–531.

37. Skylitzes 388.

38. Ter-Ghewondyan, *Emirates*, 105, 115–117; Ripper, *Marwaniden*, 37–39.

39. Konstantinos VII, *De administrando imperio* 44.125–128.

40. Skylitzes 389; Seibt, "Byzantine Thema."

41. Psellos 3.17–25; Skylitzes 389–391.

42. Christophoros Mytilenaios, *Poem* 8.32.

43. Laiou, "Marriages," 169–171.

44. Skylitzes 390–393; Psellos 4.1–5.

45. See the striking formulations in Aristakes 9.37; Kekaumenos 83.

46. Skylitzes 395; Psellos 4.9, 4.16, 4.18; Aristakes 9.38; cf. Magdalino, "Paphlagonians."

47. Psellos 4.12–14.

48. Skylitzes 393–394.

49. Ibid. 395–397; Psellos 4.22, 6.12.

50. Skylitzes 397–398; Psellos 4.17, 20–25, 31–37; Aristakes 9.38.

51. Skylitzes 404.

52. Aristakes 9.38–39; Skylitzes 402, 408 (Thessalonike); 396–397 (Myra), 408 (Ephesos); archbishop Theophanes: Kedrenos v. 1, 518–519.

53. Christophoros Mytilenaios, *Poem* 18.

54. Skylitzes 396, 403; Helene: Vannier, *Familles*, 48.

55. *Georgian Chronicles* 290–291.

56. Skylitzes 397, 399–400, 403–404; Felix, *Byzanz*, 148–152; Ripper, *Marwaniden*, 151–153.

57. Felix, *Byzanz*, 107.

58. Skylitzes 397, 399; Stephenson, *Frontier*, 81–83; Madgearu, *Organization*, 116–122.

59. Skylitzes 408; Kekaumenos 90; Stephenson, *Frontier*, 125–130.

60. Skylitzes 397–399 (probably one episode in triplicate).

61. Blöndal, *Varangians*, 59–60.

62. Harvey, *Expansion*; Laiou and Morrisson, *Economy*.

63. Feliz, *Byzanz*, 200–202; Lambakis et al., *Στρατεύματα*, 424–425.

64. Skylitzes 398, 400–401; Shepard, "Sicilian Expedition"; Felix, *Byzanz*, 205–207; Lambakis et al., *Στρατεύματα*, 426–427; Chiarelli, *History*, 122–125.

65. Felix, *Byzanz*, 208–209 n. 64; Lambakis et al., *Στρατεύματα*, 428. Harald: Kekaumenos 81; Blöndal, *Varangians*, 65–71. In Skylitzes 406, *tagma* can refer generically to any unit.

66. Skylitzes 403, 405–407; Attaleiates 8–9; Felix, *Byzanz*, 207–212; Lambakis et al., *Στρατεύματα*, 428–431; Chiarelli, *History*, 126; Troina: Odorico, "Backgammon."

67. Kekaumenos 81.

68. Skylitzes 409–411; Psellos 4.39–40; Krsmanović, *Province*, 203–205.

69. Skylitzes 411–412; Attaleiates 9; Demetrias: Kekaumenos 31. Another *strategos* defeated in *Life of Lazaros* 229.
70. Skylitzes 412.
71. Nikolaou and Tsiknakis, eds., *Βυζάντιο*; for Byzantine views, see Kaldellis, *Ethnography*, 126–139.
72. Additions to the *Synodikon*, in Petkov, *Voices*, 254.
73. Biliarsky, "St. Peter," 175, 184; milk and honey: the eleventh-century *Bulgarian Apocryphal Chronicle* in Petkov, *Voices*, 196.
74. Skylitzes 412–413; Psellos 4.42–50; Attaleiates 9–10; Alusian at Thessalonike: Kekaumenos 42; Varangians: ibid. 81; Keroularios' plot: Psellos, *Orationes funebres* 1.11.
75. Fine, *Balkans*, 205.
76. Psellos 4.53–54.
77. I have adjudicated among Skylitzes 416–421; Psellos, book 5; Attaleiates 10–17; Zonaras 17.18; cf. *Life of Lazaros* 102. Schreiner, *Kleinchroniken*, v. 1, 159, 166, dates the accession to December 11, but I do not trust it.
78. Blöndal, *Varangians*, 93–94.
79. Doxapatres, *Commentaries*, 508–509; Christophoros Mytilenaios, *Poem* 52; Krallis, "Action," for Attaleiates.

8 *"No Less Laws than Arms"*

1. Skylitzes 422; expenses: Psellos 6.5, 6.7.
2. Psellos 6.10–21; *Orationes funebres* 1.17; Skylitzes 422–423.
3. Skylitzes 423; Psellos 6.29–30.
4. Psellos, *Orationes panegyricae* 2.663–669.
5. Hondridou, *Μονομάχος*, 326–334, 339–361.
6. Psellos 6.50–65; for Skleraina, see Spadaro, *Sclerenam*, 17–47; expenses: Oikonomides, "St. George."
7. Churchill, *Annales*, 276–279, 301, based on the *Annales Barenses* and the *Annales* of Lupus Prostospatharius; Lambakis et al., *Στρατεύματα*, 432–433; for Dokeianos versus Maniakes in western sources, see Shepard, "Sicilian Expedition," 152. The Normans in southern Italy: Loud, *Robert*.
8. Skylitzes 426–427 (wrong about Bari); Churchill, *Annales*, 279–288, 301–302; Lambakis et al., *Στρατεύματα*, 433–437.
9. Loud, *Robert*, 93.
10. Skleros: Skylitzes 427–428, hinted in Attaleiates 18; Psellos 6.79–82; Churchill, *Annales*, 288–298 (but the pardon may not have been for Maniakes); Lambakis et al., *Στρατεύματα*, 437–440; double agent: Gay, *L'Italie*, 456.
11. Skylitzes 424–425, 475; Kekaumenos 29; the *Chronicle of the Priest of Dioclea (Duklja)* 38, is fanciful; Fine, *Balkans*, 202–203, 206–207; Stephenson, *Frontier*, 133–135; *katepano*: Cheynet, *Aristocracy*, XI, 192.

12. Psellos 6.83–88, *Orationes panegyricae* 2.723–724; Skylitzes 428; Attaleiates 18–20.

13. Kaldellis, "Discontinuous History."

14. Skylitzes 429–430; Attaleiates 20.

15. Skylitzes 430–433; Psellos 6.90–95; Attaleiates 20–21; *Russian Primary Chronicle* 138.

16. Shepard, "Russians" (176–178 for Harald).

17. Madgearu, *Organization*, 115.

18. Panagopoulou, Γάμοι, 195–196.

19. Psellos 6.96–98.

20. Mauropous, *Poems* 63–64; Anastasi, "Epigrammi."

21. Skylitzes 434.

22. Psellos 6.177–179, 7.19, 7.66; *Orationes funebres* 2; Criscuolo, "πολιτικὸς ἀνήρ."

23. Psellos, *Orationes funebres* 3.10; Attaleiates 21; Konstantinos IX, *Novel*; for reconstructions, see Wolska-Conus, "Écoles" and "L'école"; Lemerle, *Études*, 183–229; Hondridou, Μονομάχος, 155–253; Gkoutzioukostas, Ἀπονομή, 202–216. I am not convinced by Lefort, "Rhétorique," 279–280, and Chitwood, *Legal Culture*, 158–160, that the *Novel* should be dated to 1047 or 1048, rather than soon after the defeat of the Rus', where Attaleiates places it. Mauropous' speech on St. George (*Oration* 181.10, April 1047) refers to the law school housed in the church, and Skleraina was buried there before 1046: Oikonomides, "St. George," 240, 243 n. 44.

24. Spingou, "Snapshots," 61–62.

25. Kaldellis, *Hellenism*, chap. 4 and 225–228.

26. Psellos 6.29–30; *Orationes panegyricae* 1.79–99; *Orationes funebres* 3.8; Attaleiates 18; Christophoros Mytilenaios, *Poem* 55; Hondridou, Μονομάχος, 56–77, 98–103.

27. Vryonis, "ΔΗΜΟΚΡΑΤΙΑ" (partly overstated); Hendy, "Economy," 146.

28. Kazhdan and Epstein, *Change*; Angelidi, ed., Βυζάντιο.

29. Kekaumenos 74; past instances: Oikonomides, "Title," 201 n. 14.

30. Oikonomides, "Évolution," 125–128; Cheynet, *Aristocracy*, VI.

31. In Karpozilos, Συμβολή, 73 (v. 51); Christophoros Mytilenaios *Poem* 55.

32. Oikonomides, "Title," 208.

33. Attaleiates 21–22; cf. Psellos, *Orationes panegyricae* 5.54–60; Gkoutzioukostas, Ἀπονομή, 202–216.

34. Ahrweiler, "Recherches," 50–52, 67–78; Krsmanović, *Province*, 206–210.

35. Psellos, *Oratoria minora* 6–14; Mauropous, *Letters* 19–20.

36. Psellos, *Orationes forenses* 3.

37. Psellos, *Oratoria minora* 8; cf. Riedinger, "Quatre étapes," 47–58 (the date is uncertain).

38. For what follows, see Skylitzes 435–438; Aristakes 10.53–61; Matthew of Edessa 1.74–80, 83–85 (garbled); Attaleiates 79–80; and Shepard, "Armenia," for the chronology; Leveniotis, Κατάρρευση, 74–81.

39. Garsoïan, "Integration," 71, 76, 80–81.

40. Aristakes 10.60; Garsoïan, "Integration," 65, 87, 91, 99–100.

41. Attaleiates 80.

42. Skylitzes 437–439; Aristakes 10.62; Matthew of Edessa 1.87.

43. Felix, *Byzanz*, 165; Blaum, "Diplomacy," 5–6.

44. Curta, *Europe*, 180–188, 293–298, and "Pechenegs." Image: Kaldellis, *Ethnography*, 106–126.

45. Skylitzes 455–459; Attaleiates 30–31; Mauropous, *Oration* 182; dates: Lefort, "Rhetorique," 271–275; Tyrach crossed months after Kegen: Shepard, "John Mauropous," 75.

46. Mauropous, *Orations* 181–182; date: ibid. 186.3, 7, 9, 11, 14 (shortly before September); Lefort, "Rhétorique," 276–278. Banner: Psellos, *Poem* 27.

47. For what follows, see Skylitzes 438–442; Psellos 6.99-123; Attaleiates 22–30; Mauropous, *Orations* 186.

48. Mauropous, *Orations* 186.61, 63, 66; Psellos 6.121.

9 *"Squaring the Circle"*

1. *Georgian Chronicle* 323.

2. Peacock, *Seljuq*, 146–148.

3. Attaleiates 116.

4. Cahen, "Pénétration," 12.

5. Bosworth, "History," 41–43.

6. Leveniotis, Κατάρρευση, 147–150.

7. Skylitzes 448–449; Shepard, "Armenia," 271–274; Leveniotis, Κατάρρευση, 90, 151–152.

8. Skylitzes, 449–454; Attaleiates 148; al-Athir, *Annals*, 67–68; Aristakes 11.68–13.89; Matthew of Edessa 1.92, 94; Shepard, "Armenia," 274–279; Leveniotis, Κατάρρευση, 90–96.

9. Skylitzes 454; for the negotiations, see Leveniotis, Κατάρρευση, 43–45.

10. Cf. Attaleiates 46 with Bosworth, "History," 41, and Leveniotis, Κατάρρευση, 97, 149.

11. Skylitzes 464; *Georgian Chronicles* 295; date: Shepard, "John Mauropous," 79–81; move: Bosworth, "History," 34.

12. Kai Kawus, *Qabusnama*, 35.

13. Skylitzes 460. For what follows, see Skylitzes 460–461, 465–473, 475–476; Attaleiates 31–43; early chronology: Shepard, "John Mauropous," 76–77, 81.

14. Skylitzes is possibly confirmed by Kekaumenos 27—assuming they are referring to the same battle. Arianites would lose again the following year.

15. Additional information in Kekaumenos 28.

16. Archaeology: Curta, "Pechenegs."

17. Skylitzes 434 (Niketas Stethatos).

18. Psellos 6.69–71; *Poem* 17; Christophoros Mytilenaios, *Poem* 70.

19. Oikonomides, "St. George," 245.

20. Psellos 6.159–160, 183; date: Shepard, "John Mauropous," 67.

21. Psellos 6.128–131.

22. Psellos 6.145, 151–155; *Letters KD* 34. She might have been the daughter of Giorgi I by his second wife Alda, an Alan princess, who had moved to Constantinople with her children in the 1030s when she surrendered Anakopia to the empire.

23. *Georgian Chronicle* 291–295; Skylitzes 447–448; Attaleiates 45; *Life of Giorgi* 12.

24. Skylitzes 477; Psellos 6.177–181; *Orationes funebres* 2.9.

25. Psellos 6.191–196; Karpozilos, Συμβολή, 36–41.

26. Skylitzes 471, 473–474; Psellos 6.134–150; Cheynet, *Pouvoir*, 61–64; Hondridou, Μονομάχος, 297–299.

27. Vryonis, "Will," but others place Boïlas near Edessa: Leveniotis, Κατάρρευση, 277.

28. Attaleiates 50; Skylitzes 476; Psellos 6.5, 7–8, 29–30, 48, 63, 153–154, 157–160, 185–188, 7.55.

29. Hondridou, Μονομάχος, 326–361, 342 (no revolts).

30. *Acts of Panteleemon* 3.

31. Cf. Morrisson, "Dévaluation," with Hendy, *Studies*, 3–6, 233–236, and Kaplanis, "Debasement." A diluted version in Laiou and Morrisson, *Economy*, 149.

32. But see Cheynet, "Schisme."

33. The pro-Norman sources (Amatus, Geoffrey, and William of Apulia) barely disguise their heroes' modus operandi; a modern narrative in Loud, *Robert*, chap. 3.

34. Loud, *Robert*, 99–101; Churchill, *Annales*, 306–308; Lambakis et al., Στρατεύματα, 440–443.

35. Surveys in Morris, *Papal Monarchy*; Papadakis, *Christian East*.

36. Amatus 3.17–18.

37. Leo IX's letters to Monomachos and Keroularios are in Will, *Acta*, 85–92.

38. Psellos, *Orationes funebres* 1.17–18; in general, see Tinnefeld, "Kerullarios."

39. But see Psellos, *Orationes funebres* 1.28 and 1.46.

40. Kaldellis and Polemis, *Patriarchs*, 11–14. There is no good reason to think that Psellos and Keroularios were "friends."

41. Leon of Ohrid, *Letters on the Azyma*; Smith, *Bread*.

42. Keroularios, *Letter to Petros of Antioch*, in Will, *Acta*, 172–188, here 177.

43. J. Ryder and T. Kolbaba in *Byzantine and Modern Greek Studies* 35 (2011).

44. Kaldellis, "Keroularios."

45. Humbert, *Commemoratio* 152B, in Will, *Acta*, 150–152.

46. Edict of the Synod of Constantinople, in Will, *Acta*, 155–168.

47. Known from Leo's letter to Monomachos, in Will, *Acta*, 85–92.

48. See the reign of Isaakios I; on 1054, see Psellos, *Orationes funebres* 1.39.

49. Petros of Antioch in Chadwick, *East*, 213–216.

50. Lemerle, *Études*, chaps. 4 and 5; Hondridou, Μονομάχος.

51. Hondridou, Μονομάχος, 300–306.

52. A different (?) incursion in Skylitzes 474–475 is confused; see Felix, *Byzanz*, 173.

53. Skylitzes 462–464; Aristakes 16.92–107; Attaleiates 46–47; al-Athir, *Annals*, 93; Matthew of Edessa 2.3; Felix, *Byzanz*, 173–177; Leveniotis, Κατάρρευση, 152–157.

54. Skylitzes 474.

55. Attaleiates 44–45; Skylitzes 476; Kekaumenos 20.

56. E.g., the rebels at Paŀin in Matthew of Edessa 1.96, or the "brigands" in Michael the Syrian III:162.

57. Treadgold, *Army*, 80–84, 215–217.

58. William of Apulia, *Deeds of Robert* 134–135.

59. Grigoriou-Ioannidou, Οργανωτικά μέτρα, for many proposals.

60. Aristakes 17.108.

61. Ahrweiler, "Recherches," 19–24; Harvey, *Expansion*, 110–111; southern Italy: Lefort and Martin, "Sigillion."

62. Mentioned by Psellos, *Orationes panegyricae* 5.126–127; Aristakes 14.90.

63. Skylitzes 479.

64. Skylitzes 485, 490.

65. Ousterhout, "Temple"; Shepard, "Holy Land," 527–535.

66. In le Strange, *Palestine*, 370–375.

67. Elephant: Attaleiates 48–50; see Hendy, *Studies*, 269–270; Blaum, "Diplomacy," 15–21, 41; Drocourt, "Information," 103; Leveniotis, Κατάρρευση, 45, with different dates.

68. Psellos 6.191–203.

69. Psellos, *Orationes funebres* 1.46.

70. Skylitzes 477–478; Attaleiates 51.

10 *"With Sword Drawn"*

1. Psellos, *Orationes funebres* 1.46; cf. *Chronographia* 6A.6, 6A.17.

2. Psellos 6A.3; her official image in *Oratoria minora* 1 (a *silention*); survey: Todt, "Frau."

3. Skylitzes 479–480.

4. Aristakes 17.110–18.118; Skylitzes 479.

5. Bianquis, *Damas*, 566–568; Miotto, Ανταγωνισμός, 251–252, Todt, "Frau," 160–161.

6. Attaleiates 52; Psellos 6A.4.

7. Attaleiates 58; "Younger": Cheynet, *Aristocracy*, III, 8.

8. Psellos, *Orationes funebres* 1.47.

9. Skylitzes 481–482.

10. Skylitzes 484–486; Ripper, *Marwaniden*, 155–156; Simpson, "Sources," 184–188 for his career. Koloneia: Leveniotis, *Κλνημα*, 65 n. 67.

11. Skylitzes 483, 486–487; Psellos 7.1–5; Attaleiates 53; Aristakes 18.119; Shepard, "Suspected Source," 174–175. For the officers' careers, see *PBW*.

12. Psellos, *Orationes funebres* 1.49.

13. The war: Skylitzes 487–495 (490–491 canvassing); Psellos 7.5–14; *Orationes funebres* 1.50; Attaleiates 53–56.

14. Skylitzes 495–500; Psellos, 7.15–43; *Orationes funebres* 2.11; Attaleiates 56–59.

15. Psellos, *Orationes funebres* 1.50.

16. Spadaro, "Deposizione."

17. Psellos, *Orationes funebres* 1.51.

18. Shepard, "Coronation."

19. Kekaumenos was made *kouropalates*, Doukas a *proedros*, Bourtzes a *magistros*, and so on.

20. Psellos 7.46–49.

21. Skylitzes Continuatus 103 (who will be cited only for information not in Attaleiates); Attaleiates 60; Matthew of Edessa 2.5; Morrisson, "Displaying," 80–82; Raffensperger, *Europe*, 33–34.

22. Skylitzes Continuatus 103; his seals in the *PBW*.

23. Bryennios 1.1.

24. Psellos 7.45; Attaleiates 60.

25. Reforms: Psellos 7.51–60; Attaleiates 60–61; Skylitzes Continuatus 103–104. Stănescu, "Réformes," is outdated.

26. Zonaras 18.4.

27. Psellos 7.59–60; Attaleiates 60–61; business: Morris, *Monks*, esp. 260 a documented reduction; cf. the reflections at 240, 247–262.

28. Attaleiates 62–63; Skylitzes Continuatus 104–105; Psellos 7.65; *Orationes funebres* 1.53–55; theory: Dagron, *Emperor*, 235–247.

29. Psellos 7.65–67; *Orationes funebres* 1.55–60; *Orationes forenses* 1; Attaleiates 63–66.

30. Zonaras 18.5.

31. Psellos 7.63, 7.67.

32. Aristakes 18.122–19.130; Leveniotis, *Καττάρευση*, 188–189; the place names can be identified via Honigmann, *Ostgrenze*.

33. Aristakes 21.134–140 (likely exaggerated); Matthew of Edessa 2.8–9 (garbled and misdated); Michael the Syrian III:158–159 (even more so); Leveniotis, *Κατάρρευση*, 262–265; Vest, *Geschichte*, 1298–1315.

34. Leveniotis, *Κατάρρευση*, 262.

35. Attaleiates 66–68; Psellos 7.67–70; Skylitzes Continuatus 107; Matthew of Edessa 2.5.

36. Attaleiates 69; Psellos 6.72–91, 7A.8–14; Skylitzes Continuatus 108–109; Bryennios 1.4–5; death date: Schreiner, *Kleinchroniken*, v. 1, 160; abdication narratives: Neville, *Heroes*, 140–151.

General Considerations

1. Pure guesswork: Oikonomides, "Structure," esp. 124–125.
2. So too Howard-Johnston, "Crown Lands."
3. Skylitzes 427.
4. E.g., in Krsmanović, "Αλλαγές."
5. Skylitzes 439, 490–491 (fascinating); Psellos 6.103.
6. Well explained by Cheynet, *Pouvoir*; past views: Kaegi, "Controversy."
7. Mauropous, *Orations* 186.5, 44; Psellos 7.6; *Orationes funebres* 1.49, 2.11.
8. *On Skirmishing* 19 (216–217); see Kaldellis, *Republic*, 194–198.
9. Lemerle, *Études*, 267–271; Treadgold, *Army*, 214–217.

11 *"The Agony of a Virulent Poison"*

1. Psellos 7A.14; *Oratoria minora* 5; Attaleiates 70–71.
2. *Life of Giorgi* 25.
3. Psellos 7A.2–3, 16–18, 24; Attaleiates 71, 76–77.
4. Psellos 7A.17–18; Kaldellis, *Argument*.
5. Attaleiates 76–79; cf. Skylitzes Continuatus 112–113.
6. Psellos 7A.21, 26; Polemis, *Doukai*, 34–53.
7. Psellos, *Letters G* 8; Polemis, *Doukai*, 35 n. 4.
8. Mondrain, "Lecture."
9. Date: Cheynet, *Pouvoir*, 71.
10. Attaleiates 71–75; Psellos 7A.22.
11. Michael the Syrian III:166–168; Dagron, "Minorités," 204; Vest, *Geschichte*, 1332–1343; Xiphilinos: Psellos, *Orationes funebres* 3.18–19.
12. Psellos, *Letters G* 27.
13. Matthew of Edessa 2.12–13; taken at face value by Honigmann, *Ostgrenze*, 185; Cahen, "Pénétration," 23; Leveniotis, *Κατάρρευση*, 104, 502–504.
14. Matthew of Edessa 2.15–19; Attaleiates 78–79 alludes to this, grudgingly conceding Roman victory. For Hervé's rank and promotion, see his seals in *PBW*. Seibt, "Übernahm," proposes that he was not killed at this time but survived Mantzikert. This seal needs more discussion.
15. Al-Athir, *Annals*, 152–155; Matthew of Edessa 2.20–22; Attaleiates 79–82; Aristakes 24.163–165; *Georgian Chronicles* 299–300; Leveniotis, *Κατάρρευση*, 106–115, inscription: 108 n. 530; Peacock, *Seljuq*, 149–150.
16. Attaleiates 82.
17. Matthew of Edessa 2.23; Leveniotis, *Κατάρρευση*, 116–118.
18. Matthew of Edessa 2.13–14, 30–46; Garsoïan, "Integration," 71–72, 76, 81, 113–119; the murder may date to the 1070s: Leveniotis, *Κατάρρευση*, 448.

19. Attaleiates 83–87; Skylitzes Continuatus 113–116; Psellos 7A.23; *Orationes panegyricae* 14; Matthew of Edessa 2.24; Madgearu, *Organization*, 129–131 for the archaeology; *pace* 69, 129 on the date.

20. Kekaumenos 74.

21. Năsturel, "Valaques"; Curta, "Constantinople."

22. Loud, *Robert*, 121–134, 186–194.

23. Loud, *Robert*, 188.

24. Skylitzes Continuatus 169.

25. Maurix: Lambakis et al., Στρατεύματα, 447; an attack by Robert: Kekaumenos 74; rebellion: Amatus 5.4; Loud, *Robert*, 131–134.

26. Attaleiates 92.

27. Psellos, *Orationes panegyricae* 9–10 (almost certainly for Doukas).

28. Attaleiates 96–97.

29. Oikonomides, "Serment."

30. Psellos 7B.1–3; bishop: Attaleiates 303.

31. Michael the Syrian III:168.

32. Matthew of Edessa 2.27–29, 48–49; taken at face value by Leveniotis, Κατάρρευση, 278–281.

33. Attaleiates 100.

34. Attaleiates 93–96.

35. Psellos 7B.6.

36. Attaleiates 97–102; Psellos 7B.10.

37. Skylitzes Continuatus 123–124; Psellos 7B.6-8; see Oikonomides, "Serment," 126–127.

38. Attaleiates 106.

39. De Vries, "Psellos."

40. Psellos, *Orationes panegyricae* 19.

41. Attaleiates 103–104; elaborated by Skylitzes Continuatus 125.

42. 1068 expedition: Attaleiates 104–122.

43. Zakkar, *Aleppo*, 165–173; Bianquis, *Damas*, 581–586.

44. Al-Athir, *Annals*, 166; Miotto, Ανταγωνισμός, 255.

45. Attaleiates 119; for the later Doukas defamation of these campaigns, see Psellos 7B.12–13.

46. Psellos, *Letters G* 25.

47. Amatus 1.5–8; Attaleiates 122–125; Simpson, "Sources," 188–192.

48. Attaleiates 125–138; for Psellos on this campaign, see Jeffreys, "Psellos," 87.

49. For the "live" debate over Diogenes, see Krallis, *Attaleiates*, 79–100.

50. Attaleiates 138–142; Bryennios 1.11; Matthew of Edessa 2.54.

51. Bryennios 1.6. Diogenes' first wife was the sister of Samouel Alousianos (Skylitzes Continuatus 134), whom Diogenes sent against Crépin in 1069 and who, judging from his name, was probably related to Aikaterine, Isaakios I Komnenos' wife.

52. Bryennios 1.18; cf. Skylitzes Continuatus 141.

53. Cahen, "Pénétration," 27–28; Peacock, *Seljuq*, 143–144.

54. Foss, "Defenses," 153.

55. Attaleiates 149; Matthew of Edessa 2.56.

56. Al-Athir, *Annals*, 169–170; Matthew of Edessa 2.56; Zakkar, *Emirate*, 175–180; Bianquis, *Damas*, 590–596.

57. Leveniotis, Κατάρρευση, 169, on the variants.

58. Vryonis, "Sources for the Battle"; Leveniotis, Κατάρρευση, 159–164; eastern sources: Hillenbrand, *Turkish Myth*.

59. Skylitzes Continuatus 142.

60. The campaign in Attaleiates 142–167. Manouel: Bryennios 1.12. *Pace* Cheynet, *Aristocracy*, XIII, 417, I do not believe Bryennios 1.13. After the battle, everyone championed a different strategy.

61. Haldon, "Logistique," 14.

62. Rank: Bryennios 1.13; but I trust Attaleiates over him (1.14–15) on the order with which Bryennios and Basilakes were deployed.

63. Peacock, *Seljuq*, 95.

64. Skylitzes Continuatus 147.

65. Vratimos, "Attaleiates."

66. Bryennios 1.17.

67. Attaleiates 150–151; Psellos 7B.20; cf. Aristakes 25.168.

68. Eastern sources: Vryonis, "Captivity"; letter: Psellos 7B.26; cf. Attaleiates 164–166.

69. Leveniotis, "Συνθήκη."

70. Cheynet, *Aristocracy*, XIII, 426–432.

71. Sibt ibn al-Jawzi in Vryonis, "Captivity," 445.

72. Ibid.

73. Attaleiates 168–169; Psellos 7B.23–31; Bryennios 1.18–20; Polemis, *Doukai*, 37.

74. Attaleiates 169–179; Bryennios 1.21–25; Psellos 7B.32–42.

75. Bryennios 1.22.

76. Psellos, *Letters S* 145.

77. Ibid. 82. I am skeptical that Andronikos opposed the blinding (Bryennios 1.25); he was the father of Alexios I's wife Eirene.

78. *Timarion* 20–22.

79. Cheynet, *Aristocracy*, XIII.

80. Aristakes 25.171.

81. Skylitzes Continuatus 156–157.

12 "Squeezed by the Pangs of Death"

1. Attaleiates 303; Skylitzes Continuatus 171; cf. Psellos 7C.4.

2. Attaleiates 180–182; Bryennios 2.1–3 (Ioannes was Bryennios' wife's great-grandfather, and he may have been using Ioannes' memoirs; see below); Skylitzes Continuatus 155–156.

3. Kaldellis, "Date," 662–663.

4. Garland and Rapp, "Mary."

5. Bryennios 2.1.

6. Cheynet, *Pouvoir*, 349–350; Leveniotis, *Κίνημα*, 117–118.

7. Attaleiates 158; eastern sources: Leveniotis, *Κίνημα*, 94–102; *Κατάρρευση*, 171–172.

8. Psellos, *Orationes funebres* 3.21; Attaleiates 275–276.

9. Kaplanis, "Debasement," 770–711; Psellos' exquisite sarcasm: 7C.2.

10. Skylitzes Continuatus 162.

11. Polemis, *Doukai*, 58; Harvey, "Competition," 175.

12. *Hungarian Illuminated Chronicle* 104–112 (pp. 369–377); possible reference in Bryennios 3.1; Sirmium: Kinnamos 5.8; see Stephenson, *Frontier*, 141, 189–193; Madgearu, *Organization*, 95–97; Curta, *Europe*, 252.

13. Skylitzes Continuatus 163–166; *Chronicle of the Priest of Dioclea (Duklja)* 40; Fine, *Balkans*, 213–214.

14. Skylitzes Continuatus 121; Attaleiates 116; Vryonis, *Decline*, 103–114.

15. Anna Komnene 8.9; Leveniotis, *Κατάρρευση*, 246–251; Bryer et al., "Theodore"; in general, Cheynet, *Aristocracy*, XIV, 132–133.

16. Leveniotis, *Κατάρρευση*, 120–125.

17. Toumanoff, "Armenia," 620.

18. Bryennios 3.15; Leveniotis, *Κατάρρευση*, 556 no. 90.

19. Matthew of Edessa 2.71; Leveniotis, *Κατάρρευση*, 285–286, 588 no. 218.

20. Yarnley, "Philaretos"; Cheynet, *Société*, 390–410.

21. Miotto, *Ανταγωνισμός*, 257, 268; Zakkar, *Emirate*, 172, 180–181, 186–187.

22. Leveniotis, *Κίνημα*, 210–211.

23. Skylitzes Continuatus 135; Geoffrey Malaterra 1.3; also Anna Komnene 14.4.6; Simpson, "Sources." Shepard, "Franks," is more positive.

24. Attaleiates 183–207; Bryennios 2.3–27, Anna Komnene 1.1–3; memoirs: Neville, *Heroes*, chap. 4; in detail, see Leveniotis, *Κίνημα*.

25. Bryennios 2.14.

26. *Georgian Chronicles* 308–310; Leveniotis, *Κατάρρευση*, 120–124, 254.

27. Magdalino, *Background*, 29–32; Krallis, *Attaleiates*, 157–169.

28. Attaleiates 130–132; Bryennios 1.13.

29. Bryennios 2.23–24.

30. Ibid. 2.26.

31. Ioannes Oxeites, *Diatribes*, 23.

32. Leveniotis, *Κίνημα*, 185.

33. Flight: Attaleiates 211; Christodoulos in Miklosich and Müller, *Acta*, v. 6, 16–19, 61–62, 87; Mauropous, *Oration* 180.19, at Euchaita before 1075, refers to uprooted people and "troubles," but see Karpozilos, *Συμβολή*, 46, 152. Officials: Cheynet, *Aristocracy*, XIV, 134–141. Fleet: Michael the Syrian III:172. Chrysopolis: Attaleiates 200, 267; Leveniotis, *Κίνημα*, 182 n. 219.

34. Gautier, "Lettre"; Leveniotis, *Κίνημα*, 145–146.

35. Shepard, "Steppe-Nomads," 72–83; Cheynet, *Société*, 613–616; Hilsdale, "Social Life."

36. Attested for the mid-1070s in Bryennios 3.3.

37. See the Epilogue to this book, on the Crusade.

38. Psellos, *Orationes forenses: Actum* 5; Skylitzes Continuatus 170; Bibicou, "Page"; Falkenhausen, "Olympias"; Panagopoulou, *Γάμοι*, 224–233; the preliminary proposal is outlined in Psellos, *Letters S* 143–144.

39. Svoronos, "Recherches," 68–71.

40. Shepard, "Franks," 302–305 (among many publications).

41. Bryennios 4.4; cf. Attaleiates 211, 243.

42. Attaleiates 201–204; Laiou and Morrisson, *Economy*, 135–136, 162.

43. Attaleiates 204–209; Skylitzes Continuatus 166; Stephenson, *Frontier*, 98–100; Madgearu, *Organization*, 79–82, 131–132.

44. Attaleiates 210–212.

45. Bryennios 2.28–29; Leveniotis, *Κατάρρευση*, 341–346.

46. Cheynet, *Pouvoir*, 303–309, 333–336, 349–351; adoption: Anna Komnene 10.3.3.

47. Attaleiates 215, 240; Botaneiates' career: Karagiorgou, 'Way.'

48. Attaleiates 242–252; Bryennios 3.314; Skylitzes Continuatus 172–176.

49. Attaleiates 261–262.

50. Attaleiates 252–255, 260 (treasures); Bryennios 3.26.

51. Attaleiates 255–273, 277 (palace); Bryennios 3.15-24; Skylitzes Continuatus 171–172, 176–179, 186.

52. Krallis, *Attaleiates*, 145; career: Karagiorgou, "Way."

53. Attaleiates 273–275 (probably sarcastic), 283 (debts); Bryennios 4.1.

54. Bryennios 3.25–26, 4.2; Skylitzes Continuatus 181–182; Zonaras 18.19; Attaleiates 304 (Eudokia).

55. Polemis, *Doukai*, 50–51, 61–62, for these two.

56. Pro-Botaneiates: Attaleiates 284–294; pro-Bryennios: Bryennios 4.24.18; pro-Alexios: Anna Komnene 1.4–6.

57. Skylitzes Continuatus 181; Attaleiates 295–296; Blöndal, *Varangians*, 118–119.

58. Basilakes: Attaleiates 297–300; Bryennios 4.16–28; Anna Komnene 1.7–9.

59. Bryennios 4.30; cf. Attaleiates 300–302.

60. Yarnley, "Philaretos"; Seibt, "Philaretos"; Isaakios: Bryennios 4.29; Antioch: Leveniotis, *Κατάρρευση*, 343–346; recognition: Attaleiates 301.

61. Attaleiates 306–309.

62. Career: Leveniotis, "Θέμα/δουκάτο," 64–71, 86–87.

63. Bryennios 4.31–40.

64. Anna Komnene 2.2.1.

65. Ioannes Oxeites, *Diatribes*, 35.

66. Attaleiates 198; alluding to 2 Kings 22.6; Psalm 17.5–6.

General Considerations

1. Treadgold, "Byzantium," 228.
2. Kaldellis, *Republic*.
3. Ahrweiler, "Recherches," 19–24; Haldon, "Service," 60–64; "Approaches," 48–49; *Warfare*, 124–125.
4. A survey in Cheynet, *Aristocracy*, X.
5. E.g., Holmes, *Basil*, 364 n. 150.
6. Cf. Haldon, "Service," 62.
7. Ostrogorsky, *History*, 272–375 passim.
8. Haldon et al., "Climate," 151.
9. Kaegi, "Contribution"; Haldon, "Approaches," 54–56.
10. *Pace* Cheynet, "Conception," 63; Haldon, "Approaches," 63–65; *Warfare*, 85–90 (of course there would be fewer defenses during a civil war, as the armies were engaged in it).
11. They seem to be used interchangeably by Haldon, *Wars*, 166; *Warfare*, 92.
12. Cheynet, *Aristocracy*, VIII, 12–17; X, 61; XIII, 413–414.
13. Haldon, "Service," 61–62 n. 147.
14. Haldon, *Warfare*, 92.
15. Cf. Bryennios in Neville, *Heroes*, chap. 5.
16. Shepard, "Franks," 294.
17. Peacock, *Seljuq*, 132; Leveniotis, Κατάρρευση, 38–39.
18. Anna Komnene 2.4.8.
19. Psellos, *Orationes funebres* 3.21.
20. Harvey, "Competition," 174–177; Frankopan, "Kinship."
21. Neville, *Heroes*, 104; West, "Dynastic," 106.
22. Peacock, *Seljuq*, 151.

Epilogue

1. Magdalino, *Background*, 4.
2. Western sources are not necessarily better, but at least there are many of them.
3. Frankopan, *Crusade*. I sometimes agree with Frankopan (Alexios' decisive leadership in 1096–1097), and sometimes not (the history of Asia Minor after 1074, the letter to Robert of Flanders, etc.). But his overall argument deserves a hearing.
4. Ciggaar, *Travellers*; Riley-Smith, *Crusaders*, 25–39; Shepard, "Adventus," 338, 355–363.
5. Joranson, "German Pilgrimage," 17–18.
6. Jacoby, "Gunther."
7. William of Jumièges, *Gesta* 6.11–12 (embroidered, but, *pace* Van Houts, "Normandy," not necessarily fictitious; important pilgrims met the emperor; tr.: 558); Leveniotis, Κίνημα, 205 n. 65.

8. Anna Komnene 7.6.1.

9. I am writing a separate study of these.

10. Runciman, "Pilgrimages," 76.

11. Fulk Nerra, count of Anjou: Shepard, "Adventus," 359; Mariam, mother of Bagrat IV: *Georgian Chronicles* 78; Harald as escort: Blöndal, *Varangians*, 64–65.

12. Asbridge, *Crusade*, 19 (testing ground), 73; Riley-Smith, *Crusaders*, 42–44, 66.

13. O'Callaghan, *Reconquest*, 8–9, 18–35, for more.

14. Geoffrey Malaterra 2.33; Loud, *Robert*, 146, 164, 202; cf. Riley-Smith, *Crusaders*, 49–52; Chevedden, "Crusade," 214–217.

15. Chevedden, "Crusade," 206 (listing the concepts).

16. Cobb, *Race*, 37–41, 59.

17. Chevedden, "Crusade," 192.

18. Bernold of Constance, *Chronicle*, 520; cf. Somerville, *Piacenza*, chap. 2.

19. Sweetenham, *Robert*, 215–222; Kaldellis, *Ethnography*, 196 n. 22.

20. Shepard, "Cross-Purposes," 118; Frankopan, *Crusade*, 87–100 (I am skeptical of the Croatian episode at 23, 92).

21. Shepard, "Cross-Purposes."

22. Cowdrey, "Pope Gregory," 38–39; Latowsky, *Emperor*, 107–133.

23. Gregory VII, *Register* 1.18, 1.46, 1.49, 2.3, 2.31, 2.37; Cowdrey, "Pope Gregory," and *Gregory*, 482–486; Riley-Smith, *Crusaders*, 49–50; Leveniotis, *Κίνημα*, 147–148; Frankopan, *Crusade*, 97–99.

24. Gregory VII, *Register* 8.7, 9.17; Loud, *Robert*, 209–210; Cowdrey, *Gregory*, 434–436, 486–487.

25. Anna Komnene 10.5.4; Shepard, "Cross-Purposes," 108–109; Asbridge, *Crusade*, 356–357 n. 23.

26. For Alexios, see Mullett and Smythe, *Alexios*; Magdalino, *Empire*.

27. Anna Komnene 10.5.6.

28. Leyser, *Communications*, 77–95, on feeding the First Crusade.

29. Albert of Aachen 1.15, 1.18, 2.7, 2.17 (charity at 1.9); *Gesta* 1.1, 2.1; Robert the Monk 2.15; no complaints in Fulcher of Chartres 1.8.5–9; Anna Komnene 10.10.3.

30. Anna Komnene 10.5.9.

31. Runciman, "Journey."

32. Shepard, "Cross-Purposes," 120; Frankopan, *Crusade*, 114.

33. Albert of Aachen 1.6-15; *pace* Runciman, "Journey," 209–211; reputation: Asbridge, *Crusade*, 89. France, *Victory*, 90–91, blames the violence on Byzantine unpreparedness, but Niketas had supplies for crusaders who behaved.

34. Albert of Aachen 2.7.

35. Anna Komnene 10.7; Fulcher of Chartres 1.6.3; *Gesta* 1.3; Robert the Monk 2.6.

36. Albert of Aachen 2.7–10.

37. Anna Komnene 10.5.10, 10.9.1, 10.11.7; Robert the Monk 2.14: "you are more interested in taking his kingdom from him than in pilgrimage."

38. Geoffrey Malaterra 4.24; Riley-Smith, *Crusaders*, 17–18; Asbridge, *Crusade*, 3, 60.

39. Anna Komnene 10.8.2–10.

40. *Gesta* 1.4; Robert the Monk 2.11–15.

41. Runciman, "Journey," 216.

42. Anna Komnene 5.5–6.1; Geoffrey Malaterra 3.29.

43. Albert of Aachen 2.14; Anna Komnene 10.9.2 (Alexios worried this was happening).

44. Fulcher of Chartres 1.7.4, 1.8.5–9; Albert of Aachen 2.19; Raymond d'Aguilers 1–2; Shepard, "Greek," 205–207.

45. Fulcher of Chartres 1.8.9–1.9.1.

46. Anna Komnene 10.10.5–6.

47. Albert of Aachen 2.10–20 (here 16, soon after Christmas); *Gesta* 1.3; Robert the Monk 2.8–19; Anna Komnene 10.9 (Easter, probably inaccurately).

48. Shepard, "Greek."

49. Raymond d'Aguilers 2; Fulcher of Chartres 1.9.2; *Gesta* 2.6.

50. Stephen of Blois, *Letters to Adela* 1.

51. Anna Komnene 10.7.5, 10.11.5; Harris, "The 'Schism'," 19–20.

52. Cowdrey, "Pope Urban."

53. Fulcher of Chartres 1.9.3.

54. Robert the Monk 2.19.

55. Albert of Aachen 2.16.

56. Anna Komnene 10.11.7.

57. Ibid. 10.9.11; cf. 11.3.3, 11.4.4.

58. Albert of Aachen 1.2; *Gesta* 1.2; Robert the Monk 1.13; Anna Komnene 10.6.5 (a fleet under Konstantinos Euphorbenos Katakalon).

59. France, *Victory*; Asbridge, *Crusade*.

60. *Gesta* 2.7; Robert the Monk 3.1.

61. Anna Komnene 11.1.2–3.

62. Albert of Aachen 2.28; also Stephen of Blois, *Letters to Adela* 1; *Gesta* 2.7; Robert the Monk 3.1; Shepard, "Greek," 213, 215.

63. Alexios I, *Letter to Oderisius*, pp. 152–153.

64. France, *Victory*, 156–157, unconvincingly claims that Alexios wanted to keep good relations with the Turks by pretending that he had nothing to do with the crusaders (or even with his own armies that he had sent against Nikaia).

65. Anna Komnene 6.10. The date is unclear: Belke, "Byzanz."

66. Albert of Aachen 2.30.

67. Anna Komnene 11.2.3.

68. Ibid. 11.2.10.

69. Fulcher of Chartres 1.11.1.

70. Anna Komnene 11.3.3.
71. Location: France, *Victory*, 170–174.
72. France, *Victory*, 185; Frankopan, *Crusade*, 145.
73. France, *Victory*, 190–191.
74. Stephen of Blois, *Letters to Adela* 2; Anna Komnene 11.3.5–6.
75. *Gesta* 4.11, Robert the Monk 3.23.
76. *Gesta* 4.11; Robert the Monk 3.25; but see Shepard, "Greek," 195.
77. Albert of Aachen 3.27; Fulcher of Chartres 1.14.2; Matthew of Edessa 2.133; Leveniotis, Κατάρρευση, 313–315.
78. Leveniotis, Κατάρρευση, 270–271.
79. Matthew of Edessa 2.104–106, 2.117–118; Leveniotis, Κατάρρευση, 291–298; MacEvitt, *Crusades*, 67–68.
80. As Asbridge, *Crusade*, 140, has it.
81. Anna Komnene 6.11.2–3 (in a different context, however).
82. Raymond d'Aguilers 4; Frankopan, *Crusade*, 151; *pace* MacEvitt, *Crusades*, 55–56 (conquer them "for themselves"). MacEvitt (57–58) also excises the imperial credentials of Oshin of Adana; see Leveniotis, Κατάρρευση, 400–404; France, *Victory*, 194 (in brief).
83. Matthew of Edessa 2.117–118; Fulcher of Chartres 1.14; Albert of Aachen 3.19–25.
84. Edessa: Frankopan, *Crusade*, 151–153; MacEvitt, *Crusades*, 65–75; Antioch: Asbridge, *Creation*.
85. Raymond d'Aguilers 2.
86. Chevedden, "Crusade," 217.
87. Anna Komnene 11.5.
88. Shepard, "Father," 87–88, 125.
89. *Gesta* 2.6.
90. France, *Victory*, 220 (discussion at 208–220); Shepard, "Greek," 263, 272.
91. Magdalino, *Background*, 8, 37; Edgington, "The First Crusade," 69–72; Shepard, "Greek," 274.

GLOSSARY

A number of offices and technical terms are mentioned rarely in the narrative and are explained where they appear. But others appear with greater regularity, are integral to the dynamics of the story, and therefore are glossed here (many are also explained in the Introduction).

domestikos of the scholai: commander of the *scholai*, the most powerful *tagma* in the empire's armed forces at this time. In practice, he was often in charge of the empire's overall military planning and operations.

doukaton (pl. doukata): the regional command zone of a *doux*. Sometimes also called a *katepanaton*.

doux (pl. doukes, from Latin dux): after the reforms of ca. 970 AD, these were military officers in charge of broad regional commands that grouped together many subordinate themes and their generals (*strategoi*).

exkoubitores: a *tagma*.

hetaireia: a *tagma*.

kaisar (i.e., "Caesar"): the highest court title, given to a close relative of the emperor or designated heir. See also "titles."

katepanaton (pl. katepanata): the regional command zone of a *katepano*. Sometimes also called a *doukaton*.

katepano (pl. katepano): equivalent to a *doux*.

katholikos (or catholicos): title borne by the heads of the autocephalous Armenian and Georgian Churches.

kouropalates: high court title given to an imperial relative and to foreign rulers allied to the empire. See also "titles."

magistros: high court title (from Latin *magister*). See also "titles."

parakoimomenos: chief chamberlain of the palace, usually a eunuch, often entrusted with the empire's civilian administration and political direction.

patrikios: court title (from Latin *patricius*). See also "titles."

prefect of the City (eparchos): high-ranking member of the Senate who was in charge of aspects of public safety, law and order, and provisioning of the capital.

proedros: court title. See also "titles."

protospatharios: court title (lit. "First Swordsman"). See also "titles."

roga: a state salary associated with certain court titles and offices, sometimes obtained through the (screened) payment of a sum of gold to the court.

scholai: in this period, the leading *tagma*.

strategos (pl. strategoi): general in command of a theme (these are often just called "generals" in the narrative).

stratelatai: a *tagma*.

stratelates: literally "army commander," an ad hoc position of overall or regional military authority devised originally for a non-eunuch confidant of the emperor.

stratopedarches: literally "army commander," an ad hoc position of overall or regional military authority devised originally for a eunuch confidant of the emperor (later given to non-eunuchs too).

tagma (pl. tagmata): full-time, mobile, professional military units of a few thousand men that were stationed originally in and around Constantinople, but increasingly in the provinces as well. The most important tagma in this period were the *scholai*.

thema (pl. themata), or "themes": the militarized provinces of the empire (seventh to twelfth centuries). Each had an army of mostly local recruits and some professionals under the command of a *strategos*. Large themes were progressively subdivided into smaller units, and new themes in the conquered territories could be quite small.

titles: the imperial court granted titles that bestowed social rank, honor, and salaries but did not necessarily entail specific functions. The rank of the titles mentioned in this narrative, in descending order, was *kaisar, kouropalates, magistros, patrikios, proedros*, and *protospatharios*.

BIBLIOGRAPHY

Abbreviations

BF   *Byzantinische Forschungen*
BMGS   *Byzantine and Modern Greek Studies*
BZ   *Byzantinische Zeitschrift*
DOP   *Dumbarton Oaks Papers*
PBW   *Prosopography of the Byzantine World* (www.pbw.kcl.ac.uk)
PmbZ   Berlin-Brandenburg Academy of Sciences, *Prosopographie der mittelbyzantinischen Zeit* (Berlin 2000–).
REB   *Revue des études byzantines*
TM   *Travaux et mémoires*

Primary sources

Abû Firâs al-Hamdânî, *Les Byzantines: La voix d'un prisonnier*, tr. A. Miquel (Paris 2010).

Acts of Panteleemon, ed. P. Lemerle et al., *Actes de Saint-Pantéléêmon* (Paris 1982).

Adémar of Chabannes, *Ademari Cabannensis Chronicon*, ed. P. Bourgain (Turnhout 1999).

Albert of Aachen, *History of the Journey to Jerusalem*, ed. S. B. Edgington (Oxford 2007), and tr. S. B. Edgington (Farnham 2013).

Alexios I Komnenos, *Letter to Oderisius*, ed. H. Hagenmeyer, *Epistulae et chartae ad historiam primi belli sacri spectantes: Die Kreuzzugsbriefe aus den Jahren 1088–1100* (Innsbruck 1901) 152–153.

Anna Komnene, *Alexiad*, ed. D. R. Reinsch and A. Kambylis, *Annae Comnenae Alexias* (Berlin 2001); tr. E. R. A. Sewter, rev. P. Frankopan, *Anna Komnene: Alexiad* (London 2009).

Amatus of Montecassino, ed. V. de Bartholomaeis, *Storia de' Normanni di Amato di Montecassino* (Rome 1935); tr. P. N. Dunbar, rev. G. A. Loud, *The History of the Normans* (Woodbridge, UK 2004).

Aristakes of Lastivert, *History of the Calamities Caused by the Foreign Nations*, tr. M. Canard and H. Berbérian, *Aristakes de Lastivert: Récit des malheurs de la nation arménienne* (Brussels 1973); tr. R. Bedrosian, *Aristakes Lastivertc'i's History* (New York 1985).

al-Athir, *Annales du Maghreb et de l'Espagne*, tr. E. Fagnan, ed. A. Rebahi (Algiers 2007).

———, *Annals*, tr. D. S. Richards, *The Annals of the Saljuq Turks: Selections from al-Kamil fi'l-Ta'rikh of 'Izz al-Din Ibn Al-Athir* (London 2002).

Attaleiates, Michael, *History*, ed. and tr. A. Kaldellis and D. Krallis (Washington, DC 2012).

Balsamon, Theodoros, *Commentaries on the Church Canons*, ed. G. A. Rallis and M. Potlis, Σύνταγμα τῶν ἱερῶν καὶ θείων κανόνων etc., 6 vols. (Athens 1852–1859).

Bernold of Constance, *Chronicle*, ed. I. S. Robinson, *Die Chroniken Bertholds von Reichenau und Bernolds von Konstanz 1054–1100* (Hanover 2003).

Bryennios, Nikephoros, *Materials for a History*, ed. and tr. P. Gautier, *Nicephori Bryennii Historiarum libri quattuor (Nicéphore Bryennios: Histoire)* (Bruxelles 1975).

Campaign Organization and Tactics, ed. and tr. G. T. Dennis, *Three Byzantine Military Treatises* (Washington, DC 1985) 241–335.

Christophoros Mytilenaios, *Poems*, ed. M. de Groote, *Christophori Mitylenaii versuum variorum collectio cryptensis* (Turnhout 2012).

Chronicle of Lupus Protospatharius, ed. G. H. Pertz in *Monumenta Germaniae Historica: Scriptores* v. 5 (Hanover 1844).

Chronicle of the Priest of Dioclea (Duklja), ed. T. Zivković, *Gesta Regum Sclavorum*, 2 vols. (Belgrade 2009); ed. and tr. A. Papageorgiou, Τὸ Χρονικό του Ιερέα της Διοκλείας (Athens 2012).

Chronicle of Vat. gr. 163, ed. in Markopoulos, *History*, 91–100.

Doxapatres, Ioannes, *Commentaries on the Progymnasmata of Aphthonios*, ed. C. Walz, *Rhetores Graeci*, v. 2 (Leipzig 1835).

Fulcher of Chartres, *A History of the Expedition to Jerusalem, 1095–1127*, ed. H. Hagenmeyer, *Fulcheri Carnotensis Historia Hierosolymitana (1095–1127)* (Heidelberg 1913); tr. F. R. Ryan (Knoxville 1969).

Geoffrey Malaterra, *The Deeds of Count Roger of Calabria and Sicily and of His Brother Duke Robert Guiscard*, tr. K. B. Wolf (Ann Arbor, MI 2005).

Geometres, Ioannes, *Poems*, ed. J. A. Cramer, *Anecdota Graeca e codd. manuscriptis Bibliothecae regiae Parisiensis* (Oxford 1841) v. 4, 265–352.

Georgian Chronicles, tr. R. W. Thomson, *Rewriting Caucasian History: The Medieval Armenian Adaptation of the Georgian Chronicles. The Original Georgian Texts and the Armenian Adaptation* (Oxford 1996).

Gesta Francorum et aliorum Hierosolimitanorum, ed. and tr. R. Hill, *The Deeds of the Franks and the Other Pilgrims to Jerusalem* (London 1962).

Gregory VII, *Register*, ed. E. Caspar, *Das Register Gregors VII* (Berlin 1955); tr. H.E.J. Cowdrey, *The Register of Pope Gregory VII, 1073–1085* (Oxford 2002).

ibn Hawqal, *The Configuration of the Earth*, ed. and tr. J. H. Kramer and G. Wiet, *Ibn Hauqal: Le configuration de la terre*, 2 vols. (Paris and Beirut 1964).

Hungarian Illuminated Chronicle, ed. A. Domanovszky in E. Szentpétery, ed., *Scriptores Rerum Hungaricarum*, 2 vols. (Budapest 1937–1938) v. 1, 217–505; tr. A. West in D. Dercsényi, *The Hungarian Illuminated Chronicle* (New York 1970).

Ioannes Oxeites, ed. and tr. P. Gautier, "Diatribes de Jean l'Oxite contre Alexis Ier Comnène," *REB* 28 (1970) 5–55.

ibn Jubayr, tr. R. J. C. Broadhurst, *The Travels of Ibn Jubayr* (London 1952).

Kai Kawus, *Qabusnama*, tr. R. Levy, *A Mirror for Princes: The Qabus Nama by Kai Kai Ka'us ibn Iskandar* (London 1951).

Kedrenos, Georgios, *Chronicle*, ed. I. Bekker (Bonn 1838).

Kekaumenos, *Strategikon*, ed. and tr. D. Tsoungarakis (Athens 1993).

Kinnamos, Ioannes, *History*, ed. A. Meineke (Bonn 1836).

Konstantinos VII Porphyrogennetos, *De cerimoniis*, ed. J. J. Reiske, *Constantini Porphyrogeniti imperatoris de cerimoniis aulae byzantinae*, 2 vols. (Bonn 1829–1830); tr. A. Moffatt and M. Tall, *Constantine Porphyrogennetos: The Book of Ceremonies*, 2 vols. (Canberra 2012).

———, *De administrando imperio*, ed. G. Moravcsik and tr. R. J. H. Jenkins, *Constantine Porphyrogenitus: De administrando imperio* (Washington, DC 1967).

———, *Military Speech of 958*, ed. R. Vári, "Zum historischen Exzerptenwerke des Konstantinos Porphyrogennetos," *BZ* 17 (1908) 75–85, here 78–84.

Konstantinos IX Monomachos, *Novel on the Nomophylax*, ed. A. Salač, *Novella Constitutio saec. XI medii* (Prague 1954).

Konstantinos of Rhodes, ed. and tr. I. Vassis and L. James, *Constantine of Rhodes: On Constantinople and the Church of the Holy Apostles* (Ashgate 2012).

Lazaropoulos, Ioannes, *Synopsis of the Miracles of Eugenios*, ed. J. O. Rosenqvist, *The Hagiographic Dossier of St. Eugenios of Trebizond in Codex Athous Dionysiou 154* (Uppsala 1996) 246–358.

Leon of Ohrid, *Letters on the Azyma*, ed. E. Büttner, *Erzbischof Leon von Ohrid (1037–1056): Leben und Werk* (Bamberg 2007).

Leon of Synada, *Letters*, ed. and tr. M. P. Vinson, *The Correspondence of Leo Metropolitan of Synada and Syncellus* (Washington, DC 1985).

Leon the Deacon, *History*, ed. C. B. Hase, *Leonis diaconi Historae libri X* (Bonn 1828); tr. A.-M. Talbot and D. F. Sullivan, *The History of Leo the Deacon: Byzantine Military Expansion in the Tenth Century* (Washington, DC 2005).

Life of Giorgi, tr. T. Grdzelidze, *Georgian Monks on Mount Athos: Two Eleventh-Century Lives of the Hegoumenoi of Iviron* (London 2009).

Life of Ioane and Ep't'ime, tr. B. Martin-Hisard, "La Vie de Jean et Euthyme: Le Statut du monastère des Ibères sur l'Athos," *REB* 49 (1991) 67–142; tr. T. Grdzelidze, *Georgian Monks on Mount Athos: Two Eleventh-Century Lives of the Hegoumenoi of Iviron* (London 2009).

Life of Lazaros of Mt. Galesion: An Eleventh-Century Pillar Saint, tr. R. P. H. Greenfield (Washington, DC 2000).

Life of Loukas of Steiris, ed. and tr. C. L. Connor and W. R. Connor, *The Life and Miracles of Saint Luke of Steiris* (Brookline, MA 1994).

Life of Nikon, ed. and tr. D. F. Sullivan, *The Life of Saint Nikon* (Brookline, MA 1987).

Life of Paulos the Younger, ed. H. Delehaye, "Vita S. Pauli iunioris in monte Latro," *Analecta Bollandiana* 11 (1892) 5–74, 136–182.

Lives of Athanasios of Athos, ed. J. Noret, *Vitae duae antiquae sancti Athanasii Athonitae* (Turnhout 1982).

Liudprand of Cremona, *Antapodosis* and *Embassy to Constantinople*, tr. P. Squatriti, *The Complete Works of Liudprand of Cremona* (Washington, DC 2007).

Matthew of Edessa, *Chronicle*, tr. A. E. Dostourian, *Armenia and the Crusades, 10th to 12th Centuries: The Chronicle of Matthew of Edessa* (Lanham, MD 1993).

Mauropous, Ioannes, *Letters*, ed. and tr. A. Karpozilos, *The Letters of Ioannes Mauropous, Metropolitan of Euchaita* (Thessalonike 1990).

———, *Poems and Orations*, ed. P. de Lagarde, *Iohannis Euchaitorum Metropolitae quae in codice Vaticano Graeco 676 supersunt* (Göttingen 1882).

Michael the Syrian, ed. J.-B. Chabot, *Chronique de Michel le Syrien, Patriarche Jacobite d'Antioche (1166–1199)*, 4 vols. (Paris 1899–1910).

Miskawayh, *Experiences of the Nations*, tr. D. S. Margoliouth, in idem and H. F. Amedroz, *The Eclipse of the 'Abbasid Caliphate: Original Chronicle of the Fourth Islamic Century*, v. 5 (Oxford 1921).

Nikephoros II Phokas, *Praecepta militaria*, ed. and tr. in McGeer, *Sowing*, 12–59.

Ouranos, Nikephoros, *Taktika*, ed. and tr. in McGeer, *Sowing*, 88–163.

Psellos, Michael, *Chronographia*, ed. S. Impellizeri and tr. S. Ronchey, *Michele Psello: Imperatori di Bisanzio (Cronografia)*, 2 vols. (Milan 1984); tr. E.R.A. Sewter, *Michael Psellus: Fourteen Byzantine Rulers* (London 1966).

———, *Historia Syntomos*, ed. and tr. W. J. Aerts, *Michaelis Pselli Historia syntomos* (Berlin 1990).

———, *Letters G*, ed. P. Gautier, "Quelques lettres de Psellos inédites ou déjà éditées," *REB* 44 (1986) 111–197.

———, *Letters KD*, ed. E. Kurtz and F. Drexl, *Michaelis Pselli scripta minora*, v. 2: *Epistulae* (Milan 1941).

———, *Letters S*, ed. K. N. Sathas, Μεσαιωνικὴ Βιβλιοθήκη, v. 5 (Venice 1876).

———, *Orationes forenses et acta*, ed. G. T. Dennis (Leipzig 1994).

———, *Orationes funebres*, v. 1, ed. I. Polemis (Berlin 2014).

———, *Orationes panegyricae*, ed. G. T. Dennis, *Michaelis Pselli Orationes panegyricae* (Leipzig 1994).

————, *Oratoria Minora*, ed. A. Littlewood, *Michaelis Psellis oratoria minora* (Leipzig 1985).

————, *Poemata*, ed. L. G. Westerink (Leipzig 1992).

Pseudo-Symeon, *Chronicle* (concluding section), ed. with Theophanes Continuatus 756–760.

Raymond d'Aguilers, *Historia Francorum qui ceperunt Iherusalem*, tr. J. H. Hill and L. L. Hill (Philadelphia 1968).

Romanos II, *Funeral Oration for His Wife Bertha*, ed. S. Lambros, Ἀνέκδοτος μονῳδία 'Ρωμανοῦ Β´ ἐπὶ τῷ θανάτῳ τῆς πρώτης αὐτοῦ συζύγου Βέρθας,' *Bulletin de correspondance hellénique* 2 (1878) 266–273.

Robert the Monk, *History of the First Crusade*, ed. P. le Bas in *Recueil des historiens des Croisades: historiens occidentaux*, v. 3 (Paris 1866) 717–882; tr. C. Sweetenham (Farnham 2005).

al-Rudhrawari, *Continuation of Miskawayh's Experiences of the Nations*, tr. D. S. Margoliouth in idem and H. F. Amedroz, *The Eclipse of the 'Abbasid Caliphate: Original Chronicle of the Fourth Islamic Century*, v. 6 (Oxford 1921).

Russian Primary Chronicle (Laurentian Text), tr. S. H. Cross and O. P. Sherbowitz-Wetzor (Cambridge, MA 1953).

Schreiner, P., *Die byzantinischen Kleinchroniken*, 3 vols. (Vienna 1975–1979).

Sikeliotes, Ioannes, *Commentary on Hermogenes' Peri Ideon*, ed. C. Walz, *Rhetores Graeci*, v. 6 (Stuttgart 1834).

On Skirmishing, ed. and tr. G. T. Dennis, *Three Byzantine Military Treatises* (Washington, DC 1985) 137–239; ed. and tr. Dagron and Mihăescu, *Le traité*, 29–135.

Skylitzes Continuatus, ed. E. T. Tsolakis, Ἡ Συνέχεια τῆς χρονογραφίας τοῦ Ἰωάννου Σκυλίτζη *(Ioannes Skylitzes Continuatus)* (Thessalonike 1968).

Skylitzes, Ioannes, *Synopsis of Histories*, ed. J. Thurn, *Ioannis Scylitzae Synopsis Historiarum* (Berlin and New York 1973); tr. J. Wortley, *John Skylitzes: A Synopsis of Byzantine History, 811–1057* (Cambridge 2010).

Smbat, *The Tale of the Bagratids*, tr. S. Rapp, *Studies in Medieval Georgian Historiography: Early Texts and Eurasian Contexts* (Leuven 2003) 350–367.

Step'anos of Taron, *Universal History*, German tr. H. Gelzer and A. Burckhardt, *Des Stephanos von Taron Armenische Geschichte* (Leipzig 1907); French tr. F. Macler, *Histoire universelle par Étienne Asołik de Tarôn* (Paris 1917).

Stephen of Blois, *Letters to Adela*, ed. H. Hagenmeyer, *Epistulae et chartae ad historiam primi belli sacri spectantes: Die Kreuzzugsbriefe aus den Jahren 1088–1100* (Innsbruck 1901) 138–140, 149–152; tr. M. Barber and K. Bate, *Letters from the East: Crusaders, Pilgrims and Settlers in the 12th–13th Centuries* (Farnham 2013) 15–17, 22–25.

Stethatos, Niketas, *Life of Saint Symeon the New Theologian*, ed. and tr. R. Greenfield (Cambridge, MA 2013).

Theodosios the Deacon, *The Capture of Crete*, ed. U. Criscuolo, *Theodosius Diaconus: De Creta Capta* (Leipzig 1979).

Theophanes the Confessor, *Chronographia*, ed. C. de Boor, *Theophanis Chronographia*, 2 vols. (Leipzig 1883–1885); tr. C. Mango and R. Scott, *The Chronicle of Theophanes Confessor: Byzantine and Near Eastern History* AD *284–813* (Oxford 1997).

Theophanes Continuatus, ed. I. Bekker, *Theophanes Continuatus, Ioannes Cameniata, Symeon Magister, Georgius Monachus* (Bonn 1838).

Thietmar of Merseburg, *Chronicon*, ed. R. Holtzmann, *Thietmari Merseburgensis episcopi chronicon* (Berlin 1935); tr. D. A. Warner, *Ottonian Germany: The Chronicon of Thietmar of Merseburg* (Manchester and New York 2001).

Timarion, ed. and tr. R. Romano, *Pseudo-Luciano: Timarione* (Naples 1974).

Typikon of Tzimiskes, ed. D. Papachryssanthou, *Actes du Prôtaton* (Paris 1975) 202–215.

William of Apulia, *Deeds of Robert Guiscard*, ed. and tr. M. Mathieu, *Le geste de Robert Guiscard* (Palermo 1961).

William of Jumièges, *Gesta Normannorum Ducum*, ed. and tr. E.M.C. van Houts, 2 vols. (Oxford 1992–1995).

Yahya of Antioch, *Chronicle*; (I) the years 937–969: ed. and tr. I. Kratchovsky and A. Vasiliev, *Histoire de Yahya*, in *Patrologia Orientalis* 18.5 (1924) 699–832; (II) the years 969–1013: idem in *Patrologia Orientalis* 23.3 (1932) 347–520; and (III) the years 1013–1034: ed. I. Kratchovsky and tr. F. Michaeu and G. Trouppeau in *Patrologia Orientalis* 47 (1997) 373–559; tr. B. Pirone, *Yaḥyā al Anṭākī: Cronache dell'Egitto Fāṭimide e dell'Impero Bizantino, 937–1033* (Milan 1998).

Zonaras, Ioannes, *Chronicle*, books 13–18, ed. T. Büttner-Wobst, *Ioannis Zonarae Epitomae Historiarum libri XIII–XVIII* (Bonn 1897).

Scholarship

Adontz, N., *Études armeno-byzantines* (Lisbon 1965).

Ahrweiler, H., "Recherches sur l'administration de l'empire byzantin aux IX–XIème siècles," *Bulletin de correspondance hellénique* 84 (1960) 1–111.

Amedroz, H. F., "An Embassy from Baghdad to the Emperor Basil II," *The Journal of the Royal Asiatic Society of Great Britain and Ireland* (1914) 915–942.

Anagnostakis, I., "Μονεμβασία-Λακεδαίμων: Για μια τυπολογία αντιπαλότητας και για την Κυριακή αργία στις πόλεις," in T. Kiousopoulou, ed., *Οι βυζαντινές πόλεις, 8ος–15ος αιώνας: Προοπτικές της έρευνας και νέες ερμηνευτικές προσεγγίσεις* (Rethymno 2012) 101–137.

Anastasi, R., "Su tre epigrammi di Giovanni di Euchaita," *Siculorum Gymnasium* 25 (1972) 56–60.

Angelidi, Ch., ed., *Το Βυζάντιο ώριμο για αλλαγές: Επιλογές, ευαισθησίες και τρόποι έκφρασης από τον ενδέκατο στον δέκατο πέμπτο αιώνα* (Athens 2004).

Arnold, B., *Medieval Germany, 500–1300: A Political Interpretation* (Toronto 1997).

Arutjunova-Fidanjan, V., "Some Aspects of the Military-Administrative Districts and of Byzantine Administration in Armenia during the 11th Century," *Revue des études arméniennes* n.s. 20 (1986–1987) 309–320.

Asbridge, T., *The Creation of the Principality of Antioch, 1098–1130* (Woodbridge 2000).

———, *The First Crusade: A New History* (Oxford 2004).

Bardill, J., "The Great Palace of the Byzantine Emperors and the Walker Trust Excavations," *Journal of Roman Archaeology* 12 (1999) 216–230.

Bartlett, R., *The Making of Europe: Conquest, Colonization and Cultural Change, 950–1350* (Princeton 1993).

Baun, J., *Tales from Another Byzantium: Celestial Journey and Local Community in the Medieval Greek Apocrypha* (Cambridge 2007).

Beihammer, A., "Der harte Sturz des Bardas Skleros: Eine Fallstudie zu zwischenstaatliche Kommunikation und Konfliktführung in der byzantinisch-arabischen Diplomatie des 10. Jahrhunderts," *Römische historische Mitteilungen* 45 (2003) 21–57.

Belke, K., *Galatien und Lykaonien* (Vienna 1984).

———, "Byzanz und die Anfänge des rumseldschukischen Staates: Bemerkungen zur Chronologie von Anna Komnenes 'Alexias' in den Jahren 1084-1093," *JöB* 61 (2011) 65–79.

Bell, P. N., *Social Conflict in the Age of Justinian: Its Nature, Management, & Mediation* (Oxford 2013).

Benner, T. H., *Die syrich-jakobitische Kirche unter byzantinischer Herrschaft im 10. und 11. Jahrhundert* (Marburg 1989).

Bianquis, T., "Sayf al-Dawla," *Encyclopedia of Islam*, 2nd ed. (online reference work).

———, *Damas et la Syrie sous la domination fatimide (359–468/969–1076): Essai d'interpretation de chroniques arabes médiévales*, 2 vols. (Damascus 1986–1989).

Bibicou, H., "Une page d'histoire diplomatique de Byzance au XIe siècle: Michel VII Doukas, Robert Guiscard et la pension des dignitaires," *Byzantion* 29–30 (1959–1960) 43–75.

Bikhazi, J., *The Hamdanid Dynasty of Mesopotamia and North Syria, 868–1014* (Ph.D. thesis, University of Michigan 1981).

Biliarsky, I., "St. Peter (927–969), Tsar of the Bulgarians," in V. Gjuzelev and K. Petkov, eds., *State and Church: Studies in Medieval Bulgaria and Byzantium* (Sofia 2011) 173–188.

Blaum, P. A., "Diplomacy Gone to Seed: A History of Byzantine Foreign Relations, A.D. 1047–57," *International Journal of Kurdish Studies* 18 (2004) 1–56.

Blöndal, S., *The Varangians of Byzantium*, tr. B. S. Benedikz (Cambridge 1978).

Bonovas, N., and A. Tzitzibassi, eds., *Byzantium and the Arabs: Temporary Exhibition (October 2011–January 2012). Exhibition Catalogue* (Thessalonike 2011).

Bosworth, C. E., "The Political and Dynastic History of the Iranian World (A.D. 1000–1217)," in J. A. Boyle, ed., *Cambridge History of Iran*, v. 5 (Cambridge 1968) 1–202.

———, *The Arabs, Byzantium and Iran: Studies in Early Islamic History and Culture* (London 1996).

Božilov, I., and V. Gjuzelev, *Istorija na srednovekovna Bălgarija VII–XIV vek* (Sofia 2006).

Brett, M., *The Rise of the Fatimids: The World of the Mediterranean and the Middle East in the Fourth Century of the Hijra, Tenth Century CE* (Leiden 2001).

Brokkaar, W. G., "Basil Lacapenus," in W. F. Bakker et al., eds., *Studia Byzantina et Neohellenica Neerlandica* (Leiden 1972) 199–234.

Bryer, A., et al., "Theodore Gabras, Duke of Chaldia, and the Gabrades: Portraits, Sites and Seals," in A. Avramea et al., eds., *Byzantium, State and Society: In Memory of Nikos Oikonomides* (Athens 2003) 51–70.

Bujan, S., "La Chronique du prêtre de Dioclée: un faux document historique," *REB* 66 (2008) 5–38.

Bürgel, J. C., *Die Hofkorrespondenz 'Aḍud ad-Daulas und ihr Verhältnis zu anderen historischen Quellen der frühen Būyiden* (Wiesbaden 1965).

Burgmann, L., "Turning Sissinios against the Sisinnians: Eustathios Romaios on a Disputed Marriage," in P. Magdalino, ed., *Byzantium in the Year 1000* (Leiden and Boston 2003) 161–181.

Cahen, C., "Le première pénétration turque en Asie mineure (second moitié di XIe siècle)," *Byzantion* 18 (1946–1948) 5–67.

Canard, M., "Deux documents arabes sur Bardas Skléros," *Studi bizantini e neoellenici* 5 (1939) 55–69.

———, "La date des expéditions mésopotamiennes de Jean Tzimiscès," *Annuaire de l'institut de philologie et d'histoire orientales et slaves* 10 (1950) 99–108.

———, *Histoire de la Dynastie des H'amdanides de Jazîra et de Syrie* (Algeria 1951).

———, "Les sources arabes de l'histoire byzantine aux confins des Xe et XIe siècles," *REB* 19 (1961) 284–314.

———, "Le destruction de l'église de la Résurrection par le Calife Hakim et l'histoire de la descente du feu sacré," *Byzantion* 35 (1965) 16–43.

———, "Hamdanids," *Encyclopedia of Islam*, 2nd ed.. (online reference work).

———, "Ikritish," *Encyclopedia of Islam*, 2nd ed. (online reference work).

Cappel, A., "The Byzantine Response to the 'Arab (10th–11th Centuries)," *BF* 20 (1994) 113–132.

Chadwick, H., *East and West: The Making of a Rift in the Church* (Oxford 2003).

Charanis, P., "The Monastic Properties and the State in the Byzantine Empire," *DOP* 4 (1948) 51–118.

———, *Studies on the Demography of the Byzantine Empire: Collected Studies* (London 1972).

El Cheikh, N. M., *Byzantium Viewed by the Arabs* (Cambridge, MA 2004).

Chevedden, P. E., " 'A Crusade from the First': The Norman Conquest of Islamic Sicily, 1060–1091," *Al-Masaq* 22 (2010) 191–225.

Cheynet, J.-C., *Pouvoir et contestations à Byzance (963–1210)* (Paris 1996).

———, "La conception militaire de la frontière orientale (IXe–XIIIe siècle)," in A. Eastmond, ed., *Eastern Approaches to Byzantium* (Ashgate 2001) 57–69.

———, *Sceaux de la collection Zacos (Bibliothèque nationale de France) se rapportant aux provinces orientales de l'Empire byzantin* (Paris 2001).

———, *The Byzantine Aristocracy and Its Military Function* (London 2006).

———, "The Duchy of Antioch during the Second Period of Byzantine Rule," in K. Ciggaar and M. Metcalf, eds., *East and West in the Medieval Eastern Mediterranean*, v. 1: *Antioch from the Byzantine Reconquest until the End of the Crusader Principality* (Leuven et al. 2006) 1–16.

———, "Le schisme de 1054: un non-évenement?" in C. Carozzi et al., eds., *Faire l'évenement au Moyen Âge* (Aix 2007) 299–312.

———, *La société byzantine: l'apport des sceaux*, 2 vols. (Paris 2008).

Chiarelli, L. C., *A History of Muslim Sicily* (Malta 2011).

Chitwood, Z., *Byzantine Legal Culture under the Macedonian Dynasty, 867–1056* (Ph.D. dissertation, Princeton University, 2012).

Christides, V., "The Raids of the Moslems of Crete in the Aegean Sea: Piracy and Conquest," *Byzantion* 51 (1981) 76–111.

———, *The Conquest of Crete by the Arabs (ca. 824): A Turning Point in the Struggle between Byzantium and Islam* (Athens 1984).

———, "Raid and Trade in the Eastern Mediterranean: A Treatise by Muḥammad bn. ʿUmar, the *Faqīh* from Occupied Moslem Crete, and the *Rhodian Sea Law*, Two Parallel Texts," *Graeco-Arabica* 5 (1993) 63–102.

Christophilopoulou, A., Ἐκλογή, ἀναγόρευσις καὶ στέψις τοῦ βυζαντινοῦ αὐτοκράτορος (Athens 1956).

———, "Ἡ ἀντιβασιλεία εἰς τὸ Βυζάντιον," *Symmeikta* 2 (1970) 1–144.

Christou, E., Αὐτοκρατορικὴ ἐξουσία καὶ πολιτικὴ πρακτική: Ὁ ρόλος του παραδυναστεύοντος στη βυζαντινή διοίκηση (τέλη 8ου–αρχές 11ου αιώνα) (Athens 2008).

Churchill, W. J., *The Annales Barenses and the Annales Lupi Protospatharii* (Ph.D. thesis, University of Toronto, 1979).

Ciggaar, K., *Western Travellers to Constantinople: The West and Byzantium, 962–1204* (Leiden 1996).

Cobb, P. M., *The Race for Paradise: An Islamic History of the Crusades* (Oxford 2014).

Cowdrey, H.E.J., "Pope Gregory VII's 'Crusading' Plans of 1074," in B. Z. Kedar et al., eds., *Outremer: Studies in the History of the Crusading Kingdom of Jerusalem* (Jerusalem 1982) 27–40.

———, *Pope Gregory VII, 1073–1085* (Oxford 1998).

————, "Pope Urban II's Preaching of the First Crusade," in T. Madden, ed., *The First Crusade: Essential Readings* (Oxford and Malden, MA 2002) 15–29.

Criscuolo, U., "πολιτικὸς ἀνήρ: Contributo al pensiero politica di Michele Psello," *Rendiconti dell'Accademia di Archeologia, Lettere e Belle Arti di Napoli* 57 (1982) 129–163.

Crostini, B., "The Emperor Basil II's Cultural Life," *Byzantion* 66 (1996) 55–80.

Curta, F., *Southeastern Europe in the Middle Ages, 500–1250* (Cambridge 2006).

————, "The Image and Archaeology of the Pechenegs," *Banatica* 23 (2013) 143–202.

————, "Constantinople and the Echo Chamber: The Vlachs in the French Crusade Chronicles," *Medieval Encounters* 22 (2016) 427–462.

Cutler, A., *The Hand of the Master: Craftsmanship, Ivory, and Society in Byzantium (9th–11th Centuries)* (Princeton 1994).

Dagron, G., "Minorités ethniques et religieuses dans l'Orient byzantin à la fin du Xe et au XIe siècle: l'immigration syrienne," *TM* 6 (1976) 177–216.

————, *Emperor and Priest: The Imperial Office in Byzantium*, tr. J. Birrell (Cambridge 2003).

Dagron, G., and H. Mihăescu, *Le traité sur la guérilla (De velitatione) de l'empereur Nicéphore Phocas (963–969)* (Paris 1986).

Dark, K., "The Byzantine Church and Monastery of St. Mary Peribleptos in Istanbul," *The Burlington Magazine* 141 (1999) 656–664.

Davids, A., ed., *The Empress Theophano: Byzantium and the West at the Turn of the First Millennium* (Cambridge 1995).

Decker, M., "Frontier Settlement and Economy in the Byzantine East," *DOP* 61 (2007) 217–267.

Dédéyan, G., "Les Arméniens en Cappadoce aux Xe et XIe siècles," in C. D. Fonseca, ed., *Le aree omogenee della Civiltà Rupestre nell'ambito dell'Impero Bizantino: La Cappadocia* (Lecce 1981) 75–95.

Ditten, H., *Ethnische Verschiebungen zwischen der Balkanhalbinsel und Kleinasien vom Ende des 6. bis zur zweiten Hälfte des 9. Jahrhunderts* (Berlin 1993).

Donohue, J. J., *The Buwayhid Dynasty in Iraq, 334H./945 to 403H./1012: Shaping Institutions for the Future* (Leiden and Boston 2003).

Drocourt, N., "Passing on Political Information between Major Powers: The Key Role of Ambassadors between Byzantium and Some of Its Neighbors," *Al-Masaq* 24 (2012) 91–112.

Edgington, S., "The First Crusade: Reviewing the Evidence," in J. Phillips, ed., *The First Crusade: Origins and Impact* (Manchester 1997) 55–77.

Erdmann, C., "Das ottonische Reich als Imperium Romanum," *Deutsches Archiv für Erforschung des Mittelalters* 6 (1943) 412–441.

————, "Die nichtrömische Kaiseridee," in idem, *Forschungen zur politischen Ideenwelt des Frühmittelalters* (Berlin 1951) 1–51.

Falkenhausen, V. von, *Untersuchungen über die byzantinische Herrschaft in Süditalien vom 9. bis ins 11. Jahrhundert* (Wiesbaden 1967).

———, *La dominazione bizantina nell'Italia meridionale dal IX all'XI secolo* (Bari 1978).

———, "Olympias, eine normannische Prinzessin in Konstantinopel," in *Bisanzio e l'Italia: Raccolta di studi in memoria di Agostino Pertusi* (Milan 1982) 56–72.

———, "La vita di S. Nilo come fonte storica per la Calabria bizantina," *Atti del Congresso Internazionale su S. Nilo di Rossano* (Rossano 1989) 281–293.

———, "Between Two Empires: Southern Italy in the Reign of Basil II," in P. Magdalino, ed., *Byzantium in the Year 1000* (Leiden 2003) 135–159.

Farag, W., *Byzantium and Its Muslim Neighbours during the Reign of Basil II (976–1025)* (Ph.D. thesis, University of Birmingham, 1977).

———, "The Aleppo Question: A Byzantine-Fatimid Conflict of Interests in Northern Syria in the Later Tenth Century A.D.," *BMGS* 14 (1990) 44–60.

Felix, W., *Byzanz und die islamische Welt im früheren 11. Jahrhundert: Geschichte der politischen Beziehungen von 1001 bis 1055* (Vienna 1981).

Fine, J.V.A., *The Early Medieval Balkans: A Critical Survey from the Sixth to the Late Twelfth Century* (Ann Arbor, MI 1991).

Fögen, M.-T., "Reanimation of Roman Law in the Ninth Century: Remarks on Reasons and Results," in L. Brubaker, ed., *Byzantium in the Ninth Century: Dead or Alive?* (Aldershot 1998) 11–22.

Folz, R., *The Concept of Empire in Western Europe from the Fifth to the Fourteenth Century*, tr. S. A. Ogilvie (London 1969).

Forsyth, J. H., *The Byzantine-Arab Chronicle (938–1034) of Yahya b. Sa'id al-Antaki*, 2 vols. (Ph.D. thesis, University of Michigan 1977).

Foss, C., *Ephesus after Antiquity: A Late Antique, Byzantine and Turkish City* (Cambridge 1979).

———, "The Defenses of Asia Minor against the Turks," *Greek Orthodox Theological Review* 27 (1982) 149–204.

France, J., "The Occasion of the Coming of the Normans to Southern Italy," *Journal of Medieval History* 17 (1991) 185–205.

———, *Victory in the East: A Military History of the First Crusade* (Cambridge 1994).

Frankopan, P., "The Workings of the Byzantine Provincial Administration in the 10th–12th Centuries: The Example of Preslav," *Byzantion* 71 (2001) 73–97.

———, "Kinship and the Distribution of Power in Komnenian Byzantium," *English Historical Review* 122 (2007) 1–34.

———, "Land and Power in the Middle and Later Period," in J. Haldon, ed., *A Social History of Byzantium* (Chichester 2009) 112–142.

———, *The First Crusade: The Call from the East* (Cambridge, MA 2012).

Garland, L., and S. Rapp, "Mary 'of Alania': Woman and Empress between Two Worlds," in L. Garland, ed., *Byzantine Women: Varieties of Experience, 800–1200* (Aldershot, UK 2006) 91–124.

Garrood, W., "The Byzantine Conquest of Cilicia and the Hamdanids of Aleppo, 959–965," *Anatolian Studies* 58 (2008) 127–140.

———, "The Illusion of Continuity: Nikephoros Phokas, John Tzimiskes and the Eastern Border," *BMGS* 37 (2013) 20–34.

Garsoïan, N. G., "The Byzantine Annexation of the Armenian Kingdoms," in R. G. Hovannisian, *The Armenian People from Ancient to Modern Times*, v. 1: *The Dynastic Periods: From Antiquity to the Fourteenth Century* (New York 1997) 187–198.

———, "The Problem of Armenian Integration into the Byzantine Empire," in H. Ahrweiler and A. E. Laiou, eds., *Studies on the Internal Diaspora of the Byzantine Empire* (Washington, DC 1998) 53–124.

Gautier, P., "Lettre au sultan Malik-Shah rédigée par Michel Psellos," *REB* 35 (1977) 73–97.

Gay, J., *L'Italie méridionale et l'Empire byzantin depuis l'avènement de Basile Ier jusqu'à la prise de Bari par les Normands (867–1071)* (Paris 1904).

Gelzer, H., "Ungedruckte und wenig bekannte Bistumsverzeichnisse der orientalischen Kirchen," *BZ* 2 (1893) 22–72.

Gkoutzioukostas, A. E., *Η απονομή δικαιοσύνης στο Βυζάντιο (9ος–12ο αιώνες): Τα κοσμικά δικαιοδοτικά όργανα και δικαστήρια της πρωτεύουσας* (Thessalonike 2004).

Guillou, A., *Studies on Byzantine Italy* (London 1970).

Górecki, D., "The *Strateia* of Constantine VII: The Legal Status, Administration and Historical Background," *BZ* 82 (1989) 157–176.

Greenwood, T., "Armenian Neighbours (600–1045)," in J. Shepard, ed., *The Cambridge History of the Byzantine Empire, c. 500–1492* (Cambridge 2008) 333–364.

———, "Patterns of Contact and Communication: Constantinople and Armenia, 860–976," in R. G. Hovannisian and S. Payaslian, eds., *Armenian Constantinople* (Costa Mesa, CA 2010) 73–99.

Grierson, P., "The Tombs and Obits of the Byzantine Emperors (337–1042)," *DOP* 16 (1962) 1–63.

———, *Catalogue of the Byzantine Coins in the Dumbarton Oaks Collection and in the Wittemore Collection*, v. 3: *Leo III to Nicephorus III, 717–1081*, part 2: *Basil I to Nicephorus III (867–1081)* (Washington, DC 1973).

Grigoriou-Ioannidou, M., *Οργανωτικά μέτρα του Κωνσταντίνου Θ´ Μονομάχου: Το πρόβλημα του στρατού της Ιβηρίας* (Thessalonike 1993).

Grumel, V., "Le patriarcat et les patriarches d'Antioch sous la seconde domination byzantine (969–1084)," *Echos d'Orient* 33 (1934) 129–147.

Grumel, V., and J. Darrouzès, *Les Regestes des actes du patriarcat de Constantinople*, v. 1: *Les actes des patriarches*, fasc. II and III: 715 to 1206 (Paris 1989).

Guilland, R., *Recherches sur les institutions byzantines*, 2 vols. (Berlin and Amsterdam 1967).

————, *Études de topographie de Constantinople byzantine*, 2 vols. (Berlin and Amsterdam 1969).

Haldon, J., "Military Service, Military Lands, and the Status of Soldiers: Current Problems and Interpretations," *DOP* 47 (1993) 1–67.

————, *Warfare, State and Society in the Byzantine World, 565–1204* (London 1999).

————, "Theory and Practice in Tenth-Century Military Administration: Chapters II, 44 and 45 of the *Book of Ceremonies*," *TM* 13 (2000) 201–352.

————, "Approaches to an Alternative Military History of the Period ca. 1025–1071," in V. Vlyssidou, ed., *Η αυτοκρατορία σε κρίση (;) Το Βυζάντιο τον 11ο αιώνα (1025–1081)* (Athens 2003) 45–74.

————, *The Byzantine Wars* (Stroud, UK, 2008).

————, "Social Élites, Wealth, and Power," in idem, ed., *A Social History of Byzantium* (Chichester 2009) 168–211.

————, "La logistique de Mantzikert," in D. Barthélemy and J.-C. Cheynet, eds., *Guerre et société: Byzance—Occident (VIIIe–XIIIe siècle)* (Paris 2010) 11–25.

————, "Comparative State Formation: The Later Roman Empire in the Wider World," in S. Johnson, ed., *The Oxford Handbook of Late Antiquity* (Oxford 2012) 1111–1147.

Haldon, J., and L. Brubaker, *Byzantium in the Iconoclast Era, c. 680–850: A History* (Cambridge 2011).

Haldon, J., and H. Kennedy, "The Arab-Byzantine Frontier in the Eighth and Ninth Centuries: Military Organisation and Society in the Borderlands," *Zbornik Radova Vizantinološkog Instituta* 19 (1980) 79–116.

Haldon, J., et al., "The Climate and Environment of Byzantine Anatolia: Integrating Science, History, and Archaeology," *Journal of Interdisciplinary History* 45 (2014) 113–161.

Halkin, F., "Translation par Nicéphore Phocas de la brique miraculeuse d'Hiérapolis (BHG 3 801n)," *Subsidia hagiographica* 38 (1963) 253–260.

Harvey, A., *Economic Expansion in the Byzantine Empire, 900–1200* (Cambridge 1989).

————, "Competition for Economic Resources: The State, Landowners and Fiscal Privileges," in V. Vlyssidou, ed., *Η αυτοκρατορία σε κρίση (;) Το Βυζάντιο τον 11ο αιώνα (1025–1081)* (Athens 2003) 169–177.

Harris, J., "The 'Schism' of 1054 and the First Crusade," *Crusades* 13 (2014) 1–20.

Hendy, M. F., "Light Weight *Solidi, Tetartera*, and The Book of the Prefect," *BZ* 65 (1972) 57–80.

————, *Studies in the Byzantine Monetary Economy, c. 300–1450* (Cambridge 1985).

————, "The Economy: A Brief Survey," in S. Vryonis, ed., *Byzantine Studies: Essays on the Slavic World and the Eleventh Century* (New Rochelle, NY 1992) 141–152.

Herrin, J., *Margins and Metropolis: Authority across the Byzantine Empire* (Princeton 2013).

Hillenbrand, C., *Turkish Myth and Muslim Symbol: The Battle of Manzikert* (Edinburgh 2007).

Hilsdale, C., "The Social Life of the Byzantine Gift: The Royal Crown of Hungary Re-Invented," *Art History* 31 (2008) 603–631.

Holmes, C., "'How the East Was Won' in the Reign of Basil II," in A. Eastmond, ed., *Eastern Approaches to Byzantium* (Ashgate 2001) 41–56.

———, "Byzantium's Eastern Frontier in the Tenth and Eleventh Centuries," in D. Abulafia and N. Berend, eds., *Medieval Frontiers: Concepts and Practices* (Ashgate 2002) 83–104.

———, "Political Elites in the Reign of Basil II," in P. Magdalino, ed., *Byzantium in the Year 1000* (Leiden and Boston 2003) 35–70.

———, *Basil II and the Governance of Empire (976–1025)* (Oxford 2005).

Holo, J., "A Genizah Letter from Rhodes Evidently Concerning the Byzantine Reconquest of Crete," *Journal of Near Eastern Studies* 59 (2000) 1–12.

Hondridou, S., *Ο Κωνσταντίνος Θ´ Μονομάχος και η εποχή του (ενδέκατος αιώνας μ.Χ.)* (Thessalonike 2002).

Honigmann, *Die Ostgrenze des byzantinischen Reiches von 363 bis 1071 nach griechischen, arabischen, syrischen und armenischen Quellen* (Brussels 1935 = A. A. Vasiliev, ed., *Byzance et les Arabes*, v. 3).

Howard-Johnston, J., "Crown Lands and the Defence of Imperial Authority in the Tenth and Eleventh Centuries," *BF* 21 (1995) 75–100.

Jacoby, D., "Bishop Gunther of Bamberg, Byzantium and Christian Pilgrimage to the Holy Land in the Eleventh Century," in L. M. Hoffmann and A. Monchizadeh, eds., *Zwischen Polis, Provinz und Peripherie: Beiträge zur byzantinischen Geschichte und Kultur* (Wiesbaden 2005) 267–285.

Jeffreys, M., "Psellos and 'His Emperors': Fact, Fiction and Genre," in R. Macrides, ed., *History as Literature in Byzantium* (Farnham, UK 2010) 73–91.

Johnson, G., "Constantine VIII and Michael Psellos: Rhetoric, Reality, and the Decline of Byzantium, A.D. 1025–28," *Byzantine Studies* 9 (1982) 220–232.

Joranson, E., "The Great German Pilgrimage of 1064–1065," in L. J. Paetow, ed., *The Crusades and Other Historical Essays* (New York 1928) 3–43.

———, "The Inception of the Career of the Normans in Italy: History and Reality," *Speculum* 23 (1948) 353–396.

Kaegi, W., "The Contribution of Archery to the Turkish Conquest of Anatolia," *Speculum* 39 (1964) 96–108.

———, "The Controversy about Bureaucratic and Military Factions," *BF* 19 (1993) 25–33.

Kafesoğlu, İ, and G. Leiser, "The First Seljuk Raid into Eastern Anatolia (1015–1021) and Its Historical Significance," *Mésogeios* 25–26 (2005) 27–47.

Kaldellis, A., *The Argument of Psellos' Chronographia* (Leiden and Boston 1999).

———, "A Byzantine Argument for the Equivalence of All Religions: Michael Attaleiates on Ancient and Modern Romans," *International Journal of the Classical Tradition* 14 (2007) 1–22.

———, *Hellenism in Byzantium: The Transformations of Greek Identity and the Reception of the Classical Tradition* (Cambridge 2007).

————, *The Christian Parthenon: Classicism and Pilgrimage in Byzantine Athens* (Cambridge 2009).

————, "The Date of Psellos' Death, Once Again: Psellos Was Not the Michael of Nikomedeia Mentioned by Attaleiates," *BZ* 104 (2011) 649–661.

————, "The Original Source for Tzimiskes' Balkan Campaign (971) and the Emperor's Classicizing Propaganda," *BMGS* 37 (2013) 1–18.

————, *Ethnography after Antiquity: Foreign Lands and Peoples in Byzantine Literature* (Philadelphia 2013).

————, *The Byzantine Republic: People and Power at New Rome* (Cambridge, MA 2015).

————, "Did Ioannes I Tzimiskes campaign in the east in 974?" *Byzantion* 84 (2014) 235–240.

————, "The Byzantine Conquest of Crete (961 AD), Prokopios' *Vandal War*, and the Continuator of the *Chronicle* of Symeon," *BMGS* 39 (2015) 302–311.

————, "The Manufacture of History in the Later Tenth and Eleventh Centuries: Rhetorical Templates and Narrative Ontologies," *Proceedings of the 23rd International Congress of Byzantine Studies (Belgrade, 22–27 August 2016): Plenary Papers* (Belgrade 2016) 293–306.

————, "The Discontinuous History of Imperial Panegyric in Byzantium and its Reinvention by Michael Psellos," forthcoming.

————, "Keroularios in 1054: Nonconfrontational to the Papal Legates and Loyal to the Emperor," in preparation.

Kaldellis, A., and I. Polemis, *Psellos and the Patriarchs: Letters and Funeral Orations for Keroullarios, Leichoudes, and Xiphilinos* (South Bend, IN 2015).

Kaplan, M., "Les grands proprietaires de Cappadoce (Vie–XIe siècles)," in C. D. Fonseca, ed., *Le aree omogenee della Civiltà Rupestre nell'ambito dell'Impero Bizantino: La Cappadocia* (Lecce 1981) 125–158.

————, *Les hommes et la terre à Byzance du VIe au XIe siècle* (Paris 1992).

Kaplanis, C., "The Debasement of the 'Dollar of the Middle Ages'," *Journal of Economic History* 63 (2003) 768–801.

Karagiorgou, O., "On the Way to the Throne: The Career of Nikephoros III Botaneiates before 1078," in C. Stavrakos et al., eds., *Hypermachos: Studien zu Byzantinistik, Armenologie und Georgistik* (Wiesbaden 2008) 105–132.

Karpozilos, A., Συμβολὴ στὴ μελέτην τοῦ βίου καὶ τοῦ ἔργου τοῦ Ἰωάννη Μαυρόποδος (Ioannina 1982).

Kazhdan, A. P., and A. Epstein, *Change in Byzantine Culture in the Eleventh and Twelfth Centuries* (Berkeley 1990).

Keller, H., "Das Kaisertum Ottos des Grossen im Verständnis seiner Zeit," *Deutsches Archiv für Erforschung des Mittelalters* 20 (1964) 325–388.

Kelly, C., *Ruling the Later Roman Empire* (Cambridge, MA 2004).

Kennedy, H., "Antioch: From Byzantium to Islam and Back Again," in J. Rich, ed., *The City in Late Antiquity* (New York and London 1992) 181–198.

————, *The Prophet and the Age of the Caliphates: The Islamic Near East from the Sixth to the Eleventh Century*, 2nd ed. (London 2004).

————, "Sicily and Al-Andalus under Muslim Rule," in T. Reuter, ed., *The New Cambridge Medieval History*, v. 3 (Cambridge 2000) 646–669.

Kolias, T. G., Νικηφόρος Β΄ Φωκᾶς (963–969): Ὁ στρατηγός αὐτοκράτωρ καί τό μεταρρυθμιστικό του ἔργο (Athens 1993).

Krallis, D., "'Democratic' Action in Eleventh-Century Byzantium: Michael Attaleiates's 'Republicanism' in Context," *Viator* 40 (2009) 35–53.

————, *Michael Attaleiates and the Politics of Imperial Decline in Eleventh-Century Byzantium* (Tempe, AZ 2012).

Kresten, O., "Sprachliche und inhaltliche Beobachtungen zu Kapitel I 96 des sogenannten 'Zeremonienbuches'," *BZ* 93 (2000) 474–489.

Kreutz, B. M., *Before the Normans: Southern Italy in the Ninth and Tenth Centuries* (Philadelphia 1991).

Krsmanović, B., "Αλλαγές στη δομή της κοινωνικής κορυφής μετά την εποχή του Βασιλείου του Β΄," in V. Vlyssidou, ed., *Η αυτοκρατορία σε κρίση (;) Το Βυζάντιο τον 11ο αιώνα (1025–1081)* (Athens 2003) 87–106.

————, *The Byzantine Province in Change (On the Threshold between the 10th and the 11th Century)* (Belgrade and Athens 2008).

Kühn, H.-J., *Die byzantinische Armee im 10. und 11. Jahrhundert: Studien zur Organisation der Tagmata* (Vienna 1991).

Laiou, A. E., "The Foreigner and the Stranger in 12th Century Byzantium: Means of Propitiation and Acculturation," in M. T. Fögen, ed., *Fremde der Gesellschaft: Historische und socialwissenschaftliche Untersuchungen zur Differenzierung von Normalität und Fremdheit* (Frankfurt am Main 1991) 71–97.

————, *Mariage, amour et parenté à Byzance aux XIe–XIIIe siècles* (Paris 1992).

————, "Imperial Marriages and Their Critics in the Eleventh Century: The Case of Skylitzes," *DOP* 46 (1992) 165–176.

————, "The General and the Saint: Michael Maleinos and Nikephoros Phokas," in M. Balard et al., eds., *ΕΥΨΥΧΙΑ: Mélanges offerts à Hélène Ahrweiler*, v. 2 (Paris 1998) 399–412.

Laiou, A. E., and C. Morrisson, *The Byzantine Economy* (Cambridge 2007).

Lambakis, S., et al., *Βυζαντινά στρατεύματα στη Δύση (5ος–11ος αι.): Έρευνες πάνω στις χερσαίες και ναυτικές επιχειρήσεις· σύνθεση και αποστολή των βυζαντινών στρατευμάτων στη Δύση* (Athens 2008).

Larkin, M., *Al-Mutanabbi: Voice of the 'Abbasid Poetic Ideal* (Oxford 2008).

Latowsky, A. A., *Emperor of the World: Charlemagne and the Construction of Imperial Authority, 800–1229* (Ithaca, NY 2013).

Laurent, V., "La chronologie des gouverneurs d'Antioch sous la seconde domination byzantine," *Mélanges de l'Université Saint-Joseph de Beyrouth* 38 (1962) 219–254.

Lauxtermann, M., "John Geometres—Poet and Soldier," *Byzantion* 68 (1998) 356–380.

————, *Byzantine Poetry from Pisides to Geometres* (Vienna 2003).

————, "Byzantine Poetry and the Paradox of Basil II's Reign," in P. Magdalino, ed., *Byzantium in the Year 1000* (Leiden and Boston 2003) 199–216.

Lefort, J., "Rhétorique et politique: Trois discours de Jean Mauropous en 1047," *TM* 6 (1976) 265–303.

———, "The Rural Economy, Seventh–Twelfth Centuries," in A. Laiou, ed., *The Economic History of Byzantium from the Seventh through the Fifteenth Century* (Washington, DC 2002) 231–310.

Lefort, J., and A. Martin, "Le sigillion du catépan d'Italie Eustathe Palatinos pour le juge Byzantios (Décembre 1045)," *Mélanges de l'école française de Rome* 98 (1986) 525–542.

Lemerle, P., *Cinq études sur le XIe siècle byzantin* (Paris 1977).

Lev, Y., "The Fatimid Navy, Byzantium and the Mediterranean 909–1036 C.E./ 297–427 A.H.," *Byzantion* 54 (1984) 220–252.

Leveniotis, G. A., *Το στασιαστικό κίνημα του Νορμανδού Ουρσελίου (Ursel de Bailleul) στην Μικρά Ασία (1073–1076)* (Thessalonike 2004).

———, "Το θέμα/δουκάτο των Ανατολικών κατά το δεύτερο ήμισυ του 11ου αι.," *Byzantiaka* 25 (2005–2006) 33–101.

———, "Η συνθήκη ειρήνης Ρωμανού Δ´Διογένη και Alp Arslan μετά τη μάχη του Μαντζικέρτ (Αύγουστος/Σεπτέμβριος του 1071)," *Βυζαντιακά* 27 (2008) 167–196.

———, *Η πολιτική κατάρρευση του Βυζαντίου στην ανατολή: Το ανατολικό σύνορο και η κεντρική Μικρά Ασία κατά το Β´ ήμισυ του 11ου αι.* (Thessalonike 2007).

Leyser, K. J., *Medieval Germany and Its Neighbours, 900–1250* (London 1982).

———, *Communications and Power in Medieval Europe: The Gregorian Revolution and Beyond* (London 1994).

———, "*Theophanu divina gratia imperatrix augusta*: Western and Eastern Emperorship in the Later Tenth Century," in A. Davids, ed., *The Empress Theophano: Byzantium and the West at the Turn of the First Millennium* (Cambridge 1995) 1–27.

Lilie, R.-J., "Caesaropapismus in Byzanz? Patriarch Polyeuktos und Kaiser Ioannes I. Tzimiskes," in K. Belke et al., eds., *Byzantina Mediterranea: Festschrift für Johannes Koder zum 65. Geburtstag* (Vienna 2007) 387–397.

———, "Fiktive Realität: Basileios II. und Konstantinos VIII. in der 'Chronographia' des Michael Psellos," in M. Grünbart, ed., *Theatron: Rhetorische Kultur in Spätantike und Mittelalter* (Berlin 2007) 211–222.

Loud, G. A., "Southern Italy in the Tenth Century," in T. Reuter, ed., *The New Cambridge Medieval History*, v. 3 (Cambridge 2000) 624–645.

———, *The Age of Robert Guiscard: Southern Italy and the Norman Conquest* (New York 2000).

MacEvitt, C., "The *Chronicle* of Matthew of Edessa: Apocalypse, the First Crusade, and the Armenian Diaspora," *DOP* 61 (2007) 157–181.

———, *The Crusades and the Christian World of the East: Rough Tolerance* (Philadelphia 2008).

Macrides, R., "The Byzantine Godfather," *BMGS* 11 (1987) 139–162.

Madgearu, A., *Byzantine Military Organization on the Danube, 10th–12th Centuries* (Leiden 2013).

Magdalino, P., *The Empire of Manuel I Komnenos, 1143–1180* (Cambridge 1993).

———, *The Byzantine Background to the First Crusade* (Toronto 1996).

———, "The Byzantine Army and the Land: From *stratiotikon ktema* to Military *pronoia*," in K. Tsiknakis, ed., *Το εμπόλεμο Βυζάντιο (9ος–12ος αι.)* (Athens 1997) 15–36.

———, "Paphlagonians in Byzantine High Society," in S. Lambakis, ed., *H Βυζαντινή Μικρά Ασία (6ος–12ος αι.)* (Athens 1998) 141–150.

———, "Preface," in idem, ed., *Byzantium in the Year 1000* (Leiden and Boston 2003) ix–xv.

———, "Court Society and Aristocracy," in J. Haldon, ed., *A Social History of Byzantium* (Chichester 2009) 212–232.

Mahé, J.-P., "Basile II et Byzance vus par Grigor Narekac'i," *TM* 11 (1991) 555–573.

Makrypoulias, C. G., "Byzantine Expeditions against the Emirate of Crete c. 825–949," *Graeco-Arabica* 7–8 (2000) 347–362.

Mango, C., "The Collapse of St. Sophia, Psellus and The *Etymologicum Genuinum*," in J. Duffy and J. Peradotto, eds., *Gonimos: Neoplatonic and Byzantine Studies Presented to Leendert G. Westerink at 75* (Buffalo, NY 1988) 167–174.

Maranci, C., "The Architect Trdat: Building Practices and Cross-Cultural Exchange in Byzantium and Armenia," *The Journal of the Society of Architectural Historians* 62 (2003) 294–305.

Markopoulos, A., "Byzantine History Writing at the End of the First Millennium," in P. Magdalino, ed., *Byzantium in the Year 1000* (Leiden and Boston 2003) 183–197.

———, *History and Literature of Byzantium in the 9th–10th Centuries* (Aldershot and Burlington, VT 2004).

Martin, J.-M., *La Pouille du VIe au XIIe siècle* (Rome 1993).

———, "Les thèmes italiens: territoire, administration, population," in A. Jacob et al., eds., *Histoire et culture dans l'Italie Byzantine: acquis et nouvelles recherches* (Rome 2006) 517–558.

Martin-Hisard, B., "Constantinople et les archontes du monde caucasien dans le Livre des Cérémonies, II, 48," *TM* 13 (2000) 359–530.

Mayr-Harting, H., "Liudprand of Cremona's Account of His Legation to Constantinople (968) and Ottonian Imperial Strategy," *English Historical Review* 116 (2001) 539–556.

Mazzucchi, C. M., "Dagli anni di Basilio Parakimomenos (Cod. Ambros. B 119 sup.)," *Aevum* 52 (1978) 267–316.

McCormick, M., *Eternal Victory: Triumphal Rulership in Late Antiquity, Byzantium and the Early Medieval West* (Cambridge and Paris 1986).

McGeer, E., "Tradition and Reality in the *Taktika* of Nikephoros Ouranos," *DOP* 45 (1991) 129–140.

————, *Sowing the Dragon's Teeth: Byzantine Warfare in the Tenth Century* (Washington, DC 1995).

————, "The Legal Decree of Nikephoros II Phokas Concerning Armenian *Stratiotai*," in T. S. Miller and J. Nesbitt, eds., *Peace and War in Byzantium: Essays in Honor of George T. Dennis, S.J.* (Washington, DC 1995) 123–137.

————, *The Land Legislation of the Macedonian Emperors* (Toronto 2000).

————, "Two Military Orations of Constantine VII," in J. Nesbit, ed., *Byzantine Authors: Literary Activities and Preoccupations* (Leiden 2003) 111–135.

McGrath, S., "The Battles of Dorostolon (971): Rhetoric and Reality," in T. S. Miller and J. Nesbitt, eds., *Peace and War in Byzantium: Essays in Honor of George T. Dennis, S.J.* (Washington, DC 1995) 152–164.

Metcalf, D. M., *Byzantine Cyprus, 491–1191* (Nicosia 2009).

Miklosich, F., and J. Müller, *Acta et diplomata graeca medii aevi sacra et profana*, 6 vols. (Vienna 1860–1890).

Miles, G. C., "Byzantium and the Arabs: Relations in Crete and the Aegean Area," *DOP* 18 (1964) 1–32.

Miotto, M., *Ο ανταγωνισμός Βυζαντίου και Χαλιφάτου των Φατιμίδων στην εγγύς ανατολή και η δράση των Ιταλικών πόλεων στην περιοχή κατά τον 10ο και τον 11ο αιώνα* (Thessalonike 2008).

Mladjov, I., "Bulgarians and Magyars as Allies and Rivals across the Early Medieval Frontier," in V. Gjuzelev and G. Nikolov, eds., *South-Eastern Europe in the Second Half of 10th–the Beginning of the 11th Centuries: History and Culture* (Sofia 2015) 63–84.

Mondrain, B., "La lecture du *De administrando imperio* à Byzance au cours des siècles," *TM* 14 (2002) 485–498.

Morgan, G., "A Byzantine Satirical Song?" *BZ* 47 (1954) 292–297.

Morris, C., *The Papal Monarchy: The Western Church from 1050 to 1250* (Oxford 1989).

Morris, R., "The Powerful and the Poor in Tenth-Century Byzantium: Law and Reality," *Past and Present* 73 (1976) 3–27.

————, "The Two Faces of Nikephoros Phokas," *BMGS* 12 (1988) 83–115.

————, *Monks and Laymen in Byzantium, 843–1118* (Cambridge 1995).

Morrisson, C., "La dévaluation de la monnaie byzantine au XIe siècle: essai d'interprétation," *TM* 7 (1976) 6–48.

————, "Displaying the Emperor's Authority and Kharakter on the Marketplace," in P. Armstrong, ed., *Authority in Byzantium* (Farnham, UK 2013) 65–82.

Moutsopoulos, N, "Le tombeau du tsar Samuil dans la basilique de saint Achille à Prespa," *Études balkaniques* 3 (1984) 114–126.

Müller-Mertens, E., "The Ottonians as Kings and Emperors," in T. Reuter, ed., *The New Cambridge Medieval History*, v. 3 (Cambridge 2000) 231–266.

Mullett, M., and D. Smythe, eds., *Alexios I Komnenos* (Belfast 1996).

Năsturel, P., "Les Valaques balkaniques aux Xe–XIIIe siècles (mouvements de population et colonisation dans la Romanie grecque et latine)," *BF* 7 (1979) 89–112.

Neville, L., *Heroes and Romans in Twelfth-Century Byzantium: The Materials for a History of Nikephoros Bryennios* (Cambridge 2012).

Nicol, D. M., *Byzantium and Venice: A Study in Diplomatic and Cultural Relations* (Cambridge 1988).

Nikolaou, K., and K. Tsiknakis, eds., *Βυζάντιο και Βούλγαροι (1018–1185)* (Athens 2008).

Nikolov, G. N., "The Bulgarian Aristocracy in the War against the Byzantine Empire (971–1019)," in G. Prinzing et al., ed., *Byzantium and East Central Europe* (Cracow 2001) 141–158.

O'Callaghan, J. F., *Reconquest and Crusade in Medieval Spain* (Philadelphia 2003).

Odorico, P., "Le backgammon de Kékaumenos: à propos d'un passage peu clair et d'une bataille peu connue," *Zbornik Radova Vizantinološkog Instituta* 50 (2013) 423–431.

Ohnsorge, W., *Konstantinopel und der Okzident: Gesammelte Aufsätze zur Geschichte der byzantinisch-abendländischen Beziehung und des Kaisertums* (Darmstadt 1966).

Oikonomides, N., "Le serment de l'impératrice Eudocie: un episode de l'histoire dynastique de Byzance," *REB* 21 (1963) 73–97.

———, "Recherches sur l'histoire du Bas-Danube aux Xe–XIe siècles: La Mésopotamie de l'Occident," *Revue des études sud-est européennes* 3 (1965) 57–79.

———, *Les Listes de préséance byzantines des IXe et Xe siècles* (Paris 1972).

———, "L'organisation de la frontière orientale de Byzance aux Xe–XIe siècles et le Taktikon de l'Escorial," in M. Berza and E. Stănescu, eds., *Actes du XIVe Congrès international des études byzantines* (Bucharest 1974) 285–302.

———, "L'évolution de l'organisation administrative de l'empire byzantin au XIe siècle (1025–1118)," *TM* 6 (1976) 125–152.

———, "St. George of Mangana, Maria Skleraina, and the 'Malyg Sion' of Novgorod," *DOP* 34–35 (1980–1981) 239–246.

———, "Middle-Byzantine Provincial Recruits: Salary and Armament," in J. Duffy and J. Peradoto, eds., *Gonimos: Neoplatonic and Byzantine Studies Presented to Leendert G. Westerink at 75* (Buffalo 1988) 121–136.

———, *Fiscalité et exemption fiscale à Byzance (IXe–XIe s.)* (Athens 1996).

———, "The Social Structure of the Byzantine Countryside in the First Half of the Xth Century," *Byzantina Symmeikta* 10 (1996) 105–125.

———, "Title and Income at the Byzantine Court," in H. Maguire, ed., *Byzantine Court Culture from 829 to 1204* (Washington, DC 1997) 199–215.

———, "A propos de la première occupation byzantine de Bulgarie (971–ca 986)," in M. Balard et al., eds., *ΕΥΨΥΧΙΑ: Mélanges offerts à Hélène Ahrweiler* (Paris 1998) 581–589.

Östenberg, I., *Staging the World: Spoils, Captives, and Representations in the Roman Triumphal Procession* (Oxford 2009).

Ostrogorsky, G., "Une ambassade Serbe auprès de l'empereur Basile II," *Byzantion* 19 (1949) 187–194.

———, *History of the Byzantine State*, tr. J. Hussey (New Brunswick 1969).

Ousterhout, R., "Rebuilding the Temple: Constantine Monomachus and the Holy Sepulchre," *Journal of the Society of Architectural Historians* 48 (1989) 66–78.

Panagopoulou, A. G., *Οι διπλωματικοί γάμοι στο Βυζάντιο (6ος–12ος αιώνας)* (Athens 2006).

———, *Θεοφανώ: Η βυζαντινή αυτοκράτειρα της Γερμανίας, πρέσβειρα του βυζαντινού πολιτισμού στη Δύση* (Thessalonike 2008).

Papadakis, A., with J. Meyendorff, *The Christian East and the Rise of the Papacy: The Church A.D. 1071–1453* (Crestwood, NY 1994).

Patlagean, E., *Structure sociale, famille, chrétienté à Byzance, IVe–XIe siècle* (London 1981).

Patoura, S., *Οι αιχμάλωτοι ως παράγοντες επικοινωνίας και πληροφόρησης (4ος–10ος αι.)* (Athens 1994).

Peacock, A.C.S., *Early Seljuq History: A New Interpretation* (London 2010).

Petkov, K., *The Voices of Medieval Bulgaria, Seventh-Fifteenth Century: The Records of a Bygone Culture* (Leiden 2008).

Polemis, D. I., *The Doukai: A Contribution to Byzantine Prosopography* (London 1968).

Poppe, A., "The Political Background to the Baptism of Rus': Byzantine-Russian Relations between 986–89," *DOP* 30 (1976) 195–244.

Popović, M., "Les fortresses du système défensif byzantine en Serbie au XIe–XIIe siècle," *Starinar* 42 (1991) 169–185.

Pozza, M., and G. Ravegnani, *I trattati con Bisanzio, 992–1198* (Venice 1993).

Pryor, J. H., and E. M. Jeffreys, *The Age of the ΔΡΟΜΩΝ: The Byzantine Navy ca 500–1204* (Leiden and Boston 2006).

Raffensperger, C., *Reimagining Europe: Kievan Rus' in the Medieval World* (Cambridge, MA 2012).

Rallis, G. A., and M. Potlis, *Σύνταγμα τῶν ἱερῶν καὶ θείων κανόνων* etc., 7 vols. (Athens 1852–1859).

Rapp, S., *Imagining History at the Crossroads: Persia, Byzantium, and the Architects of the Written Georgian Past* (Ph.D. dissertation, University of Michigan 1997).

Riedel, M., "Nikephoros II Phokas and Orthodox Military Martyrs," *Journal of Medieval Religious Cultures* 41 (2015) 121–147.

Riedinger, J.-C., "Quatre étapes de la vie de Michel Psellos," *REB* 68 (2010) 5–60.

Riley-Smith, J., *The First Crusaders, 1095–1131* (Cambridge 1997).

Ripper, T., *Die Marwaniden von Diyar Bakr: Eine kurdische Dynastie im islamischen Mittelalter* (Würzburg 2000).

Runciman, S., "The First Crusaders' Journey across the Balkan Peninsula," *Byzantion* 19 (1949) 207–221.

———, "The Pilgrimages to Palestine before 1095," in K. Setton, ed., *A History of the Crusades*, v. 1 (Madison, WI 1969) 68–78.

Saradi, H., "On the '*archontike*' and '*ekklesiastike dynasteia*' and '*prostasia*' in Byzantium," *Byzantion* 64 (1994) 67–117.

Saunders, W.B.R., "The Aachen Reliquary of Eustathios Maleinos," *DOP* 36 (1982) 211–219.

Seibt, W., "Untersuchungen zur Vor- und Frühgeschichte der 'bulgarischen' Kometopoulen," *Handes Amsorya* 89 (1975) 65–99.

———, *Die Skleroi: Eine prosopographisch-sigillographische Studie* (Vienna 1976).

———, "Die Eingliederung von Vaspurakan in das byzantinische Reich (etwa Anfang 1019 bzw. Anfang 1022)," *Handes Amsorya* 92 (1978) 49–66.

———, "Philaretos Brachamios—General, Rebell, Vasall?" in E. Chrysos and E. Zachariadou, eds., *Captain and Scholar: Papers in Memory of Demetrios I. Polemis* (Andros 2009) 281–295.

———, "Übernahm der französische Normanne Hervé (Erbebios Phrangopolos) nach der Katastrophe von Mantzikert das Kommando über die verbliebene Ostarmee?" *Studies in Byzantine Sigillography* 10 (2010) 89–96.

———, "The Byzantine Thema of Soterioupolis-Anakopia in the 11th Century," *Bulletin of the Georgian National Academy of Sciences* 6 (2012) 174–178.

Seyyedi, S. M., "Abu Firas," *Encyclopedia of Islam*, 2nd ed. (online reference work).

Shepard, J., "John Mauropous, Leo Tornicius and an Alleged Russian Army: The Chronology of the Pecheneg Crisis of 1048–1049," *Jahrbuch der österreichischen Byzantinistik* 24 (1975) 61–89.

———, "Scylitzes on Armenia in the 1040s and the role of Catacalon Cecaumenus," *Revue des études arméniennes* 11 (1975–1976) 269–311.

———, "Isaac Comnenus' Coronation Day," *Byzantinoslavica* 38 (1977) 22–31.

———, "Byzantium's Last Sicilian Expedition: Scylitzes' Testimony," *Rivista di studi bizantini e neoellenici* 14–16 (1977–1978) 145–159.

———, "Why Did the Russians Attack Byzantium in 1043?" *Byzantinisch-neugriechische Jahrbucher* 22 (1985) 147–212.

———, "When Greek Meets Greek: Alexius Comnenus and Bohemond in 1097–98," *BMGS* 12 (1988) 185–277.

———, "A Suspected Source of Scylitzes' Synopsis Historion: The Great Catacalon Cecaumenus," *BMGS* 16 (1992) 171–181.

———, "The Uses of the Franks in Eleventh-Century Byzantium," *Anglo-Norman Studies* 15 (1993) 275–305.

———, " 'Father' or 'Scorpion'? Style and Substance in Alexios's Diplomacy," in M. Mullett and D. Smythe, eds., Alexios I Komnenos (Belfast 1996) 68–132.

———, "Cross-Purposes: Alexius Comnenus and the First Crusade," in J. Phillips, ed., *The First Crusade: Origins and Impact* (Manchester 1997) 107–129.

———, "Byzantium and the Steppe-Nomads: The Hungarian Dimension," in G. Prinzing and M. Salamon, eds., *Byzanz und Ostmitteleuropa, 950–1453* (Wiesbaden 1999) 55–83.

———, "Bulgaria: The Other Balkan 'Empire'," in T. Reuter, ed., *The New Cambridge Medieval History*, v. 3 (Cambridge 2000) 567–585.

———, "Emperors and Expansionism: From Rome to Middle Byzantium," in D. Abulafia and N. Berend, eds., *Medieval Frontiers: Concepts and Practices* (Ashgate 2002) 55–82.

————, "Manners Maketh Romans? Young Barbarians at the Emperor's Court," in E. Jeffreys, ed., *Byzantine Style, Religion and Civilization: In Honour of Sir Steven Runciman* (Cambridge 2006) 135–158.

————, "Holy Land, Lost Lands, *Realpolitik*," *Al-Qantara* 33 (2012) 505–545.

————, "Adventus, Arrivistes and the Rites of Rulership in Byzantium and France in the Tenth and Eleventh Century," in A. Beihammer et al., eds., *Court Ceremonies and Rituals of Power in Byzantium and the Medieval Mediterranean: Comparative Perspectives* (Leiden 2013) 337–367.

Sifonas, C., "Basile II et l'aristocratie byzantine," *Byzantion* 64 (1994) 118–133.

Simeonova, L., "The Short Fuse: Examples of Diplomatic Abuse in Byzantine and Bulgarian History," *BF* 23 (1996) 55–73.

Simpson, A., "Three Sources of Military Unrest in Eleventh Century Asia Minor: The Norman Chieftains Hervé Frankopoulos, Robert Crispin and Roussel de Bailleul," *Mésogeios* 9-10 (2000) 181–207.

Smith, J.M.H., *Europe after Rome: A New Cultural History 500–1000* (Oxford 2005).

Smith, M. H., *And Taking Bread . . . Cerularius and the Azyme Controversy of 1054* (Paris 1978).

Somerville, R., *Pope Urban II's Council of Piacenza* (Oxford 2011).

Spadaro, M. D., *Michaelis Pselli in Mariam Sclerenam* (Catania 1984).

————, "La deposizione di Michele VI: un episodio di 'concordia discors' fra Chiesa e militari?" *Jahrbuch der österreichischen Byzantinistik* 37 (1987) 153–171.

Spingou, F., "Snapshots from the Eleventh Century: The Lombards from Bari, a *chartoularios* from 'Petra,' and the Complex of Mangana," *BMGS* 39 (2015) 50–65.

Stănescu, E., "Les réformes d'Isaac Comnène," *Revue des études sud-est européennes* 4 (1966) 35–69.

Starr, J., "Notes on the Byzantine Incursions into Syria and Palestine (?)," *Archiv Orientální* 8 (1936) 91–95.

Stephenson, P., *Byzantium's Balkan Frontier: A Political Study of the Northern Balkans, 900–1204* (Cambridge 2000).

————, *The Legend of Basil the Bulgar-Slayer* (Cambridge 2003).

————, "The Balkan Frontier in the Year 1000," in P. Magdalino, ed., *Byzantium in the Year 1000* (Leiden 2003) 109–133.

Stern, S. M., "An Embassy of the Byzantine Emperor to the Fatimid Caliph al-Muʿizz," *Byzantion* 20 (1950) 239–258.

Stokes, A. D., "The Background and Chronology of the Balkan Campaigns of Svyatoslav Igorevich," *Slavonic and East European Review* 40 (1961) 43–57.

————, "The Balkan Campaigns of Svyatoslav Igorevich," *Slavonic and East European Review* 40 (1962) 466–496.

Strange, G. le, *Palestine under the Moslems: A Description of Syria and the Holy Land from A.D. 650 to 1500* (Boston 1890).

Strässle, P. M., "Raum und Kriegführung in Byzanz: Eine militärgeographische Beurteilung von Taktik und Strategie der Operation am Fluss Spercheios (996)," *BF* 26 (2000) 231–254.

———, *Krieg und Kriegführung in Byzanz: Die Kriege Kaiser Basileios II. gegen die Bulgaren (976–1019)* (Köln 2006)

Sullivan, D. F., "Siege Warfare, Nikephoros II Phokas, Relics and Personal Piety," in idem et al., eds., *Byzantine Religious Culture: Studies in Honor of Alice-Mary Talbot* (Leiden 2012) 395–409.

Svoronos, N., "Recherches sur le cadastre byzantin et la fiscalité aux XIe et XIIe siècles: Le cadastre de Thèbes," *Bulletin de correspondance hellénique* 83 (1959) 1–145.

———, *Les Novelles des empereurs macédoniens concernant la terre et les stratiotes* (Athens 1994).

Sweetenham, C., *Robert the Monk's History of the First Crusade: Historia Iherosolimitana* (Farnham 2005).

Sykoutris, I., "Λέοντος τοῦ Διακόνου Ἀνέκδοτον ἐγκώμιον εἰς Βασίλειον τον Β΄," Ἐπετηρὶς Ἑταιρείας Βυζαντινῶν Σπουδῶν 10 (1933) 425–434.

Terras, V., "Leo Diaconus and the Ethnology of the Kievan Rus," *Slavic Review* 24 (1965) 395–406.

Ter-Ghewondyan, A., *The Arab Emirates in Bagratid Armenia*, tr. N. Garsoïan (Lisbon 1976).

Thierry, N., "Un portrait de Jean Tsimiskès en Cappadoce," *TM* 9 (1985) 477–484.

Thomas, J. P., *Private Religious Foundations in the Byzantine Empire* (Washington, DC 1987)

Tibi, A., "Two Sources on Arab Crete: al-Majālis wa'l-Musāyarāt and Muʿjam al-Buldān," *Graeco-Arabica* 11 (2011) 119–122.

Tinnefeld, F., "Die Stadt Melitene in ihrer späteren byzantinischen Epoche (934–1101)," in M. Berza and E. Stănescu, eds., *Actes du XIVe Congrès international des études byzantines* (Bucharest 1974) 435–443.

———, "Michael I Kerullarios, Patriarch von Konstantinopel (1043–1058): Kritische Überlegungen zu einer Biographie," *Jahrbuch der österreichischen Byzantinistik* 39 (1989) 95–127.

Todt, K.-P., "Herrscher im Schatten: Konstantin VIII. (960/961–1028)," *Thetis: Mannheimer Beiträge zur Klassischen Archäologie und Geschichte Griechenlands und Zyperns* 7 (2000) 93–105.

———, "Die Frau als Selbstherrscher: Kaiserin Theodora, die letzte Angehörige der Makedonischen Dynastie," *Jahrbuch der österreichischen Byzantinistik* 50 (2000) 139–171.

———, "Antioch in the Middle Byzantine Period: (969–1084). The Reconstruction of the City as an Administrative, Military, Economic and Ecclesiastical Center," *Topoi* suppl. 5 (2004) 171–190.

Toumanoff, C., "The Bagratids of Iberia from the Eighth to the Eleventh Century," *Le Muséon* 74 (1961) 5–42 and 233–316.

————, "Armenia and Georgia," in J. H. Hussey, ed., *The Cambridge Medieval History*, v. 4: *The Byzantine Empire*, pt. 1: *Byzantium and Its Neighbours* (Cambridge 1966) 593–637.

Toynbee, A., *Constantine Porphyrogenitus and His World* (London 1973).

Treadgold, W., "The Army in the Works of Constantine Porphyrogenitus," *Rivista di studi bizantini e neoellenici* 29 (1992) 77–162.

————, *Byzantium and Its Army, 284–1081* (Stanford 1995).

————, "Byzantium, the Reluctant Warrior," in N. Christie and M. Yazigi, eds., *Noble Ideals and Bloody Realities: Warfare in the Middle Ages* (Leiden 2006) 209–233.

————, *The Middle Byzantine Historians* (New York 2013).

Tserebelakis, G. T., *Ο Νικηφόρος Φωκάς και η απελευθέρωση της Κρήτης από τους Άραβες (961 μ.Χ.)* (Thessalonike 2009).

Tsougarakis, D., *Byzantine Crete from the 5th Century to the Venetian Conquest* (Athens 1988).

Van Houts, E.M.C., "Normandy and Byzantium in the Eleventh Century," *Byzantion* 55 (1985) 544–559.

Vannier, J.-F., *Familles byzantines: Les Argyroi (IXe–XIIe siècles)* (Paris 1975).

Vasiliev, A. A., et al., *Byzance et les Arabes*, v. 2.1–2 (Brussels 1950–1968).

Vest, B. A., *Geschichte der Stadt Melitene und der umliegenden Gebiete vom Vorabend der arabischen bis zum Anschluss der türkischen Eroberung (um 600–1124)* (Hambourg 2007).

Vlysidou, B., *Αριστοκρατικές οικογένειες και εξουσία (9ος–10ος αι.): Έρευνες πάνω στα διαδοχικά στάδια αντιμετώπισης της αρμενο-παφλαγονικής και της καππαδοκικής αριστοκρατίας* (Thessaloniki 2001).

————, "Η πολιτική του Βασιλείου Λακαπηνού έναντι της Δύσης," *Symmeikta* 17 (2005) 111–130.

Vratimos, A., "Was Michael Attaleiates Present at the Battle of Mantzikert?" *BZ* 105 (2012) 829–840.

de Vries-van der Velden, E., "Psellos, Romain IV Diogénès et Mantzikert," *Byzantinoslavica* 58 (1997) 274–310.

Vryonis, S., "The Will of a Provincial Magnate, Eustathius Boilas (1059)," *DOP* 11 (1956) 263–277.

————, "Byzantine ΔΗΜΟΚΡΑΤΙΑ and the Guilds in the Eleventh Century," *DOP* 17 (1963) 287–314.

————, *The Decline of Medieval Hellenism in Asia Minor and the Process of Islamization from the Eleventh through the Fifteenth Centuries* (Berkeley 1971).

————, "The Greek and Arabic Sources for the Battle of Mantzikert," in idem, ed., *Byzantine Studies: Essays on the Slavic World and the Eleventh Century* (New Rochelle, NY 1992) 125–140.

————, "The Greek and Arabic Sources on the Eight Day Captivity of the Emperor Romanos IV in the Camp of the Sultan Alp Arslan after the Battle of Mantzikert," in C. Sodé and S. Takács, eds., *Novum Millennium: Studies on Byzantine History and Culture Dedicated to Paul Speck* (Farnham, UK 2001) 439–450.

Walker, P. E., "A Byzantine Victory over the Fatimids at Alexandretta (971)," *Byzantion* 42 (1972) 431–440.

———, "The 'Crusade' of John Tzimiskes in the Light of New Arabic Evidence," *Byzantion* 47 (1977) 301–327.

———, "The Ismāʿīlī Daʿwa and the Fāṭimid Caliphate," in C. F. Petry, ed., *The Cambridge History of Egypt*, v. 1 (Cambridge 1998) 120–150.

———, *Caliph of Cairo: Al-Hakim bi-Amr Allah, 996n1021* (Cairo and New York 2012).

Wander, S. H., *The Joshua Roll* (Wiesbaden 2012).

Wasilewski, T., "Le thème de Sirmium-Serbie au XIe et XIIe siècles," *Zbornik Radova Vizantinološkog Instituta* 8 (1964) 465–482.

West, C., "Dynastic Historical Writing," in S. Foot and C. F. Robinson, eds., *The Oxford History of Historical Writing*, v. 2 (Oxford 2012) 496–516.

Whittow, M., *The Making of Byzantium 600–1025* (Berkeley 1996).

———, "How the East Was Lost: The Background to the Komnenian *reconquista*," in M. Mullett and D. Smythe, eds., Alexios I Komnenos (Belfast 1996) 55–67.

Will, C., *Acta et scripta quae de controversiis ecclesiae graecae et latinae saeculo undecimo composita extant* (Leipzig and Marburg 1861).

Wolska-Conus, W., "Les écoles de Psellos et de Xiphilin sous Constantin IX Monomaque," *Travaux et Memoires* 6 (1976) 233–243.

———, "L'école de droit et l'enseignement du droit à Byzance au XIe siècle: Xiphilin et Psellos," *Travaux et Memoires* 7 (1979) 1–107.

Yarnley, C. J., "Philaretos: Armenian Bandit or Byzantine General?" *Revue des études arméniennes* 9 (1972) 331–353.

Yuzbashian, K. N., "L'administration byzantine en Arménie aux Xe–XIe siècle," *Revue des études arméniennes* n.s. 10 (1973–1974) 139–183.

Zaimov, I., *Bitolski nadpis na Ivan Vladislav samodurzhets bulgarski: starobulgarski pametnik ot 1015–1016 godina* (Sofia 1970).

Zakkar, S., *The Emirate of Aleppo, 1004–1094* (Beirut 1971).

Zivković, T., *Gesta Regum Sclavorum*, 2 vols. (Belgrade 2009).

INDEX